INFORMATION LITERACY: RESEARCH AND COLLABORATION ACROSS DISCIPLINES

PERSPECTIVES ON WRITING
Series Editors, Susan H. McLeod and Rich Rice

The Perspectives on Writing series addresses writing studies in a broad sense. Consistent with the wide ranging approaches characteristic of teaching and scholarship in writing across the curriculum, the series presents works that take divergent perspectives on working as a writer, teaching writing, administering writing programs, and studying writing in its various forms.

The WAC Clearinghouse, Colorado State University Open Press, and University Press of Colorado are collaborating so that these books will be widely available through free digital distribution and low-cost print editions. The publishers and the Series editors are committed to the principle that knowledge should freely circulate. We see the opportunities that new technologies have for further democratizing knowledge. And we see that to share the power of writing is to share the means for all to articulate their needs, interest, and learning into the great experiment of literacy.

Recent Books in the Series

Justin Everett and Cristina Hanganu-Bresch (Eds.), *A Minefield of Dreams: Triumphs and Travails of Independent Writing Programs* (2017)

Chris M. Anson and Jessie L. Moore (Eds.), *Critical Transitions: Writing and the Questions of Transfer* (2017)

Joanne Addison and Sharon James McGee, *Writing and School Reform: Writing Instruction in the Age of Common Core and Standardized Testing* (2017)

Lisa Emerson, *The Forgotten Tribe: Scientists as Writers* (2017)

Jacob S. Blumner and Pamela B. Childers, *WAC Partnerships Between Secondary and Postsecondary Institutions* (2015)

Nathan Shepley, *Placing the History of College Writing: Stories from the Incomplete Archive* (2015)

Asao B. Inoue, *Antiracist Writing Assessment Ecologies: An Approach to Teaching and Assessing Writing for a Socially Just Future* (2015)

Theresa Lillis, Kathy Harrington, Mary R. Lea, and Sally Mitchell (Eds.), *Working with Academic Literacies: Case Studies Towards Transformative Practice* (2015)

Beth L. Hewett and Kevin Eric DePew (Eds.), *Foundational Practices of Online Writing Instruction* (2015)

Christy I. Wenger, *Yoga Minds, Writing Bodies: Contemplative Writing Pedagogy* (2015)

INFORMATION LITERACY: RESEARCH AND COLLABORATION ACROSS DISCIPLINES

Edited by Barbara J. D'Angelo, Sandra Jamieson,
Barry Maid, and Janice R. Walker

The WAC Clearinghouse
wac.colostate.edu
Fort Collins, Colorado

University Press of Colorado
upcolorado.com
Boulder, Colorado

The WAC Clearinghouse, Fort Collins, Colorado 80523-1040

University Press of Colorado, Boulder, Colorado 80303

© 2017 by Barbara J. D'Angelo, Sandra Jamieson, Barry Maid, and Janice R. Walker. This work is licensed under a Creative Commons Attribution-NonCommercial-NoDerivatives 4.0 International.

Library of Congress Cataloging-in-Publication Data

Names: D'Angelo, Barbara J., editor. | Jamieson, Sandra, editor. | Maid, Barry M., editor. | Walker, Janice R., editor.
Title: Information literacy : research and collaboration across disciplines / edited by Barbara J. D'Angelo, Sandra Jamieson, Barry Maid, and Janice R. Walker.
Other titles: Perspectives on writing (Fort Collins, Colo.)
Description: Fort Collins, Colorado : The WAC Clearinghouse ; Boulder : University Press of Colorado, [2016] | Series: Perspectives on writing | Includes bibliographical references.
Identifiers: LCCN 2016048671| ISBN 9781607326571 (pbk.) | ISBN 9781607326588 (ebook)
Subjects: LCSH: Information literacy—Study and teaching (Higher)
Classification: LCC ZA3075 .I544 2016 | DDC 028.7071173—dc23
LC record available at https://lccn.loc.gov/2016048671

Copyeditor: Brandy Bippes
Designer: Mike Palmquist
Series Editors: Susan H. McLeod and Rich Rice

This book is printed on acid-free paper.

The WAC Clearinghouse supports teachers of writing across the disciplines. Hosted by Colorado State University, and supported by the Colorado State Univeristy Open Press, it brings together scholarly journals and book series as well as resources for teachers who use writing in their courses. This book is available in digital formats for free download at wac.colostate.edu.

Founded in 1965, the University Press of Colorado is a nonprofit cooperative publishing enterprise supported, in part, by Adams State University, Colorado State University, Fort Lewis College, Metropolitan State University of Denver, Regis University, University of Colorado, University of Northern Colorado, Utah State University, and Western State Colorado University. For more information, visit upcolorado.com.

CONTENTS

Introduction..3
    Barbara J. D'Angelo, Sandra Jamieson,
    Barry Maid, and Janice R. Walker

PART I. SITUATING INFORMATION LITERACY

Chapter 1. Writing Information Literacy: A Retrospective and
a Look Ahead..15
    Rolf Norgaard and Caroline Sinkinson

Chapter 2. Threshold Concepts: Integrating and Applying
Information Literacy and Writing Instruction 37
    Barry Maid and Barbara D'Angelo

Chapter 3. Employer Expectations of Information Literacy:
Identifying the Skills Gap....................................51
    Dale Cyphert and Stanley P. Lyle

Chapter 4. Creating and Exploring New Worlds: Web 2.0,
Information Literacy, and the Ways We Know 77
    Kathleen Blake Yancey

Chapter 5. Information Literacy in Digital Environments:
Construct Mediation, Construct Modeling, and Validation Processes......93
    Irvin R. Katz and Norbert Elliot

PART II. RESEARCHING INFORMATION LITERACY

Chapter 6. What the Citation Project Tells Us about Information
Literacy in College Composition 115
    Sandra Jamieson

Chapter 7. Preliminary Paths to Information Literacy: Introducing
Research in Core Courses......................................139
    Katt Blackwell-Starnes

Chapter 8. Approximating the University: The Information Literacy
Practices of Novice Researchers 163
    Karen Gocsik, Laura R. Braunstein,
    and Cynthia E. Tobery

Chapter 9. Understanding and Using Sources: Student Practices and Perceptions.. 185
    Patti Wojahn and Theresa Westbrock, Rachel Milloy,
    Seth Myers, Matthew Moberly, and Lisa Ramirez

Chapter 10. Writing Information Literacy in First-Year Composition: A Collaboration among Faculty and Librarians 211
    Donna Scheidt, William Carpenter, Robert Fitzgerald,
    Cara Kozma, Holly Middleton, and Kathy Shields

PART III. INCORPORATING AND EVALUATING INFORMATION LITERACY IN SPECIFIC COURSES

Chapter 11. Up the Mountain without a Trail: Helping Students Use Source Networks to Find Their Way............................237
    Miriam Laskin and Cynthia R. Haller

Chapter 12. Ethics, Distribution, and Credibility: Using an Emerging Genre to Teach Information Literacy Concepts 257
    Christopher Toth and Hazel McClure

Chapter 13. Information Literacy Preparation of Pre-Service and Graduate Educators 271
    Susan Brown and Janice R. Walker

Chapter 14. Not Just for Citations: Assessing Zotero while Reassessing Research...287
    Rachel Rains Winslow, Sarah L. Skripsky,
    and Savannah L. Kelly

Chapter 15. Quantitative Reasoning and Information Literacy in Economics...305
    Diego Méndez-Carbajo

PART IV. COLLABORATING TO ADVANCE PROGRAMMATIC INFORMATION LITERACY

Chapter 16. Moving Ahead by Looking Back: Crafting a Framework for Sustainable, Institutional Information Literacy...........325
    Lori Baker and Pam Gladis

Chapter 17. Supporting Academics to Embed Information Literacy to Enhance Students' Research and Writing Process 345
    Angela Feekery, Lisa Emerson, and Gillian Skyrme

Chapter 18. Building Critical Researchers and Writers Incrementally:
Vital Partnerships Between Faculty and Librarians 371
    Alison S. Gregory and Betty L. McCall

Chapter 19. Impacting Information Literacy through Alignment,
Resources, and Assessment 387
    Beth Bensen, Denise Woetzel, Hong Wu,
    and Ghazala Hashmi

Chapter 20. Bridging the Gaps: Collaboration in a Faculty and
Librarian Community of Practice on Information Literacy. 411
    Francia Kissel, Melvin R. Wininger, Scott R. Weeden,
    Patricia A. Wittberg, Randall S. Halverson, Meagan Lacy,
    and Rhonda K. Huisman

Afterword 429
    Trudi E. Jacobson

Contributors 435

INFORMATION LITERACY: RESEARCH AND COLLABORATION ACROSS DISCIPLINES

INTRODUCTION

Barbara J. D'Angelo, Sandra Jamieson, Barry Maid, and Janice R. Walker

When we began discussing our vision for a collection on information literacy (IL), our initial conversations revolved around the incredible amount of scholarship and practice that already existed in both Writing Studies (WS) and in Library/Information Science (LIS). Yet, while librarians, writing faculty, and other disciplinary faculty had presented and/or published together, there was still not enough cross-over in disciplinary literature addressed to both faculty and librarian audiences.

One of our goals for this collection, then, was to bring together the rich scholarship and pedagogy from multiple perspectives and disciplines to provide a broader and more complex understanding of IL in the second decade of the 21st century. Further, we hoped that a collection that bridged the disciplinary divide would advance the notion of shared responsibility and accountability for the teaching, learning, and research of IL in the academy: faculty, librarians, administrators, and external stakeholders such as accrediting agencies and the businesses/industries that employ our graduates.

As we issued the call for contributions for the collection, our view of IL was guided by the Association of College & Research Libraries (ACRL) *Information Literacy Standards for Higher Education* (*IL Standards*) which defines IL as the ability to "determine the extent of information needed, access the needed information effectively and efficiently, evaluate information and its sources critically, incorporate selected information into one's knowledge base, use information effectively to accomplish a specific purpose, understand the economic, legal and social issues surrounding the use of information, and access and use information legally" (ACRL, 2000). Widely cited since its formal approval by the ACRL Board, the *IL Standards* has seen widespread acceptance by librarians, faculty, administrators, and accrediting bodies. As a result, librarians and faculty have created strong partnerships to develop pedagogy related to IL and the *IL Standards* have been adapted to meet disciplinary contexts.

However, the *IL Standards* also have faced considerable criticism as both research and practice began to highlight and illustrate the shortcomings of a standards- and competencies-based approach. Critiques of the *IL Standards*, theoretically and research-based, have focused on the de-contextualized nature of standards that potentially emphasize a prescribed set of skills. Research demonstrated that IL is a contextual concept situated in specific information landscapes. For example, Carol Kuhlthau's ground-breaking research on the information search process (Kuhlthau, 2004) clearly demonstrated the process-oriented nature of research and has shaped IL pedagogy within LIS. Christine Bruce's (1997) landmark work on the relational nature of IL, along with the work of others in Australia and Europe (see, for example, Lupton, 2004; Limberg, 2008; Lloyd, 2010), further demonstrated that IL is contextual and that individuals "experience" IL in ways that are dependent on the context of the situation.

Not long after we began work on this collection, ACRL established a task force to review the *IL Standards* and to make recommendations to update them. In recognition of the broad constituency that is impacted by and responsible for IL, the task force consisted of librarians, administrators, and external constituents from accrediting agencies and other relevant associations. Our development of the collection and the Task Force's work to review and make recommendations about the *IL Standards* ensued nearly simultaneously and it became clear to us that the emerging framework based on threshold concepts and metaliteracy was consistent with trends we were seeing in WS and in higher education in general. Recognition of the roles of faculty and librarians within the academy and of the rapidly changing dynamic information landscape all contributed to the impetus for the Task Force's work, resulting in the *Framework for Information Literacy for Higher Education* (*Framework for IL*).

The *Framework for IL* is divided into six frames, each with a set of related knowledge practices and dispositions:

- Authority is constructed and contextual
- Information creation as a process
- Information has value
- Research as inquiry
- Scholarship as conversation
- Searching as strategic exploration

The *Framework for IL* draws upon both threshold concepts (foundational concepts within a discipline that serve as portals to thinking and practice) and the concept of metaliteracy (Mackey & Jacobson, 2011; Mackey & Jacobson, 2014). Metaliteracy presents a vision for IL as an overarching literacy that places students in the role of both consumer and producer of information within today's collaborative information environments. Metaliteracy also emphasizes four domains of engagement within the information environment: behavioral, affective, cognitive, and metacognitive with metacognition as particularly important for individuals to become self-directed learners required in today's rapidly changing landscape.

Rather than focus on discrete skills, the *Framework for IL* is grounded in core concepts with the intent that implementation would be flexible to allow local contexts to influence the development of teaching and learning practices. The revised, expanded definition of IL accompanying the *Framework for IL* also explicates current thinking of IL as a more sophisticated and contextual concept relevant to student learning throughout their academic careers (and beyond):

> Information literacy is the set of integrated abilities encompassing the reflective discovery of information, the understanding of how information is produced and valued, and the use of information in creating new knowledge and participating ethically in communities of learning. (ACRL, 2015)

The adoption of the *Framework for IL* presents a challenge to all of us who research, teach, and assess IL. The use of the word "framework" intentionally emphasizes that the document is a structure to set the context for ongoing discussions and collaborations between librarians, faculty, administrators, and other stakeholders to connect and to partner for the development of IL programs that are relevant within each program and institution. The *Framework for IL* further challenges all of us involved in IL to learn about and envision what threshold concepts and metaliteracy mean in order to develop pedagogy that facilitates transfer of learning across contexts as well as how these concepts influence and shape research studies and projects related to IL. As the Task Force worked, releasing drafts for discussion, the *Framework for IL* was received positively by many librarians, who began using it to discuss and shape instruction programs even before its approval by the ACRL Board. While it would be easy to view the *Framework for IL* as a marked shift away from the *IL Standards*, in reality it is an evolution based on nearly 20 years of research and practice.

As this collection moved to fruition, we realized, as editors, how much of an exigence the *Framework for IL* was and continued to be. Themes that authors explore in chapters mirror the threshold concepts and metaliteracy principles that ground the *Framework for IL*. The scope of the collection began as an attempt to bridge disciplinary boundaries, which is also a goal of the *Framework for IL*. As we read the submissions, a further vision for the collection emerged as a bridge between past/current knowledge and the future. As such, we defer to Rolf Norgaard and Caroline Sinkinson, the authors of the first chapter, who refer to the Roman god Janus as a potential presiding deity for their essay. We would suggest that Janus, with one face looking back and one looking to the future, further serves as the presiding deity for the collection as a whole: one face looking back and celebrating past and current work on IL and one looking forward to the continued evolution of IL as the *Framework for IL* continues to take hold and influences our pedagogy, research, and assessment practices.

ORGANIZATION OF THE COLLECTION

Within the dual exigencies of bridging boundaries and creating connections past and future, the chapters presented in this collection facilitate an understanding of how IL has evolved and continues to evolve. Chapters address the core concepts articulated in the *Framework for IL* and demonstrate the relevance of it to higher education; indeed, chapters emphasize how the foundational underpinnings of the *Framework for IL* have been part of our understanding and work in IL, even if unarticulated. Chapters also address related threshold concepts, metacognition, large-scale research studies, programmatic and institutional efforts to institutionalize IL, and pedagogical innovations. Above all, this collection should be viewed as part of the conversation about IL as we adapt to and implement the *Framework for IL*. In that spirit, the book begins with a conversation between WS and LIS as Rolf Norgaard and Caroline Sinkinson engage in dialogue to look back over more than a decade of teaching and learning related to IL and ponder the future.

To continue and build upon the dialogue, we have organized the collection into four sections, each representing a core focus area of IL. Section I situates IL and provides us with understanding of how and why IL is a contextual concept based on threshold concepts and metaliteracy. Section II presents results of research projects which help us to further our understanding of IL and of student learning related to it, particularly the threshold concept of Scholarship as Conversation. Section III explores the already rich collaborations taking place to define IL locally within programs and institutions and to define shared responsibility for IL. Chapters in Section IV describe pedagogical strategies and evaluation of them. This section ends by returning us back to the notion of conversation and collaboration between WS and LIS. Finally, in the afterword, Trudi Jacobson wraps up the collection by reminding us of the complex information landscape we and our students now find ourselves in and how the *Framework for IL* and metaliteracy are providing us with a new lens to facilitate our teaching and learning of IL as shared responsibility.

SECTION I. SITUATING INFORMATION LITERACY

Authors in Section I bring together past theory and practice to situate IL for us by articulating what the *Framework for IL* means for the evolution of IL pedagogy, research, and assessment. Just over a decade ago, in one of the few notable pieces of scholarship to cross disciplinary boundaries, Rolf Norgaard contextualized IL rhetorically in his seminal paired articles in *Reference and User Services Quarterly* (2003, 2004). Norgaard and librarian Caroline Sinkinson begin our collection in conversation to look back at the ensuing decade and the progress that has (or hasn't) been made, and to speculate on what the future may hold. Barry Maid and Barbara D'Angelo then articulate how the *Framework for IL* connects with the Writing Program Administrator's Outcomes Statement and "Habits of Mind," furthering their work to contextualize and rhetoricize IL for WS. Maid and D'Angelo's explanation of the threshold concepts foundational in the *Framework for IL* as portals to knowledge construction deeply connected to WS, reminds us that our pedagogy and assessment of IL should acknowledge the situated nature of the concept and the ways it extends beyond the classroom to our students' professional, personal, and civic lives. Following on this theme, Dale Cyphert and Stanley Lyle articulate IL within a business context, reminding us that the IL landscape expands beyond academia and WS and that "the functional role of any individual within a large, complex organization is neither linear nor independent, and information is only occasionally objective. . . . Organizational activities are not simple collections of acts performed by discrete individuals, each carrying an individual set of skills, but collectively constituted patterns of interaction, affordance, and social interpretation" (Chapter 3, this collection). The recognition of IL's situated nature within a landscape and contextualized by social, political, and other factors emphasizes the threshold concept that knowledge is constructed within discourse communities and that types of authority may differ based on those communities. As such, they remind us that the conversation related to IL extends beyond academia to the workplace and other contexts.

Kathleen Blake Yancey considers the current moment of information literacy as an ecology by outlining three "periods" in its recent history: (1) the period of all-vetting-all-the-time where gatekeepers assured the credibility of the sources; (2) the period of online access of information; and (3) the most recent, ongoing current period located in an ecology of interacting sources—academic; mainstream; and "alternative." Yancey situates this history within the context of source analysis and the challenge all researchers face when establishing source credibility.

Irvin Katz and Norbert Elliot round out Section I by articulating the importance of defining constructs for assessment and using assessment methods that are capable of evaluating complex concepts such as IL in a way that respects its contextual and process-oriented nature. Their case study is particularly timely as the *Framework for IL* shifts IL away from a skills-based foundation to one that is grounded in metaliteracy. Their chapter addresses the question of how we—librarians, faculty, and administrators—adapt and employ assessments that can effectively evaluate IL within the academy. Katz and Elliot describe Educational Testing Service's iSkills to demonstrate how assessment within a

Introduction

digital environment can go beyond the mechanized skills-testing of paper bubble tests to a richer and more robust assessment of a construct that is situated, mediated, and remediated—i.e., that information creation is a process in which an information need and data collection and analysis are constantly revisited and revised based on feedback and effectiveness. Katz and Elliot conclude that IL is a threshold concept that requires holistic instruction, a conclusion that is consistent with metaliteracy as an overarching literacy serving as the theoretical underpinning of the *Framework for IL*.

SECTION II. RESEARCHING INFORMATION LITERACY

Section II focuses on large-scale research projects that are contributing to our understanding of IL, in particular, our understanding of students' ability to use information to construct knowledge. The threshold concept of Scholarship as Conversation is clearly evident in the work of these researchers and scholars. Sandra Jamieson leads off Section II with a discussion of results of Citation Project research concerning the kinds of sources students selected for source-based papers in first-year writing, how they incorporated them, and the implications for IL. Following this chapter, Katt Blackwell-Starnes reports on the results of a pilot study for the LILAC Project revealing the impact of students' focus on final product rather than process when completing a research project. Karen Gocsik, Laura Braunstein, and Cynthia Tobery report on the results of a six-year study to research and code wiki assignments to determine how students analyze and use sources. Then Patti Wojhan, Theresa Westbrook, Rachel Milloy, Matthew Moberly, Seth Myers, and Lisa Ramirez describe the results of an analysis of student research diaries and self-assessments to identify trends in students' use of information. Maintaining the focus on student perceptions, Donna Scheidt, William Carpenter, Robert Fitzgerald, Cara Kozma, Holly Middleton, and Kathy Shields describe a collaboration between composition faculty and librarians to study students' perceptions of research with an emphasis on source use.

What all of these authors highlight in their work is the importance of the threshold concept related to the use of information and entering into a scholarly conversation, making them timely and, perhaps, leading to strategies that allow us to adapt practices to help students become information literate.

SECTION III. INCORPORATING AND EVALUATING INFORMATION LITERACY IN SPECIFIC COURSES

Section III highlights pedagogical enactments and collaborations to incorporate IL into the classroom, both in first-year composition and disciplinary subject courses. The frame Scholarship as Conversation again dominates the themes of these chapters.

Miriam Laskin and Cynthia Haller describe their strategy to help students identify citation trails and the failure of students to identify and work within source networks. From a multimodal perspective, Christopher Toth and Hazel McClure challenge us to consider the use of infographics as a tool for IL pedagogy and provide an example of IL in a digital environment in which information is presented in ways other than text. In a demonstration of the metaliteracy that underlies the *Framework for IL*, they show that students are producers of information through remixing and remediation of information graphically.

Susan Brown and Janice R. Walker describe yet another collaboration for instruction exploring IL in pre-service teacher education classes. They raise the concern that absent a common terminology across disciplines, the focus on IL in both K-12 and higher education is fragmented. Brown and Walker call for "scaffolded, cross-disciplinary, teacher-librarian collaborative interventions" (Chapter 13, this collection) to facilitate shared language and ownership of IL. As such, like so many other authors in this collection, they point to the shared responsibility for IL and for the importance of dialogue.

Rachel Winslow, Sarah Skripsky, and Savannah Kelly describe a collaboration between a librarian and teaching faculty in WS and social science to incorporate the citation manager Zotero to help students learn to use sources. Finally, Diego Méndez-Carbajo raises another issue regarding discipline specificity, noting that the relationship between IL and quantitative reasoning is one that has not been fully explored previously. He provides an effective example of how IL can be integrated into an intermediate level economics course with the use of quantitative case studies. His model is based on how the *Framework for IL* frame Research as Inquiry relates to the economics course as students learn to collect, manipulate, and analyze quantitative information in order to contextualize and apply it.

SECTION IV. COLLABORATING TO ADVANCE PROGRAMMATIC INFORMATION LITERACY

Chapters in Section IV highlight collaborative efforts to develop IL on a programmatic level. Authors in this section describe the partnerships involved in creating and evolving shared ownership of IL within their institutions. In light of the *Framework for IL*, the challenge of encouraging broad-based ownership of IL beyond librarians and individual librarian-faculty partnerships is a timely one, and these chapters give us interesting models that are potentially replicable at other institutions.

Introduction

Lori Baker and Pam Gladis describe a programmatic effort to institutionalize IL at their small liberal arts college. In particular, they discuss a key issue associated with IL instruction—that of ownership and the required shift of perspective required when the agency of IL becomes institutional. From a different perspective again, Angela Feekery, Lisa Emerson, and Gillian Skyrme explore issues related to the integration and scaffolding of IL throughout a degree program in New Zealand. The results of their action research revealed the shifting perspectives of faculty related to the responsibility for IL within the curriculum as they were introduced to holistic views of the concept. Feekery et al. show us the power of collaboration and conversation to advance IL practices.

Alison Gregory and Betty McCall describe collaborative work to integrate IL vertically into the curriculum at their institution, discussing their recognition that developing IL skills are progressive and the process cannot be taught in one-shot sessions or in one course. Their results also point to the value of collaboration when faculty are pro-active in viewing their role in the development of IL. Beth Bensen, Denise Woetzel, Hong Wu, and Ghazala Hashmi describe the impetus for the Quality Enhancement Plan at their institution and the first step in its implementation in the second semester first-year writing course as part of a planned vertical implementation of IL.

Francia Kissel, Melvin Wininger, Scott Weeden, Patricia Wittberg, Randall Halverson, Meagan Lacy, and Rhonda Huisman round out the collection by presenting a model for faculty-librarian-administrator collaboration related to IL through the establishment of a community of practice, a volunteer work group to develop pedagogical strategies for teaching in courses with research assignments. Kissel et al., then, brings our collection full circle. The community of practice they describe embodies the notion of shared responsibility for IL and for the importance and power of collaboration and dialogue to engage us in advancing IL teaching and learning.

WHITHER IL?

As we reflect on the tremendous amount of research, pedagogical planning, teaching and learning that has enveloped IL since the *IL Standards* were initially adopted, we are impressed with the inroads and advancements that have been made in a short period of time. Yet, we also recognize how much work there is still to be done as Norgaard and Simkinson have so aptly described in their reflective conversation to open this collection. As we finish our work on this collection, the *Framework for IL* has been approved, discussion surrounding it continue at conferences and in webinars, and plans for implementation and development of related resources to facilitate adoption are underway. The

Framework for IL serves not just as a vehicle for evolving our conception of IL and how we help students to become information literate, it serves as a potential vehicle for sharing ownership of the responsibility for IL. Recalling our presiding deity Janus, we believe this collection, as part of the ongoing conversation on IL, serves to help us—librarians, faculty, administrators, external collaborators—to meet the challenge by looking back and learning from the past and looking forward to envision the future.

REFERENCES

Association of College and Research Libraries (2015). *Framework for information literacy for higher education*. Retrieved from http://www.ala.org/acrl/standards/ilframework.

Association of College and Research Libraries. (2000). *Information literacy competency standards for higher education*. Retrieved from http://www.ala.org/acrl/standards/informationliteracycompetency.

Kuhlthau, C. C. (2004). *Seeking meaning: A process approach to library and information services*. Westport, CT: Libraries Unlimited, Inc.

Limberg, L., Alexandersson, M., Lantz-Andersson, A. & Folkesson, L. (2008). What matters? Shaping meaningful learning through teaching information literacy. *Libri, 58*(2), 82.

Lloyd, A. (2010). *Information literacy landscapes: Information literacy in education, workplace and everyday contexts*. Oxford: Chandos Publishing.

Lupton, M. J. (2004). *The learning connection: Information literacy and the student experience*. Blackwood, South Australia: Auslib Press.

Mackey, T. P. & Jacobson, T. E. (2011). Reframing information literacy as a metaliteracy. *College & Research Libraries, 72*(1), 62–78.

Mackey, T. P. & Jacobson, T. E. (2014). *Metaliteracy*. Chicago, IL: Neal Schuman.

Norgaard, R. (2003). Writing information literacy: Contributions to a concept. *Reference & User Services Quarterly, 43*(2), 124–130.

Norgaard, R. (2004). Writing information literacy in the classroom: Pedagogical enactments and considerations. *Reference & User Services Quarterly, 43*, 220–226.

PART I.
SITUATING INFORMATION LITERACY

CHAPTER 1

WRITING INFORMATION LITERACY: A RETROSPECTIVE AND A LOOK AHEAD

Rolf Norgaard and Caroline Sinkinson
University of Colorado at Boulder

Roughly a decade ago, two paired articles published in *Reference and User Services Quarterly* under the title "Writing Information Literacy" voiced what became a rather widespread call for more broadly shared ownership of and responsibility for information literacy (IL) on our college campuses (Norgaard, 2003; Norgaard, 2004). In these articles, Rolf Norgaard claimed that enhanced collaboration between librarians and writing faculty would yield improved educational opportunities for students. By pairing Rhetoric and Writing Studies with IL, Norgaard argued that a more robust understanding of IL as a situated, process-oriented, and relevant literacy would ensue. More specifically, he encouraged a collaboration that extended beyond librarian service to the discipline and course structures. He envisioned a collaboration that was steeped in dialogue on both theory and practice, going far beyond our more traditional roles as "classroom colleagues" or "curricular compatriots" (Norgaard, 2003, p. 124).

The call voiced in those paired articles, although appreciatively recognized, has not been fully realized. Therefore, in the spirit of collaboration, this chapter engages Rhetoric and Writing Studies scholar Norgaard (RN) and librarian Caroline Sinkinson (CS) in a dialogue that explores reactions and outcomes in the intervening decade. In doing so, the authors hope to identify barriers which hindered progress and to identify suggestions for the decade which lies ahead.

ORIGINS

CS: Your articles resonate with many librarians who are eager to break down the perception of IL as a generic, skills-based, and normative behavior. Instead, many view IL as a critical habit of mind, which functions within situated and contextual information landscapes (Lloyd, 2006, p. 572). I return often to your articles, and each time I reread your words, I am curious about what factors invited you, a Rhetoric and Writing Studies scholar, to so deeply engage with IL.

RN: The paired articles were the direct result of a very powerful moment of radical institutional change. Rather high-level, campus-wide discussions led to the formation of a new Program for Writing and Rhetoric. With the new program we engaged in a fundamental reconceptualization of our suite of first-year writing courses, which provided the initial platform for working with IL. These efforts have since expanded to our upper-division curriculum. The prior writing program had no investment in IL. Indeed, I doubt if its leaders and much of its faculty would even have recognized the term.

The opportunity to fashion a new program and a new curriculum made it possible to integrate IL into our pedagogy and our program mission, instead of treating it, as it most often is, as a supplement, an add-on. We were fortunate at the time to have forward-looking IL advocates, at the highest levels of campus discussions. Additionally, we had dedicated librarians to shepherd our IL efforts during the early stages of program building. So, when I speak of partnerships in these two articles, the call for reconceptualizing and broadly sharing IL is not merely abstract or theoretical. It is grounded in an institutional landscape and in deeply rewarding personal and intellectual friendships. But it goes well beyond those particularities to advance a vision of IL that has been widely appreciated, if not always implemented.

CS: Well, your articles have influenced many librarians, both pedagogically and conceptually. Your work helped librarians frame IL rhetorically, to justify enhanced collaborations with writing colleagues, and to build or revise programs, which is evidenced by the several examples in the literature (Jacobs & Jacobs, 2009; O'Connor et al., 2010; Holliday & Fagerheim, 2006; Gruber et al., 2008; Artman, 2010; Davidson & Crateau, 1998). In addition to practical applications, your work has had significant influence on IL theorists, specifically in the discussions surrounding critical IL (Elmborg, 2006; Elmborg, 2012; Jacobs, 2008; Accardi et al., 2010).

RN: As truly gratifying as that reception has been, it is unfortunate that the two articles failed to elicit a similarly robust discussion in my own field, Rhetoric and Writing Studies. Important work is being done; Rebecca More Howard and the Citation Project come to mind (Howard et al., 2010; Jamieson & Howard, 2013). Nevertheless, we have a ways to go to foster the disciplinary dialogue and disciplinary cross-fertilization that I envision in the two articles.

With a decade of hindsight, I now realize that I should have written not two but three articles. The first article focused on how Rhetoric and Writing Studies can contribute to the conceptualization of IL (Norgaard, 2003). The second focused on pedagogical enactments of that concept in the classroom (Norgaard, 2004). That missing third article should have focused on the institutional identities and roles whose transformations are likewise necessary if we are to make progress in IL, both conceptually and pedagogically. I am imagining an article that maps strategies and methods for institutionalizing IL, and as Sharon Weiner (2012) has argued, these strategies must acknowledge specific institutional contexts and cultures in order to meet success.

INSTITUTIONAL IDENTITIES AND DISCIPLINARY ROLES

RN: Both of our faculties—in Writing and Rhetoric and in University Libraries—have historically been marginalized groups whose identities, roles, and "place" have been defined more by others than by ourselves. We are in some sense natural allies. But as each faculty seeks to overcome its historical burden in distinctive ways, address new institutional challenges, and realize disciplinary aspirations, our roles and identities may in part conspire against the dialogue and partnership we seek, and the more robust understandings of IL that we wish to enact.

LIBRARIANS IN INSTITUTIONAL PERSPECTIVE

CS: At the very least, traditional roles compound our challenges. If asked, students might describe the library as a location for study or as a resource for accessing course materials; faculty might describe the library as a service in support of their research, scholarship and teaching. These descriptions reinforce the pervasive image of the traditional campus library as a storehouse of resources offered up to support and serve. However, the iconic library image obscures the work of librarians, specifically the work of teaching librarians. To an individual walking through the stacks or even posing a question at the research desk, that work is not visible or apparent. Libraries have historically been rooted in concepts of information, knowledge, and learning, but the librarian as an active educator invested in pedagogy and praxis has not fully matured. We continue to confront perceptions of the librarian role that undermine IL, both internally in the profession and externally with campus colleagues.

Internally, as Courtney Bruch and Carroll Wilkinson (2012) observe, tensions may exist between librarians who embrace a teaching identity and those who resist it (p. 14). This tension is increased when library structures and administration do not demonstrate a commitment to a culture of teaching. It is not uncommon for institutions to employ one individual, an instruction coordinator, primarily responsible for instruction programming and coordination. Bruch and Wilkinson (2012) point out that these positions often lack the authority and management oversight necessary to impact change (p. 21). Furthermore, for other library positions, teaching is a peripheral responsibility, if one at all, and must compete with other more traditional library tasks such as reference, collections or cataloging. Structures across library organizations and institutions vary widely, but these observations highlight an ongoing tension surrounding librarians' identity as teachers and educators. Equally, the emphasis placed on teaching roles within Masters of Library and Information Science curricula varies drastically across institutions. For example the University of Missouri, Columbia School of Information Science and Learning Technologies offers a robust slate of courses on instructional design, assessment and pedagogy which clearly demonstrate an expectation of librarian as educator. Yet, several other programs offer only one or two course options related to IL theory and practice (ACRL Instruction Section, Professional Development Committee, 2013). These variations underscore an unequal approach to the librarian's teaching role within the profession at large.

Despite these barriers, some individual instruction librarians have embraced a teaching identity and have developed as experts in the scholarship of teaching and learning.

RN: And as this expertise grows, our institutions and our students stand to lose if we don't tap into and highlight that expertise. Librarians occupy a unique and distinctly valuable position in the university. Your active integration of several domains—knowledge construction, new media, information networks, and information technologies—places you at the center of the educational enterprise, not at its periphery. Disciplinary faculty members across campuses are slow to recognize this expertise.

CS: Indeed. Even as librarians work to advocate for internal support of our teaching role, we also must work to showcase our value as pedagogical partners to disciplinary teaching faculty. A frequent narrative in the literature is that faculty members do not understand the librarian's teaching role or are unaware of our pedagogical knowledge (Elmborg, 2003, p. 77; Derakhshan & Singh, 2011, p. 227; Phelps & Campbell, 2012, p.16). However, as librarians, we need to consider how our actions reinforce perceptions of the librarian simply as a service provider. For example, more often than not, librarians adjust teaching strategies to faculty-outlined objectives and goals, which are typically bound up in research assignments. Yvonne Meulemans and Allison Carr (2013) suggest that if libraries truly value collaboration, they must become more brazen in their approach with faculty. If librarians disagree with an assignment design, or wholeheartedly find fault with a stand-alone tour, they should converse with faculty about those opinions and their beliefs as educators (Meulemans & Carr, 2013, p. 82). This approach might be very fruitful if, as Laura Saunders (2012) found, the lack of faculty-initiated collaboration is not a result of disrespect but rather a lack of awareness about how librarians can help in teaching and learning (p. 232).

WRITING TEACHERS IN INSTITUTIONAL PERSPECTIVE

RN: If librarians struggle to make their role as educators visible and appreciated, writing teachers suffer from a role definition that is different but equally problematic. Our role as teacher and educator is a given, but what we are expected to teach, and who is seen as qualified to teach, have been shaped by disciplinary, campus, and public expectations. Rhetoric and Writing Studies differs from any other discipline in that our field has historically been tied to but one course: first-year writing or freshman English. This traditional curricular moment, occurring in the first year, tends to privilege a narrow perspective on IL, emphasizing preparation for general academic work in college but neglecting broader civic and workplace contexts for IL. Moreover, the focus on the first-year composition course tends to promote a skills-oriented "inoculation" approach to IL, and tends to obscure how IL ought to be seen as a rich, multifaceted literacy that is responsive to changing contexts and opportunities. Writing across the Curriculum (WAC) programs and Writing in the Disciplines (WID) initiatives do offer a far more expansive set of contexts for IL. But here too, writing faculty are often seen as merely providing a service to various disciplines, and are relegated to secondary status with respect to their expertise and their pedagogical roles. As Rhetoric and Writing Studies expands its curricular offerings, it can embrace a more capacious understanding of IL, for example by developing a more vertical curriculum that engages writing and IL at various points and for various purposes throughout the undergraduate experience (Gregory & McCall, Chapter 18, this collection). At our institution, we are fortunate to have a robust upper-division curriculum, and as a free-standing program not located, as most are, within an English department, we may have greater latitude to seize new opportunities for teaching IL. The growing number of Writing Studies majors, as well as certificate programs, provides fertile ground for greater integration of IL throughout the writing curriculum. Likewise, the growing number of free-standing writing programs provides an opportunity to reach beyond the orbit of English departments to reach whole campuses.

CS: I can easily understand how this historical emphasis on first-year writing tends to place a lot of expectations on that single course. My sense is that writing teachers often feel overwhelmed by the many goals and objectives they are expected to meet, and that IL adds but one more item to an already full plate.

RN: Yes, feeling overwhelmed comes with the territory. First-year writing is one of the very few courses that nearly all students take on campus, and campus administrators often look to the course as a platform for a variety of campus initiatives.

With these external pressures, writing instructors continue to deal with misunderstandings of our role on campus. For a surprisingly large number of faculty members, we are still the grammar police whose purview extends little further than correct style, organization, and, yes, citations. Writing is still all too often seen as the transcription of finished thought rather than central to the generation of insight. What matters to all too many disciplinary faculty are that the citations are in correct shape, not that the process of acquiring and evaluating information has given students insight into the discursive and cognitive features of a discipline. Ten years ago, in the first of the two paired articles, I noted how the still widely entrenched "current-traditional" paradigm of writing instruction limits our ability to enact a more robust approach to IL. That very same paradigm also limits our institutional roles and identities.

As to internal pressures, one of the greatest ongoing concerns is staffing. Our field is all too reliant on contingent labor—part-time lecturers and graduate students for whom writing instruction and IL may not be central to their long-term career interests. This reliance on contingent faculty has only gotten worse in the last ten years, especially with the Great Recession, and has become the subject of explicit concern and national discussion. Turn-over in personnel is constant, and puts pressure on effective training, professional development, and quality control and assessment. At large state universities, the sections of first-year writing offered during any one semester can easily reach well over 100 (Bousquet, 2008; Bousquet, Scott & Parascondola, 2004; Palmquist & Doe, 2011; Schell & Stock, 2001). Last minute accommodations to enrollment demand can easily lead to the impression that virtually anyone can teach writing. No matter how well conceived, an IL initiative in a writing program can only succeed if it has buy-in and intellectual engagement from people in the trenches, not just the writing program administrator, several tenure-track faculty, and a handful of full-time instructors.

As a discipline, Rhetoric and Writing Studies has continued to mature over these last ten years, with more graduate programs, and more undergraduate majors and certificate programs. The very limitations to our institutional roles that I note above are gradually being addressed on campuses that have active writing centers, and robust WAC and WID programs. But the higher disciplinary profile that Rhetoric and Writing Studies has achieved can also limit intellectual partnerships. However gregarious we might be by nature, an interest in establishing disciplinary authority adds just one further disincentive to institutional and disciplinary partnerships. Incentives and reward structures tend to recognize work done on one's own home turf. Librarians and writing faculty are natural partners, but historically determined identities and campus roles can conspire against that partnership.

MOVING FORWARD ON CAMPUS

CS: Despite the barriers that we have discussed, librarians and writing teachers across the country are engaged in successful partnerships. For some, the collaborations are the outcome of campus level change. For example, at Purdue University there was a "perfect storm" of campus curricular initiatives, library-invested initiatives, and local experts engaged in IL which resulted in a broad campus initiative as well as an endowed chair of IL (Seamans, 2012, p. 228; "W. Wayne Booker Chair," 2014). On our own campus, a similar "perfect storm" enabling new approaches to IL accompanied the formation of a new Program for Writing and Rhetoric.

However, other local or individual IL partnerships shared in the literature describe a different story. A solitary librarian is driven by intrinsic motivations to actively extend IL education. She may identify an amenable faculty member with whom she shares her ideas for collaboration in the classroom. Often, these efforts may end successfully and work as exemplars for other librarians and faculty. For example, Heidi Jacobs and Dale Jacobs (2009) describe a partnership that grew organically from a casual conversation but resulted in significant curricular and programmatic change to IL integration in English Composition courses. In this example, had the process begun with a goal to impact full programmatic change, the authors admit that the magnitude, and one may assume the associated time commitment, may have halted their efforts (p. 79). For that reason, the authors argue for initiatives led by individuals and stakeholders who pursue manageable commitments and responsibilities in unison with existing workloads.

RN: But as effective as "stealth innovation" can be (and I'm a fan of working undercover until the right institutional moment emerges), this approach can have its downsides. Unless IL initiatives become part of core identities and core budgets, they easily get pushed to the side. The impact of accreditation agencies on an institution's commitment to IL can have significant impact on local buy-in. For example, in 2002 the Southern Association of Colleges and Schools required "Quality Enhancement Plans" from its member institutions (SACS, 2012). Colleges and schools were asked to create proposals that broadly improved student learning. As a result, 18 institutions focused the plan on IL while at least 100 institutions included IL to some degree (Harris, 2013, p. 175). Similarly, organizations and IL leaders are encouraging librarians to actively participate on local national assessment and curriculum reform committees in order to explicitly include IL in student learning outcomes (GWLA, 2013; Iannuzzi, 2013). Placing IL at the core of a writing program's mission helps to create a more cohesive sense of IL and helps guard against this notion that it is a peripheral add-on.

Also, it is worth noting that we have endured a modest budget crisis in 2003 and the Great Recession starting in 2008. Fiscal crises tend to have administrators circle the wagons to protect core responsibilities and identities.

CS: Moreover, Barbara D'Angelo and Barry Maid (2004) caution that when change is led by individuals, it is typically the individual who "absorbs the increased workload and time commitment without institutional change or support" (p. 212). Similarly, Barbara Fister (1995) warns that these programs will dismantle when collaborators withdraw due to burnout, career advancement or general turnover. Or alternatively, the programs will be handed off to junior colleagues who may view the project as superfluous to their core functions (p. 34). While it is clear that energetic individuals are essential to sparking improvements to IL teaching and learning, like you, I agree that garnering institutional support is essential.

RN: I believe the trick is to find the institutional "sweet spot": high enough on the institutional food chain to garner real support, visibility, continuity, and investment, but also low enough so that on-the-ground expertise is not neglected and can be leveraged effectively through personal relationships.

CS: Assuming we can find that "sweet spot," Fister (1995) suggests a few central characteristics and conditions for collaboration. The first is a "need to trust one another and have a sense of shared ownership" (p. 47). In order to reach that trust, writing instructors need to understand the evolution of librarians as educators. Similarly, it will be helpful for librarians to appreciate the demands and expectations placed on the writing teachers. Second, Fister recommends that goals be set together by librarians and writing instructors, which will inevitably encourage a sense of shared ownership and understanding. Third, Fister encourages the sharing of "insights both practical and theoretical" (p. 16).

ADVANCING CONCEPTUAL DISCUSSIONS

RN: As we continue our discussion here, the need looms large for more clearly articulated shared goals and understandings between librarians and writing instructors. Only by sharing conceptual discussions can we improve student learning.

LACK OF SHARED LITERATURE

CS: Alas, that shared conceptual discussion has not developed as we hoped. In your first article, you recognize that few IL-related articles have successfully invoked theoretical foundations or pedagogical frameworks from Rhetoric and Writing Studies. I believe that your observation prompted many to begin doing just that, with the intention of theorizing IL to a greater degree. (Here I'm thinking of the work of Jacobs (2008), Veach (2012), Elmborg (2012), and Fister (1993, 1995), to name a few.) However, while both writing instructors and librarians have pursued investigations into IL, they have failed to directly speak to one another through this work.

RN: Quite true. The literature produced by both fields has largely remained siloed and directed to an audience of peers within their home disciplines, rather than reaching beyond these boundaries. The politics of publication and the reward systems of, and criteria for, tenure may play a role in this.

CS: That seems like a solid assumption, and represents a problem not unique to Rhetoric and Writing Studies faculty. According to Sue Phelps and Nicole Campbell (2012), the models of successful librarian-faculty partnerships for IL are mainly written by librarians (72%) and appear in library journals (82%) (p. 15).

RN: My own paired articles from ten years ago share in that dynamic: although writing as a rhetorician and writing teacher, those articles appeared in a library journal that goes largely unread by my colleagues in Rhetoric and Writing Studies. The library community has warmly received this "interloper"; I just wish that such work would no longer be seen as interloping!

CS: These findings might be interpreted to mean that collaborative partnerships are of a higher priority to librarians, or perhaps, they may simply indicate a lack of awareness from writing instructors, or the lack of shared language and understanding between fields. Regardless, we can safely conclude that formal written collaborations have not yet crossed disciplinary boundaries to the extent you encourage. However, conference presentations and papers offer evidence that cross-disciplinary conversations are taking place in less formal settings. For example, papers from the Georgia International Conference on Information Literacy (2013) include works co-authored by librarians and writing teachers as well as presentations that indicate a desire for increased collaborations (Dew et al., 2013; McClure & Toth, 2013; Carter & Schmidt, 2013; Gola & Creelman, 2013). Similarly, the 2013 Conference on College Composition and Communication included at least three sessions that integrated IL into composition and curriculum discussions (CCCC, 2013). This evidence reveals that collaborations continue to grow between cross-disciplinary colleagues, yet, perhaps still not to the degree that you suggest.

LACK OF SHARED DEFINITION

RN: A prerequisite for that discussion, but also a valuable outcome, is a shared definition of IL. Definitions—acts of naming—are not trivial, and carry with them political and disciplinary dimensions (Scheidt et al., Chapter 10, this collection; Kissel et al., Chapter 20, this collection).

CS: Clarifying a definition of IL has indeed been an area of debate and conversation in librarianship (Owusu-Ansah, 2005). There are numerous standards and definitions devised by international, national, regional, and state organizations (International Federation of Library Associations (IFLA), Australian and New Zealand Information Literacy (ANZIL), Society of College, National and University Libraries (SCONUL), Association of College and Research Libraries (ACRL), Middle States Commission). Scholars and practitioners, on a global scale, have devoted considerable energy without reaching a uniformly accepted definition or understanding of IL. A reader of the complementary and competing definitions will quickly understand that IL is a complex concept interwoven with myriad other literacies.

RN: In a similar vein, Rhetoric and Writing Studies was plagued by disparate understandings of what the outcomes of first-year composition should be. After broad consultation, the national Council of Writing Program Administrators adopted in April 2000 the "WPA Outcomes Statement for First-Year Composition" (2000). This statement has had an amazing galvanizing influence on curricular design in writing programs across the country. It omits the term IL, and yet the original document, and the several revisions that have followed it, remain quite amenable to the concept.

CS: While it is unfortunate that the WPA Outcomes Statement and the *Information Competency Standards for Higher Education* (ACRL, 2000) were written in isolation, writing instructors and librarians have taken it upon themselves to mesh these two documents while pursuing local initiatives (McClure, 2009; Jacobs & Jacobs, 2009; Gruber et al., 2008; D'Angelo & Maid, 2004). The documents provide a strong means for one to enter discussion in the other's community, because the precepts and beliefs had already been endorsed by the broad professional community. While many faculty members may not be familiar with the term "information literacy," when the concept is defined they easily comprehend the value and importance. Furthermore, Laura Saunders (2012) surveyed faculty from 50 colleges and universities and found that a faculty member's awareness of standards or defining documents increased her enthusiasm for integrating IL (p. 232).

RN: A more recent foundational document in the Rhetoric and Writing Studies community, the *Framework for Success in Postsecondary Writing*, published by the Council of Writing Program Administrators, the National Council of Teachers of English, and the National Writing Project (2011), holds much promise for collaboration. Although this document, too, fails to highlight IL as I would like, it does a great service by highlighting "habits of mind" that underpin success, among them the need for metacognition. Such habits of mind are necessary complements to the more instrumental definitions that have dominated IL discussion thus far.

CS: Indeed, such "habits of mind" are similar to elements found in the American Association of School Libraries Standards for the 21st Century Learner (2007). So we can clearly identify overlap between professional documents authored by writing teachers and those written by librarians.

RN: Perhaps it is not enough to recognize the similarities in our reform impulses; we need to advocate strongly for our associations and national groups to join in intellectual partnership through shared documents (Maid & D' Angelo, Chapter 2, this collection).

CS: Yes, I think that would prove very fruitful and could add depth to our existing guiding documents. While the *IL Standards* have been invaluable in developing momentum for IL initiatives, the standards are problematic due to their decontextualized and linear structure. The document's performance indicators suggest that an individual's IL might be measured against precise action, regardless of circumstance or context; one may be judged to have or not have IL based on measured performance. Furthermore, the *IL Standards* fail to clearly articulate that information is bound in conversations between ourselves and others and between varied contexts or situations. Information is not represented as a "product of socially negotiated epistemological processes and the raw material for further making of new knowledge" (Elmborg, 2006, p. 198). Rather, it is presented as a static entity, which learners may acquire and evaluate based on codified and imposed criteria. In 2011, the ACRL, having noted the shortcomings of the *IL Standards*, took initial steps to consider a revised document. Beginning March 2013, a taskforce, whose membership included an array of stakeholders, not only librarians, worked to develop the *Framework for Information Literacy for Higher Education* (ACRL, 2015), which approaches IL through conceptual understandings rather than standards. In the *Framework for IL*, IL is defined as "a spectrum of abilities, practices, and habits of mind that extends and deepens learning through engagement with the information ecosystem" (ACRL, 2015).

Because the *Framework for IL* resists defining IL through a "prescriptive enumeration of skills," it may strengthen your argument against misconceptions of IL as a neutral, on/off skill (ACRL, 2015). Perhaps, the *Framework for IL* will encourage advocacy for a situated literacy as you have done.

RN: The academy, however, situates IL in narrow ways. And the historical connection, indeed identification, between Rhetoric and Writing Studies and but one first-year course further limits how we might situate IL in innovative and genuinely useful ways. To broaden our approach, we might tap into WAC and WID programs and writing center activities, which offer more expansive and differentiated venues for discussing IL.

CS: You also call for a process-oriented approach to IL rather than a product-focused approach. The *IL Standards* present IL as neatly packaged skills which result in a successful product, performance, or presentation. Yet, lived information experiences are far more complex, problematic, and entwined with one's own identity, beliefs, and experiences. Instead of an intellectual process in which the learner is an active agent, as written in the *IL Standards*, IL positions the learner as passive recipient. A brief nod to an individual's past experiences and beliefs is given in standard three: the information literate individual "determines whether the new knowledge has an impact on the individual's value system and takes steps to reconcile differences" (ACRL, 2000). The *Framework for IL* improves that shortcoming by recognizing that "students have a greater role in creating new knowledge" (ACRL, 2015). Still, a process-centered IL needs to place great attention on the learner's construction of knowledge, whether in past information experiences, current experiences, or through reflection on experiences (See Yancey, Chapter 4, this collection).

RN: As you suggest, the myth of the student as "blank slate" pervades higher education, and is related to our focus on purveying information, the domain content of a field, and not on cultivating rhetorical and cognitive aptitudes and strategies. Our traditional approaches to IL have much in common with the "banking concept of education" that Paolo Freire (1970) so roundly criticized. We have much to gain by leveraging students' varied IL activities, and by better understanding how they might misinterpret contexts and misuse tools. Appreciating how people construct their world through information is where we need to begin, not end.

CS: The third dimension of your interest in rhetoricizing IL is the need for a relevant literacy—that is, relevant to a "broad range of social, political, and intellectual endeavors," and appreciative of the dynamic early moments of invention when we launch inquiry and formulate problems (Norgaard, 2003, p. 128).

RN: It is not surprising given the intended audience of the *IL Standards*—higher education—that they have been used within one particular context and have become representative of one information landscape alone, namely academic. To be genuinely useful, our conception of IL needs to be attentive to what we might call "information ecologies," in all their varied forms. Higher education, broadly speaking, is becoming more aware of the need for a new culture of learning that has similar ecological impulses. All of this underscores the exigence of extending our understandings of IL, and the relevance of the *Framework for IL*, as it defines IL as situated and contextualized.

CS: Indeed. Much of the practice surrounding IL in higher education has privileged textual and codified norms of information such as the peer reviewed article and academic research databases. And very little attention is paid to the social, economic, political, and cultural influences on the creation, dissemination, and the use of information (Luke & Kapitzke, 1999, p. 11).

An essential aspect of IL is a critical stance towards information systems (Elmborg, 2006, p. 196). In other words, learners would scrutinize information systems, in any mode, understand the systems' norms (what counts as knowledge), and identify the voices included or excluded (Luke & Kapitzke, 1999, p. 484; Simmons 2005, p. 301). Students are not provided the opportunity to do so when academic values are imposed without question, and students are told to use peer-reviewed articles and to limit searching to academic databases.

Accepting one frame or focusing on one information landscape is not only a misrepresentation; it may alienate students and deter the transfer of critical dispositions to other contexts. As students enter alternate information landscapes, they will need to examine the unique contextual information and learning tools therein and to acclimate to the specific "skills, practices and affordances" required (Lloyd, 2006, p. 572). In order to offer a more holistic and authentic view, IL education should expand across domains as well as to new information modes and formats. As educators, if we hold our focus to textual information only, we ignore the "mediascapes and infospheres" in which students live presently, not to mention the new modes they will encounter in the future (Luke & Kapitzke, 1999, p. 469).

RN: As you mentioned, ACRL has filed the *Framework for IL*. What promise does this revision hold for fostering the kind of collaboration I called for a decade ago?

CS: The current draft revision strongly encourages librarians to introduce the document at home institutions in order to identify "synergies" with other educational initiatives (ACRL, 2015) The task force chairs recognize that the *IL Standards* limited conversation between librarians and course instructors because of their skills-based approach (Jacobson & Gibson, 2013). The new model abandons the "standards-like inventory" in favor of identifying core dispositions that may be cultivated in varied information contexts, including workplace and lifelong learning (Jacobson & Gibson, 2013). The goal is to be more flexible and responsive given the current environment and the speed with which the information ecologies change. Additionally, the intended audience is all educators, not only librarians, as evidenced by sections dedicated to faculty and administrators, "For Faculty: How to Use the Framework" and "For Administrators: How to Support the Framework" (ACRL, 2015). According to the task force chairs, the new document provides "a conceptual approach for collaboration, pedagogical innovation, curriculum planning, and a weaving together of literacies that is critical for today's Information Literacy" (Jacobsen & Gibson, 2013). Given these guiding principles, the revised *Framework for IL* has the potential to foster conversations between course instructors and librarians (Maid & D'Angelo, Chapter 2, this collection).

REFINING PRACTICE AND PEDAGOGY

RN: New national standards are most welcome. Indeed, the *Framework for IL* is especially promising in that it resonates with the "habits of mind" stressed in the 2011 *Framework for Success in Postsecondary Writing* developed by the Council of Writing Program Administrators (2011). Yet there remains the issue of what is often the yawning gap between concept and implementation, theory, and the practical demands of the classroom. Many inherited and now ossified norms compete with the more holistic and dynamic view of IL and writing to which we have been pointing. Ten years ago I felt the need to complement my first article on "Contributions to a Concept" with a second on "Pedagogical Enactments and Implications." Today, that need to connect concepts with classrooms is as pressing as ever.

CS: And it is pressing because of the disconnect that we see. The process we dearly hope students experience is one in which information seeking, reading, and writing are recursive and intertwined. Through these experiences, students would begin to build their own meaning, their own knowledge, and contribute their own voices into a wider conversation. Yet, in failing to deeply engage in reciprocal relationships, writing teachers and librarians present a fragmented process to students in which writing and information may appear vastly disconnected.

RN: One culprit in this disconnect is the sedimentation of classroom practice. We tend to recycle our pedagogy—handouts are photocopied yet again, and while files may now be posted electronically, with all the speed and freshness that such technology implies, those files (and the classroom approaches that inform them) may themselves be years old.

CS: The research paper, another inherited practice, has significant influence on the ways in which librarians and writing teachers collaborate. The common one-shot library seminar is often designed to directly support students' completion of the research paper (Blackwell-Starnes, Chapter 7, this collection).

RN: I would have hoped that the old ghost of the research paper would have by now faded away, for it has been under such intense criticism in Rhetoric and Writing Studies. Yet the old ghost continues to haunt us, and with it outmoded notions of IL.

CS: The same sentiments have been echoed in librarianship as well, perhaps most compellingly by Fister (2013). She spoke at the 2013 LOEX conference, making several "outrageous claims," one of which was to abandon the research paper in first-year experiences. Fister identifies many ways that the research paper is not suited to first-year students, because they are novices to academic communication norms and because the assignment de-emphasizes research as an intellectual and knowledge-building act. When we couple the research paper with one shot library seminars, where the focus is information retrieval, it is no wonder that students fail to comprehend sources as rhetorical acts or to see their own information interactions as rhetorical choices (Fister, 2013).

RN: If the ghost of the traditional research paper endures, what I saw ten years ago as the new specter of plagiarism has grown even larger. Of course, we wish to instill a sense of academic values in our students, and with it the ethical obligation and practical ability to document sources according to codified rules of citation. Yet this goal has privileged procedure in much the same way as has information gathering. Students are fearful of breaking the rules to the point that they cut and paste citations into a paper without comprehending the pragmatics inherent in these academic practices. There is ample evidence provided by the Stanford Writing Project, the Citation Project, and Project Information Literacy that students do struggle with understanding citation and plagiarism fully (Lunsford, 2008, Jamieson et al., n.d.; Project Information Literacy, n.d.). Students patchwrite rather than summarize sources, and quote sentences with little awareness of their rhetorical role in the original sources (Jamieson & Howard, 2013). Students are taught about plagiarism with fear tactics, threatening punishment for infringement. Students hear this warning. They do not hear that citation is a means to support claims, track scholarly discourse, and create allegiances with other writers. If students obsess with "covering their behinds" so as not to get caught by Turnitin.com, they will not appreciate how real authors use citations and why (Jamieson, Chapter 6, this collection).

CS: And the most pernicious aspect of this narrow focus on plagiarism is the way it disenfranchises student writers. Students construct citations because "knowledge belongs to other people," so they must follow the rules (Fister, 2013). When writing and IL become divorced from knowledge making, we've lost far more than the battle against plagiarism.

RN: Plagiarism-detection software loomed large ten years ago, and is still with us. What looms large now, ten years later, is the specter of automated or machine grading of student writing. News reports now happily claim that this or that software can lighten the burden of teachers as they respond to student writing—neglecting all the while the crucial distinction between grading or scoring and responding. As Common Core State Standards sweep into high school classrooms, so too do heavily marketed software products that purport to evaluate the writing that is meant to meet those standards. Although the Rhetoric and Writing Studies community has responded to these developments with cogent arguments in both scholarly venues and the public press, the more specific impact of this new technology on IL has yet to be fully discussed (Strauss, 2013). Even as we endorse a more nuanced, context-sensitive approach to IL, if machines are grading the writing that is meant to foster and showcase those capacities, our efforts will not be valued, and may even be undermined.

CS: And to note but another barrier, a significant failure of the coupling between the research paper and the one-shot library session is an intense privileging of academic enactments of IL. First, as already noted, this is an environment foreign to first-year students and one which requires a great deal of acculturation in order for students to authentically engage. Second, it ignores the expertise and experiences that students have in other contexts and through other information interactions. Third, it does not support students' future needs in alternate contexts. At the core of IL is discerning what to learn, seeking patterns across information (people, text, places), generating knowledge, and acting in the world (Elmborg, 2003, p. 73). If we focus our efforts in IL on academic contexts, students may come to view its importance as relevant only in that context, rather than being transferable and broadly relevant. Take, for example, Project Information Literacy's "Passage Studies," which found employer dissatisfaction with recent graduates' IL in the workplace. Employers interviewed in this study value employees who are agile, collaborative, flexible, nimble, patient, persistent, and resourceful. However, recent graduates lacked sophisticated habits of analyzing information across sources, distinguishing important information from "noise," synthesizing information for problem solving, and finding patterns. This example captures only one alternate information landscape, the workplace, but there are many others that students will encounter after graduation in which a critical disposition towards information will be vital (Cyphert & Lyle, Chapter 3, this collection).

RN: As important as workplace contexts are, I also worry that our privileging of the academic context renders students underprepared for civic life and advocacy. Students deserve an approach to IL that will support broad engagement and collaboration in our communities, not just in classrooms with access to academic databases.

CS: Indeed. As we take into account civic, social, and workplace contexts, our potential strategies should ensure that the multiple actions inherent in IL—questioning, seeking, reading, thinking, and writing—are not presented as separate. These are in fact "non-consecutive acts," which are not neatly delimited or linear (Fister, 1993, para. 19). To support students through these messy activities, collaborations may help to scaffold and to slow down students' inquiry, allowing for time to reflect, pause, reverse or proceed. These are habits and functions much more authentic to self-motivated acts of inquiry transferable across contexts and information landscapes.

All of this leads us back to your initial claim, some ten years ago, that we form intellectual partnerships.

RN: Yes, the metaphor—and real act—of conversation is central to ensuring progress and surmounting barriers. Our students best appreciate the relevance of IL when they read information environments as invitations to converse, and when we prepare them to enter those conversations fully aware of their obligations and opportunities. But to do so, we ourselves must enter into a more robust and sustained conversation with each other.

COMMON GROUND GOING FORWARD

CS: We started our conversation by looking back ten years. We noted in your two articles a call that, if appreciated, went largely unheeded. And we've observed more than a few obstacles along the path to intellectual partnerships, engaged classroom teaching, and a more nuanced sense of IL.

RN: But our conversation has also demonstrated that there has been considerable progress as well. We have a better sense of the challenges as well as the rewards of an IL actively shaped by collaboration between our two fields.

RN and CS: And, now speaking in one voice, we've also arrived at several desiderata that can inform our efforts going forward:

Community
- Share our educational identities, and our hopes with one another.
- Formulate integrated guiding documents that lead to shared understanding.
- Establish locations for shared conversation and collaboration, in formal literature, organizations, and institutions.

Change
- Reflect on our strategies through feedback from one another and students.
- Experiment and revise so as to resist fossilized approaches.
- Attend to student-centered approaches which call on contexts outside of our academic ones.

Context
- Embrace the rich environments in which students use technology and information.
- Look beyond college to dynamic, life-long relevance and application.
- Emphasize knowledge making in collaborative and interactive information environments.

If there were to be a presiding deity for our article it would Janus, the Roman god of transitions, thresholds, and new beginnings. Janus is usually depicted as having two faces, one that looks to the past, and one that looks forward into the future. We have likewise looked back ten years to a pair of articles that had a formative influence, if not on IL practices then at least on IL discussions. And from our current position we have also looked forward. IL is itself similarly positioned at a threshold moment. The promise of the next decade is bright indeed if collaboration and conversation drive our efforts, as they have in these pages.

REFERENCES

Accardi, M. T., Drabinski, E. & Kumbier, A. (2010). *Critical library instruction: Theories and methods*. Sacramento, CA: Library Juice Press, LLC.

Association of College and Research Libraries (ACRL). (2000). *Information literacy competency standards for higher education*. Retrieved from http://www.ala.org/acrl/standards/informationliteracycompetency.

ACRL. (2015). *Framework for information literacy for higher education*. Retrieved from http://www.ala.org/acrl/standards/ilframework.

ACRL, Instruction Section, Professional Education Committee. (2013). *Library instruction courses. ACRL Instruction Section, Professional Education Wiki*. Retrieved from http://wikis.ala.org/acrl/index.php/IS/Library_Instruction_Courses.

American Association of School Libraries. (2007). *Standards for the 21st-century learner*. Retrieved from http://www.ala.org/aasl/standards-guidelines/learning-standards.

Artman, M., Frisicaro-Pawlowski, E. & Monge, R. (2010). Not just one shot: Extending the dialogues about information literacy in composition classes. *Composition Studies/Freshman English News*, *38*(2), 93–110.

Australian and New Zealand Institute for Information. (2004). *Australian and New Zealand information literacy framework*. Retrieved from http://archive.caul.edu.au/info-literacy/InfoLiteracyFramework.pdf.

Blackwell-Starnes, K. (2016). Preliminary paths to information literacy: Introducing research in core courses. In B. J. D'Angelo, S. Jamieson, B. Maid & J. R. Walker (Eds.), *Information literacy: Research and collaboration across disciplines*. Fort Collins, CO: WAC Clearinghouse and University Press of Colorado.

Bousquet, M. (2008). *How the university works: Higher education and the low-wage nation*. New York: New York University Press.

Bousquet, M., Scott, T. & Parascondola, L. (2004). *Tenured bosses and disposable teachers: Writing instruction in the managed university*. Carbondale: Southern Illinois University Press.

Bruch, C. & Wilkinson, C. W. (2012). Surveying terrain, clearing pathways. In C. Bruch (Ed.), *Transforming information literacy programs: Complex frontiers of self, library culture, and campus community* (pp. 3–44). Chicago: ACRL.

Carter, T. & Schmidt, G. (2013). Transforming students through two literacies: The integration of sustainability literacy into information literacy classes. Georgia Inter-

national Conference on Information Literacy. Retrieved from http://digitalcom mons.georgiasouthern.edu/cil-2012-2/6.
CCCC. (2013). 2013 CCCC convention program. Conference on College Composition and Communication. Retrieved from http://www.ncte.org/cccc/review/2013program.
Council of Writing Program Administrators. (2008). WPA outcomes statement for first-year composition. Retrieved from http://wpacouncil.org/positions/outcomes.html.
Council of Writing Program Administrators & National Writing Project. (2011). *Framework for success in postsecondary writing.* Retrieved from http://wpacouncil.org/framework.
Cyphert, D. & Lyle, S. P. (2016). Employer expectations of information literacy: Identifying the skills gap. In B. J. D'Angelo, S. Jamieson, B. Maid & J. R. Walker (Eds.), *Information literacy: Research and collaboration across disciplines.* Fort Collins, CO: WAC Clearinghouse and University Press of Colorado.
D'Angelo, B. J. & Maid, B. M. (2004). Moving beyond definitions: Implementing information literacy across the curriculum. *Journal of Academic Librarianship, 30*(3), 212–217. doi:10.1016/j.acalib.2004.02.002.
Davidson, J. R. & Crateau, C. A. (1998). Intersections: Teaching research through a rhetorical lens. *Research Strategies, 16*(4), 245–257. doi:10.1016/S0734-3310(99)00013-0.
Derakhshan, M. & Singh, D. (2011). Integration of information literacy into the curriculum: A meta-synthesis. *Library Review, 60*(3), 218–229. doi:10.1108/00242531111117272.
Dew, D., Belzowski, N., Mileham, T. & Bull, J. (2013). Panel: Going vertical together: An interdisciplinary infusion of information literacy with research writing in the disciplines. Georgia International Conference on Information Literacy. Retrieved from http://digitalcommons.georgiasouthern.edu/cil-2012-2/23.
Elmborg, J. (2012). Critical information literacy: Definitions and challenges. In C. W. Wilkinson & C. Bruch (Eds.), *Transforming information literacy programs : Intersecting frontiers of self, library culture, and campus community.* Chicago: Association of College and Research Libraries.
Elmborg, J. (2006). Critical information literacy: Implications for instructional practice. *Journal of Academic Librarianship, 32*(2), 192–199. doi:10.1016/j.acalib.2005.12.004.
Elmborg, J. (2003). Information literacy and writing across the curriculum: Sharing the vision. *Reference Services Review, 31*(1), 68–80. doi:10.1108/00907320310460933.
Fister, B. (1993). Teaching the rhetorical dimensions of research. Retrieved October 9, 2012, from http://homepages.gac.edu/%7Efister/rs.html.
Fister, B. (1995). Connected communities: Encouraging dialogue between composition and bibliographic instruction. In J. Sheridan (Ed.), *Writing across the curriculum and the academic library: Implications for bibliographic instruction* (pp. 33–51). Westport, CT: Greenwood Press.

Fister, B. (2013). Decode academy. Presented at the LOEX, Nashville, TN. Retrieved from http://homepages.gac.edu/~fister/loex13.pdf.

Freire, P. (1970). *Pedagogy of the oppressed.* New York: Seabury Press.

Gola, C. & Creelman, K. (2013). Building a culture of IL assessment: Establishing buy-in for programmatic change. Georgia International Conference on Information Literacy. Retrieved from http://digitalcommons.georgiasouthern.edu/cil-2012-2/13.

Greater Western Library Alliance (GWLA). (2013). *GWLA student learning outcomes task force.* Retrieved from http://www.gwla.org/Committees/slo.

Gregory, A. S. & McCall, B. L. (2016). Building critical researchers and writers incrementally: Vital partnerships between faculty and librarians. In B. J. D'Angelo, S. Jamieson, B. Maid & J. R. Walker (Eds.), *Information literacy: Research and collaboration across disciplines.* Chapter 18. Fort Collins, CO: WAC Clearinghouse and University Press of Colorado.

Gruber, A. M., Knefel, M. A. & Waelchli, P. (2008). Modeling scholarly inquiry: One article at a time. *College & Undergraduate Libraries, 15*(1–2), 99–125. doi:10.1080/10691310802177085.

Harris, B. R. (2013). Subversive infusions: Strategies for the integration of information literacy across the curriculum. *Journal of Academic Librarianship, 39*(2), 175–180. doi:10.1016/j.acalib.2012.10.003.

Head, A. J., Van Hoeck, M., Eschler, J. & Fullerton, S. (2013). What information competencies matter in today's workplace? *Library and Information Research, 37*(114), 74–104.

Holliday, W. & Fagerheim, B. A. (2006). Integrating information literacy with a sequenced English composition curriculum. *portal: Libraries and the Academy, 6*(2), 169–184.

Howard, R. M., Serviss, T. & Rodrigue, T. K. (2010). Writing from sources, writing from sentences. *Writing & Pedagogy, 2*(2), 177–192.

Iannuzzi, P. (2013). Info Lit 2.0 or Deja Vu? *Communications in Information Literacy,* 1–17.

Jamieson, S. (2016). What the Citation Project tells us about information literacy in college composition. In B. J. D'Angelo, S. Jamieson, B. Maid & J. R. Walker (Eds.), *Information literacy: Research and collaboration across disciplines.* Fort Collins, CO: WAC Clearinghouse and University Press of Colorado.

Jamieson, S., Howard, R. M. & Serviss, T. (n.d.). *The Citation Project: Preventing plagiarism, teaching writing.* Retrieved from http://site.citationproject.net/.

Jamieson, S. & Howard, R. M. (2013). Explorations of what NextGen students do in the undergraduate writing classroom. In R. McClure & J. P. Purdy (Eds.), *The new digital scholar: Exploring and enriching the research and writing practices of NextGen students* (pp. 109–127). Medford, NJ: ASIST.

Jacobs, H. L. & Jacobs, D. (2009). Transforming the one-shot session into pedagogical collaboration. *Reference & User Services Quarterly, 49*(1), 72–82. doi:10.5860/rusq.49n1.72.

Jacobs, H. L. M. (2008). Information literacy and reflective pedagogical praxis. *Journal of Academic Librarianship, 34*(3), 256–262. doi:10.1016/j.acalib.2008.03.009.

Jacobson, T. & Gibson, C. (2013). A prospectus for revision. ACRL Information Literacy Competency Standards for Higher Education Task Force. Retrieved from http://connect.ala.org/files/Doc%205.0a%20Info%20Lit%20Standards%20Prospectus%20for%20Revision.pdf.

Kissel, F., Wininger, M. R., Weeden, S. R., Wittberg, P. A., Halverson, R. S., Lacy, M. & Huisman, R. (2016). Information literacy community of practice. In B. J. D'Angelo, S. Jamieson, B. Maid & J. R. Walker (Eds.), *Information literacy: Research and collaboration across disciplines.* Fort Collins, CO: WAC Clearinghouse and University Press of Colorado

Lloyd, A. (2006). Information literacy landscapes: An emerging picture. *Journal of Documentation, 62*(5), 570–583. doi:10.1108/00220410610688723.

Luke, A. & Kapitzke, C. (1999). Literacies and libraries: Archives and cybraries. *Pedagogy, Culture & Society, 7*(3), 467–491. doi:10.1080/14681369900200066.

Lunsford, A. A. (2008). *Stanford study of writing.* Stanford, CA: Stanford University. Retrieved from https://ssw.stanford.edu/about

Maid, B. & D'Angelo, B. J. (2016). Threshold concepts: Integrating and applying information literacy and writing instruction. In B. J. D'Angelo, S. Jamieson, B. Maid & J. R. Walker (Eds.), *Information literacy: Research and collaboration across disciplines.* Fort Collins, CO: WAC Clearinghouse and University Press of Colorado

McClure, R. (2009). Examining the presence of advocacy and commercial websites in research essays of first-year composition students. *WPA: Writing Program Administration, 32*(3). Retrieved from http://muwriting.wdfiles.com/local--files/annotated-readings/mcClure.pdf.

McClure, H. & Toth, C. (2013). Panel: Bridging the gap: Collaborative teaching of an emerging genre to empower students with information literacy skills. Georgia International Conference on Information Literacy. Retrieved from http://digitalcommons.georgiasouthern.edu/cil-2012-2/19.

Meulemans, Y. N. & Carr, A. (2013). Not at your service: Building genuine faculty-librarian partnerships. *Reference Services Review, 41*(1), 80–90. doi:10.1108/00907321311300893.

Middle States Commission on Higher Education. (2000). *Developing research and communication skills: Guidelines for information literacy in the curriculum.* Retrieved from http://www.msche.org/publications/devskill050208135642.pdf.

International Federation of Library Associations and Universities. (2005). *Alexandria Proclamation on Information Literacy and Lifelong Learning.* Retrieved from http://archive.ifla.org/III/wsis/BeaconInfSoc.html.

Norgaard, R. (2003). Writing information literacy contributions to a concept. *Reference & User Services Quarterly, 43*(2), 124–130.

Norgaard, R. (2004). Writing information literacy in the classroom: Pedagogical enactments and considerations. *Reference & User Services Quarterly, 43*, 220–226.

O'Connor, L., Bowles-Terry, M., Davis, E. & Holliday, W. (2010). "Writing information literacy" revisited. *Reference & User Services Quarterly, 49*(3), 225–230.

Owusu-Ansah, E. K. (2005). Debating definitions of information literacy: Enough is enough! *Library Review, 54*(6), 366–374.

Palmquist, M. & Doe, S. (Eds.). (2011). Special Issue. *College English, 73*(4).

Phelps, S. F. & Campbell, N. (2012). Commitment and trust in librarian–faculty relationships: A systematic review of the literature. *Journal of Academic Librarianship, 38*(1), 13–19. doi:10.1016/j.acalib.2011.11.003.

Project Information Literacy. (n.d.). Retrieved from http://projectinfolit.org.

Purdue University Libraries. (2014). W. Wayne Booker. *Purdue University Libraries W. Wayne Booker Chair in Information Literacy.* Retrieved from https://www.lib.purdue.edu/infolit/bookerChair

Saunders, L. (2012). Faculty perspectives on information literacy as a student learning outcome. *Journal of Academic Librarianship, 38*(4), 226–236. doi:10.1016/j.acalib.2012.06.001.

Schell, E. E., Stock, P. L. & National Council of Teachers of English. (2001). *Moving a mountain: Transforming the role of contingent faculty in composition studies and higher education.* Urbana, IL: National Council of Teachers of English.

Scheidt, D. L., Carpenter, W., Fitzgerald, R., Kozma, C., Middleton, H. & Shields, K.. (2016). Writing information literacy in first year composition: A collaboration among faculty and librarians. In B. J. D'Angelo, S. Jamieson, B. Maid & J. R. Walker (Eds.), *Information literacy: Research and collaboration across disciplines.* Chapter 10. Fort Collins, CO: WAC Clearinghouse and University Press of Colorado

SCONUL Working Group on Information Literacy. (2011). *SCONUL Seven pillars of information literacy: Core model.* Retrieved from http://www.sconul.ac.uk/sites/default/files/documents/coremodel.pdf.

Seamans, N. H. (2012). Information literacy reality check. In C. Bruch & C. W. Wilkinson (Eds.), *Transforming information literacy programs: Complex frontiers of self, library culture, and campus community* (pp. 221–241). Chicago: ACRL.

Simmons, M. H. (2005). Librarians as disciplinary discourse mediators: Using genre theory to move toward critical information literacy. *Portal: Libraries and the Academy, 5*(3), 297–311. doi:10.1353/pla.2005.0041.

Southern Association of Colleges and Schools Commission on Colleges. (2012). *Principles of accreditation: Foundations for quality enhancement.* Retrieved from http://sacscoc.org/pdf/2012principlesof acreditation.pdf.

Strauss, V. (2013, May 4). Grading writing: The art and science—and why computers can't do it. *The Answer Sheet, Washington Post* [Blog]. Retrieved from http://www.washingtonpost.com/blogs/answer-sheet/wp/2013/05/02/grading-writing-the-art-and-science-and-why-computers-cant-do-it/.

Todorinova, L. (2010). *Writing center and library collaboration: A telephone survey of academic libraries* (Masters). University of North Carolina Chapel Hill. Retrieved from http://works.bepress.com/ltodorinova/1.

Veach, G. (2012). At the intersection: Librarianship, writing studies, and sources as topoi. *Journal of Literacy and Technology, 13*(1), 102.

Weiner, S. A. (2012). Institutionalizing information literacy. *Journal of Academic Librarianship, 38*(5), 287–293. doi:10.1016/j.acalib.2012.05.004.

CHAPTER 2

THRESHOLD CONCEPTS: INTEGRATING AND APPLYING INFORMATION LITERACY AND WRITING INSTRUCTION

Barry Maid and Barbara D'Angelo
Arizona State University

Originally approved in 2000, the Association of College and Research Libraries (ACRL) *Information Literacy Standards for Higher Education* (*IL Standards*) have been adopted by libraries in higher education as the basis of instructional programs and for collaboration between librarians and instructional faculty for student learning. In particular, librarians and writing faculty have collaborated in what can be seen as natural partnerships due to mutual interest to develop student research skills. The *IL Standards* have also been recognized by regional accreditation agencies and serve as a foundation for many Southern Association of Colleges and Schools (SACS)-accredited Quality Enhancement Plans (QEP), a plan each member school must develop and submit as part of the reaccreditation process. In 2012, the ACRL Board of Directors initiated the process to review and revise the *IL Standards* with the formation of a task force, resulting in the evolution away from standards towards a framework. The *Framework for Information Literacy for Higher Education* (*Framework for IL*) is based on a cluster of interconnected concepts intended to provide a skeleton for flexible implementation based on local context. Conceptually, the *Framework for IL* is grounded in current learning theory which stresses threshold concepts and metaliteracy as a way to enhance skills and knowledge transfer. As a result, the *Framework for IL* presents librarians, instructional faculty, and administrators with challenges to rethink how IL has been taught and assessed at their institutions and what it means more broadly for accreditation.

For those of us in Writing Studies, the *Framework for IL* provides an exigence to consider our pedagogical and assessment practices within a changing information landscape and a shifting higher education landscape. An understanding of the *Framework for IL* and the concepts it is based upon, is, therefore, called for within the context of the seminal documents grounding writing programs:

The Writing Program Administrators' (WPA) *Outcomes Statement for First Year Composition* (WPA OS) and the *Framework for Success in Postsecondary Writing*.

WHAT'S A THRESHOLD CONCEPT?

The *Framework for IL* establishes six frames, each with a designated threshold concept. In addition, recent research and scholarship in Writing Studies has focused on threshold concepts within the context of transfer. What, though, is a threshold concept?

In the early years of this century, British researchers Jan Meyer and Ray Land (2006) proposed the idea of threshold concepts. Conceived as a way to understand why some students "get stuck" and have trouble negotiating concepts, threshold concepts represent a transformed way of viewing or understanding something. This transformed understanding is required for a learner to progress and may be seen as the way individuals think and practice within a disciplinary (or other) community. Meyer and Land talk about a threshold concept as a "conceptual gateway" or "portal" which a learner progresses through as they learn and integrate the concept and are transformed by it. Importantly, threshold concepts are not the same as core concepts. A threshold concept represents "seeing things in a new way." When accepted by the individual, threshold concepts may lead to an individual adopting a new way to see the world and/or changes the way s/he may think about their own and others' choices. Core concepts are building blocks on which learning progresses but that do not lead to a different view of the subject or to transformation in perspective. While threshold concepts will be unique to each discipline, it is possible to identify the properties of a threshold concept. According to Meyer and Land (2006a; 2006b), features of threshold concepts are that they are:

- **Transformative:** once understood, a threshold concept represents a significant shift in the way an individual perceives a subject. The shift may be affective, as in a shift in identity, or it may be performance-related in the way that an individual behaves.
- **Troublesome:** a threshold concept may be seen as troublesome for a couple of reasons. One, moving through a portal to a new way of thinking results in letting go of the old way of thinking, something that students may find difficult to do. In addition, threshold concepts may constitute or lead to the acquisition of troublesome knowledge that is conceptually difficult to understand, is "alien" or from a perspective that conflicts with the one currently held, or is complex and seemingly inconsistent or counter-intuitive. Threshold concepts

may also be troublesome due to "troublesome language"; that is, while disciplinary discourse practices may facilitate communication between members of a discipline, the language may make familiar concepts seemingly foreign and conceptually difficult to understand.
- **Irreversible:** once an individual has understood and adapted the transformation, it cannot be reversed without considerable effort. An individual may feel loss initially at leaving the old perspective or understanding behind.
- **Integrative:** once acquired, a threshold concept reveals interrelatedness between concepts or ideas in ways that were previously hidden or unclear.
- **Bounded:** threshold concepts have boundaries, bordering with threshold concepts from other areas. These boundaries may represent the divisions between disciplines.
- **Discursive:** the transformation brought about by the acquisition of threshold concepts results in new and empowering forms of expression for the learner.
- **Reconstitutive:** Discursive practices distinguish disciplinary thinking. A learner's identity within a discipline is interrelated to their thinking and use of language.
- **Liminal:** Learners pass through a liminal stage when acquiring a threshold concept during which there is uncertainty as the individual leaves the old ways behind and passes through the portal to the new. This liminal stage can be viewed in the same light as a "rite of passage" in which there is a change in status and the learner has been transformed—acquired their new identity and "thinks" and "practices" in their new identity (i.e., "thinks like a rhetorician").

What is important to understand is that since a threshold concept transforms a learner, that concept becomes a part of an individual's thought process about a subject. It requires a shift in worldview and can be quite difficult. It also often feels as though one has gone through a passage; hence, the gateway or portal metaphor.

THRESHOLD CONCEPTS AND WRITING

To this point there have only been a handful of Writing Studies researchers that have addressed threshold concepts and how they may be used to help in writing instruction. Most notably they are Linda Adler-Kassner, Elizabeth Wardle, and Irene Clark.

Researchers have suggested certain traits of threshold concepts as important. Linda Adler-Kassner, John Majewski, and Damian Koshick (2012) tend to focus on the traits of "troublesome" and "liminality." Based on a study of linked first-year writing and history classes, they point out that these traits can be useful in helping students understand the writing concepts of genre, discourse community, audience, purpose and context. They look at the threshold concepts the students face in each course as "snapshots." Irene Clark and Andrea Hernandez (2012) focus on the same traits but also include "transformative," while they suggest writing instructors should think about "genre awareness" rather than "teaching genre." By analyzing survey data and student reflections, they suggest that students are taught and learn about genres in a defined context and are not able to transfer that knowledge. They suggest students would be more likely to transfer genre skills if the focus was on the context rather than the surface features.

In addition, scholars have connected threshold concepts to transfer. Adler-Kassner et al. (2012) explore threshold concepts as a frame to consider writing and transfer in the context of troublesome knowledge. Most recently, Linda Adler-Kassner and Elizabeth Wardle, along with thirty other Writing Studies scholars have presented five threshold concepts of writing (2015). Those threshold concepts are

- Writing is a Social and Rhetorical Act
- Writing Speaks to Situations through Recognizable Forms
- Writing Enacts and Creates Identities and Ideologies
- All Writers Have More to Learn
- Writing Is (Also Always) a Cognitive Activity

ACRL STANDARDS REVISION, THRESHOLD CONCEPTS, AND METALITERACY

While the ACRL *IL Standards* were widely accepted by academic librarians and have formed the basis of many collaborations between librarians and faculty from across disciplines, the *IL Standards* have also faced significant criticism. In particular, research and theory has shown that rather than a prescriptive and de-contextualized set of skills, IL is a contextualized and situated concept (Bruce, 1997; Lloyd, 2010; Lupton, 2004; Norgaard, 2003), In addition, Carol Kuhlthau's (2004) research has shown that like writing, research is a process. In addition, the information environment has changed significantly since the inception of the *IL Standards*, both in the context of collecting information and in its analysis and use. Individuals are no longer the consumers of pre-packaged information; they are also producers of information in dynamic and ever changing landscapes.

In recognition of the evolving definition and understanding of IL based on research and theory, the *Framework for IL* moves away from a standards-based approach to one that is grounded in threshold concepts and metaliteracy. Rather than a prescriptive set of standards, the *Framework for IL* is intended to be situational; that is, the intent is that each institution implement it and develop learning outcomes based on local context. The new definition of IL emphasizes the dynamic and flexible nature of the concept:

> Information literacy is the set of integrated abilities encompassing the reflective discovery of information, the understanding of how information is produced and valued, and the use of information in creating new knowledge and participating ethically in communities of learning. (ACRL, 2015)

For Writing Studies, the shift represented in the *Framework for IL* should be a comfortable one as it is similar to developments within the discipline to emphasize rhetorical (and contextual) pedagogy. However, the *Framework for IL* presents challenges to the discipline of Writing Studies. Clearly, how we approach IL as a pedagogical concept within curricula and for assessment will be challenged. In particular, the place of the traditional "research paper" assignment may continue to be contested and evolve as we help students adopt and adapt to the threshold concepts and metaliteracy. This challenge potentially benefits student learning by instilling a richer and fuller understanding of information and its use and presentation and their own role as both consumer and producer of information.

THE FRAMEWORK FOR IL THRESHOLD CONCEPTS

The *Framework for IL* is divided into six frames; each frame consists of associated knowledge practices and dispositions.

Authority Is Constructed and Contextual recognizes that information is produced within a context and that authority—expertise and what is accepted as expertise—differs based on discipline or context. Novices rely on superficial characteristics to identify authority such as publication type or academic credentials; experts rely on and are open to changes in schools of thought and discipline- or context-specific paradigms. The concept that authority is contextual is a comfortable one for Writing Studies as it recognizes that authority comes from disciplinary values, conversations that evolve with research and theory building within a discipline, industry, or other context. Yet, in too many cases, students are taught to evaluate authority based on rote mechanical criteria such as an author's degree or affiliation rather than situating a source within the broader disciplinary context/conversation.

Information Creation as a Process recognizes that information is an intentional act of message creation that may take place in any format/media and that is the result of a process that involves research, creation, revision, and dissemination. Experts understand and evaluate the process of creation as well as the final product to evaluate the usefulness of information whereas novices frequently focus on the finished product (or don't recognize that a product may be dynamic). In today's information landscape, in which information may be produced, disseminated and continually evolve within a dynamic medium, the ability to understand process and how format/media impacts information (as both a producer of it and a consumer of it) is critical. Even when assignments involve dynamic media, often the constraints of a classroom mean that conceptually they appear to be static (one author or team of authors producing a finished product that is graded and forgotten) rather than the type of process that may take place within the workplace or in personal lives (creating a product that is then continually commented upon and/or revised). The ability to understand this has implications for evaluating information. In addition, as a threshold concept for IL, Information Creation as a Process evolves beyond the traditional interpretation of the "writing process" or "research process" to incorporate a more realistically dynamic process that is potentially never-ending.

Information Has Value recognizes that information may have several different types of value: economic, educational, as a means to influence, or as a way to negotiate and understand the world. The value of information is impacted by legal and sociopolitical interests for both production and dissemination. This threshold concept is clearly associated with critical thinking aspects of the WPA OS as well as Knowledge of Conventions outcomes to understand legal implications of intellectual property and attribution.

Research as Inquiry emphasizes that research is an iterative process of ongoing inquiry and extends beyond academics. For Writing Studies, this threshold concept is most closely associated with what is traditionally viewed as "research process"—that is, the establishment of a need (research question or thesis) and a plan to collect data/information based on that need.

Scholarship as Conversation recognizes the role of discourse communities and the evolution of discourse over time resulting from different perspectives and interpretations of information. Seemingly overlapping with "Authority is Constructed and Contextual, Scholarship as Conversation focuses on the broader disciplinary/social/industry conversation of relevant topics/interests rather than on the evaluation of individual pieces or sources.

Searching as Strategic Exploration recognizes that the search for information is iterative and non-linear and is based on the evaluation of information sources to adapt searches and collection of information. Similar to Research as Inquiry, this threshold concept focuses on the search process itself and the mechanics of that process.

Metaliteracy

The *Framework for IL* draws upon metaliteracy as a foundational principle in conjunction with threshold concepts. Similar to the way that metacognition is defined as "thinking about thinking," metaliteracy refers to "literacy about literacy." It has become almost a commonplace in recent years to identify or describe certain skill sets as literacies: visual literacy, critical literacy, and digital literacy are just a few. How these literacies are defined and understood is dependent on the community of practice to which they are most associated; many reflect similar and overlapping skills and abilities.

As defined by Thomas Mackey and Trudi Jacobson (2011, 2014), metaliteracy re-envisions IL as an overarching literacy in which individuals are both consumers and producers of information. The four domains that form the basis of metaliteracy are behavioral, cognitive, affective, and metacognitive. Metaliteracy also forms the theoretical foundation for the *Framework for IL* in conjunction with the six frames and related dispositions. These four domains serve to integrate spheres of learning in a way that fosters student development. This makes sense in terms of teaching for transfer. When we cross through the portal, to use Jan Myer and Ray Land's metaphor, we have changed the way we think, the way we perceive things, the way we act, and the way we reflect about what we have done and need to do. Further, the domains are familiar to Writing Studies as they also form the basis of the WPA OS and Habits of Mind.

ACRL *Framework for IL* and the WPA OS/Habits of Mind

In previous work, we have noted the connections between the original *IL Standards* and the WPA OS (D'Angelo & Maid, 2004; Maid & D'Angelo, 2012) there seem to be real differences in the movement of the revisions for both groups. Both documents emerged in the 90s, partly as a result of the general environment that called for more accountability and assessment in higher education. Both standards and outcomes nicely fit the model for assessment purposes. Both disciplines were able to use their respective standards and outcomes for that purpose. However, while assessment is a good thing, especially when groups need accountability with a variety of constituencies, neither document really speaks to pedagogical concerns or learning theory.

WPA Outcomes: What They're Good For and What They're Not Good For

The original impetus for the WPA OS came from a grassroots effort of writing program administrators who were convinced that even though they oversaw programs with widely diverse curricula, there was an unarticulated agreed-upon sense of what it was that students were supposed to learn in first-year composition. The original WPA OS articulated that previously unspoken sense of "what it was that students should know when they finish the course."

We can see, by looking at the original statement adopted by WPA, how easy it would be for both students and teachers to interpret the outcomes as goals that can be checked off. In this sense it is similar to the *IL Standards* and the potential to see it as a discrete set of skills instead of contextualized set of outcomes. The outcomes are defined by four categories: Rhetorical Knowledge; Critical, Thinking, Reading, and Writing; Processes; and Knowledge of Conventions; each category is divided into explicit statements articulating individual outcomes (http://wpacouncil.org/positions/outcomes.html).

Not seeing the outcomes as skills to be learned so students can move on to other things is crucial when we are concerned with the idea of transfer—the idea that something learned in one context can be effectively adapted and applied in another context. One of the most common complaints WPAs hear is that students "can't write" even though they've successfully completed first-year writing or disciplinary writing courses. This phenomenon certainly isn't unique to writing; anecdotally it is not uncommon for instructors to complain that students don't carry what they learn in one course to another even within their disciplinary courses. Of course, faculty in all disciplines have undoubtedly heard or read similar complaints from employers about students who haven't learned or "can't write, can't research, can't do whatever it was they were supposed to have learned." But learning is not a linear lock-step process. Is it, then, that students don't learn? Or have they, in fact, learned but not transferred that learning for some reason?

In 2011, driven by the need to determine what constitutes "readiness for college success," The Council of Writing Program Administrators, the National Council of Teachers of English, and the National Writing Project jointly adopted the *Framework for Success in Postsecondary Writing*. The hallmark of this document are the "Eight Habits of Mind" that mark the processes of successful writers:

- Curiosity—the desire to know more about the world
- Openness—the willingness to consider new ways of being and thinking in the world
- Engagement—a sense of investment and involvement in learning
- Creativity—the ability to use novel approaches for generating, investigating, and representing ideas
- Persistence—the ability to sustain interest in and attention to short- and long-term projects
- Responsibility—the ability to take ownership of one's actions and understand the consequences of those actions for oneself and others
- Flexibility—the ability to adapt to situations, expectations, or demands
- Metacognition—the ability to reflect on one's own thinking as well as on the individual and cultural processes used to structure knowledge

We can easily see these habits of mind are not something that can be checked off as an assessment of skills. They are clearly difficult to demonstrate and/or assess. How, for example, would a program assess "curiosity" or "openness"? Of course, they weren't intended to be assessed; instead they are intended to be descriptors of behaviors of successful writers that should be emulated. Unlike outcomes articulated in the WPA OS, the habits of mind are attributes or behaviors. If we view the habits of mind in the context of metaliteracy, they fall into the affective and metacognitive domains. In the context of the *Framework for IL*, the habits of mind are similar to and serve the same purpose as the dispositions articulated for each frame. The *Framework for IL*, however, took a different approach by integrating specific dispositions associated with each frame rather than a separate document. As such, it presents a more integrated whole in terms of contextualizing student learning.

While the habits of mind or dispositions may be less teachable, clearly possessing them, since they are not context dependent, theoretically will more likely allow students to transfer skills. In fact, Dana Driscoll and Jennifer Wells (2012) suggest that individual dispositions should be an area of writing transfer research. Wardle (2012) further called for more research on how educational systems encourage specific dispositions within students with an emphasis on "problem-exploring dispositions" vs. "answer-getting dispositions" and the influence of standardized testing as facilitating answer-getting dispositions in students.

In *Writing across Contexts*, Kathleen Yancey, Liane Robertson, and Kara Taczak (2014) emphasize writers' needs to take control or their own learning processes and that, as instructors, we need to construct pedagogies that will help them do so. Yancey, Robertson, and Taczak describe a "teaching for transfer" model for writing classes which they believe guides students to learn and transfer knowledge about their writing. A key component of this model is metacognition to facilitate students' reflection upon what they have learned and how it can be applied to other contexts. Metacognition, or reflection, has of course been well-documented as a strategy to facilitate student learning. The work of Yancey et al. is based, for example, on the National Research Council's *How People Learn* (2000) and Yancey's own extensive work on reflection and its use in writing classrooms. Their work points to the realization that students must first learn the appropriate language in order to be able to articulate their learning. Further, they acknowledge the role of prior knowledge in student learning (a nod to dispositions) as either a conduit or barrier to learning.

MAKING SENSE OUT OF RELATED CONCEPTS

So we see some hints at how these related ideas—threshold concepts, metaliteracy, habits of minds/dispositions—might have an impact on developing a writing pedagogy that would not only stress the ability to be information literate but also allow student writers to transfer learned concepts from one context to another. Where do we go from here? An example may help to illustrate how these concepts are related in practice.

The *Framework for IL* identifies Information Creation as a Process as a threshold concept. For ages, writing instructors have been trying to teach students that "writing is a process." Many of us have crossed that portal and can't understand how writing can be viewed in any other way. However, how many of us always really believed that in practice writing is a process? Can we articulate when we really passed through the portal? Can we point to not when we learned about process in an "I can come up with the right answer on a test" way (based on the work of Flower and Hayes), but truly changed our thinking to understand that effective writing can only be undertaken through a process? Do our students really understand this? Can we articulate what process means in an era in which information is communicated in media that is not static or fixed so that there may not be, in reality, a "final product"? We can assess it by requiring drafts and peer review and the like, but do they "really get it" or are they simply meeting a course requirement to get the grade?

Let us offer a personal anecdote to show how it might really be working based on Barry's experience with "crossing the threshold" of understanding writing (information creation) as a process. He's not quite sure when he was first introduced to the idea that writing is a process since high school teachers and college TAs didn't then teach process as we have come to understand it. They talked about formal outlines, first drafts, and final drafts. That didn't connect with Barry; instead his process included lots of reading and thinking. Eventually, close to when the writing was due, he'd type up (using first a manual and eventually an electric typewriter) a draft, go over the draft for typos and the like. Then he'd retype the final draft and hand it in. Perhaps since there were identifiable steps, that was a process. But when he first started teaching writing, he was introduced to the whole process idea as a disciplinary construct. But he taught it without really believing in it since the process that worked for him didn't fit the model that was generally accepted as "writing process." In a sense, he was in a liminal state—he understood the concept intellectually but didn't fully accept it. In part this may be due to the concept of "writing process" as troublesome knowledge. What he was being told was writing process didn't fit his conception of it. Whether this was due to teaching that didn't quite resonate or his own ties to his own prior knowledge, for Barry, the concept wasn't fully sinking in.

Then one day as a relatively new assistant professor he received a manuscript he had submitted back with a "revise and resubmit" verdict. Most of the revisions were simple and easy to do. However, there was one paragraph, where the editor asked several questions that required some serious thinking in order to answer the concerns. Typing a new paragraph on an electric typewriter didn't work so after a couple of tries, he then tried to insert longhand comments on the typescript. Nothing worked, other than growing frustration until he had an idea. The department had just received two TRS-80 computers with a word processing program so he decided to word process the troublesome paragraph. After typing it in and printing it out to read it, he made some additional changes and was easily able to rewrite the text on the screen—in fact, he wrote at least a dozen versions of that paragraph.

What does this have to do with crossing the threshold of "writing process" or Information Creation as a Process? First came the recognition of the power in using the new technology. He now understood the capabilities and constraints of creating information through various processes and with various technologies. But then came an additional realization, and the threshold was finally crossed. Barry finally realized that this was what people were talking about when they were talking about "writing as process": the reiterative and dynamic process of revision, feedback, revision, and dissemination. Barry was transformed in the way Meyer and Land describe as crossing the threshold to not only understand a concept but be transformed by it. He could never go back to the old way of seeing and practicing writing as a process.

The question is, now that the threshold was crossed, could he teach it better? The honest answer is he doesn't know for sure. Which leads us to the connection to dispositions and to habits of mind. The passage through the portal, attaining the threshold concept and never being able to look back, is an incredibly individual act. That doesn't mean we should not attempt to help our students understand the concepts and be transformed; it just means that doing so is neither easy nor "canned." Interestingly, "Process" is not listed as a "threshold concept of writing" in the Adler-Kassner and Wardle book. This may be one more indication of the incredibly individual nature of what we are describing.

And therein lies the challenge of the *Framework for IL*. The integration of threshold concepts and dispositions is a significant evolution in our understanding of student learning. To understand what makes up a concept as complex as IL, we need a way to articulate it. Using language which breaks down threshold concepts into knowledge practices and dispositions may on the surface appear to be similar to the standards model: a listing of skills or abilities or practices that can be discretely assessed. However, the challenge is to go beyond that surface appearance to understand how deeply situated and contextualized IL is based on the information landscape (discipline, industry, personal life of the individual) *and* on the individualized dispositions of each person.

So, while we have seen two different professional organizations, who have often had intertwined instructional goals, develop their own statements about what students should know, we now see both of these professional organizations slightly diverge as their statements get revised. Both ACRL and WPA created their original documents out of the need for assessment and accountability. It appears that the latest revision of the WPA Outcomes Statement is still in that mode. ACRL, on the other hand, has moved to a new framework that stresses threshold concepts—or ways of changing how students think about information. Still, it would be wrong to assume that while ACRL has evolved in a slightly different direction from 15 years ago that WPA has simply tweaked and stagnated. The creation of the *Framework for Success in Postsecondary Writing* with its Habits of Mind, clearly moves WPA in the same direction as ACRL. Finally, then, we can see disciplinary leadership moving beyond assessment to transfer, and in some ways embracing the importance threshold concepts have in the way students not only learn but transfer skills and knowledge beyond a single classroom setting. Looking at transfer really means looking at education in a different way. It moves beyond teaching students identifiable and quantifiable facts and skills that are easily assessed within the classroom context and towards a pedagogy that teaches students how to apply what they have learned in the classroom to other classrooms and other areas of life.

The *Framework for IL* has the potential to open new dialogs between faculty, librarians, and administrators to share responsibility for the teaching and assessment of IL. As Rolf Norgaard and Caroline Sinkinson (Chapter 1, this collection) have pointed out, those dialogs and action resulting from them have more often than not been aspirational rather than reality or limited to individual initiatives. Still, progress has been made and the *Framework for IL* with its foundation in core principles of threshold concepts and metaliteracy provides an opportunity for those of us in Writing Studies and in Library and Information Science to do more than simply focus on a common concern related to transfer as we investigate ways to use seminal documents within both fields. It will no longer be enough to understand one another's perspectives and only to engage in dialogue. We now need to actively partner together to move forward with helping our students become information literate.

REFERENCES

Adler-Kassner, L., Majewsi, J. & Koshnick, D. (2012). The value of troublesome knowledge: Transfer and threshold concepts in writing and history. *Composition Forum, 26*. Retrieved from http://compositionforum.com/issue/26/troublesome-knowledge-threshold.php.

Adler-Kassner, L. & Wardle, E. (Eds.). (2015). Naming what we know: Threshold concepts of writing studies. Logan, UT: Utah State University Press.

Association of College and Research Libraries. (2015). *Framework for information literacy for higher education*. Retrieved from http://www.ala.org/acrl/standards/ilframework.

Bruce, C. (1997). *The seven faces of information literacy.* Adelaide, Australia: Auslib Press.

Clark, I. L. & Hernandez, A. (2012). Genre awareness, academic argument, and transferability. *WAC Journal, 22*, 65–78.

D'Angelo, B. J. & Maid, B. M. (2004). Moving beyond definitions: Implementing information literacy across the curriculum. *Journal of Academic Librarianship, 30*(3), 212–217.

Driscoll, D.L. & Wells, J. (2012). Beyond knowledge and skills: Writing transfer and the role of student dispositions. *Composition Forum, 26*. http://compositionforum.com/issue/26/beyond-knowledge-skills.php.

Kuhlthau, C. C. (2004). *Seeking meaning. A process approach to library and information services.* Westport, CT: Libraries Unlimited, Inc.

Limberg, L., Alexandersson, M., Lantz-Andersson, A. & Folkesson, L. (2008). What matters? Shaping meaningful learning through teaching information literacy. *Libri, 58*(2), 82.

Lloyd, A. (2010). *Information literacy landscapes: Information literacy in education, workplace and everyday contexts.* Oxford: Chandos Publishing.

Lupton, M. J. (2004). The learning connection: Information literacy and the student experience. Blackwood, South Australia: Auslib Press.

Mackey, T. P. & Jacobson, T. E. (2011). Reframing information literacy as a metaliteracy. *College & Research Libraries, 72*(1), 62–78.

Mackey, T. P. & Jacobson, T. E. (2014). *Metaliteracy.* Chicago: Neal Schuman.

Maid, B. M. & D'Angelo, B. J. (2012). The WPA outcomes, information literacy, and challenges of outcomes-based curricular design. In N. Elliott & L. Perelman (Eds.),

Teaching and assessing writing: A twenty-fifth anniversary celebration (pp. 99–112). New York, NY: Hampton Press.

Meyer, J. H. F. & Land, R. (2006a). Threshold concepts and troublesome knowledge. An introduction. In J. H. F. Meyer & R. Land (Eds.), *Overcoming barriers to student understanding. Threshold concepts and troublesome knowledge* (pp. 3–18). New York, NY: Routledge.

Meyer, J. H. F. & Land, R. (2006b). Threshold concepts and troublesome knowledge. Issues of liminality. In J. H. F. Meyer & R. Land (Eds.), *Overcoming barriers to student understanding. Threshold concepts and troublesome knowledge* (pp. 19–32). New York: Routledge.

Norgaard, R. (2003). Writing information literacy: Contributions to a concept. *Reference and User Services Quarterly, 43*(2), 124–130.

Wardle, E. (2012). Creative repurposing for expansive learning: Considering "problem-exploring" and "answer-getting" dispositions in individuals and fields. *Composition Forum, 26.* Retrieved from http://compositionforum.com/issue/26/creative-repurposing.php.

Yancey, K., Robertson, L. & Taczak, K. (2014). Writing across contexts: Transfer, composition, and sites of writing. Logan, UT: Utah State University Press.

CHAPTER 3
EMPLOYER EXPECTATIONS OF INFORMATION LITERACY: IDENTIFYING THE SKILLS GAP

Dale Cyphert and Stanley P. Lyle
University of Northern Iowa

The 21st century finds renewed discussion of the importance of a liberal arts education. Citing the demands of a "complex and volatile" global economy, the Association of American Colleges and Universities (AACU) presented the case in terms of "essential learning outcomes," including information literacy (IL), that cross all areas of study (National Leadership Council for Liberal Education and America's Promise, 2007, p. 12). A survey of business executives conducted by the American Management Association (2010) names the crucial skills, "critical thinking, creativity, collaboration, and communication skills" (p. 2), and acknowledges four-year colleges as the educational institutions most likely to develop a proficient workforce. Employers surveyed by the AACU (Hart Research Associates, 2013) overwhelmingly felt these capacities to be more important than a candidate's undergraduate major (p. 1).

Unfortunately, the resurging interest in these broad language, thinking, and interpersonal skills is largely driven by a sense that universities are not adequately preparing the nation's students. Even in an economy beset by persistently high unemployment, employers complain that jobs cannot be filled because applicants lack these critical "soft skills" (American Society for Training and Development, 2012, p. 7). They also report that recent college graduates rarely demonstrate expected and needed research competencies (Head, 2012). The persistent concern for graduates' career readiness suggests that traditional liberal arts education is not meeting the needs of the 21st century's information economy.

Within liberal arts universities, library faculty have been among the first to address the issue, perhaps because they were first impacted by the same technologies that have so dramatically altered the global business environment. Over the past thirty years, academic librarians have expanded their role as information curators to embrace research and instruction within a broader notion of "information skills" (Rader, 2002) or IL (Pinto, Cordón & Díaz, 2010). By 1987, the American Library Association (ALA) had appointed a committee to study the role of IL in business, government, and education (American Library Association, 1989).

Two years later, Patricia S. Breivik and E. Gordon Gee (1989) called for an IL revolution, pointing to academic libraries as the "key to achieving higher education reform goals" (p. 3) necessitated by the exploding information age, along with public librarians who would be instrumental in locating and organizing their communities' economic development data. The resulting IL would help workers engage in *lifelong learning* and allow them to become the flexible, easily trainable workforce that business leaders were calling for. Subsequent work showed a "vital link between higher education, information literacy and lifelong learning" (Head, Van Hoeck, Eschler & Fullerton, 2013, p. 75) with some researchers focusing on the need to "guarantee a competitive workforce in times of turbulent global change" and others on the desire to promote "personal growth and social equality and enrich society" through learning (p. 6).

Agreement that IL is important in the workplace has not offered, however, much guidance to universities seeking to prepare their students for professional success. Over the past two decades, efforts to better integrate IL into business curricula have resulted in limited change. There has been no "collective impact on business curricula in general," and business, trade and professional leaders continue to describe IL with a vocabulary of desirable but generic soft skills (Sokoloff, 2012). The lack of curricular and business attention to IL has been attributed to accreditation pressure to focus on more easily measurable outcomes (Sokoloff, 2012), an overemphasis on technology issues (Association of College and Research Libraries, 1998), differences in terminology (Conley & Gil, 2011; Klusek & Bornstein, 2006; Leveson, 2000; O'Sullivan, 2002), and the overwhelming nature of the task (Fiegen, Cherry & Watson, 2002).

Qualitative research (Head et al., 2013) suggests the mismatch between academic preparation and employer expectations is not a simple matter of incommensurate vocabularies, or even the more embarrassing but equally simple problem of inadequate education. As a concept, IL grew from roots in bibliographic instruction, but the contemporary domain encompasses functional, critical, and rhetorical "multiliteracies" that extend across multiple purposes, technologies, and disciplines (Selber, 2004). The specific issues of differing priorities, knowledge bases, and vocabularies have been clearly shown to be factors in the academic/employer mismatch, but more fundamental issues involve the use of information in a specific professional context. Extensive interviews conducted across a wide variety of professional settings have revealed consistent challenges (Head et al., 2013); college graduates are not well prepared for the social nature of information storage, the ambiguities inherent in the search for information, or the rigors of timely thoroughness.

Recognizing these challenges, the *Framework for Information Literacy for Higher Education* (ACRL, 2015) marks a significant broadening from functionally defined IL skills toward an appreciation for the context in which information will be used and a capacity for contextualized interpretation of information that leads to reasonable conclusions. The domain of IL still encompasses the functional literacy of where and how to get information as well as the critical literacy of assessing the nature and use of information, but it is the rhetorical literacy of constructing meaning from contextualized data that seems to matter most in the workplace.

ONE UNIVERSITY'S RESPONSE

The University of Northern Iowa's College of Business Administration helps students develop their soft skills with a program designed to introduce all business majors to the broader thinking, communication, and interpersonal skills associated with professional success. Begun in 2010, the College's Professional Readiness Program (Hillyer, 2013) relies on an advisory board of business faculty, a network of alumni and corporate partners, and a staff of faculty and graduate assistants from the liberal arts disciplines to create programming and resources that support students' professional development efforts across their entire college experience.

Relying on published survey research with Fortune 500 companies, the program addresses 37 skill sets in the areas of professional attitude, communication and presentation skills, writing and reasoning skills, and organizational awareness. Business research is classified as a writing and reasoning skill, along with business documents, problem solving, clear descriptions, audience analysis, critical thinking, persuasive arguments, and message construction (Cyphert, 2011). New business majors attend a series of mandatory meetings while they are taking their liberal arts courses, followed by activities and resources designed to integrate professional context and expectations into the major courses over the junior and senior years. At both levels, professionals serve as speakers and meeting facilitators, solidifying the students' ability to apply the skills during interviews, internships, and ultimately in their business careers.

Business research skills are one area of professional readiness, so a faculty member and the library's business specialist began a project to develop professionally relevant resources for the program. It became apparent that neither the general academic research skills that were part of the liberal arts curriculum, nor the business-specific research tools that had been created to support the academic curriculum were targeting workplace research priorities as described by professionals. A project was undertaken to systematically define the career-relevant skill sets, determine the skills gap that existed for business majors taking professional positions in the region, and develop program resources to prepare them more appropriately.

The skill set that emerged encompassed broad notions of IL, unsurprising based on the previous work that had been done regarding workplace readiness. A subsequent survey of employers identified a somewhat more surprising pattern of relatively small gaps between the skills desired by employers and those held by college-educated entry-level employees, suggesting that a collaborative process to define workplace skills from a professional perspective might resolve some of the terminology problems. On the other hand, the project also demonstrates the degree to which ongoing collaboration will be necessary to provide instruction that prepares students for a socially and rhetorically complex workplace environment.

DEFINING THE SKILL SET

The project began with a straightforward request within a professional network of business librarians. In retrospect, the assumptions inherent in that request for advice are illustrative. We asked about employer expectations regarding databases, research reports, key trade journals, and automated information sources. Our own focus on students' ability to use specific information sources belies a *functional* orientation that we ultimately found to be out of sync with the professional community's more *rhetorical* understanding of the skill set. A review of the research on IL in business contexts illustrates the degree to which IL differs in work and educational settings (Weiner, 2011) as well as the degree to which employers describe a wide range of intellectual, technical, and social behavior as just a few key categories of worker preparation. More recent studies, such as the Project Information Literacy Research Report on recent college graduates, also have found a "distinct difference between the information competencies and strategies today's graduates bring with them to the workplace and the broader skill set that more seasoned employers need and expect" (Head, 2012, p. 24).

RESEARCH ON INFORMATION LITERACY IN THE BUSINESS PROFESSIONS

In 1989, the American Library Association (ALA) committee's final report warned that "a lack of timely and accurate information is costly to American businesses" (American Library Association, 1989, para. 8) and promised that "those who learn how to achieve access to the bath of knowledge that already envelops the world will be the future's aristocrats of achievement" (para. 12). Noting the role of libraries "as the potentially strongest and most far-reaching community resource for lifelong learning" (para. 19) as well as the dearth of attention in the business discussion of the emerging information society, the ALA called for efforts to raise awareness of the importance of IL.

A review of the research conducted over the following decade found that businesses were focused on the pragmatic issues of technology adoption, leaving the exploration of the uses of information to the academics (Bruce, 1999; 2000). Theoretical and educational models of IL thus continued to develop, but they were based primarily on data collected in academic settings and analyzed by professional librarians. Over the same decade, a few business faculty began to explore the importance of research skills and IL in a contemporary business environment (for example Ali & Katz, 2010; Burke, Katz, Handy & Polimeni, 2008; Hawes, 1994; Karakaya & Karakaya, 1996; Katz, Haras & Blaszczynski, 2010; Schlee & Harich, 2010; Walker et al., 2009), leading to expanded research on workplace information use.

The most obvious feature of this initial research is the broadened scope of knowledge, skills, and attitudes involved in professional contexts. Acknowledging that "libraries and dedicated librarians have taken the lead," one organizational development consultant deemed it "not enough" in a business environment where "information comes from many sources and can be obtained in many ways" (Goad, 2002, p. x). Abigail J. Sellen, Rachel Murphy, and Kate L. Shaw (2002) used diaries of knowledge workers to categorize the complex information tasks involved in their use of the Internet, which included steps to maintain and monitor the business environment as well as seek, evaluate, and retain specific information. Similarly, O'Sullivan (2002) pointed out that workers "are faced with information overload, have difficulty finding what they need quickly and efficiently, and are struggling with issues of quality and credibility" (p. 9).

The solution seemed to be an expansion of the concept of IL to encompass the "peripheral" skills that allow a worker to "do the steps" involved in accessing, evaluating, and using information (Goad, 2002, p. 30). Soft skills of time management, business outlook, delegation, and teamwork (O'Sullivan, 2002) as well as communication, critical thinking, risk-taking, computer literacy, and business literacy (Goad, 2002, p. x) were proposed as essential. O'Sullivan concluded that it is possible to "massage" the concepts of learning organizations, knowledge management, and lifelong learning so that they encompass the terminology of IL, but "this approach only skirts around the edges" of IL as a "holistic concept" (p.11).

O'Sullivan (2002) proposed a framework to reconcile business and academic perspective as an issue of organizational level, suggesting that

> businesses have been concentrating on implementing knowledge strategies and have not yet got past the infrastructure

> and management buy-in hurdles to the question of individual capability and contribution. When they do start to look at how individuals are coping with life in a knowledge company, and at the employee's ability to contribute positively, the information literacy gap will be self-evident. (p. 11)

Within an organizational context, however, individuals' goals, capacities, and procedural choices do not lead to organizational outcomes in an additive way. The success of a *learning organization* depends on tapping its complex internal interrelationships to foster long-term collective success (Senge, 1994), and *knowledge management* is distinguished by the opacity of the underlying tasks (Drucker, 1973). Peter F. Drucker later referred to the need to be "information literate" in today's organization (Harris, 1993, p. 120), but any link between individual skill development and enterprise-level outcomes is necessarily complicated by the economic and political environment of the business, the contextual complexity of work, and the systems nature of organizations.

Economic and political environment. The initial formulation of IL was itself a function of a changing workplace where technology was shifting labor from routine manual and cognitive tasks toward more sophisticated behaviors (Autor, Levy & Murnane, 2003). During the 1980s, U.S. business leaders had recognized that global competitiveness would increasingly rely on a flexible, quality-minded workforce and became concerned about worker readiness (Johnston & Packer, 1987). Anthony Carnevale's (1991) influential report described the shift as one from "job-specific to more general capabilities" and "personal skills" that could be applied across a variety of "fluid contexts" (p. 101). In the new technologically enhanced workplace, the "collecting, recording, analyzing, and communicating of information" was just one more "labor-intensive" task that was being "subsumed in information-based or communications technology" (p. 102).

Although the vocabulary of *lifelong learning* seemed to reflect the academic learning that libraries traditionally supported, organizational goals were quite different. The concern was not for workers to become better at information processing tasks; computers were expected to take over those functions. Instead, workers previously educated to do those jobs would be required to gain the "self-management and interpersonal skills" needed for the increasing levels of social interaction the new workplace required (p. 103).

Similarly, business' call for more *empowered* workers was not a simple corollary to educators' notion of learners with information-gathering skills that would allow them to learn on their own. Cost savings from an increased use of technology could be amplified with a decrease in organizational levels. As production workers gained communication, teamwork, and problem-solving skills, they would be able to take on the autonomous, decision-making required in a lean organization—one that aimed to replace multiple layers of expensive management with computers and empowered workers.

Complexity of information work. The last decade has seen a shift toward more fine-grained attempts to identify the discrete information skills needed in business contexts, fleshing out the relationship between traditional library-based definitions of IL and the business community's concern for more broadly defined communication and critical thinking attributes. The results highlight differences in vocabulary and conceptualization of the tasks, but illustrate as well the complexity of workplace information use.

In one attempt to prove the importance of IL in the business environment (Klusek & Bornstein, 2006), elements of IL were mapped to the U.S. Department of Labor's O*Net job categories. Louise Klusek and Jerry Bornstein (2006) observed that those outside academe do not recognize that IL is neither library-centered nor information technology-centered, and they concluded that while the "business community has not embraced the concept of information literacy, IL skills are in fact highly valued in the field" (p. 19). However, their analysis does not fully account for differences in the perceived sophistication of various skills. To some extent, academics and professionals simply reverse the skill hierarchy. The O*Net descriptions place explicit search and manipulation of information within larger categories of *Complex Problem Solving* and *Critical Thinking and Instructing*, while the librarian authors argue that, "critical thinking and communication are core concepts of information literacy" (p. 5). Conversely, employers classify many IL skills as basic work readiness and learning skills (e.g. reading comprehension, listening), rather than sophisticated knowledge processing skills that might be expected of college graduates.

In Carnevale's precursor to the O*Net database development, key components of "learning to learn" were "the cognitive domain of skills we use to collect, know, and comprehend information" (1991, p. 111), understood as foundational to gaining the more sophisticated skills needed in the New Economy and included in the O*Net catalog of basic skills (Askov, 1996). Carnevale's competency description was not focused on the manipulation of complex information, but on leveraging individual learning styles and using learning strategies and tools to effectively apply new knowledge to new job requirements. Conversely, Carnevale's description of problem solving skills focused on the use of various business-specific problem-solving methods (i.e., Juran and Friedman & Yarborough Comprehensive Models, as well as more general Dewey-based processes). Beyond a first step to "recognize, define, and analyze problems" (1991, p. 115), there is no overlap with the accepted elements of IL.

An ability to use popular management tools is thought to prepare a newly empowered worker for broader responsibilities, but the fundamental abilities to think logically, critically, and systematically are seemingly subsumed in the very basic elements of worker readiness to learn. In short, differences in vocabulary and priority seem to involve implicit assumptions about the relative teachability of cognitive skills. Academic librarians understand problem-solving skills to be learned steps in the development of IL, while the business community seems to perceive them as a general capacity to learn a variety of relevant, technical skills such as computer use, managerial methods, and communication processes.

Theresa M. Conley and Esther L. Gil (2011) parse this dichotomy further in a recent employer survey. Employers agree on the importance of the skill set, but when challenged to provide a more business-oriented term for "information literacy," their top two choices were "critical thinking" and "decision-making." Meanwhile, the most traditional aspect of IL, the location and retrieval of information from a wide variety of sources, was deemed the easiest part of the process. The important and more difficult skills were the abilities to recognize the need for information and to use it effectively.

Jason Sokoloff (2012), after surveying employers, concluded, "non-librarians have little awareness of information literacy and instead conflate technology and communication skills as essential qualifications for mastering information and managing knowledge in the work place" (p. 6). In the work context, information use is not understood as a cognitive ability, but as a set of relatively complicated technical tasks to be accomplished. Information technology consultant Craig Roth (2011), for instance, describes the contemporary information worker's job as an "active, conscious effort at subscribing to the right sources, setting filters, creating watch lists, setting bookmarks, tagging, friending, and developing the right social networks to get and analyze information" (para. 5). Roth warns against an "old-fashioned" assumption that the knowledge worker's only "'real' job is to define problems, analyze the information, find alternatives, etc." (para. 4) using information easily at hand. At the same time, his description of workplace information gathering emphasizes the contextual and cultural experience of a worker whose "intuition about what is of value, and applying years of accumulated knowledge about where to look and (more importantly) who to pay attention to is of tremendous value in a knowledge economy" (para. 7).

Organizational systems. IL has been primarily concerned with the personal development of an individual information seeker or learner, especially with respect to text-based information resources (Ferguson, 2009). The skills are typically defined within a predominant paradigm of computing and telecommunications that understands information processing as a staged progression from "noise (unorganized data) to perceived data, to (organized) information, to knowledge" (Marcum, 2002, p. 3). The result is a linear model; independent assembly and use of objective information is the ultimate goal. In contrast, the functional role of any individual within a large, complex organization is neither linear nor independent, and information is only occasionally objective. Instead, contemporary business organizations are better understood from a complex systems perspective (Axelrod & Cohen, 1999; Gharajedaghi, 1999). Organizational activities are not simple collections of acts performed by discrete individuals, each carrying an individual set of skills, but collectively constituted patterns of interaction, affordance, and social interpretation (Taylor & Van Every, 2000; Wilson, Goodman & Cronin, 2007).

Professionals seem to intuitively recognize that social skills make it possible for individuals to negotiate the complex "knowledge ecosystem" of "people, processes, technology and content" (Standards Australia, 2005, p. 8), and workplace research has begun to demonstrate the limitations of the individual-based model of IL in a contemporary organization. A survey of corporate librarians and information professionals (Matesic, 2005), for example, found that IL was understood as the special domain of the company library, while non-specialists were seen as needing communication and context knowledge to effectively utilize the library staff's information resources. Similarly, Sokolof (2012) found that new employees were not expected to engage in information tasks alone, but instead to assist and rely on senior colleagues who had developed the company and industry experience needed for effectively accessing and evaluating information.

Christine Bruce (2011) has noted that two key lines of research have emerged that contradict the "traditional skills and competency approach" (p. 335). One is her own "phenomenographic" framework; the other is Annemaree Lloyd's sociocultural research (2006; 2011). This literature illustrates the degree to which IL does not exist separately from an organizational environment, and "its many dimensions are closely related to the contexts in which it is experienced" (Bruce, 2011, p. 335). The takeaway is a distinction between *information experience*, which is the collective, context-bound, and socially constructed environment within which a set of embodied *information behaviors* utilize individual knowledge, skills, and attributes. There is no simple translation of individual IL skills to the collective, distributed negotiation of knowledge as it occurs at an organizational level. The recently developed *Framework for IL* (2015) recognizes this complexity by presenting flexible core concepts, such as the constructed and contextual nature of authority, rather than a prescriptive set of decontextualized skills.

EMPLOYER EXPECTATIONS AND EMPLOYEE SKILLS

Research thus shows that any transition from academic preparation to workplace application involves considerably more than a simple transfer of objective, individual skills to a new context, and pedagogical success will require more than simply translating IL vocabulary from library to workplace contexts or acknowledging differing priorities. The economic and political environment, information task complexity, and organizational systems create a dynamic professional setting that is fundamentally different from the academic; professional preparation requires a holistic understanding of the *tasks* expected as well as a contextually relevant sense of the levels of *mastery* required. Relevant and workable definitions of IL in the workplace will necessarily require the input of business professionals who are familiar with both the contextualized tasks and the organizational expectations of mastery.

In our college's effort to prepare business majors for the information work they will be expected to do, an important first step was thus to clarify employer expectations with respect to information tasks and the mastery levels involved. The university had recently piloted a protocol for assessing career-relevant skill preparation of its students. The authors elected to use the methodology which allowed us to simultaneously determine employer expectations and gain a baseline assessment of graduates' skill levels.

METHODOLOGY: THE TARGETED SKILLS GAP ANALYSIS

The assessment framework is derived from SERVQUAL (Parasuraman, Zeithaml & Berry, 1985; 1988), a commonly used model for measuring outcomes in service industries, including libraries, which have derived the LIBQUAL+ quality instrument from the same framework (Association of Research Libraries, 2013). In applying the SERVQUAL model to the service provided by an educational institution, the service provider is understood to be the university, while the regional employers seeking a ready workforce are understood as the customers. The service delivery process involves mutually constructed relationships, behaviors, and features, which might be understood by an education provider as the learning process. The resulting framework (Manning et al., 2012) includes seven potential gaps in the delivery of educational services to the State's employers.

Each of the gaps represents a point at which there can be differences in the expectations of service. Gap 1 illustrates the differences between what employers expect of new employees and what the University perceives those expectations to be. That is, a gap occurs when faculty do not know which skills are most critical to employers or the level of skill that would be required for success in the job.

Employer Expectations

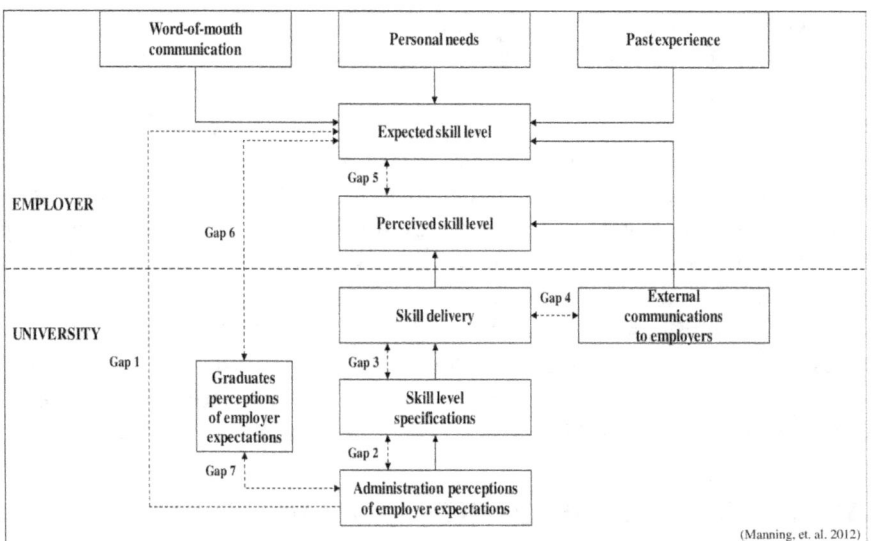

Figure 3.1. Potential employer-university service gaps.

Gaps 2, 3, and 4 represent potential discrepancies within the service provider's operation. Gap 2 represents a difference in the faculty understanding of an employer's skill requirements and the learning objectives within the curriculum, while Gap 3 indicates the degree to which instructional processes do not result in the targeted learning objectives. Gap 4 reflects an important insight from the service quality research: there can be discrepancies between the actual education delivered and the educational outcomes that are advertised by the institution. Although the model illustrates this as a single gap, it could be a complicated three-way interaction among a university's recruiting division, faculty perceptions, and actual learning outcomes.

The expectational discrepancy on the consumer side, represented here as Gap 5, has been shown to have the most impact on customer satisfaction (Parasuraman et al., 1988). This is the difference between the employers' *expectations* of graduates' skill levels and their *perceptions* of the actual skill levels possessed. This implies a somewhat different relationship from the way educational assessment is typically framed. When a student's performance in the classroom setting is assumed to indicate capacities or behaviors that will be observable upon graduation, the model is that of a student as a tangible product who carries certain assessable characteristics. Assuming the assessment process to have been accurate, any failure to express those characteristics after graduation is presumed to be a function of the student's personality or the employment context.

61

By contrast, the service model understands service delivery and the customer's perception of that service as simply two perspectives on the same transaction. That is, the student's *performance as perceived by the eventual employer* is the outcome of the educational service delivery process. There is no implicit transfer of responsibility from educator to student, but an integration of the teacher/learner process within a holistically understood educational outcome. As any educator will quickly realize, this represents a more complex situation than the more typical service industry product where a single person or employee team delivers the service. In an effort to represent this unique aspect of educational service delivery, two additional gaps are added to the original SERVQUAL model. Gap 6 illustrates differences between employers' expectations and graduates' expectations of the skills required for a position, and Gap 7 represents differences between the graduates' and faculty's expectations (Manning et al., 2012).

TARGETED SKILLS AS SERVICE CHARACTERISTICS

Service dimensions were conceptualized in terms of the functional and technical aspects of the students' performance of their education within the workplace. Development of an appropriate set of general but workplace-relevant IL skills was a three-stage process. A first round of meetings was held with professional staff from the college's Business and Community Services division, a self-supporting unit that offers consulting and research services in marketing, entrepreneurship, economic development, and a variety of business operations throughout the state and the upper midwest (US).

Still working with our initial expectation that specific research tools or data resources would be professionally desirable, we were surprised by the broad range of critical thinking and communication skills that were actually sought. The ability to recognize what information would be needed to answer a specific business question was identified as the most problematic element of research skill. If given a specific information request, graduates were able to locate the data, but seemed unable to determine what information was needed in the first place. Further, their tendency was to try to solve the problem with whatever information they knew how to find, regardless of its appropriateness or adequacy for the task.

The second step was to incorporate the full range of IL skills into our scope, specifically seeking out those operationalized skill descriptions that had been developed in workplace contexts. The aim was to insure that we were addressing the full range of skills that might be desired by our statewide employer stakeholder group. Further, the utility of the survey items required that we use terminology that would be clear and consistent across a variety of companies and industries. A matrix was developed that lined up aspects of IL as described by multiple resources. Sources included four academic efforts (Association of American Colleges and Universities, n.d.; Association of College and Research Libraries, 2000; Goad, 2002; Head, 2012), four that utilized research with business contexts (Coplin, 2003; Graveline, 2013; Malcom, 2012; Sokoloff, 2012), and two industry-specific lists for competitive intelligence and information technology (Chung & Ripperger, 2013; Committee on Information Technology Literacy of the National Research Council, 1999).

The final step was to partner with professionals drawn from the college's alumni community. We wished to verify our interpretation of each skill description, insuring that we understood the behavior in a business context and that we were describing it in a way that would be clearly understood by our employer respondents. As a result of these meetings, the skill matrix was reordered somewhat to reflect a more common job-related task sequence, and wording was changed to reflect some important business distinctions. Initial steps in the research process involved gathering *data*, while *information* was the preferred term for the product of evaluation and integration steps that occurred later in the process. A distinction was also introduced between *secondary* and *primary* research, in large part because secondary research would typically be conducted to determine the need for additional primary research. Finally, communication skills were expanded to reflect what employers perceived as distinct skills involved in *choosing* just that information appropriate to a specific audience or context and effectively *delivering* the result. The categories involved in the ethical use of information were deemed acceptable, although the point was made that attribution of sources was exclusively related to secondary research tasks, while the ethical issues of most importance to the business environment had to do with primary research, including ethical gathering of data, as well as confidentiality and ethical dissemination of information. The final list of 24 skills was used to determine gaps between employer expectations and employee readiness.

IL Skills Defined by Employers

Know
1. Detects the need for research through regular workplace interaction
2. Recognizes and articulates a research question
3. Identifies appropriate secondary research sources

Access
4. Develops a research plan
5. Considers practical costs/benefits of various research methods
6. Identifies appropriate primary research methods

7. Able to effectively use appropriate secondary research resources, technologies
8. Uses appropriate data recording, storage methods

Evaluate
9. Evaluates information and sources according to stated criteria
10. Evaluates information for fallacies and limitations with deductive and inferential logic
11. Accurately extracts data from sources
12. Synthesizes information from multiple sources
13. Recognizes value of information with respect to what is already known
14. Recognizes data that are sensitive to social, cultural, personal influence or bias
15. Revises search methods on the basis of information assessment

Use
16. Selects contextually relevant new knowledge for communication to others
17. Clearly, effectively communicates research results to others
18. Able to engage in meaningful interpretation of data with others
19. Uses analytical methods to utilize information
20. Uses information to make strategic business decisions

Ethics
21. Recognizes ethical and legal issues of information gathering
22. Follows professional and/or legal guidelines for ethical behavior
23. Follows appropriate rules for attribution and acknowledgement of sources
24. Recognizes moral and ethical implications of new knowledge

PRIORITIZING THE SERVICE GAPS

The service gaps for each skill dimension were measured with survey questions that asked respondents to indicate both the *expected* level of skill and their *perceptions* of the actual skill delivered. The average difference score provides a measure of the gap for that dimension. This measure alone is not sufficient to prioritize management attention. A large gap could exist in an area that is not particularly important to the customer, and management resources might be more effectively spent on reducing a smaller gap in an area of greater customer concern. The Targeted Skills Gap Analysis (Manning et al., 2012) thus calls for results of the expectations/perceptions gap survey to be plotted on a two-dimensional decision matrix that displays the gap in customer expectations as well as the relative importance to the customer, prioritizing those service elements that are most deserving of management attention.

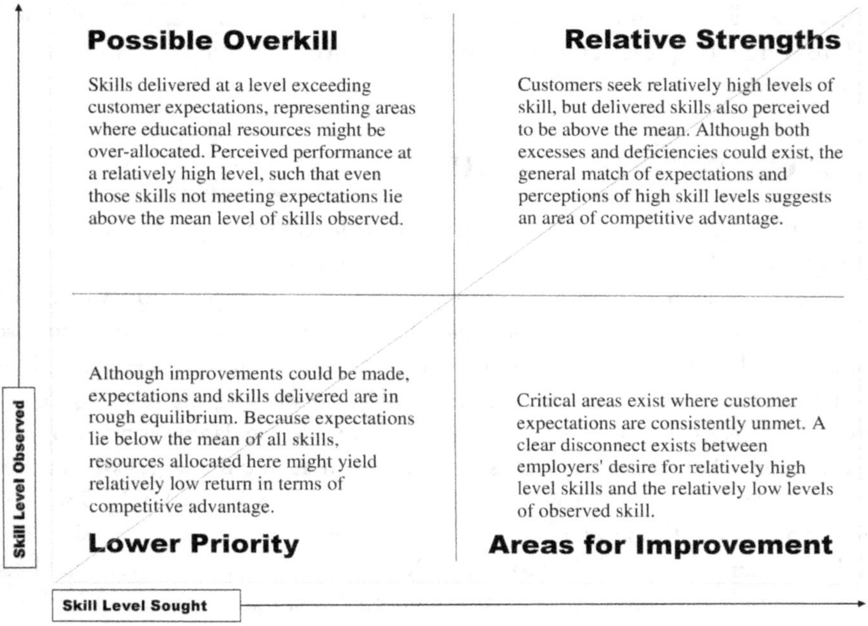

Employer Expectations

Possible Overkill

Skills delivered at a level exceeding customer expectations, representing areas where educational resources might be over-allocated. Perceived performance at a relatively high level, such that even those skills not meeting expectations lie above the mean level of skills observed.

Relative Strengths

Customers seek relatively high levels of skill, but delivered skills also perceived to be above the mean. Although both excesses and deficiencies could exist, the general match of expectations and perceptions of high skill levels suggests an area of competitive advantage.

Although improvements could be made, expectations and skills delivered are in rough equilibrium. Because expectations lie below the mean of all skills, resources allocated here might yield relatively low return in terms of competitive advantage.

Lower Priority

Critical areas exist where customer expectations are consistently unmet. A clear disconnect exists between employers' desire for relatively high level skills and the relatively low levels of observed skill.

Areas for Improvement

Skill Level Observed

Skill Level Sought

Figure 3.2. Skill gap analysis quadrants.

The service expectation, the skill level sought in University graduates, is plotted on the x-axis; the perception of the skill performance actually received from those same graduates is plotted on the y-axis. A perfect match is represented as the dashed diagonal line, x=y, and the perceived gap appears as the vertical distance between the dashed diagonal line and the plotted point. Four decision quadrants are then created by drawing vertical and horizontal lines at the mean values of skill levels sought and delivered. Skills for which customers desire a level of skill higher than the mean are deemed more salient to their operations, while observed skills that are below the mean are areas of more concern. The resulting quadrants assist management in prioritizing the gaps that require attention.

A full map of the service delivery process would involve data collection on each of the expectational gaps discussed above, but for practical reasons, most data collection efforts focus first on customers' perceptions and satisfaction with the service experience, designated as Gap 5. The results drive management investigation of the remaining gaps to determine causal relationships and develop effective solutions. We sought the most salient measure of employer satisfaction with the university's ability to provide information literate employees to create a baseline measure, and we will use these results to refine the IL skill definitions before conducting research with respect to faculty perceptions, alumni perceptions, current student self-efficacy, and direct skill assessment.

RESULTS: IDENTIFYING THE SKILLS GAP

With IRB approval, a web-based survey was distributed by email to the university Career Center's list of 1,306 employers and recruiters. Although this list includes some education and government employers, a large majority of Career Center activities involve business majors. Given our desire to create a skill set that could be generalized across multiple industries and business functions, we felt all employers could be included without distorting the results. We also invited the recipients, many of whom are recruiters associated with the human resource function, to forward the survey link to first-line managers within their organizations. Survey data was collected from 168 recipients, a 12.9% overall response rate. Respondents worked for companies that ranged in size from under 100 employees (46.7%) to over 1,000 (21.2%). New employees had been hired in all O*Net career clusters, although business, management, and administration and marketing, sales, and service dominated the mix.

Some respondents did not provide ratings for one or more skills, suggesting that not all entry-level jobs necessarily encompass the full scope of IL, and for each item at least a few respondents selected "don't know" as their answer. While total numbers of responses on each item differ, their range from 74 to 106 was deemed both adequate and sufficiently balanced. The average ratings of employer expectations and perceived new employee skill were calculated for each (See Tables 3.1 through 3.4) and plotted into quadrants of the Skill Gap Analysis (Figure 3.3).

Overall, the results demonstrated a relatively consistent result across all elements of IL. Employers expected only "moderate" IL skills, averaging only a 2.09 on our five-point scale. Across all skill categories, entry-level employees were not fully meeting employer expectations, but in no case was the gap larger than .51, barely more than half a rating category. Employers found new graduates to be working at the moderate level desired, albeit not at optimal performance. An evaluation of the results by skills area, along with comments from respondents, provides additional insight.

In the general category of knowing when to seek information, employers acknowledge the need to learn the business context before a new employee can be fully productive. As one respondent summarized it, "Knowledge of college students is not industry specific. The [research] tools used vary by company, and it would be impossible to teach every tool to students," further, says another, "We can teach some technical [skills]." Employers see a key skill as the social

Table 3.1: Knowing information needs

	Average Level Expected	Average Level Observed	Skill Gap
1. Detects the need for research through regular workplace interaction	2.10	1.69	0.41
2. Recognizes and articulates a research question	2.07	1.63	0.44
3. Identifies appropriate secondary research sources	1.91	1.54	0.37
All knowledge awareness skills	2.03	1.62	0.41

Rating Scale: None (0), Novice (1), Moderate (2), Advanced (3), Master (4), Expert (5)

Table 3.2. Accessing information

	Average Level Expected	Average Level Observed	Skill Gap
4. Develops a research plan	1.80	1.54	0.26
5. Considers practical costs/benefits of various research methods	1.77	1.42	0.35
6. Identifies appropriate primary research methods	1.82	1.58	0.24
7. Able to effectively use appropriate secondary research resources, technologies	1.93	1.70	0.23
8. Uses appropriate data recording, storage methods	2.02	1.83	0.20
All information access skills	1.87	1.61	0.26

Rating Scale: None (0), Novice (1), Moderate (2), Advanced (3), Master (4), Expert (5)

capacity that allows new employees to engage productively in "regular workplace interaction" such that they are able to read the implicit and contextual cues that cause them to "detect the need for research." Respondents named, in particular, asking questions, teamwork, and getting along well with others.

In the realm of accessing information, employers expected slightly less than moderate skills, and graduates came closest to meeting expectations in this area. Employers were most concerned with an ability to document results, with one noting, "We find that typically college grads are enthusiastic about doing the research and not so much on documenting it in a way that will be helpful to others in the future." Although employee skills rated lower than moderate in all other access skills, several employers admitted that their organizations' planning or cost analysis practices were also less than optimal.

Table 3.3. Evaluating information

	Average Level Expected	Average Level Observed	Skill Gap
9. Evaluates information and sources according to stated criteria	2.18	1.86	0.32
10. Evaluates information for fallacies and limitations with deductive and inferential logic	1.89	1.56	0.33
11. Accurately extracts data from sources	2.16	1.83	0.34
12. Synthesizes information from multiple sources	2.08	1.74	0.33
13. Recognizes value of information with respect to what is already known	2.19	1.81	0.38
14. Recognizes data that are sensitive to social, cultural, personal influence or bias	2.11	1.74	0.37
15. Revises search methods on the basis of information assessment	2.05	1.70	0.35
All information evaluation skills	2.10	1.75	0.35

Rating Scale: None (0), Novice (1), Moderate (2), Advanced (3), Master (4), Expert (5)

Employers consistently desired moderate information evaluation skills. As suggested by previous research in workplace IL, however, the focus seems to be on reporting the results of evaluation, distinguishing those tasks from whatever cognitive processes are involved in the evaluation of information. As one employer put it, "Not all positions require a research component. However, all positions require problem-solving skills." The ability to evaluate data for social, cultural, and personal bias is rather obviously context-bound, but comments suggest that employers understand each of these skills in terms of relationship and communication skills. Employers emphasized the need for "understanding the corporate culture and doing it the way that is generally accepted by our company" as well as functional elements of "grammar and spelling mistakes" in the written documents used to report the evaluation.

The largest gap in the uses of information involved the analytical methods, but the lowest expectations lie in use of information for business purposes. The highest expectations involved graduates' ability to communicate their findings to others. Comments further emphasized respondents' concern for communication with general remarks that "people skills and exceptional communication skills are absolutely necessary for every employee" and more specific complaints that new employees were unable to format their communications so that colleagues could easily use the information being provided.

Table 3.4. Using information

	Average Level Expected	Average Level Observed	Skill Gap
16. Selects contextually relevant new knowledge for communication to others	2.15	1.83	0.32
17. Clearly, effectively communicates research results to others	2.28	1.84	0.44
18. Able to engage in meaningful interpretation of data with others	2.21	1.75	0.46
19. Uses analytical methods to utilize information	2.18	1.67	0.51
20. Uses information to make strategic business decisions	2.03	1.63	0.40
All information use skills	2.17	1.74	0.43

Rating Scale: None (0), Novice (1), Moderate (2), Advanced (3), Master (4), Expert (5)

Table 3.5. Information ethics

	Average Level Expected	Average Level Observed	Skill Gap
21. Recognizes ethical and legal issues of information gathering	2.27	1.87	0.40
22. Follows professional and/or legal guidelines for ethical behavior	2.55	2.23	0.31
23. Follows appropriate rules for attribution and acknowledgement of sources	2.31	2.00	0.31
24. Recognizes moral and ethical implications of new knowledge	2.28	1.94	0.34
All information ethics skills	2.35	2.01	0.34

Rating Scale: None (0), Novice (1), Moderate (2), Advanced (3), Master (4), Expert (5)

Employers' highest expectations lay in the area of information ethics, but this was also the only area in which new employees possessed moderate skills, overall. Confidentiality was the largest ethical concern, especially with respect to the careless use of social media.

Each of the 24 skill gaps were plotted onto the Skill Gap Analysis Quadrants. The resulting diagram, designed to highlight areas for managerial attention, finds the entire scope of IL to be highly clustered.

The average level of skill sought, 2.09, and the average level of skill observed, 1.74, define the vertical and horizontal midlines, respectively. Entry-level

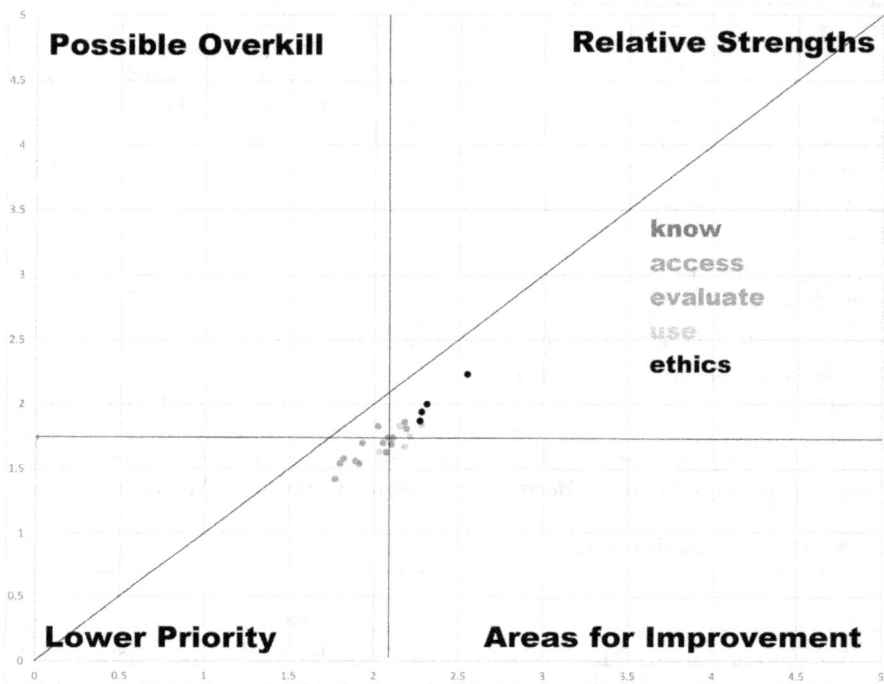

Figure 3.3. Plotted skill gap results.

employees are performing all skills below the diagonal, which represents a match between skills and expectations, but the gap is not large. Further, IL skills fall primarily in the *relative strength* and *lower priority* quadrants. That is, although all are lower than desired, those skills that are rated the lowest, generally falling in the area of information access, are also those least expected by employers. Meanwhile ethics skills, expected to be somewhat higher, are also observed to be somewhat higher.

Just three skills fall in the *areas for improvement* where the employers' expectations are the highest (i.e., at or above the overall average of 2.09) but skills are observed to be the lowest (i.e., at or below the overall average 1.74):

- Detects the need for research through regular workplace interaction (Skill #1, Know)
- Recognizes data that are sensitive to social, cultural, personal influence or bias (Skill #14, Evaluate)
- Uses analytical methods to utilize information (Skills #19, Use)

These areas of concern and employer comments are similar to those reported by the Project Information Literacy Research Report on college graduates (Head, 2012). Of the 4 competencies rated as highly needed by employers, but rarely demonstrated by recent hires (p. 12), two were identified by the employers in this study as well. The communication aspects of "engaging team members during the research process" are reflected in skills #1 and #18, while "finding patterns and making connections" seems to appear as skills #19, #20, and possibly #18 as well. One area, "retrieving information using a variety of formats," appears to be encompassed by skill #7, but the fourth, "taking a deep dive into the 'information reservoir,'" does not appear to have a direct corollary. It is possible that our methodology, which was specific to the skill levels of new college graduates, might have reduced employer expectations of the more independent research skills implied in that descriptor.

DISCUSSION

Based on the survey data, the College's Professional Readiness Program staff will be developing relevant and effective preparation in the area of business research practices. The results seem to lead us toward action in four areas:

1. *Frame instruction in terms of the information tasks that will be common for new employees.* One of our most interesting findings was that employers perceived new graduates as consistently but only slightly less qualified than expected. Given the concerns reported in previous research, this was gratifying, but probably says more about the survey methodology than about students' preparation. Because we had taken steps to describe elements of IL with a generic but typical business vocabulary, we believe that employers were responding in terms of generic but recognizable tasks. Just as workers' skills cannot be easily differentiated from the overall information experience, employers' evaluation of information skills cannot be easily differentiated from overall performance of a task.

2. *Combine IL with communication skills.* Employers see information-related skills as different and perhaps more limited than the "soft" skills of critical thinking and communication, which might still be reported as problematic. A communication skill survey is planned, and the comparison will be informative. In the meantime, the creation of task-related skill definitions suggests that if academic institutions are going to prepare students to participate effectively, they cannot neglect the communicative and problem-solving context in which information is used. As Marcum (2002) puts it, "librarians must ratchet up their standards and expectations from literacy to sociotechnical fluency" (p. 20).

3. *Provide IL skills in a business context.* A consistent point made in both published research and conversations with professionals was that information

use is fully embedded in a specific organizational context. This does not seem to mean that skills are impossibly specific; we were able to develop a set of sufficiently generic business tasks to create a survey instrument that was usable across multiple industries and job titles. We nevertheless believe that students will be better equipped to transfer skills if the terminology and task vocabulary are consistently maintained across academic and workplace contexts.

4. *Continue the collaboration.* Finally, the most salient conclusion is probably the most straightforward: we must continue to work closely with the professional stakeholders who can provide contexts, terminologies, experiential learning, mentoring, and coaching. To the extent that IL develops through a process of socialization into a discursive community, the involvement of that community is crucial to the success of any instruction.

IMPLICATIONS FOR RESEARCH IN IL

The *Framework for IL* addresses the contextualized nature of IL that we have described here with six "frames" that are relevant to information use across academic disciplines as well as to civic and professional contexts. Our project suggests that research must continue to explore the complicated nature of information use in context. As our employer perceptions demonstrate, there seems to be no effective way to separate IL from the social skills that allow individuals to gain that literacy within a knowledge community. Nor are there useful distinctions between the effective use of information and its effective application in a specific context. We have demonstrated here that employers perceive IL in terms of purposeful information use, and we expect that the same will be true of faculty and student perceptions of their instructional and learning activities. Further, expectations of IL vary with a trajectory of experience, maturity, and socialization into the rhetorical practices of a community.

For those of us who work to prepare students for non-academic futures, it is not enough to recognize that academic tasks are different from workplace tasks, or even to translate academic skills into a more typically professional vocabulary. Neither addresses the more important step of preparing students to undertake the process of joining a socially and rhetorically complex workplace community. As with any other professional behavior, IL develops as new workers learn to pay attention to the salient features of their environment and respond in accordance with social and rhetorical norms.

Some argue that "the critical ground for information literacy is the workplace and not the education sector" (Lloyd, 2011, p. 280), but that does not imply there is no research to be done within the academic environment. Rolf Norgaard and Caroline Sinkinson (Chapter 1, this collection) review the necessary relationships between IL and writing instruction, as well as the historical and institutional barriers that conspire against students' participation in the rhetorical community that is academia. As we solve these pedagogical problems, we are poised to learn a great deal about how individuals master threshold concepts to negotiate an information context and successfully adopt normative practices. Students entering the university are learning to recognize the epistemological frameworks of their new academic community in the same way any worker learns to recognize and effectively use information to accomplish relevant tasks within a specific context. We can understand how that happens—or doesn't happen—not merely to better prepare students for academic work, but to translate that understanding into general principles of IL as the *process* of becoming literate in the ways of a knowledge-using community.

REFERENCES

Ali, R. & Katz, I. R. (2010). Information and communication technology literacy: What do businesses expect and what do business schools teach? Research Report 10–17. Princeton, NJ, Educational Testing Service.

American Library Association. (1989). *Presidential Committee on Information Literacy: Final report.* Retrieved from http://www.ala.org/acrl/publications/whitepapers/presidential.

American Management Association. (2010). *AMA 2010 critical skills survey.* Retrieved from http://www.amanet.org/training/articles/3727.aspx.

American Society for Training and Development. (2012). *Bridging the skills gap.* Alexandria, VA: ASTD.

Askov, E. N. (1996). *Framework for developing skill standards for workplace literacy.* University Park, PA: National Institute for Literacy.

Association of American Colleges and Universities. (n.d.). *Information literacy value rubric.* Retrieved from http://www.aacu.org/value/rubrics/pdf/InformationLiteracy.pdf.

Association of College and Research Libraries. (1998). *A progress report on information literacy: An update on the American Library Association Presidential Committee on Information Literacy: Final report.* Retrieved from http://www.ala.org/acrl/publications/whitepapers/progressreport.

Association of College and Research Libraries. (2000). *Information literacy competency standards for higher education.* Retrieved from http://www.ala.org/acrl/standards/informationliteracycompetency.

Association of College and Research Libraries. (2015). *Framework for information literacy for higher education.* Retrieved from http://www.ala.org/ilstandards/ilframework.

Association of College and Research Libraries Information Literacy Competency Standards Review Task Force. (2012). *Recommendations of the ACRL Information Literacy Competency Standards Review Task Force.* Retrieved from http://www.ala.org/acrl/sites/ala.org.acrl/files/content/standards/ils_recomm.pdf.

Association of Research Libraries. (2013). *History of LibQUAL*. Retrieved from http://www.libqual.org/about/about_lq/history_lq.

Autor, D. H., Levy, F. & Murnane, R. J. (2003). The skill content of recent technological change. *Quarterly Journal of Economics, 118*, 1279–1333.

Axelrod, R. & Cohen, M. D. (1999). *Harnessing complexity: Organizational implications of a scientific frontier.* New York: Free Press.

Breivik, P. S. & Gee, E. G. (1989). *Information literacy: Revolution in the library.* New York: American Council on Education.

Bruce, C. S. (1999). Workplace experiences of information literacy. *International Journal of Information Management, 19*, 33–47.

Bruce, C. S. (2000). Information literacy programs and research: An international review. *The Australian Library Journal, 49*(3), 209–218.

Bruce, C. S. (2011). Information literacy programs and research: Reflections on "Information literacy and research: An international review" by Christine Bruce. 2000. *The Australian Library Journal, 49*(3), 209–218. *The Australian Library Journal, 60*(4), 334–338.

Burke, J. A., Katz, R., Handy, S. A. & Polimeni, R. S. (2008). Research skills: A fundamental asset for accountants. *The CPA Journal, 78*(1), 66–69.

Carnevale, A. P. (1991). *America and the new economy.* Alexandria, VA: American Society for Training and Development.

Chung, J., Gella, C. & Ripperger, K. (2013). *Competitive intelligence as a profession.* Des Moines, IA: Strategic and Competitive Intelligence Professionals (SCIP) Iowa Chapter.

Committee on Information Technology Literacy of the National Research Council. (1999). *Being fluent with information technology.* Washington, DC: National Academy Press.

Conley, T. M. & Gil, E. L. (2011). Information literacy for undergraduate business students: Examining value, relevancy, and implications for the new century. *Journal of Business & Finance Librarianship, 16*(3), 213–228. doi: 10.1080/08963568.2011.581562.

Coplin, B. (2003). *10 things employers want you to learn in college.* Berkeley: Ten Speed Press.

Cyphert, D. (2011). *Professional Readiness Program.* Retrieved from http://business.uni.edu/prp/pages/studentresources/skilldevelopment/skilldevelopment.cfm.

Drucker, P. F. (1973). *Management: Tasks, responsibilities, practices.* New York: Harper & Row.

Ferguson, S. (2009). Information literacy and its relationship to knowledge management. *Journal of Information Literacy, 3*(2), 6–24.

Fiegen, A. M., Cherry, B. & Watson, K. (2002). Reflections on collaboration: Learning outcomes and information literacy assessment in the business curriculum. *References Services Review, 30*(4), 307–318. doi: 10.1108/00907320210451295.

Gharajedaghi, J. (1999). *Systems thinking: Managing chaos and complexity: A platform for designing business architecture.* Boston: Butterworth-Heinemann.

Goad, T. W. (2002). *Information literacy and work performance.* Westport, CT: Quorum Books.

Graveline, J. (2013). Business research certificate program fall 2013 [blog entry]. Retrieved from http://blogs.mhsl.uab.edu/business/?page_id=664.

Harris, T. (1993). The post-capitalist executive: An interview with Peter F. Drucker. *The Harvard Business Review, 71*(3), 114–122.

Hart Research Associates. (2013). *It takes more than a major: Employer priorities for college learning and student success.* Washington, DC: Hart Research. Retrieved from http://www.aacu.org/leap/documents/2013_ EmployerSurvey.pdf.

Hawes, D. K. (1994). Information literacy and the business schools. *Journal of Education for Business, 70*(1), 54–62.

Head, A. J. (2012). *Learning curve: How college graduates solve information problems once they join the workplace* (Project Information Literacy Research Report). Retrieved from http://projectinfolit.org/pdfs/PIL_fall2012_workplaceStudy_Full Report.pdf.

Head, A. J., Van Hoeck, M., Eschler, J. & Fullerton, S. (2013). What information competencies matter in today's workplace? *Library and Information Research, 37*(114), 74–104.

Hillyer, K. (2013) About the Professional Readiness Program. Retrieved from http://business.uni.edu/prp/pages/about/about.cfm.

Johnston, W. B. & Packer, A. E. (1987). *Workforce 2000: Work and workers for the 21st century.* Indianapolis, IN: The Hudson Institute.

Karakaya, F. & Karakaya, F. (1996). Employer expectations from a business education. *Journal of Marketing for Higher Education, 7*(1), 9–16.

Katz, I. R., Haras, C. & Blaszczynski, C. (2010). Does business writing required information literacy? *Business Communication Quarterly 73*(2): 135–149.

Klusek, L. & Bornstein, J. (2006). Information literacy skills for business careers: Matching skills to the workplace. *Journal of Business & Finance Librarianship, 11*(4), 3–21. doi: 10.1300/J109v11n04-02.

Leveson, L. (2000). Disparities in perceptions of generic skills: Academics and employers. *Industry & Higher Education, 14*(3), 157–164.

Lloyd, A. (2006). Information literacy landscapes: An emerging picture. *Journal of Documentation, 62*(5), 570–583. doi: 10.1108/00220410610688723.

Lloyd, A. (2011). Trapped between a rock and a hard place: What counts as information literacy in the workplace and how is it conceptualized? *Library Trends, 60*(2), 277–296.

Malcom, J. B. (2012). Syllabus for GBUS 574-Competitive Business Intelligence. Retrieved from http://syllabi.oru.edu/?id=37502.

Manning, D., Meyer, S. & Verma, R. (2012). *University of Northern Iowa targeted skill gap analysis.* MBA Capstone Report. Cedar Falls: University of Northern Iowa

Marcum, J. W. (2002). Rethinking information literacy. *Library Quarterly, 72*(1), 1–26.

Matesic, M. (2005). What are you looking for? Summary of a brief survey of new hires. *The Courier, 42*(3), 16–19.

National Leadership Council for Liberal Education and America's Promise. (2007). *College learning for the new global century.* Washington, DC: American Association of Colleges and Universities.

O'Sullivan, C. (2002). Is information literacy relevant in the real world? *Reference Services Review, 30*(1), 7–14.

Parasuraman, A., Zeithaml, V. A. & Berry, L. L. (1985). A conceptual model of service quality and its implications for future research. *Journal of Marketing, 49*(4), 41–50.

Parasuraman, A., Zeithaml, V. A. & Berry, L. L. (1988). SERVQUAL: A multi-item scale for measuring consumer perceptions of service quality. *Journal of Retailing, 64*(1), 12–40.

Pinto, M., Cordón, J. A. & Díaz, R. G. (2010). Thirty years of information literacy (1977–2007): A terminological, conceptual and statistical analysis. *Journal of Librarianship & Information Science, 42*(1), 3–19. doi: 10.1177/0961000609345091.

Rader, H. B. (2002). Information literacy 1973–2002: A selected literature review. *Library Trends, 51*(2), 242–259.

Roth, C. (2011). Attention information workers: Your job description has changed [blog entry]. Retrieved from http://blogs.gartner.com/craig-roth/2011/04/22/attention-information-workers-your-job-description-has-changed/.

Schlee, R. P. & Harich, K. R. (2010). Knowledge and skill requirements for marketing jobs in the 21st century. *Journal of Marketing Education, 32*(3), 341–352. doi: 10.1177/0273475310380881.

Selber, S. A. (2004). *Multiliteracies for a digital age.* Carbondale, IL: Southern Illinois University Press.

Sellen, A. J., Murphy, R. & Shaw, K. L. (2002, 22–25 Apr). *How knowledge workers use the web.* Proceedings of CHI '02, Conference on Human Factors in Computing Systems, Minneapolis: Association for Computing Machinery, 227–234.

Senge, P. M. (1994). *The fifth discipline: The art and practice of the learning organization.* New York: Doubleday.

Sokoloff, J. (2012). Information literacy in the workplace: Employer expectations. *Journal of Business & Finance Librarianship, 17*(1), 1–17. doi: 10.1080/08963568.2011.603989.

Standards Australia. (2005). *Success through knowledge: A guide for small business* (2nd ed.). Sydney: Author.

Taylor, J. R. & Van Every, E. J. (2000). *The emergent organization: Communication as its site and surface.* Mahwah, NJ: Lawrence Erlbaum.

Walker, I., Tsarenko, Y., Wagstaff, P., Powell, I., Steel, M. & Brace-Govan, J. (2009). The development of competent marketing professionals. *Journal of Marketing Education, 31*(3), 253–263. doi: 10.1177/0273475309345197.

Weiner, S. (2011). Information literacy and the workforce: A review. *Education Libraries, 34*(2), 7–14.

Wilson, J. M., Goodman, P. S. & Cronin, M. A. (2007). Group learning. *Academy of Management Review, 32*(4), 1041–1059.

CHAPTER 4
CREATING AND EXPLORING NEW WORLDS: WEB 2.0, INFORMATION LITERACY, AND THE WAYS WE KNOW

Kathleen Blake Yancey
Florida State University

This chapter—more of a story, perhaps, than a dialogue between two disciplines interested in writing, although informed by each—identifies the current moment of information literacy (IL) as an ecosystem requiring new ways of researching, including new means of determining credibility of sources. It begins by outlining three periods in the recent history of IL as experienced by the researcher: (1) the period when gatekeepers were available to help assure credibility of sources; (2) the period of online access to information held in brick and mortar libraries, with digitized information providing new ways of organizing information and thus new ways of seeing; and (3) the most recent period located in a wide ecology of interacting sources—academic; mainstream; and "alternative"—sources that include texts, data, and people inside the library, of course, but ranging far beyond it. In such an ecology, as we see in the information ecologies presented in both the *Framework for IL* (ACRL, 2015) and Rolf Norgaard's chapter (Chapter 1, this collection), students trace some sources and actively identify and invite others: research, in other words, has become a variegated set of processes, including searching and confirming credibility, but including as well initiating contact with and interacting with sources. Given this new context for research, I also consider how we can introduce students to this new normal of researching and identify some tasks we might set for students so that they learn how to determine what's credible and what's not—in addition to considering how, if in the future students are not only knowledge-consumers but also knowledge-makers, we can support this development, too.

RESEARCH ONE: THE TRADITIONAL SCENE

In the fall of 2006, I spent the better part of a day in the Victoria and Albert Museum (V&A) in London, my purpose there to review some sources from

Figure 4.1. Victoria and Albert Museum in London.

the V&A special collection for an article I was writing (see Figure 4.1). To put it more simply, I was conducting a kind of humanities research in a very conventional way—identifying a purpose, tracing textual sources in a sanctioned library, drafting and revising. (Research in other fields takes various forms, of course, including field work and lab work.)

As I learned, the V&A library is very generous with its resources: it shares materials with anyone who can show a simple identity card. This sharing, however, comes with three very noteworthy stipulations. The first is that one can borrow materials only when the V&A is open, and they pretty much keep banker's hours five days a week, so while access to materials is possible, it is only so within a limited number of days and hours—and this assumes one can travel to London. Second, the materials can be used only onsite; they can be copied on library-approved copying machines, but they cannot be checked out, even overnight. The third is that assuming a patron can get to the V&A at the appointed days and hours, accessing the materials requires an elaborated process. Each item requires a specific protocol, as the V&A (2015) explains:

> In the interests of security and conservation, materials from
> Special Collections are issued and consulted near the Invigila-

tion Desk. A seat number will be allocated by the invigilator when the material ordered is ready for consultation. Readers are asked to sign for each item issued. Readers who find that works ordered are "Specials in General Stock" will be asked to collect them from the Invigilation Desk and consult them at the desks provided for the purpose.

In other words, the materials are there, but obtaining them isn't an expeditious exercise, and using them requires a specific setting. As suggested, this is not an open-shelf library, where the patron might wander among the stacks and peruse the shelves, both practices that can lead to serendipitous discoveries: here the material in question is requested by the researcher and then retrieved by someone else. Some serendipity could occur as the researcher works with the V&A's materials themselves, of course, but then that discovery could prompt another request protocol.

Nonetheless, it's worth noting that the materials at the V&A offer an important value: they promise credibility. Of course, this library is a very specific one with a very specific mission; it is very unlike my academic library, which includes materials both credible (e.g., *Scientific American*) and incredible (e.g., *The National Enquirer*). If I am in doubt about the credibility of the materials, however, the V&A, like my FSU library, employs faculty and staff who can assist in reviewing materials and determining their credibility. What I thus need to do in such a scenario is identify and access the materials, ask for assistance if needed, and use the materials. Moreover, given its specific mission, a library like the V&A offers print collections that are relatively stable: their materials change with additions, but they don't change very rapidly; their very permanence promotes a kind of confidence in the research process. Not least, such a research process is built on a tradition that also promotes confidence. Such a scene has supported research for several hundred years; to say that we have re-enacted and participated in such a scene in and of itself endows the researcher with a certain authority.

In sum, the V&A library provides one scene of research, a scene where materials are not always easily accessed, but where the materials themselves endow a kind of authority and whose credibility can be authenticated with the assistance of a library specialist.

RESEARCH TWO: THE TRADITIONAL SCENE DIGITIZED

When I returned home from London, I needed to do more research, and fortunately, the materials I needed were available in Florida State University's Strozier Library; even more fortunately, they were available online. In other words, because the digital resources are available 24/7, I could access them even when the brick and mortar library was closed. In this case, assuming I have access—here defined quite differently, not as physical location, but rather as a set of factors all working together: a computing device, Internet access, and an FSU ID—I can read articles and ebooks, often the same research materials available in the brick and mortar library, and I can do so at any time in a 24-hour day. Moreover, because the electronic materials are located in a database, they come with affordances unavailable in print. For example, in accessing an issue of *College Composition and Communication* (*CCC*) through JSTOR, a database available through the FSU library that mimics the print resources in the library stacks, I can read the articles online; I can save them; and I can print them; I can export citations via email, BibTex, RefWorks, or Endnote. More important for situating an idea or author, there is a search engine inside both journal and complete database (e.g., *CCC*; JSTOR) that enables looking for authors, topics, and key terms: I can thus trace a given idea or author throughout a set of articles, and if the source is digitized and in the FSU library—two big conditions, admittedly—I can access it immediately. Other journals offer even more options. For example, someone researching the relationship between medical doctors and patients might consult the *Journal of the American Medical Association* (*JAMA*) and, if so, find an article published in 2005, available in FSU's proxy for *JAMA*, and, again, read or download it. The reader can also immediately link to the articles that it cites in its references since most of them are in the database; the process of finding other sources is thus even easier than the one described above, and by engaging in this process, the reader can begin to create his or her own context for the reading of the article, although it's worth noting that in terms of reading, we haven't explored the impact on a reader of links supplied by others. In other words, there is likely a difference between reading a text that is unmarked and reading one with links provided by someone else, as I suggested in reviewing a digitized version of *Hill's Manual of Social and Business Forms*:

> An addition to the text is a set of links taking the reader to surprising places inside *Hill's*—in one case, to an explanation of letters, in another to information about resorts. In that sense, reading this *Hill's* is like reading a text with links functioning as annotations: it's a text of someone else's reading. Do we find the links others have planted for us an annoyance or an opportunity to read differently and more richly?

JAMA also provides a citation index (see Figure 4.2) showing the number of times the article has been cited in other articles and a graph showing how often per year, and it provides links to most of those articles as well.

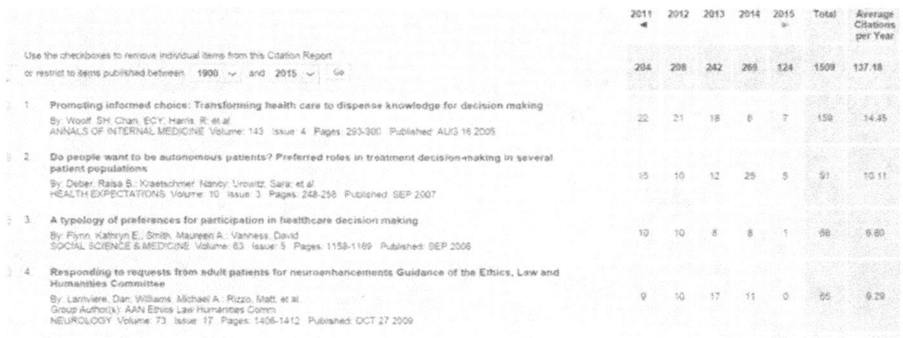

Use the checkboxes to remove individual items from this Citation Report
or restrict to items published between 1900 and 2015 Go

	2011	2012	2013	2014	2015	Total	Average Citations per Year
	204	208	242	269	124	1509	137.18
1. **Promoting informed choice: Transforming health care to dispense knowledge for decision making** By: Woolf, SH; Chan, ECY; Harris, R; et al. ANNALS OF INTERNAL MEDICINE Volume: 143 Issue: 4 Pages: 293-300 Published: AUG 16 2005	22	21	18	8	7	159	14.45
2. **Do people want to be autonomous patients? Preferred roles in treatment decision-making in several patient populations** By: Deber, Raisa B.; Kraetschmer, Nancy; Urowitz, Sara; et al. HEALTH EXPECTATIONS Volume: 10 Issue: 3 Pages: 248-258 Published: SEP 2007	15	10	12	25	5	91	10.11
3. **A typology of preferences for participation in healthcare decision making** By: Flynn, Kathryn E.; Smith, Maureen A.; Vanness, David SOCIAL SCIENCE & MEDICINE Volume: 63 Issue: 5 Pages: 1158-1169 Published: SEP 2006	10	10	8	8	1	68	6.80
4. **Responding to requests from adult patients for neuroenhancements Guidance of the Ethics, Law and Humanities Committee** By: Larriviere, Dan; Williams, Michael A.; Rizzo, Matt; et al. Group Author(s): AAN Ethics Law Humanities Comm NEUROLOGY Volume: 73 Issue: 17 Pages: 1406-1412 Published: OCT 27 2009	9	10	17	11	0	65	9.29

Figure 4.2. JAMA Citation Index.

In this Janus-like way, *JAMA* provides access to both the research the article draws on and the research to which it contributes: the article thus literally appears not as a stand-alone piece of research, but as one contribution to a larger set of research questions. Moreover, for 25 medical topics, *JAMA* includes videos of authors discussing the research. And not least, in the FSU online library, there is information available in independent databases, those not linked to journals, including newspapers from around the world, unpublished dissertations, and the like. The resource bank of the online library is thus very full.

As useful as the online library is, however, it's not without disadvantages to the researcher. For one, the stacks and open shelves of the FSU brick and mortar library have been replaced by links created by others: as indicated above, those may or may not reflect the interests of the researcher, and in any event, online texts preclude the kind of serendipitous self-motivated browsing supported by brick and mortar libraries with open shelves, although it's fair to note that the online files can promote a modified electronic bread crumbing that may be a kind of digital equivalent. But not all materials are digitized: many articles are not, and most books, at least for the moment, are not; the resources are thus simultaneously fuller and diminished. And for yet another concern, the life span of electronic materials in any given library is not assured: subscriptions to e-materials can change. Print, the library owns; electronic, it rents. If a journal's price goes up or the library's budget goes down (or both), the library may be forced to stop the rental. For yet another, as with print, formats that have been very useful may disappear: four years ago, *JAMA* offered a citation map (see Figure 4.3) for each of its articles, a very useful graphical representation visualizing an article's influence. That affordance is now gone.

And for one last, the digitized materials themselves are often selectively digitized and thus are incomplete. Including only the "important" texts, they

Figure 4.3. JAMA Citation Map

exclude materials, like advertisements, that were a part of each journal issue and that at the least provide information about context. But such excluded materials can also prompt or locate research projects: without such information, for example, it's not only impossible to complete a project tracing advertisements for textbooks during the advent of writing process in the 1970s and 1980s, but likewise impossible to see how publishers translated and marketed scholars' research back to the field, and impossible as well for any reader of the digitized journal to develop a fuller sense of the moment's zeitgeist.

In sum, this scene of research is both richer and poorer than the traditional scene; it offers materials 24/7, and through its database representations, new ways of contextualizing materials—as long as it can offer them.

A RESEARCH ECOLOGY

In terms of research, what we see in academic libraries is by definition limited in other ways as well, principally because libraries stock publications: they are not sites of research themselves, but rather places we go to consult research materials, including databases, primary texts, rare books, journal runs, newspapers, and monographs. Put another way, there's research and there's publication: research materials are available in libraries, but research itself takes place outside them in many sites—laboratories, field sites (from the Arctic to the neighborhood cemetery), community centers, classrooms, and so on. Historically, research has been reported in many venues, some of them the long form, peer-reviewed journals and books characteristic of traditional library holdings, but also in informal texts—in letters predating journals (Bazerman, 2000); in diaries; in logs; in newspapers and magazines. Such sites of research-making and distribution have always existed, but are now, with the affordances of the Internet, more visible, inclusive, and interactive. It's commonplace now for researchers to share raw data and early findings in multiple venues ranging from scholarly websites to personal or professional blogs, personally hosted websites, and other social media outlets. Florida State University's Rhetoric and Composition program, for example, hosts a Digital Postcard Archive (http://fsucardarchive.org/), and two graduate students in our program have created the Museum of Everyday Writing (https://museumofeverydaywriting.omeka.net/), which they personally host on Omeka, and which links to Facebook and Twitter. Likewise, I knew about Henry Jenkins' theory of convergence culture over a year before his book on the topic was released because I'd been reading his blog. Of course, given these sources, a researcher needs to determine how credible the information is.

To help students explore this issue, which the Association of College and Research Libraries' (ACRL, 2015) threshold concept "Research as Inquiry" articulates, I have often assigned a "map of reading and researching" task: each student is to pose a question and trace online where the question takes him or her. As we can see from the map composed by Liane Robertson in Figure 4.4, a question about the impact of personal genetic testing leads to a robust ecology of sources, including academic sources like the *New England Journal of Medicine*; institutional blogs like Wired Science; newspapers like the *Los Angeles Times* online; and personal blogs like The Medical Quack. These resources are not all alike nor equivalent in credibility; sorting through them is one research task, and a very large part of that task entails determining the credibility of both claims and evidence that are displayed. Later versions of this assignment have asked students to research in another way: by writing to a source to obtain

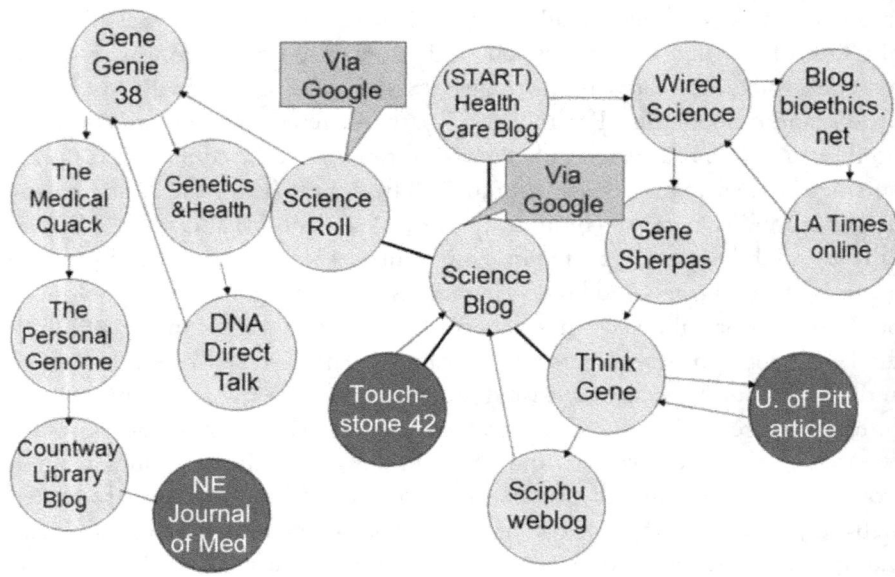

Figure 4.4. Circulation map.

information that isn't yet published, a task I have taken up myself. When I read about research on contextualized pedagogical practice and its role in supporting students in science, I emailed Steve Rissing, the researcher quoted in the *Inside Higher Ed* story, and he replied, helpfully, within a day. Another option in researching, in other words, is to contact a researcher or informant, and with electronic communication, it's never been easier.

In this new ecosystem, establishing credibility of sources is a larger challenge, but there are frameworks available to help. The ACRL, for example, includes this kind of task in its threshold concept Authority Is Constructed and Contextual. Likewise, building on the thinking about IL created by the National Forum on Information Literacy, the Association of American Colleges and Universities (AAC&U) has issued a definition of IL, and a rubric to match, entirely congruent with the ACRL's approach. The AAC&U definition (2009) is fairly straightforward: "The ability to know when there is a need for information, to be able to identify, locate, evaluate, and effectively and responsibly use and share that information for the problem at hand." And as operationalized in the AAC&U VALUE (Valid Assessment of Learning in Undergraduate

Education) scoring guides, IL includes five components or dimensions expanding the definition: (1) Determine the extent of information needed; (2) Access the needed information; (3) Evaluate the information and its sources critically; (4) Use information effectively to accomplish a specific purpose; and (5) Access and use information ethically and legally. Although this heuristic for the activities required in research is useful, it doesn't speak very specifically to the issue of credibility of sources, which is always at play, and never more so than in the current research ecology with its mix of sources and materials. Indeed, speaking to this research ecology, the ACRL (2015) observes that students have a new role to play in it, one involving "a greater role and responsibility in creating new knowledge, in understanding the contours and the changing dynamics of the world of information, and in using information, data, and scholarship ethically."

EXPLORING CREDIBILITY

When considering the credibility of sources, researchers find four questions in particular helpful:

1. What sources did you find?
2. How credible are they?
3. How do you know?
4. And what will you do with them?

In thinking about credibility—which we can define as the accuracy or trustworthiness of a source—the key question may be "How do you know," a question that historian Sam Wineberg (1991) can help address. Wineberg's particular interest is in how students, in both high school and college, understand the making of history, which he locates in three practices useful in many fields. First is corroboration: "Whenever possible, check important details against each other before accepting them as plausible or likely" (p. 77), a standard that is very like the philosopher Walter Fisher's (1995) "fidelity," that is, looking for consonance between the new information and what we know to be accurate. Second is sourcing: "When evaluating historical documents, look first to the source or attribution of the document" (p. 79), a practice of consulting attributions that is just as important for scientists studying global warming and sociologists examining police arrest records as it is for historians. Moreover, Wineberg has also found the sequence of checking attribution important in evaluating credibility: historians predictably read attributions *before* reading a text whereas students, if they check for attributions at all, do so at the conclusion of the reading. Put another way, historians rely on the attribution to contextualize their reading, while students barely attend to it if they do attend to it at all. Third is contextualization: "When trying to reconstruct historical events, pay close attention to *when* they happened and *where* they took place" (p. 80). Here Wineberg is, in part, emphasizing the particulars of any given case, and recommending that in researching we attend to those, not to some preconceived idea that we brought to the text with us.

Equally useful is working with Wineberg's practices in the context of case studies: using these questions together with case studies can help students (and other researchers) learn to use the questions as a heuristic to help decide the credibility of sources and identify which sources to use and how—tasks that the *Framework for IL* addresses in two threshold concepts, Authority is Constructed and Contextual and Searching as Strategic Exploration. Here I highlight two case studies: one in which students compare kinds of encyclopedias and contribute to one of them, and a second focused on some thought experiments raising epistemological questions related to credibility.

A first case study focuses on an analysis of an encyclopedia entry and a Wikipedia entry: as defined in the assignment, this comparison provides "an opportunity to consider how a given term is defined in two spaces purporting to provide information of the same quality"; the task is "to help us understand how they are alike and different and what one might do in creating a Wikipedia entry." A simple comparison taps what we all suspect: a conventional encyclopedia, written by experts, presents an authorized synopsis on multiple topics, whereas Wikipedia shares information identified by several people, none of whom may bring any credentialed expertise to the topic. But this comparison isn't an evaluation. It's not that one of these is credible and one is not: each has different virtues, as students discover. An encyclopedia may be credible, but its entries are usually short, including very few references; it's largely a verbal text; and it could be outdated. Wikipedia typically includes longer entries (often longer by a factor of 3) and includes links to other sources so that more exploration is easily possible, and its entries are often timely—assuming that they are not removed. But are the entries credible? In Wineberg's terms, can we corroborate their claims? What do their attributions tell us?

Often students arrive at the same conclusion as Clay Shirkey (2009) in *Here Comes Everybody*:

> Because Wikipedia is a process, not a product, it replaces guarantees offered by institutions with probabilities supported by process: if enough people care enough about an article to read it, then enough people will care enough to improve it, and over time this will lead to a large enough body of good

enough work to begin to take both availability and quality of articles for granted, and to integrate Wikipedia into daily use by millions. (p. 140)

This latter claim is untested, of course, and can lead to discussions about the value, or not, of peer review: what is the relationship between a scholarly process of peer review and a Wikipedian crowdsourcing, and why is such a question important? Likewise, Shirkey's claim is easier to consider when someone has experience in the process, that is, if students are asked not only to compare Wikipedia with another like text, but also to contribute to it themselves, either by adding to or modifying an existing entry or by beginning a new one. What students learn is twofold, about composing, of course, and a very different composing than they are accustomed to, but also about the making of knowledge—about, for example, how a claim that seems neutral to them is deleted as biased by one of Wikipedia's editors or about how they too have to provide a credible, "neutral" source in order for a claim to be published on the site. In other words, asking students to compare different kinds of encylclopedias and to contribute to one of them helps them understand firsthand the processes of sourcing and of establishing credibility. And in terms of applying this assignment to their own research, students find that there are no easy answers to Weinberg's questions and that one encyclopedia, whether a traditional encyclopedia or Wikipedia, isn't inherently better than the next. They also learn that in conducting their own research, it might be useful to consult both as starting places, to corroborate them against each other, and to explore the resources identified in each.

THOUGHT EXPERIMENTS AS CASE STUDIES

Other kinds of case studies, which I have used with students and in faculty workshops, raise other kinds of questions, especially about the relationship of credibility and epistemology. To introduce this issue, I call on topical issues from a variety of fields. For example, we might consider issues raised by a movie. Several years ago, the movie *Bright Star* portrayed the life of John Keats: is it an accurate portrayal? Is it a good movie? These different questions, both related to the ACRL (2015) threshold concept Research as Inquiry, call for different approaches. To explore the first, we might consult Keats' poetry and his personal writings; we might consult accounts of Keats provided by colleagues and friends; we might consult histories of the period. To explore the second, its value as a movie, we might view movies that have received awards, especially other biographical movies, like *Amadeus* and *The Imitation Game*. And more philosophically, we might consider the relationship between accuracy and value, especially in the context of adaptation studies, which take as their focus questions about the relationship between a print literary text, like *Pride and Prejudice*, and its movie version(s). A single movie and two related questions, as a thought experiment, pointing us in very different directions, helps demonstrate how we know what (we think) we know, and in Wineberg's terms, helps us consider how we might (1) corroborate; (2) authenticate in terms of attribution; and (3) employ the specifics of the movie in the context of historical and literary records.

A second thought experiment is less canonical: it focuses on the website "Patients like Me" (http://www.patientslikeme.com/). Late in the 1990s, James Heywood's brother Stephen was diagnosed with ALS (Lou Gehrig's disease); frustrated by his inability to be helpful, Heywood collaborated with two friends to create the site, a

> free online community for people with life-changing diseases, including ALS, Multiple Sclerosis, Parkinson's disease, HIV/AIDS, Mood Disorders, Fibromyalgia and orphan diseases (such as Devic's Neuromyelitis Optica, Progressive Supranuclear Palsy and Multiple System Atrophy). Our mission is to improve the lives of patients through new knowledge derived from their shared real-world experiences and outcomes. To do so, we give our members easy-to-use, clinically validated outcome management tools so they can share all of their disease-related medical information. Our website is also designed to foster social interaction for patients to share personal experiences and provide one another with support. The result is a patient-centered platform that improves medical care and accelerates the research process by measuring the value of treatments and interventions in the real world. (2015)

In other words, this is a site that for the first time in history compiles patients' accounting of their own diseases; that's impressive. But is the information on it credible? Again, ACRL threshold concepts are useful here, especially Authority Is Constructed and Contextual and Searching as Strategic Exploration. Speaking to the first threshold concept, for instance, one ALS patient claims to have had ALS for 21 years: given the disease's typical trajectory—most patients die within five years—he is a very unusual person. Here, we might consider the value of self-reported data, both on this site and in other, more conventional studies, like those that informed early accounts of composing processes. In addition, we might consider what we learn and how credible the aggregated information based on such data is. PatientsLikeMe offers considerable data; each disease community page, for example, includes statistics speaking to how many members of the site have the disease, how recently profiles have been updated, and how many new patients with the disease have joined, as well as a bar graph showing the age range of patients and a pie chart showing the percentage of patients reporting gender. Patients themselves provide considerable information, including treatment types and their efficacy, which is then compiled into treatment reports with treatment descriptions and efficacies, numbers of patients who use the treatment and for what purpose, reported side effects of use and so on. Some think that the information is credible: as Heywood (2009) explains, it's shared with pharmaceutical companies (which is how the site is financially viable): "We are a privately funded company that aggregates our members' health information to do comparative analysis and we sell that information to partners within the industry (e.g., pharmaceutical, insurance companies, medical device companies, etc.)" (p. 1). But do we find this information credible? In Wineberg's terms, how might we corroborate these data?

Not least is the thought experiment regarding global warming, an exercise that has changed over time. In the 1990s, the question was whether the planet was experiencing the beginnings of global warming and how we would assess that. Today, the question has shifted to how quickly global warming is affecting the earth. Is a massive flood just experienced in India a sign of or an index to global warming? In the millions of years of earth-time, haven't we seen global warming before? What are the effects of global warming, and what do they mean for public policy? And a related question that seems to be asked daily in all parts of the world: is our current weather normal? What is normal, and normal for what period of time—the last 10, 100, 1,000, or million years? What is current—this hour, this day, this week, this month? What is weather and how is it related to climate? Would we create our own records, consult back issues of *The Farmer's Almanac*, examine diaries from centuries ago, log onto the records available on weather.com or accuweather or wunderground, or would we prefer data accumulated by the U.S. government? Would we include some mix of these data? Many questions like these are taken up by citizen scientists who are guided by rudimentary scientific protocols, as they have historically: Charles Darwin, for example, relied on 19th century homemakers in the U.S. to collect data for him. More generally, however, examining such protocols provides another window into how credibility is established, a window that seems increasingly wide given the availability of raw data and the role of interested laypeople in gathering them. Thus, Wineberg's questions are helpful here as well, but they also prompt new ways of thinking, too. Given that much of history isn't recorded, corroboration will probably need to include multiple kinds of materials, person-made and nature-recorded. What signs in nature might help us—rings on trees, for example? Given that attribution is important, what is the relative value to this project of a 17th century diary, a weather.com report, and U.S. government data? And given Wineberg's interest in specifics, what are the signs of warming that we may have missed? What are signs that we may have mis-interpreted?

CONCLUSION

As we see through the concept of a research ecosystem, establishing credibility is increasingly difficult. In a very short period of time—less than the lifetime of many current academics—we have gone from a formalized IL system with human interpreters to an ecology constituted of the valuable and the incredible—facts, data, personal narrative, rumors, information, and misinformation, all inhabiting the same sphere, each info bit circulating as though it carried the same value as all the others, each info bit connected to other info bits and also disconnected from others in a seemingly random way. The good news, of course, is that more information is available: the more challenging, that we are all called on to make more sense of that information, to decide what's credible, how it's credible, and how we know that, a task that—given the thought experiments closing this chapter—is new not only for students, but for most of us.

One way to begin taking up this challenge is through the use of case studies, which raise very different kinds of questions and which are put into dialogue with Sam Wineberg's (1991) schema for establishing credibility. Testing claims and evidence—that is, establishing credibility—isn't easy, but with the lenses of corroboration, attribution, and specifics, it is more likely.

NOTE

1. As explained by AAC&U, the VALUE project is "a campus-based assessment initiative sponsored by AAC&U as part of its LEAP initiative. VALUE provides needed tools to assess students' own authentic work, produced across their diverse learning pathways and institutions, to determine whether and how well they are progressing toward graduation-level achievement in learning outcomes that both employers and faculty consider essential. VALUE builds on a philosophy of learning assessment that privileges multiple expert judgments and shared understanding of the quality of student work through the curriculum, cocurriculum, and beyond over reliance on standardized tests administered to samples of students disconnected from an intentional course of study."

REFERENCES

American Council of Research Libraries (ACRL). (2015). *Framework for information literacy for higher education.* Retrieved from http://www.ala.org/acrl/standards/il framework#introduction.

Association of American Colleges and Universities. (2009). VALUE Rubrics. Retrieved from https://www.aacu.org/value/rubrics

Bazerman, C. (2000). Letters and the social grounding of differentiated genres. In D. Barton & N. Hall (Eds.), *Letter writing as a social practice* (pp. 15–31). London: John Benjamins.

Fisher, W. & Goodman, R. F. (Eds.). (1995). *Rethinking knowledge: Reflections across the disciplines.* New York: State University of New York Press.

Heywood, J. (2009). Testimony before the National Committee on Vital and Health Statistics Subcommittee on Privacy, Confidentiality and Security. Retrieved from http://www.ncvhs.hhs.gov/wp-content/uploads/2014/05/090520p04.pdf.

Robertson, L. (2008). Circulation Map. Digital Revolution and Convergence Culture.

Shirkey, C. (2009). *Here comes everybody: The power of organizing without organizations.* New York: Penguin Books.

Victoria and Albert Museum. (2007). National Art Library Book Collections. Retrieved from http://www.vam.ac.uk/content/articles/n/national-art-library-book-collections/.

Wineberg, S. (1991). Historical problem solving: A study of the cognitive processes used in the evaluation of documentary and pictorial evidence. *Journal of Educational Psychology, 83*(1), 73–87.

Yancey, K. B. (Forthcoming 2016). Print, digital, and the liminal counterpart (in-between): The lessons of Hill's Manual of Social and Business Forms for rhetorical delivery." *Enculturation.*

CHAPTER 5
INFORMATION LITERACY IN DIGITAL ENVIRONMENTS: CONSTRUCT MEDIATION, CONSTRUCT MODELING, AND VALIDATION PROCESSES

Irvin R. Katz
Educational Testing Service

Norbert Elliot
New Jersey Institute of Technology

Information literacy (IL) is a 21st century skill most often conceptualized and measured through 20th century assessment practices. Designed by the Association of College and Research Libraries (ACRL) in 1999 and approved by its board in 2000, the *Information Literacy Competency Standards for Higher Education* (*IL Standards*) is a *fin de siècle* statement. A construct caught between the print-based world of the 20th century and the digitally based networks of the 21st, IL is framed as a skill that, once mastered, will allow those who possess it to stem the tide of the "uncertain quality and expanding quantity of information" that will surely "pose large challenges for society" (ACRL, 2000, p. 2). Those who have this skill will be able to locate, evaluate, and use information effectively to sort through the "abundance of information" that "will not in itself create a more informed citizenry" (p. 2). With the advent of Web 2.0 over the intervening 13 years—its social media, virtual communities, blogs, wikis, podcasts, folksonomies, and mashups—the *IL Standards* look as if they had been cast by Gutenberg.

In response, in 2013 the ACRL chartered a task force to begin the process of updating the *IL Standards*. Noting the limits of the "competency and skill-based approach," the revision promises a "conceptual approach" that provides not just a detailed listing of skills but, rather, "a set of archetypal of core abilities that will serve students well in a continuously changing information environment" (Jacobson & Gibson, 2013, p. 1). The new *Framework for*

Information Literacy for Higher Education (*Framework for IL*) (ACRL, 2015) advances six threshold concepts, transformative perspectives discussed by Barry Maid and Barbara J. D'Angelo (Chapter 2, this collection). Defined as "a spectrum of abilities, practices, and habits of mind that extends and deepens learning through engagement with the information ecosystem" (p. 1), IL is advanced as these threshold concepts are advanced: Authority Is Constructed and Contextual; information is created through intentional acts; information has value; research is a process of inquiry; scholarship is conversational; and searching is strategic. Key to the *Framework for IL* in its present form is the recognition that IL is a contextualized, complex experience in which the cognitive, affective, and social dimensions of the searcher have distinct roles.

The emphasis on underlying cognitive abilities as they are identified, studied, and used in digital environments is the subject of this chapter. To identify important conceptual and validation practices associated with the construct of IL, in this chapter we focus on our experience with iSkills™, a digitally based assessment that uses real-time, scenario-based tasks to measure a defined IL construct.

iSkills: INFORMATION LITERACY IN A DIGITAL ENVIRONMENT

In 2002, Educational Testing Service (ETS) recognized that digital environments made public since the early 1990s presented a unique opportunity for test delivery (ETS, 2002). Instead of simply digitizing the bubble and booklet test format that had been used since its charter in 1947, ETS researchers recognized that emerging information and communication technologies held the potential for new forms of assessment. In digital environments, items could be presented that required a series of actions—not simply the identification of a single correct answer. If a student were to be examined on ability to access information, that student could be required to enact a process of decision-making within rhetorical contexts sensitive to aim, genre, and audience. The student could be placed in a context—as an employee, for instance, seated before a computer at a fictitious company named Restoration Demolition in which a request had been made from a customer to find stained glass panels in good condition. Faced with a choice of databases from which information may be drawn, increasingly precise searches might yield exactly those results needed by the customer (Figure 5.1).Performing a simulation of information retrieval within databases, the candidate demonstrates search capability and then selects information to meet the customer request.

Information Literacy in Digital Environments

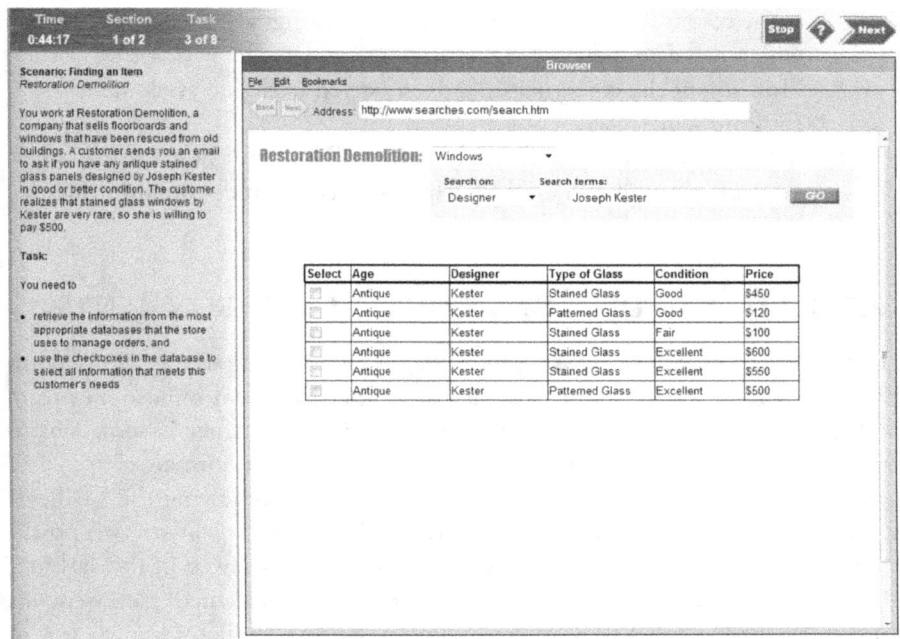

Figure 5.1. Restoration Demolition: iSkills assessment task. © 2015, Educational Testing Service. All rights reserved. Used with Permission.

In a print-based environment, the candidate would select a single correct answer from a list; in this digital environment, the candidate selects the appropriate database from a list of alternatives, types search terms, reviews results and may try an alternative search strategy, and then selects the responses from the results that answers the customer's query—while the machine records database selection, search terms, the number and characteristics of the potentially multiple searches conducted, and the relevance and appropriateness of reviewed and selected results. Blending process and product, the resulting system, iSkills, represents a type of next-generation assessment in which real-life applications track the learning process as it occurs in the digital environments (Tucker, 2009) that exist within the ecologies of interacting information sources identified by Kathleen Blake Yancey (Chapter 4, this collection). From the design of tasks to the delivery of results, digital environments provide a new way of thinking about large-scale assessment programs.

For those responsible for the selection of assessment instruments in specific institutional sites, answers to three questions will be helpful when assessment of IL occurs in digital environments:

1. Is the construct of IL itself mediated by the digital environments in which it is assessed?
2. How might the construct of IL be modeled in digital assessment environments?
3. What do present theories of validation tell us about how institutional assessments might be used to help students become more information literate?

CONSTRUCT MEDIATION IN DIGITAL ENVIRONMENTS

For purpose of exposition, it is useful to begin by returning to the 1955 definition of a construct as proposed by the psychometrician and philosopher team of Lee J. Cronbach and Paul E. Meehl (1955): "A construct is some postulated attribute of people, assumed to be reflected in test performance" (p. 283). Broadly speaking, all constructs are mediated—that is, following the Medieval Latin origin of the word, the construct is divided in the middle, with part postulated (or targeted) and part performed (and measured). Viewed in this fashion, all environments mediate constructs, and the extent of the mediation depends on standpoint. To use a well-known example, writing mediates knowledge, as Walter Ong (1982) famously demonstrated in his study of orality and literacy. Writing restructures consciousness, he boldly proposed, and backed it up by calling to mind distinctions between orally based thought and literacy-based practices: Oral cultures are empathetic, he claimed, while writing establishes objectivity. A list of such dualisms, his psychodynamics of orality illustrate that all constructs exist in domains that are mediated by—and reflected in—performance. For Ong, the mediation of language by writing was of paramount importance; for his critics (Scribner & Cole, 1981), the generalized cognitive effects of the technology of literacy could not be substantiated.

By the mid-1990s, it was becoming clear that the digital world—a new environment—was emerging as the latest in a series of contextual shifts that had begun 5,300 years ago with the writing on the clay tablets of Uruk (Woods, 2010). Whether the technology was the visible language created by stylus or pixel, all mediation, Jay David Bolter and Richard Grusin (1996) claimed, is remediation (p. 346). As a theory of media, remediation is a concept that allows us to investigate the promise of digital representation: the way digital environments import and refashion other media into digital space; the ways these environments suggest reality itself with image, sound, and haptic technology; and the ways they allow participants to reform reality as they synchronously participate in events. So powerful are these digital environments today that it is difficult to imagine a context in which a user could avoid mediation when engaging the IL construct. The question thus becomes one of agency: How is the IL construct mediated?

Here Herbert A. Simon's parable of the ant is useful. In *The Sciences of the Artificial* (1996), Simon offered the following narrative and its interpretation:

> We watch an ant make his laborious way across a wind- and wave-molded beach. He moves ahead, angles to the right to ease his climb up a steep dune, detours around a pebble, stops for a moment to exchange information with a compatriot. Thus he makes his weaving, halting way back to his home. (p. 51)

In coming to terms with the journey of the ant, we wonder at the irregular, complex series of traced and retraced steps and realize that the wandering is due to the encountered obstacles of pebble and path. Simon offers an hypothesis: "An ant, viewed as a behaving system, is quite simple. The apparent complexity of its behavior over time is largely a reflection of the complexity of the environment in which it finds itself" (p. 52).

In the case at hand, let's imagine that Simon's ant parable is about the IL construct and how it reveals itself through behavior. Let's narrow the construct to the variable of information access as the employee of Restoration Demolition engages it. Following Simon, the seeming elementalist (bubble and booklet) or complex (constructed response) behaviors comes not from different constructs but from the complexity of the environments in which the construct is assessed. As such, print and digitally based samples of the construct used in a given assessment reflect a different beach and therefore lead to different behavior. Effectively, each measures a different construct—the measured construct requiring, let's say, its own smaller circle of behavior—although the constructs may certainly be related, if only because they derive from the same underlying domain.

So, to answer the first question—is the construct of IL mediated in digital assessment environments?—we offer the following answer: Measured constructs are indeed mediated by the way the assessment designers sample the construct. As such, depending on how the assessment designers view the digital scene of action, there may be differences in what is being measured.

CONSTRUCT MODELING IN DIGITAL ENVIRONMENTS

The concept of mediation is extremely helpful in allowing us to reflect on the impact of digital environments on constructs. However, that concept alone is insufficient if we are to examine assessment of learning in digital environments. Required is an additional concept: modeling.

Susan E. Embretson (1983) recognized that the impact of the information processing perspective described by Simon led to a shift from "explaining antecedent/consequent relationships to explaining performance from the systems and subsystems of underlying processes." "As a paradigm shift," she continued, "the information-processing view entails changes not only in the questions that are asked but also in the type of data that are deemed relevant" (p. 179). Because construct modeling was, in fact, the equivalent of theory building, Embretson proposed that a sound construct model must account for individual performance, allow for comparison of alterative models, yield quantification of the constructs in the model, and provide information about individual differences in performance. In the study of writing—a field familiar to readers of this volume—the most significant modeling work has been that of John R. Hayes (2012) who has been modeling the writing construct for over three decades (Hayes & Flower, 1980). Delineation of cognitive processes—writer's control of task, writing processes, composition environment, and resource level—has transformed our concept of writing. Because of the work of Hayes and his colleagues, we now know that writing is not a series of mechanically executed displays of knowledge of conventions but, rather, a complex socio-cognitive process.

While the concept of mediation is one of scene (where IL occurs), the concept of modeling is one of agency (how the construct is modeled). While the digital environment of iSkills involves pebbles on a new beach, the differences in performance we see are due to differences in the way the construct is sampled by iSkills. Ultimately, the targeted construct—information access, for example—is nevertheless identical to those for print communication, inasmuch as the digital and print assessments both intend to assess IL. Even if the assessment-makers' intentions are to assess IL, differences in performance are artifacts of the assessment environment and may result in different measured constructs.

Here is the key: the assessment environment of iSkills introduces nontrivial performance differences within the constructed-response task (Bennett, 1993). Knowing how to avoid pebbles and navigate the paths is essential to the performance of the student and, in turn, to an institution's assessment of that candidate's level of IL. Just because two assessments are labeled "information literacy" by their respective developers does not mean that the mediated construct of IL (the measured construct) is the same—and, thus, may be modeled differently.

Two examples are in order to bring this theoretical discussion into their practical application.

Comparison of two tests—the print-based Standardized Assessment of Information Literacy Skills (SAILS) test (O'Connor, Radcliff & Gedeon, 2002) and the digitally based iSkills (Katz, 2007b)—demonstrates the distinction between construct representation in print and digital environments. (Although

SAILS is delivered now exclusively online, the test maintains similar organization and formatting as when it was delivered on paper.) Based on a strategy of identifying the correct answer, a SAILS item asks the candidate, for instance, to identify the best source of information about an event that took place two days ago by asking the candidate to fill in the bubble next to the term "newspaper." In identifying the answer, the candidate internalizes a correct response by an analytic process of exclusion of incorrect answers. The response, distanced and non-situated, is executed by a single action of identification. In contrast, in the digital environment of iSkills the student is examined on ability to access information experiences, both in a realistically simulated context and in a robust constructed response environment. The task begins with just a description of the customer need and an empty search screen. As the student selects databases, keystrokes search terms, and reviews results over potentially multiple search-and-review cycles, that student engages one aspect of the IL construct in continuous process of mediation (the original approach) and re-mediation (the original approach restructured by the constructed response task). Immersed, the student adopts the persona of an employee of Restoration Demolition (Figure 5.1), a digitally created reality.

In essence, the IL experience is transformed by that created environment. Both the SAILS item and the iSkills constructed response task tap the IL variable of information access but in distinctly different ways. Indeed, the distinction between print and digital environments is also carried into the function of test scoring: SAILS allows only one correct answer; iSkills yields a competency score based on levels of ability encompassing both efficacy of process and correct answer identification.

Contrast of two assessments—the print-based IL assessment at New Jersey Institute of Technology (NJIT, 2012; Scharf, Elliot, Huey, Briller & Joshi, 2007) and iSkills (Katz, 2007b)—demonstrates the distinction between construct assessment in print and digital environments. In 2005, NJIT researchers conducted a study of the relationship between a model of writing informed by Hayes and a model of IL informed by ACRL, as both constructs were represented in a sample of 100 portfolios of senior undergraduate students enrolled in humanities courses. Similar to the curricular project reported by Beth Bensen, Hong Wu, Denise Woetzel, and Ghazala Hashmi (Chapter 19, this collection), the research was the result of collaboration between English faculty and librarians. The overall score on the writing model correlated with the overall score on the IL model at 0.50 ($p < 0.01$), evidence that the two models were related. Based on this print-based system of assessment, NJIT and ETS researchers then collaborated to investigate the relationship between holistic portfolio scores (designed to capture both writing and IL skills) and iSkills scores of students enrolled in humanities courses (Katz, Elliot, et al., 2008). After controlling for students' overall ability as measured by SAT scores, analysis revealed near zero correlations between the portfolio scores and iSkills scores of first-year students as well as upper-division students. At the time of the study, we concluded that the constructs were related yet distinct. In the print-based environment of the portfolios, students had been asked to read novels, search databases for peer-reviewed articles, and integrate those articles to develop various interpretations of elements within the novels. One of the iSkills digitally based constructed response tasks had asked students to compare advertisements from competing vendors' websites by summarizing information into a table, or students had been asked to present results from a sporting event into a spreadsheet to clarify standings and decide the need for playoffs. From task to scoring, the two assessments could not have been more different. Although the target construct domain of IL was the same, it was mediated by the respective assessments, resulting in different measured constructs.

Based on these two studies, our answer to the second question—how is the construct of IL modeled in digital assessment environments?—is as follows: While identification of the construct of IL, viewed as a system of behavior, can be made in straightforward terms, the observed complexity of the behavior of students as they perform in print and digital environments is a reflection of the complexity of the environment in the assessment. While the core variables—those postulated attributes of Cronbach and Meehl—exist in the larger domain, their representation in the digital environment of the measured construct of assessment systems such as iSkills is unique. The extent to which the construct is digitally mediated depends on the extent to which the assessment leverages, in Bolter and Grusin's terms, the delivery of other media, realistic simulation, and participation in that created reality. And, while the target construct (the intended construct domain) is shared among environments, in digitally mediated environments there may indeed be differences in exactly what is being measured, as the NJIT study demonstrated.

While that somewhat long-winded answer is conceptually useful, institutional assessment staff and their instructional colleagues who are deciding on how to assess IL must consider practical strategies of providing a clearer picture of the underlying construct and its representation in the test at hand. Through validation—the process of gathering evidence for the interpretation and use of an assessment—institutions can begin to make such evaluations.

As we will now show, such evaluations are as nuanced as is the representation of the construct in unique forms of assessment. Through validation, assessment stakeholders can make important decisions leading to claims about the IL of their students. We turn now to present theories of validation and how they can

Information Literacy in Digital Environments

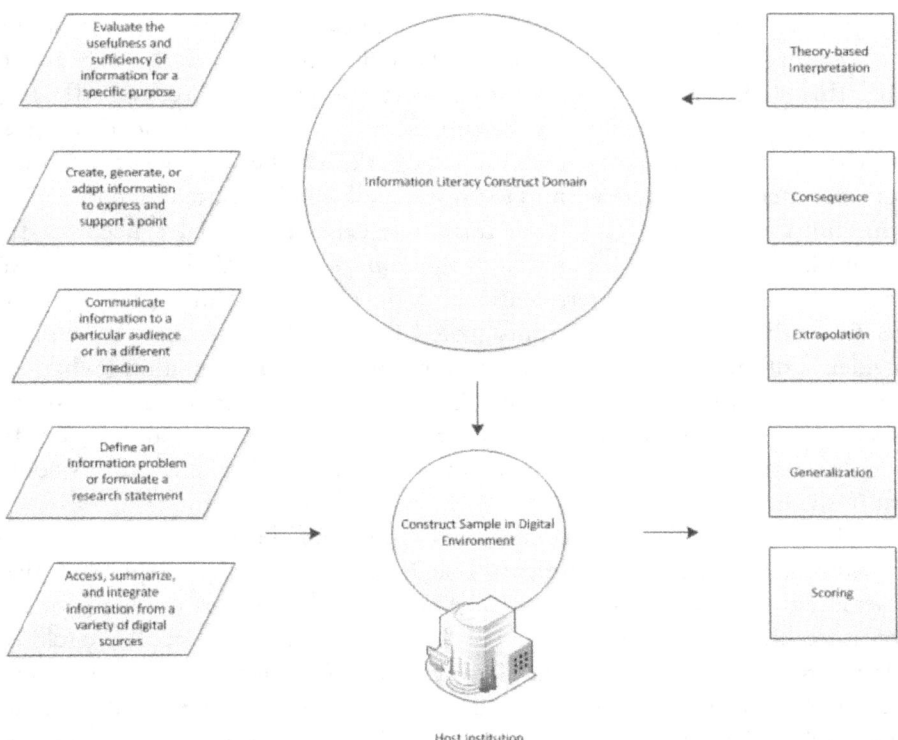

Figure 5.2. Information literacy: A validation model.

support institutional assessment efforts to help students become more information literate.

CONSTRUCT VALIDATION IN DIGITAL ENVIRONMENTS

Michael T. Kane (2013) proposed an Interpretation/Use Argument (IUA) as the most current form of validation. In presenting his case for an evidentiary system of gathering validity evidence, he treated the concept of construct validity in some detail. Tracing the idea of construct representation offered by Cronbach and Meehl (1955), Kane identifies three legacies of their model: test-score interpretations cannot be taken as self-evident; validation is a process that is dependent upon claims made in a defined interpretative framework; and critical inquiry is the appropriate result of validation.

Application of Kane's concepts of representation and validation to the study of IL in digital environments is shown in Figure 5.2.

The large circle represents the construct *domain*—the postulated attribute of developed knowledge, intended to be reflected in test performance—of IL. This circle—the targeted construct—represents the full scope of IL: the not-directly observable knowledge and skills in a student's mind that drive observable performance on any IL-related task, whether real-world activities or assessment tasks. Here we find the work of all who have attempted to define this full construct of IL. Within this circle exists the initial concept of IL found in the *IL Standards*, as well as the *Framework for IL*. Here, too, stand particular institutional interpretations of IL, such as the one established at NJIT, with its emphasis on traits scored in portfolio assessments: citation; evidence of independent research; appropriateness; and integration (Scharf et al., 2007). In the large circle we also find all forms of print and digital assessment—those that have been examined, those that are emerging, and those that can be imagined. Put another way, all the concepts of IL offered in this book fit in the large circle.

The smaller circle represents a single sample of the IL construct as it is reflected in a digital environment. That is, the smaller circle represents the measured construct—those knowledge and skill elements of the range of IL measureable by a digitally based assessment. Note that the smaller circle is drawn from the larger domain; although we would like the measured construct to be a perfect subset, the reality is that the assessed construct might also include knowledge and skills not described in the larger domain. In the case of iSkills, the construct sample includes the five variables of IL that drive the test: access, summarize, and integrate information from a variety of digital sources; define an information problem or formulate a research statement; communicate information to a particular audience or in a different medium; create, generate, or adapt information to express and support a point; and evaluate the usefulness and sufficiency of information for a specific purpose (adapted from ETS, 2002).

The host institution represents the specific site in which the assessment takes place. It is there that the construct takes meaning for users of the assessment. As we will demonstrate, this context shifts the validity framework from that of the assessment designer to that of the assessment user.

Institutional researchers who want to measure and guide improvement of students' IL skills should create their own IUAs that will guide decisions about sampling plans, use of scores, and needed curricular changes. However, because the use of scores for a system such as iSkills—or any test, for that matter—is not simply an up or down vote regarding validity, Kane (2013) offers a process of validation attentive to sources of evidence that guide interpretation and score use. We have illustrated these five sources on the right of Figure 5.2:

1. *Scoring inferences* take us from the observed performances on a test to an observed score. These inferences include evidence about the appropriateness of the scoring criteria and the principles for combining scores. These inferences provide evidence that test scores reflect test performance. This inference might not be as obvious as it might initially seem, as we illustrate below.
2. *Generalization inferences* take us from the observed sample of performances (as reflected in the test score) to claims about expected performance in the construct sample (e.g., that the test score reflects expected performance not only on the current digital IL assessment tasks, but on similar digital IL assessment tasks).
3. *Extrapolation inferences* extend the interpretation into the full construct domain, and are likely among the most common assumption made about test scores—that they reflect actual, real-world ability in the domain of interest.
4. *Consequence inferences* extend the interpretation into the larger assessment environment, thereby strengthening the IUA. (Of course, unintended consequences that threaten validity should be considered and, when possible, avoided.)
5. *Theory-based inferences* extend the interpretation even further, into hypothesized relationships between the construct domain and other areas of interest.

Kane proposed these five categories of evidence as a way to validate the interpretation and use of test scores. We propose that instructors and administrators may use these categories to design a program of research that will yield information about the IL abilities of their students. As we show in the following examples, the extension is not hard to make.

Scoring inferences conceptually refer to the idea that test scores reflect students' performance on the test. Although, traditionally, evidence for this inference includes technical issues such as scoring procedures, in an accreditation context a key factor is motivation: Are students trying their best on an assessment that might have no direct consequences for them? And, if they are not, then how meaningful are the scores themselves? Because more motivated students perform better on such tests (Liu, Bridgeman & Adler, 2012), one type of evidence for sufficient motivation is to investigate the reception of a test by students. Table 5.1 presents a feedback survey (N = 1823) gathered by ETS during early field trials of iSkills. As the responses indicate, the students gave the test their best effort, found it innovative and challenging, and realized that success required both technical and critical thinking skills. The software—the

Table 5.1. iSkills feedback survey: Percentage of responses

Considering the test overall, please indicate how much you agree or disagree with each of the following statements:	N	Agree	Somewhat Agree	Somewhat Disagree	Disagree
I gave this test my best effort.	1823	59%	32%	6%	3%
I have never taken a test like this one before.	1813	77%	15%	4%	4%
This test was appropriately challenging.	1810	53%	35%	9%	3%
The unfamiliar software made it difficult for me to do well on this test.	1804	21%	35%	26%	18%
To perform well on this test requires thinking skills as well as technical skills.	1794	62%	31%	5%	2%
I found the overall testing interface easy to use (even if the tasks themselves might have been difficult).	1800	38%	40%	15%	7%
I enjoyed taking this test.	1804	18%	34%	23%	26%
My performance on this test accurately reflects my ability to solve problems using computers and the Internet.	1801	17%	40%	26%	17%
The tasks reflect activities I have done at school, work, or home.	1803	32%	46%	14%	9%
I encountered a lot of system glitches while taking this test (e.g., system freeze, long time for tasks to load).	1548	23%	25%	19%	34%

digital environment—nevertheless presented problems that may have resulted in interference with construct measurement. Using such information allows a more complete representation of the meaning of the scores themselves.

Evidence for *generalization inferences* would include information about student performance on iSkills in relation to the level of test performance expected to be considered "information literate." A large scale study (N = 1,442) of 14 tasks covering the five variables in Figure 5.2 tells us a good deal about student performance on iSkills.

Figure 5.3 shows the distribution of scores from 1,442 college students and high school seniors. The mean score on this sample was 260, with a standard

Information Literacy in Digital Environments

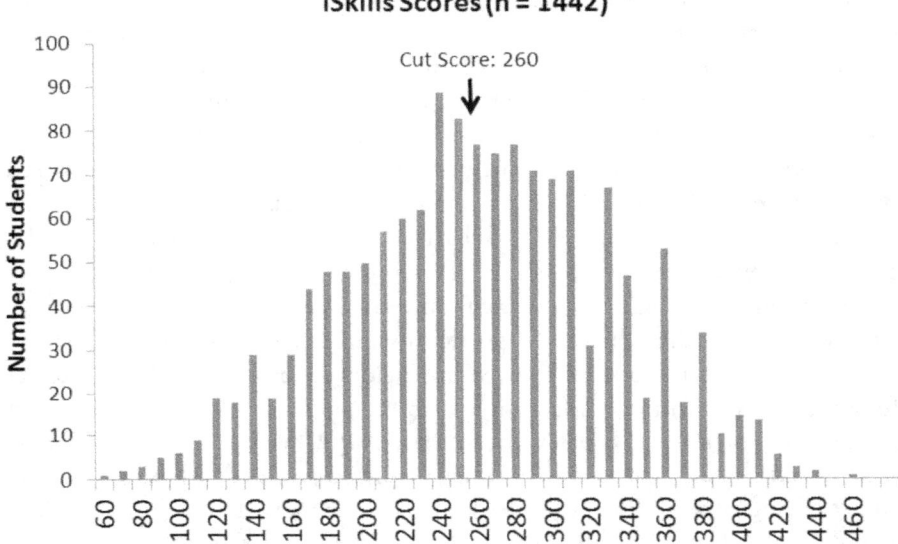

Figure 5.3. iSkills passing rate, April 2011 through March 2012 (N = 1,442).

deviation of 72; scores were approximately normally distributed across the possible score range of 0–500. Approximately 50% of students achieved a level of foundational ICT literacy expected of entering college freshmen. (See Tannenbaum & Katz, 2008, for details on the definition and establishment of the foundational level.) Generalization inferences are supported because the distribution of scores is consistent with what is expected on the distribution of IL. While many librarians would not be surprised at this number, that only half the students "passed" the exam suggests that the so-called digital natives are not uniformly proficient at the effective use of technology (see Katz, 2007a, for more descriptions of strengths and weaknesses of these test takers). At the same time, this percentage is higher than what was observed in previous research (e.g., 27–40% on earlier versions of the assessment; Tannenbaum & Katz, 2008). While we cannot definitively attribute a cause of this rise in passing rates among iSkills test takers, we would hope that the increase is due to increased attention to IL and ICT literacy skills by accreditation agencies as well as by colleges and universities who place these skills in the general education curriculum, such as the work of Alison S. Gregory and Betty L. McCall (Chapter 18, this collection) and Lori Baker and Pam Gladis (Chapter 16, this collection).

However, generalization inferences need not rely on large-scale sampling plans or inferential statistics alone, as a study of 88 undergraduates who responded to iSkills assessment tasks and to more open-ended "naturalistic" tasks revealed (Snow & Katz, 2009). In that study, analysis of student interviews revealed the response process used to answer both standardized tests and locally developed classroom assignments. In learning more about student response process, instructors can design a curriculum that will allow success on both test types.

Extrapolation inferences would include observations of relationships between performance on iSkills and the performances in a related domain. As noted above, the NJIT portfolio study (Scharf et al., 2007) documented the relationship between writing scores and IL scores. However, the writing scores correlated more strongly with curriculum-related scores (current course grade and overall GPA) than did the IL portfolio scores. The extrapolation inference from these criterion measures allowed instructors to realize that IL was not yet fully integrated into the curriculum and to design a way for librarians to help increase the intensity of coursework in that area. A related study (Katz, Haras & Blaszczynski, 2010) found that iSkills predicted grades in a business writing course, demonstrating the type of connection between IL and business skills explored by Dale Cyphert and Stanley P. Lyle (Chapter 3, this collection). Thus, extrapolation inferences become a significant part of the validation process as IL becomes an enabling construct suggesting across-the-curriculum expansion.

Stemming from the use of iSkills at NJIT and the impact of the assessment on the institution and the assessment itself, identification of *consequential inferences* strengthen the IUA (American Educational Research Association, American Psychological Association & National Council on Measurement in Education, 2014; Haertel, 2013). For NJIT, our studies contrasting the IL construct as measured through print (Scharf et al., 2007) and as measured through a digital environment (Katz, Elliot, et al., 2008) revealed shortcomings in the institutions' view of the IL construct. Accordingly, the iSkills assessment was made part of the NJIT suite of assessments, a decision that strongly reinforced an information-literacy-across-the-curriculum framework that librarians had been building since 2009. This integration had two consequences: digitally based IL became part of the core curriculum for student learning adopted at NJIT; and iSkills served as a key assessment component of the institution's 2012 successful re-accreditation by the Middle States Commission on Higher Education (NJIT, 2012). To bolster student motivation on assessments, the institution is now examining how Certificates of Achievement—awards for predefined performance levels on iSkills—might provide additional motivation for students to try their best. Because enhancing motivation strengthens the validity argument (Liu et al., 2012), case studies from institutions such as NJIT transformed the environment of the assessment itself at ETS and led to certificates awarded for levels of ICT literacy (ETS, 2014).

Theory-based inferences are also of great importance to instructors and administrators as they help make explicit the connection between the construct domain and strategies for curricular change. In the case at hand, a theory of IL postulates the underlying framework that drove Simon's little ant, as well as our students, in certain ways when encountering, respectively, pebbles and constructed response tasks.

An example drives home the importance of theory-building. To investigate the nature of IL, as measured by iSkills, ETS researchers (Katz, Attali & Rijmen, 2008) used factor analysis to identify patterns in a set of items and establish which combinations of items tend to be highly correlated. In the case of iSkills, there were two primary ideal models to consider. First, a seven-factor model arranged the items into the groups corresponding to postulated IL subskills (define, access, evaluate, manage, integrate, create, and communicate; see Katz, 2007b). The iSkills assessment was originally designed with these seven skills, with each task (and the items within a task) corresponding to one of the skills. This model postulates that a student could do well on, say, finding information (access) tasks but do poorly on tasks that require adapting materials to an audience (communicate). Second, the one-factor model took the view that all of the items in the iSkills assessment together measure a single, integrated construct of IL: Students are strong or weak at IL generally, with all of the items on the test being highly correlated (e.g., high performance on one type of item implies high performance on all types of items). Both exploratory and confirmatory factor analyses suggest that IL, as measured by iSkills, consists of a single factor (Katz, Attali, et al., 2008). That is, based on data from a sample of more than 600 test takers, exploratory factor analyses suggested that the entire set of iSkills tasks measure a single, integrated construct: students might have greater or lesser IL, but there was no evidence that the seven IL skill areas were distinct from one another. Similarly, in confirmatory factor analyses, the one-factor ideal model fit the data much better than did the seven-factor ideal model.

What does this research mean for instruction? Interpretatively, it appears that IL is an integrated skill: improving one's IL is a matter of holistic, comprehensive instruction, rather than piecemeal training on component skills. IL appears to be a truly significant threshold concept (Towsend, Brunetti & Hofer, 2011). Such an integrated outlook on IL might reflect either a stronger, more sophisticated view of information generally or a weaker, simplistic view. Of course, instruction cannot ignore the various activities that make up IL skill, as outlined in such documents as the *Framework for IL* or the particular ways that NJIT humanities instructors teach and assess the construct. However, focusing on those foundational skills alone might not be the quickest (or best) path to IL. Instead, a balanced approach that points out the usefulness of more sophisticated attitudes toward IL might help students recognize the value in, say, trying to figure out alternative descriptors for information (which, in turn, should lead to better search results).

Evidence that IL, as measured by iSkills, is a unified construct impacts how that assessment should be administered. Institutional researchers should explicate theory-based inferences about IL that postulate characteristics of students and their experiences that lead to stronger or weaker IL. Are students who complete a particular set of courses, compared with those that do not, more information literate? Are transfer students entering with weaker IL skills, leading them to struggle in programs compared with students who, from freshmen year, benefit from the university's core curriculum in IL? Which majors tend to have the most information literate students, and is that a function of students who tend to go into that major or a function of the courses in that major? These are just examples of theory-based inferences that could be investigated using an appropriate sampling plan in the administration of IL assessments such as iSkills. They directly tie assessment results to the institutional improvement plans.

Returning to Figure 5.2, we note that the arrows indicate that the interpretation/use argument, and associated evidence, should be used by institutional instructors and administrators to help them reconsider and redefine, as needed, the construct domain itself and the elements of it that are most relevant to their admitted students. Without that feedback loop, the gathered information will only result in reports completed and papers published; with it, stakeholders can work to ensure that the results of the assessment are used to improve learning.

And so we conclude by answering our third question: What do present theories of validation tell us about how institutional assessments might be used to help students become more information literate? Present theories such as IUA reveal the vital importance of a carefully planned program of research, based at the institution, when complex constructs are under examination. In the field of writing studies, such calls for contextualization have been well developed and may serve as basis for IL research (Condon, 2013; Huot, 1996; White, Elliot & Peckham, 2015). In similar fashion, each of the sources of evidence identified by Kane suggests distinct programs of research focusing on areas of validation. Research in these areas provides the level of detail necessary to identify ways to help students improve their IL performance.

Nevertheless, it is an error to conclude with triumphalism because so very much remains to be done. Valuable as it is, the IUA perspective is that of an assessment designer, not an assessment user. For those stakeholders at the host institution shown in Figure 5.2, for example, motivation is of enormous importance. While the assessment designer will justifiably be concerned with technical issues such as scoring procedures, making sure that students are willing to engage the construct sample of iSkills is of paramount importance. Indeed, cultivating student motivation is one aspect of the assessment over which institutional stakeholders have great influence. As Mariëlle Leijten, Luuk Van Waes, Karen Schriver, and John R. Hayes (2014) have observed of the writing model, however, educators have not adequately learned how to combine motivation with cognitive processes in our construct models in both academic and workplace communication settings. If we follow the recommendations of the National Research Council (2012) and attend to the broad spectrum of cognitive, intrapersonal, and interpersonal domains—as the *Framework for IL* has proposed in its emphasis on cognitive, affective, and social dimensions—we come to realize that we must continue to broaden our investigation of the IL construct mediation and its domain. And, in doing so, we must also continue to conceptualize the IUA perspective in terms of all those who will be influenced by its use: advisory boards, administration, faculty and instructional staff, parents, students, and the public. Depending on audience, the IUA for an assessment may have to be refashioned if it is to have meaning. When perspective is added, we realize that we are only just beginning to understand our parables.

REFERENCES

American Educational Research Association, American Psychological Association & National Council on Measurement in Education (2014). *Standards for educational and psychological testing*. Washington, DC: American Educational Research Association.

Association for College and Research Libraries (2000). *Information literacy competency standards for higher education*. Chicago, IL: American Library Association.

Association for Colleges and Research Libraries (2015). *Framework for information literacy for higher education*. Chicago, IL: American Library Association.

Baker, L. & Gladis, P. (2016). Moving ahead by looking back: Crafting a framework for sustainable, institutional information literacy. In B. J. D'Angelo, S. Jamieson, B. Maid & J. R. Walker (Eds.), *Information literacy: Research and collaboration across disciplines*. Fort Collins, CO: WAC Clearinghouse and University Press of Colorado.

Bennett, R. E. (1993). On the meanings of constructed response. In R. E. Bennett & W. C. Ward (Eds.), *Construction vs. choice in cognitive measurement: Issues in constructed response, performance testing, and portfolio assessment* (pp. 1–27). Hillsdale, NJ: Erlbaum.

Bensen, B., Woetzel, D., Wu, H. & Hashmi, G. (2016). Impacting information literacy through alignment, resources, and assessment. In B. J. D'Angelo, S. Jamieson, B. Maid & J. R. Walker (Eds.), *Information literacy: Research and collaboration across disciplines*. Fort Collins, CO: WAC Clearinghouse and University Press of Colorado.

Bolter, J. D. & Grusin, R. (1996). Remediation. *Configurations, 4,* 133–358.

Condon, W. (2013). Large-scale assessment, locally-developed measures, and automated scoring of essays: Fishing for red herrings? *Assessing Writing, 18,* 100–108.

Cronbach, L. J. & Meehl, P. E. (1955). Construct validity in psychological tests. *Psychological Bulletin, 52,* 281–302.

Cyphert, D. & Lyle, S. P. (2016). Employer expectations of information literacy: Identifying the skills gap. In B. J. D'Angelo, S. Jamieson, B. Maid & J. R. Walker (Eds.), *Information literacy: Research and collaboration across disciplines.* Fort Collins, CO: WAC Clearinghouse and University Press of Colorado.

Educational Testing Service (2002). *Digital transformation: A framework for ICT literacy.* Princeton, NJ: Author. Retrieved from http://www.ets.org/Media/Tests/Information_and_Communication_Technology_Literacy/ictreport.pdf.

Educational Testing Service (2014). *iSkills™ Certificates of achievement.* Retrieved from http://www.ets.org/iskills/scores_reports/certificates.

Embretson, S. E. (1983). Construct validity: Construct representation versus nomothetic span. *Psychological Bulletin, 93,* 179–197.

Gregory, A. S. & McCall, B. L. (2016). Building critical researchers and writers incrementally: Vital partnerships between faculty and librarians. In B. J. D'Angelo, S. Jamieson, B. Maid & J. R. Walker (Eds.), *Information literacy: Research and collaboration across disciplines.* Fort Collins, CO: WAC Clearinghouse and University Press of Colorado.

Haertel, E. (2013). How is testing supposed to improve schooling? *Measurement: Interdisciplinary Research and Perspectives, 11,* 1–18.

Hayes, J. R. (2012). Modeling and remodeling writing. *Written Communication, 29,* 369–388.

Hayes, J. R. & Flower, L. S. (1980). Identifying the organization of writing processes. In L. W. Gregg & E. R. Steinberg (Eds.), *Cognitive processes in writing* (pp. 3–30). Hillsdale, NJ: Erlbaum.

Huot, B. (1996). Toward a new theory of writing assessment. *College Composition and Communication, 47,* 549–566.

Jacobson, T. & Gibson, C. (2013). *ACRL information literacy competency standards for higher education task force.* Retrieved from http://connect.ala.org/node/205100.

Kane, M. T. (2013). Validating the interpretation and uses of test scores. *Journal of Educational Measurement, 50,* 1–73.

Katz, I. R. (2007a). ETS research finds college students fall short in demonstrating ICT literacy: National Policy Council to create national standards. *College and Research Libraries News, 68,* 35–37. Retrieved from http://crln.acrl.org/content/68/1/35.full.pdf.

Katz, I. R. (2007b). Testing information literacy in digital environments: ETS's *iSkills* assessment. *Information Technology and Libraries, 26,* 3–12.

Katz, I. R., Attali, Y. & Rijmen, F. (2008, April). *ETS's iSkills™ assessment: Measurement of information and communication technology literacy.* Paper presented at the meeting of the Society for Industrial/Organizational Psychology, San Francisco, CA.

Katz, I. R., Elliot, N., Attali, Y., Scharf, D., Powers, D., Huey, H., . . . Briller, V. (2008). *The assessment of information literacy: A case study* (Research Report RR-08-03). Princeton, NJ: Educational Testing Service.

Katz, I. R., Haras, C. M. & Blaszczynski, C. (2010). Does business writing require information literacy? *Business Communication Quarterly, 73,* 135–149.

Leijten, M., Van Waes L., Schriver, K. & Hayes, J. R. (2014). Writing in the workplace: Constructing documents using multiple digital sources. *Journal of Writing Research, 5,* 285–337.

Liu, O. L., Bridgeman, B. & Adler, R. M. (2012). Measuring outcomes in higher education: Motivation matters. *Educational Researcher, 41,* 352–362.

Maid, B. & D'Angelo, B. J. (2016). Threshold concepts: Integrating and applying information literacy and writing instruction. In B. J. D'Angelo, S. Jamieson, B. Maid & J. R. Walker (Eds.), *Information literacy: Research and collaboration across disciplines.* Fort Collins, CO: WAC Clearinghouse and University Press of Colorado.

National Research Council (2012). *Education for life and work: Developing transferable knowledge and skills in the 21st century.* Washington, DC: National Academies Press.

New Jersey Institute of Technology (2012). *A science and technology research university for the 21st Century: Final report.* Retrieved from http://www.njit.edu/middlestates/docs/2012/NJIT_Middle_States_Self_Study_FinalReport.pdf.

O'Connor, L. G., Radcliff, C. J. & Gedeon, J. A. (2002). Applying systems design and item response theory to the problem of measuring information literacy skills. *College and Research Libraries, 63,* 528–543.

Ong, Walter. (1982). *Orality and literacy: The technologizing of the word.* London, UK: Methuen.

Scharf, D., Elliot, N., Huey, H., Briller, V. & Joshi, K. (2007). Direct assessment of information literacy using writing portfolios. *Journal of Academic Librarianship, 33,* 462–477.

Scribner, S. & Cole, M. (1981). *The psychology of literacy.* Cambridge, MA: Harvard University Press.

Simon, H. A. (1996). *The sciences of the artificial* (3rd. ed.). Cambridge, MA: MIT Press.

Snow, E. & Katz, I. R. (2009). Using cognitive interviews to validate an interpretive argument for the ETS™ assessment. *Communications in Information Literacy, 3,* 99–127.

Tannenbaum, R. J. & Katz, I. R. (2008). *Setting standards on the core and advanced iSkills™ assessments* (Research Memorandum RM-08-04). Princeton, NJ: Educational Testing Service. Retrieved from http://www.ets.org/Media/Research/pdf/RM-08-04.pdf.

Townsend, L., Brunetti, K. & Hofer, A. R. (2011). Threshold concepts and information literacy. *portal: Libraries and the Academy, 11,* 853–869.

Tucker, B. (2009). The next generation of testing. *Educational Leadership, 67,* 48–53.

White, E. M., Elliot, N. & Peckham, I. (2015). *Very like a whale: The assessment of writing programs.* Logan, UT: Utah State University Press.

Woods, C. (2010). *Visible language.* Chicago, IL: University of Chicago Press.

Yancey, K. B. (2016). Creating and exploring new worlds: Web 2.0, information literacy, and the ways we know. In B. J. D'Angelo, S. Jamieson, B. Maid & J. R. Walker (Eds.), *Information literacy: Research and collaboration across disciplines.* Fort Collins, CO: WAC Clearinghouse and University Press of Colorado.

PART II.
RESEARCHING INFORMATION LITERACY

CHAPTER 6
WHAT THE CITATION PROJECT TELLS US ABOUT INFORMATION LITERACY IN COLLEGE COMPOSITION

Sandra Jamieson
Drew University

INTRODUCTION

In the introduction to the *Framework for Information Literacy for Higher Education* (*Framework for IL*) (ACRL, 2015), the ACRL Board explains (through footnotes) that the thinking behind the *Framework for IL* is indebted to Thomas Mackey and Trudi Jacobson's (2011, 2014) work on metaliteracy. That work, it notes,

> expands the scope of traditional information skills (i.e., determine, access, locate, understand, produce, and use information) to include the collaborative production and sharing of information in participatory digital environments (collaborate, produce, and share). This approach requires an ongoing adaptation to emerging technologies and an understanding of the critical thinking and reflection required to engage in these spaces as producers, collaborators, and distributors (footnote 7, citing Mackey & Jacobson, 2014).

As writing teachers and librarians develop ways to help students acquire the dispositions identified in the *Framework for IL*, it is useful to look closely at the kind of researched writing produced before its introduction. In addition to providing a sense of the kinds of resources being consulted in response to specific writing contexts, such analysis provides a baseline to work beyond—and instructors against. We have learned a lot about attitudes, practices, and expectations from student interviews such as those by Project Information Literacy (Head & Eisenberg, 2009, 2010; Head, 2013) and protocol analysis (see

Blackwell-Starnes, Chapter 7, this collection), but analysis of the final product—the research paper—offers insight into how those various habits of mind play out. Review of student research papers produced before the *Framework for IL* reveals why the shift to a metacognitive information literacy (IL) is welcomed by many involved in IL instruction. It also demonstrates the impact of some of the limitations of the ACRL *Information Literacy Competency Standards for Higher Education* (*IL Standards*) (ACRL, 2000).

As others have noted (see Norgaard & Sinkinson, Chapter 1, this collection), there are many institutional challenges preventing faculty and librarians from working together to develop shared IL pedagogy. Not the least of these is the common location of IL instruction in the required first-year writing course (FYW) where IL assignments and too often product-based, focusing attention away from IL as a process (Blackwell-Starnes, Chapter 7, this collection) and obscuring the vision of IL as "a rich multifaceted literacy that is responsive to changing contexts and opportunities" (Norgaard & Sinkinson, Chapter 1, this collection). Yet the location of IL instruction is not likely to change with the introduction of the new *Framework for IL*, making it essential for those who would develop a more responsive IL pedagogy to understand what happens in this current context. For this reason, analysis of the research papers produced in first-year writing (FYW) prior to 2011 is particularly instructive. FYW is the one college-level course that almost always includes a researched project (Hood, 2010). Whether the instruction takes the form of the "one shot" library visit (Gavin, 1995; Jacobs & Jacobs, 2009), a program-wide IL component (Holliday & Fagerheim, 2006; Jacobson & Mackey, 2007), embedded librarians (Deitering & Jameson, 2008; Kesselman & Watstein, 2009), or team-taught courses (Alvarez & Dimmock, 2007; Jacobson & Mackey, 2007), final papers are expected to reflect what students have learned about research writing (Howard & Jamieson, 2014) and IL. Because IL instruction is often formally or informally assessed based upon those papers, we can also use them to assess the *IL Standards*.

Articles published by librarians and by writing teachers that focus on or include data on papers produced in FYW courses (Grimes & Boening, 2001; Carlson, 2006; McClure & Clink, 2009) or other lower-level introductory courses mostly populated by first-year students (Davis & Cohen, 2001; Jenkins, 2002; Davis, 2002, 2003; Carlson, 2006; Knight-Davis & Sung, 2008) can help us begin this assessment, but all report on single-institution studies, so they may be too limited to allow broad conclusions. Such single-site research has important local relevance, permitting the campus community to explore questions about the kinds of sources selected and retrieved at a specific moment in a specific place and develop responsive pedagogies and policies. Individually, though, they reveal little about national patterns or trends. These studies occur in isolation and are designed to address local concerns rather than being developed in response to other research. Indeed, single-institution studies are so inward-focused that very few replicate the methods or coding categories of other studies with which they might compare data. Lacking such overlap, existing studies cannot be easily aggregated as part of an evolving national picture of source use. The two exceptions to this are Project Information Literacy and the Citation Project, both of which are engaged in multi-institution study of student research practices and products.

This chapter reports on data from a study of the Citation Project Source-Based Writing (CPSW) Corpus. The study in question explores the types of sources selected and cited in 800 pages of source-based writing by 174 students enrolled in FYW courses at 16 U.S. institutions, ranging from community colleges to Ivy Leagues. Source codes replicate coding categories of earlier studies (Carlson, 2006; McClure & Clink, 2009). Sub-codes allow the data to be broken out for comparison with other studies (Davis & Cohen, 2001; Jenkins, 2002; Davis, 2002, 2003; Knight-Davis & Sung, 2008), extending their reach and reinforcing some of their findings while challenging other oft-repeated claims. This research allows us to understand the limits of decontextualized and linearly focused IL instruction (Norgaard & Sinkinson, Chapter 1, this collection). The data indicate that, nationally, students are broadly able to identify, locate, and access information from apparently appropriate sources in sanctioned ways; however, a closer look at which texts are cited and the ways they are incorporated into the papers reveals the need to go beyond what has for many become a checklist mentality to what the *Framework for IL* describes as "an expanded definition of information literacy [that] emphasize[s] dynamism, flexibility, individual growth, and community learning" ("Introduction").

THE CITATION PROJECT DATA

CITATION PROJECT SOURCE-BASED WRITING (CPSW) CORPUS

As reported elsewhere (Jamieson & Howard, 2013; Jamieson, 2013), the Citation Project Source-Based Writing Corpus (CPSW) gathered research papers from 16 institutions distributed regionally and representing 12 states throughout the United States and also distributed across 2008-2010 Carnegie classifications (see Table 6.1). The papers were produced at the end of whatever the institution identified as the standard FYW course, requiring a 7–10-page research paper using at least five sources. Only decontextualized final research papers were collected; Institutional Research Board (IRB) approvals required researchers to

Table 6.1. Institution types in the Citation Project Source-Use Study

Carnegie classification (data from 2008–2010)			
Level	Control	Classification & Description	N
2-year	Public	Assoc/Pub-R-M (Associate's—Public Rural-serving Medium)	2
4-yr	Private	Bac/A&S (Baccalaureate Colleges—Arts & Sciences)	2
4-yr	Public	Bac/Diverse (Baccalaureate Colleges—Diverse Fields)	1
4-yr plus	Public	Master's L (Master's Colleges & Universities, larger programs)	4
4-yr plus	Public	DRU (Doctoral/Research Universities)	1
4-yr plus	Public	RU/H (Research Universities, high research activity)	2
4-yr plus	Private	RU/VH (Research Universities, high research activity)	2
4-yr plus	Public	RU/VH (Research Universities, very high research activity)	2
TOTAL			16

Carnegie classification	Number of papers available for study	Papers whose sources could not all be retrieved	Number of papers coded	Number of pages coded
Assoc/Pub-R-M	54	31	23	100
Bac/A&S Private	80	23	20	100
Bac/Diverse Public	85	16	10	50
Master's L Public	136	43	40	200
DRU Public	43	4	16	50
RU/H Public Public	37	15	20	100
RU/VH Private	58	23	20	100
RU/VH Public	68	16	25	100
Total	561	171	174	800

protect students and faculty from possible repercussion should plagiarism be detected, which prevented collection of any demographic information, syllabi, or assignments. The study focuses only on the finished product of the research process—the papers—gathered between Spring 2008 and Spring 2010, and the source use in a total of 50 pages from each participating institution was coded. In all, 174 papers and works cited lists were examined, along with the 1,911 citations they included and the 930 sources cited.

LOCATING SOURCES CITED

In order to generate the 174 papers used in this study, 171 papers were rejected (Table 6.1) because researchers were unable to retrieve all of the sources listed. In some cases, the irretrievable sources were part of localized databases set up by the participating institution but not accessible to researchers, or were part of larger collections behind a prohibitive pay-wall. In other cases, citations provided inadequate documentation, especially URLs containing typographical errors; many others pointed to URLs that no longer exist or had been overwritten. Other bibliographic studies spend considerable time discussing concerns about unretrievable Internet sources. Grimes and Boening (2001) note that 30% of the URLs cited in their sample could not be found "due to either student misreporting of the URL or inactive links" (p. 19); and when Davis (2003) checked URLs for "accuracy and persistence" six months after collecting the papers in his 2001 study, he found that 35% did not take him to the original source (p. 55).

In general, these researchers attribute their difficulty locating cited sources to errors on the part of the students or imply that the difficulty reveals the inadequacy of the source itself, citing both as further evidence of the need to strengthen IL instruction. It is possible, though, that many of the URLs were correct when the students listed them. Lepore (2015) notes that "the average life of a webpage is 100 days," and Zittrain, Albert, and Lessig (2014) found that 70% of the 1,002 sampled URLs cited in the *Harvard Law Review*, the *Harvard Journal of Law and Technology*, and the *Harvard Human Rights Journal* failed to send readers to the information originally cited (what they term "reference rot"). The same was true of 49.9% of the 555 URLs in all published United States Supreme Court opinions. Instead of jumping too quickly to conclusions about the quality of Internet sources selected by the students or blaming student honesty or IL skills for irretrievable sources, these findings suggest that teachers and librarians should revise IL instruction to include discussion of the role of accurate citations, the problem of "reference rot," and the importance of listing DOIs if they exist.

The fact that, using the information provided, Citation Project researchers were able to locate most of the Internet sources in the sample papers using the Internet Archive (http://archive.org/), suggests that reference rot might have been part of the problem in other studies as well. Successful retrieval of sources by Citation Project researchers was higher when papers used MLA-style works cited lists that note access date, but approximate searches based on the date of the paper were also largely effective. The Internet Archive allowed Citation Project researchers to read Internet sources as they appeared the day the student consulted them.

Coding Categories

Data on source use has been reported elsewhere, along with a discussion of methods (Jamieson & Howard, 2013, Jamieson, 2013). This chapter focuses on the sources themselves, which were classified into one of 14 types (see Table 6.2). The category "book" is uniformly described across studies of student source use (Davis & Cohen, 2001; Jenkins, 2002; Davis, 2002, 2003; Carlson, 2006; Knight-Davis & Sun, 2008; McClure & Clink, 2009); Citation Project coding replicated this category and, like other studies, included books accessed in any format. The definition of journal article as peer-reviewed and written for an academic audience is also quite standard, although Citation Project coding replicated Jake Carlson's (2006) language, "written by an academic expert in the field, incorporating scholarly perspectives such as theory or research, and having an intended audience of other individuals knowledgeable in the field" (p. 16). The category "Specialized News Source and other periodicals" is defined by Citation Project coding the way Carlson defines "Magazine article" ("reporting an event, opinion, or other issue from a non-scholarly perspective . . . written in a way that would be accessible to a general audience," p. 16), and includes articles from publications such as *The Economist, Nature, Mother Jones, The New Yorker*, and *Harpers*, regardless of how they were accessed. In the case of encyclopedia, dictionaries, and government documents, again no distinction was made between those consulted electronically and those consulted in print, although almost all of the citations indicated that they were consulted online. The category "General News Source" includes traditional newspapers that appear in print and electronically, as well as news delivered by television and radio and related websites (where broadcast news and related information is repeated and updated), and via apps, social media, and email and text updates. Neither the reputation nor the politics of the news source were noted, although sources were also coded using a slight modification of the categories developed by McClure and Clink (2009) as "information (apparently without bias)," "opinion," "advocacy," "commercial," and "self-help."

While Davis (2003) does note that some websites in his studies would probably be deemed sufficiently informational to be included in student papers, he does not break out URLs in this way, nor do Carlson (2006) or Knight-Davis and Sung (2008). McClure and Clink (2009) do make that distinction, and Citation Project research followed their lead and used the categories they developed. Informational Internet sites are defined as sources that seem to be presenting information without bias or commercial backing, such as the American Cancer Society, and the CDC. Researchers also coded an additional category not included by McClure and Clink, "Internet, multiple-author," special interest websites or eZines that include articles by a number of contributors but do not have a print version and are not associated with any news or entertainment organizations (most notably fan sites for sports, collectables, or activities). This category includes commercially produced multi-user fandom sites associated with films, books, or television shows, although such sites were also coded as commercial following McClure and Clink.

Data was analyzed using SPSS (Statistical Package for Social Science 14.0).

LIMITATIONS OF THE STUDY

Although it includes students from 16 institutions, this study only provides a snapshot of first-year college students in the U.S. as they leave a specific course in a given year. As Carlson (2006) notes about his own study, the data are potentially skewed by the fact that the instructors from whose classes the papers were drawn and the students who submitted their papers were volunteers rather than being randomly selected (randomizing occurred after papers had been submitted). Instructors who felt they were doing a good job teaching research skills were probably more likely to volunteer than those who had doubts; experienced instructors were also probably more likely to volunteer. As for the students, those who were misusing sources or who had very low confidence in their research and citation skills probably selected out of the study. Papers were drawn from the standard FYW course, which is sometimes the second writing course for those deemed weaker writers and which in some institutions stronger writers place out of and English Language Learners or multilingual writers are tracked out of. These factors provided a fairly evenly prepared pool of writers for the study, but also limit what might be learned from outliers.

FINDINGS

TYPES OF SOURCES SELECTED AND RETRIEVED

Surveys of faculty expectations for the FYW research paper (see Howard & Jamieson, 2014) and conversations with librarians about sources they recommend indicate that, in general, books, journal articles, government documents, and specialized news sources (accessed either electronically or in print) are considered appropriate sources for FYW research papers. As Head and Eisenberg (2010) among others have found, many assignments still require that students use a specific number of types of sources, often one book and at least two journal articles. Once those requirements are satisfied, many faculty also consider newspaper articles appropriate, although of course this depends on the context and the nature of the topic selected. The majority of FYW research papers address general interest topics selected by the student, and 85% of the assignments studied by Head and Eisenberg (2010) either expected students to generate their own topic or provided acceptable topics from which they could choose (p. 8). This

Table 6.2. Categories of sources selected and used at least once

	Frequency	Percent	Cumulative Percent
Book (single author or anthology)	128	13.76	13.76
Journal *	219	23.55	37.31
Specialized news source or periodical *	105	11.29	48.60
Government document or publication *	63	6.77	55.37
General news source *	141	15.17	70.54
Visual images (still and moving)	7	0.75	71.29
Encyclopedia *	18	1.93	73.22
Dictionary *	10	1.07	74.29
Informal print or oral (email, text mess., etc.)	4	0.43	74.72
Public Internet	235	25.28	100.00
TOTAL	930	100.0	

accessed electronically or in print

also appears to describe the papers in the CPSW, whose topics are frequently abortion, gun control, Title IX, global warming, marijuana (legalization/health benefits), and Internet privacy. Some papers focus on literature or discipline-specific topics requiring specialized sources, but these are the minority.

As Table 6.2 shows, source types that fit the category "appropriate for FYW" as described above dominate the list of sources selected, retrieved, and cited at least once in the 800 pages coded. Of the 930 sources cited in coded extracts written by the 174 student participants, 55% fall into this category. Of those, books make up 14%; articles from scholarly journals, 24%; specialized news sources and periodicals, 11%; and government documents, 7%. If general news sources (15%) and visual images, mostly films (0.75%) are added to the list of generally acceptable source types, as they often are in FYW courses, the percentage of the 930 sources that would be considered appropriate types for FYW rises to 71%. Relatively few students cite encyclopedia and dictionaries (2% and 1%), or informal print or oral sources (0.5%), although this does not mean they do not use them; only cited sources were studied.

A CLOSER LOOK AT SOURCES

Where sources were available in print or electronically, they were coded by source type (e.g., journal article) rather than method of retrieval, but sources that listed a URL were also coded as "Internet" following previous research. Table 6.3

What the Citation Project Tells Us

Table 6.3. Categories of public internet sources selected and used at least once

	Frequency	Percent of all internet sources (n=235)	Percent of all 930 sources (Table 6.2)	Cumulative percent of all sources (n=930)
Informational website	128	54.47	13.76	13.76
Personal website incl. social media	5	2.13	0.54	14.30
Blog (personal or professional)	14	5.96	1.50	15.80
Multiple-author (eZine, wiki, etc.)	32	13.62	3.45	19.25
Other (not classified above)	56	23.82	6.03	25.28
TOTAL	235	100.00	25.28	

Table 6.4. Sponsorship categories of public internet sources selected and used at least once

	Frequency	Percent of all internet sources (n=235)	Percent of all 930 sources (Table 6.2)	Cumulative percent of all sources (n=930)
Informational (no obvious bias)	128	54.47	13.76	13.76
Advocacy	21	8.94	2.26	16.02
Personal	19	8.08	2.04	18.06
Company or commercial	7	2.98	0.75	18.81
Online journal (unsponsored)	32	13.62	3.45	22.26
Other (not classified above)	28	11.91	3.02	25.28
TOTAL	235	100.00	25.28	

reveals more about the 235 Internet sources cited at least once within the coded pages. More than half (54%) are informational websites, which is 14% of all of the sources cited at least once. Such informational sources (including the American Cancer Society and the CDC) are generally also acceptable in FYW courses, raising the percentage of the 930 sources that would be considered appropriate types of sources by most writing teachers today to 85%.

Of the 107 Internet sites not classified as "informational," Table 6.4 shows that 21 (9% of all 235 Internet sites) fit McClure and Clink's (2009) classification of "advocacy website," and 7 (3%) are websites with clearly commercial motivation. While many websites are sponsored or include advertising, this

Table 6.5. Categories of books selected and used at least once

	Frequency	Percent of all Books (n=128)	Percent of all 930 sources (see Table 6.2)	Cumulative percent of all sources (n=930)
Fiction	16	12.50	1.72	1.72
Drama	2	1.56	0.22	1.94
Poetry	2	1.56	0.22	2.16
Creative non fiction	1	.78	0.10	2.26
Literary criticism	12	9.38	1.29	3.55
Information (non-academic)	17	13.29	1.83	5.38
Information (Curated collections)	15	11.71	1.61	6.99
Information (scholarly books and edited collections)	63	49.22	6.77	13.76
TOTAL	128	100.00	13.76	

category focuses on websites whose purpose is directly or indirectly commercial (selling or promoting an item, brand, person, location, activity, etc.). These findings are significantly lower than McClure and Clink's, revealing again the influence of context on single-institution data.

A CLOSER LOOK AT BOOKS

When the category "book" is sub-divided, the question of acceptable source type is further complicated, as Table 6.5 shows. Of the 128 books selected, retrieved, and used at least once in the 800 coded pages, 49% are the traditional scholarly texts probably imagined as the result of the instruction to "include at least one book." Such texts make up 7% of the total 930 sources. A further 16% of the 128 books cited are works of literature, and 9% are literacy criticism focusing on them. Of the remaining books, 13% are non-academic (self-help or popular press books that do not cite sources or include notes regarding sources), and 12% are curated collections, such as the *Opposing Viewpoints* and *At Issue* series, and short single-topic textbooks that arrange extracts from longer texts into a "conversation" for the students.

Perhaps unsurprisingly, while some books are cited frequently in literature-based papers, of the 930 sources only 14% are cited more than three times, and 56% are cited only once (Table 6.6).

Table 6.6. Frequency of citation for each of the 930 sources

	Frequency	Percent	Cumulative Percent
Once	525	56.45	56.45
Twice	185	19.89	76.34
Three times	89	9.57	85.91
Four times	48	5.16	91.07
Five times	34	3.66	94.73
Six times	19	2.04	96.77
Seven times	10	1.08	97.85
Eight times	9	.97	98.82
Nine times	4	.43	99.25
Ten or more times	7	.75	100.00
TOTAL	930	100.00	

DISCUSSION

IDENTIFYING, LOCATING AND RETRIEVING SOURCES

Bibliographic coding provides information about the kinds and combinations of sources used in each of the 174 papers and also aggregate data about the 930 sources used within the coded pages (sources not used in the coded pages were not retrieved or coded). It also reveals the frequency of use of each source across the 1,911 citations in the sample, allowing comparison between what was selected for the works cited list and what was actually used by the student to build an argument within the paper itself. This allowed researchers to track what percentage of citations drew on scholarly and non-scholarly sources and also to explore the relationships among the sources cited.

On the face of it, the data in Tables 6.2 to 6.5 indicate that students seem to be able to retrieve *types* of sources that meet faculty requirements and that would probably be recommended by librarians, thereby demonstrating an ability to identify, locate, and access source types appropriate for their academic projects. In spite of the inclusion of obviously non-academic sources and commercial and advocacy websites, Tables 6.2 to 6.5 reveal that the majority of the sources being cited at least once are of a type that most instructors of FYW courses would consider "acceptable." Tables 6.2 and 6.3 reveal that 85% of the 930 sources (791) would appear to be of acceptable types (although this does not mean that the individual sources would be acceptable to support or build the argument in question). Even when adjusted to remove non-academic books (see Table 6.5), that number is still 80% (774 sources).

While sources classified as "magazines" (such as *Business Week, The Economist*, and *National Geographic*) may not be appropriate for research papers in courses like those in economics studied by Davis and Cohen (2001) and Davis (2002, 2003), following McClure and Clink's (2009) lead, the Citation Project classifies "specialized news sources or periodicals" as generally appropriate for FYW. These differences are, of course, institution-specific (and sometimes instructor-specific), and lacking assignments and handouts, researchers cannot speak to what was acceptable in each case. At the same time, although literature-based and discipline-specific courses skew the data a little, the overall pattern described here persists across sites.

Because they classify sources by type (book, journal) rather than content, the majority of scholars who study student researched-writing focusing on source use or sources cited classify sources that can be accessed freely from the public Internet as "websites" or "web" if a URL is listed with no further subdivision. This means that the category includes everything from self-help blogs to sites that would be considered appropriate for a paper in a FYW course, such as government- or university-sponsored website. Just as the category "book" tends to be considered appropriate without analysis of content, so "web" tends to be considered inappropriate, and "sources from the Internet" are *still* forbidden or limited by some faculty, particularly beyond the first year. While Davis (2003) does note that some Internet sources would probably be sufficiently informational to be included in first-year economics papers, his study does not break out URLs in this way, nor do those of Carlson (2006) or Knight-Davis and Sung (2008). McClure and Clink (2009), focus most of their attention on the 48% of sources they coded as "websites," offering a more granular classification and when Citation Project sources are coded using those classifications (Table 6.4) it is obvious that not all Internet sources should be considered unacceptable for source-based papers in FYW courses. The decision to exclude sources found "online" from studies, and still from some classes, seems increasingly limited given the ubiquity of the Internet, the quality of sources available through it, and the growing sophistication of the so-called "digital natives." Where earlier studies found cause for concern in the types of Internet sources selected, the research reported in this chapter echoes Carlson's (2006) observation that the quality of sources revealed in single-institution studies do not appear to be generalizable to a national level. The national snapshot provided by the Citation Project suggests less cause for concern about the Internet and also records a high percentage of sources classified as informational (websites from national organizations such as the American Cancer Institute, or from government sponsored sites like the Center for Disease Control).

Perhaps because they were distracted by the Internet, earlier researchers have not focused on the books students select, apparently imagining "books" by definition to be scholarly. In fact, data regarding this category (Table 6.5) suggests the need to revisit the traditional instruction to "include at least one book." Some of the courses in the sample were literature-focused, producing papers using literary criticism (including *SparkNotes* and *Cliff's Notes*, which are frequently used as criticism) to discuss literary texts. Another subset of courses aid the "research" process by selecting curated collections such as *Opposing Viewpoints* and *At Issue* series or single-topic textbooks. While these collections include scholarly sources, they do most of the IL work for students, arranging extracts from longer texts into a "conversation" rather than asking students to conduct research in order to discover possible conversations themselves. Such collections may help students understand the *Framework for IL* threshold concept Scholarship as Conversation, and many of the papers also draw on other sources that the students may have selected. The use of curated collections in FYW alongside additional student-selected sources is worth further consideration as part of IL pedagogy, especially if students learn to develop source networks from the works cited lists of texts in those collections (Laskin & Haller, Chapter 11, this collection). Books make up only 14% of the 930 sources, and of those, half are monographs and edited collections that are sufficiently scholarly, although a closer look at the books that would not be acceptable is instructive.

Overall, the Citation Project research indicates that in the area of traditional sources (books and journals) and in non-traditional sources (websites), first-year students are mostly able to identify, find, access, and cite sources in ways that would satisfy traditional bibliographic instruction. If the purpose of IL instruction is to help students navigate library databases and stacks along with the Internet, select sources of an appropriate type on a specific topic, and access and cite them correctly, then it seems to have succeeded. Studies of student bibliographies produced in intermediate- and upper-level courses report a high percentage of books and appropriate scholarly journals (Hovde, 2000; Jenkins, 2002; Kraus, 2002; Carlson, 2006; Mill, 2008), confirming that this skill appears to transfer beyond the first year. While Davis (2003) found that students were using more Internet sources, he reports that they did not do so at the expense of traditional sources but as part of an increase in the total number of sources cited (p. 47). Of course, the *IL Standards* go far beyond simple information retrieval, calling for a sophisticated understanding of sources and listing characteristics of an equally sophisticated "information literate student" within the performance indicators and outcomes. It is on this level that the Citation Project data suggests the *IL Standards* have been less than successful in transforming both practice and habits of mind. This observation reinforces critiques that the *IL Standards* present a set of "neatly packaged skills which result in a successful product" (Norgaard & Sinkinson, Chapter 1, this collection) rather than encouraging a process-oriented pedagogy. Such a recursive, rhetorically based IL pedagogy is, of course, harder to measure using the kinds of checklists so common in FYW and IL assessment, yet it is more in line with the process-oriented pedagogy called for by Writing and Composition theorists, and perhaps a similar focus on process in the *Framework for IL* will encourage radical pedagogical revision in both areas.

A Deeper Look at Source Use

A closer look at Tables 6.5 and 6.6 suggests that there is still much IL work to be done. The fact that the papers in this study demonstrate an ability to retrieve appropriate types of sources does not mean students can do that work alone. When instructed to include a certain number of books and peer-reviewed articles on their works cited list, most students will comply; however, if they are not part of a brief literature review it is unlikely that a single citation was what the professor intended. Overall, 56% of the 930 sources and 50% of the 128 books were cited only once, although the 21 works of literature were cited with greater frequency. This finding suggests, again, that students need to be exposed to a more sophisticated model of IL that teaches them to retrieve information as needed from types and numbers of sources appropriate to the topic at hand, not to satisfy a decontextualized checklist.

Other studies (Sherrard, 1986; Hull & Rose, 1990; Pecorari, 2003; Howard, Serviss & Rodrigue, 2010) reveal that students working with sources write from sentences within those sources rather than summarizing extended passages, and in this expanded study they were found to do so in 94% of the citations (Jamieson & Howard, 2013; Jamieson 2013). Together, these data suggest that the focus of concern should not be the sources *per se* but the ways students engage with them and use them to trace connections and create a conversation among them. As Maid and D'Angelo (Chapter 2, this collection) observe, IL is a "contextualized and situated concept," and by replacing the "prescriptive and de-contextualized set of skills" with a deeper attention to metaliteracy, the new *Framework for ILs* may begin to address this.

Information Literacy Dispositions and Habits of Mind

Because most of the students used the citation guidelines included in the 7th edition of the *MLA Handbook for Writers of Research Papers* (2009), which require the inclusion of the medium (print, Web, DVD) and the date a source was consulted, it is possible to track the order that sources were retrieved and the ways papers were constructed. Jenkins (2002), Davis (2003), and Carlson (2006) all caution that there is no "average bibliography," and that observation holds for the Citation Project papers as well; there are, though, patterns within the kinds of sources selected and the way those sources are used. A look at papers that use "acceptable source types" reveals an often torturous research process and paper-writing formula that is far from the "set of integrated abilities encompassing the reflective discovery of information, the understanding of how information is produced and valued, and the use of information in creating new knowledge and participating ethically in communities of learning" identified as a goal of the *Framework for IL*.

One such paper, Z24, while not being typical, is representative of the many struggles revealed in the coded papers, and reflects many of the concerns that indicate the need to move beyond a checklist model of IL. A review of the works cited list (Appendix A) suggests that few of us would find a problem with it unless we looked at the sources themselves. It includes two books, one scholarly journal article, two additional journal/periodical articles, one government website, two informational sources from the Internet, an article from *The New York Times*, and a website whose title at least would appear appropriate to the paper topic (obesity).

"Authority Is Constructed and Contextual"

A closer look reveals the problems that can result from an over-dependence on source type to assess authority. Neither of the two books cited in this paper is scholarly, the first obviously so from the title—*Skinny Bitch*. The second, *Compulsive Overeating* by Judith Peacock, is 64 pages long but may have appeared reliable to the student because s/he used *LexisNexis Academic* to access the (8-page) chapter "Who is at Risk?" cited in the paper. The publisher, Life Matters, explain "each book defines the problem, describes its effects, discusses dilemmas teens may face, and provides steps teens can take to move ahead," giving it a Citation Project classification of "book-self help." It could have been a useful source for a paper analyzing the kinds of advice given to teens suffering from eating disorders; however, that was not the focus of the paper, and it appears that the student did not assess the contextual nature of the data in this source.

One other source was also retrieved from *LexisNexis Academic*. Listed as being from *Biotech Business Week*, the title is "Salad Bars in Every School: United Fresh Applauds New Child Nutrition Bill," and no author is included by the student, although it is actually listed as the United Fresh Produce Association. *Biotech Business Week* notes on its "about" page that it publishes "News and information from pharmaceutical and biotechnology companies, with a focus on business trends and analysis." The article reports on United Fresh's president's visit to Capital Hill to thank legislators for including fresh produce in the New Child Nutrition Bill, crediting Congressman Farr and United Fresh lobbying for this legislation. The student introduces unattributed data about the importance of fresh produce from the article with "research shows. . . ." This source should have raised flags about authority when the student found it (Citation Project researchers classified it as "company or commercial"). A student with a deeper understanding of IL might have considered the role of context and purpose and rejected it.

While Z24 is an outlier in some ways, it reflects the impact of findings by other researchers that students tend to trust the authority of all sources they find "through the library" (Tolar-Burton & Chadwick, 2000). Head and Eisenberg (2009) found that 84% of students reported that scholarly research databases were the library resource they used most frequently (p. 22) and 78% reported that such databases "contain more credible content than the internet" (p. 27). Four of the sources in Z24 were retrieved via Academic Search Complete, which notes that it "provides complete coverage of multidisciplinary academic journals . . . [and] supports high-level research in the key areas of academic study by providing *peer-reviewed* journals, full-text periodicals, reports, books, and more" (ebscohost). Two others came from *The LexisNexis-Academic* "about" page notes that it allows researchers to "quickly and easily search full-text documents from over 15,000 *credible* sources of information and pinpoint relevant information for a wide range of academic research projects . . . [from] comprehensive, authoritative news content, including current coverage and deep archives" (LexisNexis). A final source was retrieved from a third "database," *about.com* ("the largest source for *Expert* content on the Internet that helps users answer questions, solve problems, learn something new or find inspiration" according to the "about" page). In fact, *about.com* led the student to a government document published by the Center for Nutrition Policy and Promotion, which is part of the USDA, but the student does not even mention that this is government research. Do students know the difference between "peer-reviewed," "credible," and "expert"? This student appears not to have, nor to have been able to make any judgment call about these different databases when looking at the sources themselves or seen the difference between a government document and a company-sponsored promotion.

The student does introduce *Skinny Bitch* as "*New York Times* Best Selling book," but aside from that does not appear to consider the authority of the sources selected, and only cites one 23-page chapter entitled "Have no Faith: Government Agencies Don't Give a Shit About Your Health." (While this might have been used in dialogue with the government data, it was not.) Source assessment has always been part of IL instruction and is central to the *IL Standards*, but as Head and Eisenberg's (2010) data show, if it is not accompanied by a larger metacognitive discussion of the role of research and what we hope students will learn through the process of researching a topic, they are unlikely to incorporate such assessment into their normal research habits or the way they think about information in general.

INFORMATION CREATION AS A PROCESS AND INFORMATION HAS VALUE

Each of the sources in Z24 is used to introduce a reason why people might be obese (eating disorders, high cost of healthy food, low cost of burgers, lack of government concern), but the very different kinds of sources and the lack of acknowledgement of their context or purpose undermines the argument. While some of the sources selected are appropriate in terms of content and type, the remaining sources are isolated voices on the general topic of the student's paper, and the information in them is created and presented for a very different audience and purpose. One such source is a self-help blog, "Eat without Guilt," which promises to help readers "make peace with food, your body, and your weight." A second comes from *The New York Times* Well blog and is entitled "A High Price for Healthy Food," and a third is the book chapter "Compulsive Overeating," which is cited twice in the paper, with both quotations taken from the same page. Blogs and self-help sources would be appropriate for some kinds of paper (an analysis of the rhetoric of "help," or the kinds of resources available for people with eating disorders), but to mix self-help with academic research in a paper whose stated aim is to explore the causes of obesity is a questionable decision, and to do so without acknowledgment of the different context or recognition of the different scholarly weight assigned to each, reveals a student who still needs to develop IL skills. If students are able to "assess the fit between an information product's creation process and a particular information need" they are also on the way to developing "an understanding that their choices impact the purposes for which the information product will be used and the message it conveys" (*Framework for IL*). Such an awareness may have guided this student to different source choices.

SEARCHING AS STRATEGIC EXPLORATION AND SCHOLARSHIP AS CONVERSATION

Perhaps more interesting than the student's inability to evaluate the sources s/he cites is the story about the process of construction of the paper that the works cited list suggests. The student accessed four sources on 5 April, 2010, all four of them via *Academic Search Complete*. Two come from academic journals (*Pediatrics* and *New Scientist*), and the other two are from the *Proceedings of the National Academy of Sciences of the United States of America* and the *Tufts University and Nutrition Letter*. The *New Scientist* article, introduced by the student as "a recent study by *New Scientist*" is a book review of *Supersize Me*. If one looks at these four sources, a story appears to be emerging, moving from comments in *Supersize Me* about corn to "Corn Content of French Fry Oil from National Chain vs. Small Business Restaurants" (*Proceedings*), and from there to "Who's Losing the Burger Battle?" (*Tufts*) and "Nutrition Labeling May Lead to Lower-Calorie Restaurant Meal Choices for Children" (*Pediatrics*). All of these sources were published in 2010 making it impossible for them to cite or reference each other; however, all seem appropriate to begin an exploration of the topic of obesity, and all are in some ways part of a larger dialogue on the given topic. It would appear that on April 5, the student spent some quality time with a reliable database beginning the process of strategically exploring an evolving topic and entering an ongoing conversation on that topic. Perhaps the class visited the library to start their research or a librarian came to the classroom; certainly someone introduced the student to this database and perhaps helped focus the research question. So far, so good.

But the next reported access of source material is not for another three weeks. On April 25 the *Biotech* article on salad bars was added to the list, appearing to continue the conversation begun on April 5; however, by April 27 when the four remaining sources were accessed the paper seems to be on the way to its final disconnected list of possible causes of obesity, one per paragraph, each supported by a different source. Two of the sources accessed on April 5 (and still listed as "works cited") do not appear in the final paper (the *Proceedings* article and the *Pediatrics* article). Instead, on April 27 the student lists accessing the blogs "Eat without Guilt" and the *The New York Times* Well blog, the book chapter "Compulsive Overeating," and the report on fruit and vegetables from the USDA. The book *Skinny Bitch* is listed as having been read in print so has no access date. It is cited four times in the paper in two different paragraphs drawing from 4 pages in one 23-page chapter. None of the authors of these sources is directly cited by others, none of the student sources is drawn from the works cited lists of other sources, and no citations from one source appear in any of the other sources.

Because the sources selected in late April do not explicitly respond to other sources about obesity or healthy living, it is easier for them to be used to provide "evidence" for one item on the list of causes of obesity that ultimately organize the paper. Perhaps the need for a list-like outline came externally, but had the student been reading the sources as part of a conversation on the topic of healthy eating and explicitly creating source networks (Laskin & Haller, Chapter 11, this collection), paper Z24 might have evolved very differently. The student concludes by stating agreement with the author of *Skinny Bitch* that ultimately Americans are responsible for the "obesity epidemic" by remaining naive and ill-informed, but this claim contradicts many of the "causes" that organize the paper. The student neither counters that lack of information by adding to the conversation about obesity, nor makes the argument expressed in the conclusion.

It is this concept of research, and academic sources, as part of an ongoing conversation that seems most missing from the papers in the Citation Project study. The organization of Z24 with one source per paragraph (and one paragraph per source) makes it typical. When each source is a discrete item, and even a "type" to be checked off, the possibility of those sources entering into conversation is slim. If assignments do not specify why we do research or how research questions and conversations evolve as Head (2010) found to be the case, and if IL instruction emphasizes identifying, finding, and assessing discrete sources rather than developing metacritical frameworks for thinking about research (Kleinfeld, 2011), it should be no surprise that the resulting papers tend to be "information dumps" rather than forays into academic conversation and the intellectual work the research paper is imagined to be (Robinson & Schlegl, 2004). Diametrically opposite to the image of scholarship as a conversation is the model of research as formulaic, demanding particular types of sources and "killer quotes," which can mostly be extracted from the first page of the source. This latter version of "The Research Paper" characterizes the papers in the CPSW corpus.

CONCLUSION

The data generated by the Citation Project's multi-institution research suggests that students who received IL instruction in the era of the *IL Standards* have adopted a limited checklist mode of research rather than the nuanced appreciation of sources and source selection included in that document. This suggests that the *IL Standards* themselves did not totally displace the kind of bibliographic instruction that preceded them in 2000. The papers in the CPSW corpus demonstrate that students have the ability to select, retrieve, and cite the right kinds of sources, many of them appropriately academic for first-year papers; however, the papers evidence little or no relationship among those sources. Analysis of the incorporation of information from the sources into the papers reveals students working at the sentence-level, and segregating each source into one paragraph, mostly by including quotation or paraphrase rather than by summarizing larger ideas in a text or comparing arguments with those of other sources. Furthermore, most of the references to sources are to the first one or two pages and most of the sources are cited only once or twice, suggesting little engagement with them as part of a broader scholarly conversation.

It may be, as I have argued elsewhere (Howard & Jamieson, 2014), that the first-year research paper itself bears more responsibility for this state of affairs than the IL instruction that tries to support it. It is certainly the case that shorter source-based papers could be used to introduce students to IL practices and habits of mind; however, it is also the case that the introduction of threshold concepts in writing pedagogy (Adler-Kassner, Majewsi & Koshnick, 2012) and in the *Framework for IL* increases the likelihood that students may gain a "vision of information literacy as an overarching set of abilities in which students are consumers and creators of information who can participate successfully in collaborative spaces" ("Introduction"). Had the students writing the papers studied by the Citation Project evidenced the kinds of critical self-reflection described in the *Framework for IL* and embedded in the description of what constitutes IL, it is difficult to believe they could have produced the papers in the sample. We might hope that with the revised instruction associated with threshold concepts, future papers will show evidence of the "dynamism, flexibility, individual growth, and community learning" described in the *Framework for IL* document ("Introduction").

This optimism is unlikely to bear fruit unless we ask some difficult questions of IL instruction and the FYW courses where it so frequently becomes ghettoized. What is the role of real IL (not bibliographic instruction) in FYW? How can we ensure that the skills and habits of mind are transferrable to other courses (and to work, life, etc.)? When included amongst many other elements of a writing course, how can threshold concepts be introduced without overwhelming the students—or the course? And if institutions recognize that IL cannot be "delivered" in one library visit, assignment, or even semester, how can it be advanced programmatically or throughout a student's education (and beyond to lifelong learning)? Finally, how can the *Framework for IL* be introduced to all faculty—including library faculty, administrators, and students in a way that will help us all to recognize our shared responsibility for IL and our shared stake in successful IL pedagogy? Unless these questions are addressed, I fear that the 2019 FYW research papers will not look significantly different from those produced in 1999 or 2010.

REFERENCES

About.com. http://www.about.com/.
Academic Search Complete. https://www.ebscohost.com/academic/academic-search-complete.

Adler-Kassner, L., Majewsi, J. & Koshnick, D. (2012). The value of troublesome knowledge: Transfer and threshold concepts in writing and history. *Composition Forum 26*.

Association of College and Research Libraries. (2015). *Framework for Information Literacy for Higher Education*. Retrieved from http://www.ala.org/acrl/standards/ilframework.

Association of College and Research Libraries. (2000). *Information Literacy Competency Standards for Higher Education*. Retrieved from http://www.ala.org/acrl/standards/informationliteracycompetency.

Alvarez, B. & Dimmock, N. (2007). Faculty expectations of student research. In N. Foster & S. Gibbons (Eds.). *Studying Students: The Undergraduate Research Project at the University of Rochester* (pp. 1–7). Chicago: Association of College and Research Libraries.

Blackwell-Starnes, K. (2016). Preliminary paths to information literacy: Introducing research in core courses. In B. J. D'Angelo, S. Jamieson, B. Maid & J. R. Walker (Eds.), *Information literacy: Research and collaboration across disciplines*. Fort Collins, CO: WAC Clearinghouse and University Press of Colorado.

Carlson, J. (2006). An examination of undergraduate student citation behavior. *Journal of Academic Librarianship, 32*(1), 14–22.

Davis, P. (2002). The effect of the web on undergraduate citation behavior: A 2000 update. *College & Research Libraries, 63*(1), 53–60.

Davis, P. (2003). Effects of the web on undergraduate citation behavior: Guiding student scholarship in a networked age. *portal: Libraries and the Academy, 3*(1), 41–51.

Davis, P. & Cohen, S. (2001). The effect of the web on undergraduate citation behavior 1996–1999. *Journal of the American Society for Information Science and Technology, 52*(4), 309–14.

Deitering, A. & Jameson, S. (2008). Step-by-step through the scholarly conversation: A collaborative library/writing faculty project to embed information literacy and promote critical thinking in first-year composition at Oregon State University. *College and Undergraduate Libraries, 15*(1–2), 47–59.

Gavin, C. (1995). Guiding students along the information highway: Librarians collaborating with composition instructors. *Journal of Teaching Writing, 13*(1/2), 225–236.

Grimes, D. & Boening, C. (2001). Worries with the web: A look at student use of web resources. *College & Research Libraries, 62*(1), 11–23.

Head, A. (2013). *Learning the ropes: How freshmen conduct course research once they enter college*. Project Information Literacy Research Report (pp. 1–48).

Head, A. & Eisenberg, M. (2010). *Assigning inquiry: How handouts for research assignments guide today's college students*. Project Information Literacy Progress Report: University of Washington Information School (pp. 1–41).

Head, A. & Eisenberg, M. (2009). *Lessons learned: How college students seek information in the digital age*. Project Information Literacy Progress Report: University of Washington Information School (pp. 1–42).

Holliday, W. & Fagerheim, B. (2006). Integrating information literacy with a sequenced English composition curriculum. *portal: Libraries and the Academy, 6*(2), 169–184.

Hood, C. (2010). Ways of research: The status of the traditional research paper assignment in assignment in first-year writing/composition courses. *Composition Forum, 22.*

Hovde, K. (2000). Check the citation: Library instruction and student paper bibliographies. *Research Strategies, 17*(1), 3–9. Doi: http://dx.doi.org/10.1016/S0734-3310(00)00019-7.

Howard, R. & Jamieson S. (2014). Research writing. In G. Tate, A. Rupiper-Taggart, B. Hessler & Schick, K. (Eds.), *A guide to composition pedagogies* (2nd ed.) (p. 231–247). New York: Oxford.

Howard, R., Serviss, T. & Rodrigue, T. (2010). Writing from sources, writing from sentences. *Writing & Pedagogy, 2*(2), 177–192.

Hull, G. & Rose, M. (1990). "This wooden shack place": The logic of unconventional reading. *College Composition and Communication, 41*(3), 286–298.

Internet Archive. http://archive.org/.

Jacobs, H. & Jacobs, D. (2009). Transforming the library one-shot into pedagogical collaboration: Information literacy and the English composition class. *Reference & Users Quarterly, 49*(1), 72–82.

Jacobson, T. & Mackey, T. (Eds.). (2007). *Information literacy collaborations that work.* New York: Neal-Schuman.

Jamieson, S. (2013). Reading and engaging sources: What students' use of sources reveals about advanced reading skills. *Across the Disciplines, 10.* Retrieved from http://wac.colostate.edu/atd/reading/jamieson.cfm.

Jamieson, S. & Howard, R. (2013). Sentence-mining: Uncovering the amount of reading and reading comprehension in college writers' researched writing. In R. McClure & J. Purdy (Eds.), *The new digital scholar: Exploring and enriching the research and writing practices of nextgen students* (pp. 111–133). Medford, NJ: American Society for Information Science and Technology.

Jenkins, P. (2002). They're not just using web sites: A citation study of 116 student papers. *College and Research Libraries News, 63*(3), 164.

Kesselman, M. & Watstein, S. (2009). Creating opportunities: Embedded librarians. *Journal of Library Administration, 49*(4), 383–400.

Kleinfeld, E. (2011). Writing Centers, ethics, and excessive research. *Computers and Composition Online.* Retrieved from http://www.bgsu.edu/departments/english/cconline/ethics_special_issue/Kleinfeld/.

Knight-Davis, S. & Sung, J. (2008). Analysis of citations in undergraduate papers 1. *College & Research Libraries, 69*(5), 447–458; Doi:10.5860/crl.69.5.447.

Kraus, J. (2002). Citation patterns of advanced undergraduate students in biology, 2000–2002. *Science & Technology Libraries, 22*(3–4), 161–179. http://dx.doi: 10.1300/J122v22n03_13.

Laskin, M. & Haller, C. (2016). Up the mountain without a trail: Helping students use source networks to find their way. In B. J. D'Angelo, S. Jamieson, B. Maid & J. R. Walker (Eds.), *Information literacy: Research and collaboration across disciplines.* Fort Collins, CO: WAC Clearinghouse and University Press of Colorado.

Lepore, J. (2015, January 15). Can the Internet be archived? *The New Yorker.* Lexis-Nexis. Retrieved from http://www.lexisnexis.com/en-us/about-us/about-us.page.

Mackey, T. & Jacobson, T. (2011). Reframing information literacy as a metaliteracy. *College and Research Libraries, 72*(1), 62–78.

Mackey, T. & Jacobson, T. (2014). *Metaliteracy: Reinventing information literacy to empower learners.* Chicago: Neal-Schuman.

Maid, B. & D'Angelo, B. (2016). Threshold concepts: Integrating and applying information literacy and writing instruction. In B. J. D'Angelo, S. Jamieson, B. Maid & J. R. Walker (Eds.), *Information literacy: Research and collaboration across discipline.* Fort Collins, CO: WAC Clearinghouse and University Press of Colorado.

McClure, R. & Clink, K. (2009). How do you know that? An investigation of student research practices in the digital age. *Portal: Libraries and the Academy, 9*(1), 115–132.

Mill, D. (2008). Undergraduate information resource choices. *College & Research Libraries, 69*(4), 342–355. Doi: 10.5860/crl.69.4.342.

Modern Language Association. (2009). *MLA handbook for writers of research papers* (7th ed.). New York: MLA.

Norgaard, R. & Sinkinson, C. (2016). Writing information literacy: A retrospective and a look ahead. In B. J. D'Angelo, S. Jamieson, B. Maid & J. R. Walker (Eds.), *Information literacy: Research and collaboration across disciplines.* Fort Collins, CO: WAC Clearinghouse and University Press of Colorado.

Pecorari, D. (2003). Good and original: Plagiarism and patchwriting in academic second language writing. *Journal of Second Language Writing, 12,* 317–345.

Robinson, A. & Schlegl, K. (2004). Student bibliographies improve when professors provide enforceable guidelines for citations. portal: *Libraries and the Academy, 4*(2), 275–290.

Sherrard, C. (1986). Summary writing: A topographical study. *Written Communication, 3,* 324–343.

Tolar-Burton, V. & Chadwick, S. (2000). Investigating the practices of student researchers: Patterns of use and criteria for use of Internet and library sources. *Computers and Composition, 17*(3), 309–328. Doi: 10.1016/S8755-4615(00)00037-2.

Zittrain, J., Albert, K. & Lessig, L. (2014) Perma: Scoping and addressing the problem of link and reference rot in legal citations. *Legal Information Management, 14*(02), 88–99. Doi: 10.1017/S1472669614000255.

APPENDIX: WORKS CITED LIST FOR PAPER Z24 (AS SUBMITTED)

Citation Project

Z24

Works Cited

Biotech Business Week. "Salad Bars in Every School: United Fresh Applauds New Child Nutrition Bill." *News Rx* 4 Jan. 2010. LexisNexis Academic. Web. 25 Apr. 2010.

Center for Nutrition Policy and Promotion. "Eating Fruits and Vegetables." About. com Pediatrics. Medical Review Board. 26 Jan. 2008. Web. 27 Apr. 2010.

Dineen. Eat Without Guilt. N.p. 29 Mar. 2010. Web. 27 Apr. 2010.

Freedman, Rory, and Kim Barnouin. Skinny Bitch. Pennsylvania: Running Press Book Publishers, 2005. Print.

Jahren, A. Hope & Brian A. Schubert. "Corn Content of French Fry Oil from National Chain vs. Small Business Restaurants." Proceedings of the National Academy of Sciences of he United States of America 107.5 (2010): 2099-210. Academic Search Complete. Web. 5 Apr. 2010.

Motluk, Allison. "Supersize Me." New Scientist 184.2471 (2004): 46. *Academic Search Complete*. Web. 5 Apr. 2010.

Parker-Pope, Tara. "A High Price for Healthy Food." Well Blog. The New York Times. 5 Dec. 2010. Web. 27 Apr. 2007.

Peacock, Judith. "Chapter #2: Who is at Risk?" Compulsive Overeating 2000: 12+. LexisNexis Academic. Web. 27 Apr. 2007.

Tandon, Pooja, et al. "Nutrition Labeling May Lead to Lower-Calorie Restaurant Meal Choices for Children." Pediatrics 125.2 (2010): 244–248. Academic Search Complete. Web. 5 Apr. 2010.

"Who's Losing the Burger Battle?" Tufts University & Nutrition Letter 27.12 (2010): 6. Academic Search Complete. Web. 5 Apr. 2010.

CHAPTER 7
PRELIMINARY PATHS TO INFORMATION LITERACY: INTRODUCING RESEARCH IN CORE COURSES

Katt Blackwell-Starnes
Lamar University

Writing faculty multitask teaching information literacy (IL) skills with academic writing skills through scaffolded assignments that include a formal research project as an assessment tool. However, results from the Learning Information Literacy across the Curriculum (LILAC) Project pilot study illustrate that students turn to the formal research project requirements rather than IL skills as they conduct research.1 This formal research assignment holds the students' focus in such a way they work toward the assignment requirements with rote, quick, research, an approach that hinders their IL skills. Devoting class time to assignments that guide preliminary research and reiterate, through grades, the importance of early research to writing an academic research paper can improve students IL skills.

    Studies in information-seeking behaviors emphasize students' reliance on Internet search engines to conduct academic research and indicate a cognitive rationale for these beginnings. J. Patrick Biddix, Chung Joo Chung, and Han Woo Park's (2011) 282 respondents report beginning research with a search engine to construct a source outline and locate initial sources. Twelve of Huri-Li Lee's (2008) 15 interviewees cite search engines as a convenient starting point. Patrick Corbett's (2010) respondents assert the Internet is both more dependable and effective in terms of time and feedback than library research. Conversely, Alison J. Head and Michael Eisenberg's (2009) respondents cite familiarity and habit as their rationale; however, these respondents also indicate they turn to course textbooks before Internet searches. Research also suggests students lack engagement with academic research. Randall McClure and Kellian Clink's (2009) analysis of student source use found 48% of citations in 100 composition papers were web sources. Sandra Jamieson and Rebecca Moore Howard's (2012) Citation Project study finds 77% of citations in 174 papers came from the first three pages of sources, regardless of source length (p. 4). Head and Eisenberg's (2010) research handout study finds that students rely—from the beginning of a research assignment—on the handout to guide them through how much time to spend on research and requirements for a passing grade. Taken together, this research emphasizes students' reliance on quick Internet research, and quick results from the first few pages of their sources.

Quick research and lack of source engagement prevents students from acquiring and applying IL skills to academic research. The Association of College and Research Libraries' (2015) *Framework for Information Literacy for Higher Education* reframes IL as six threshold concepts—Scholarship Is a Conversation, Research as Inquiry, Authority Is Contextual and Constructed, Format as a Process, Searching as Exploring, and Information Has Value. These threshold concepts reconceptualize IL for higher education to better prepare students to apply IL in a broader range of situations. IL does not benefit only academic research, but professional and personal research as well; therefore, furthering college students' IL skills provides crucial learning and critical thinking necessary beyond the college degree.

SACRIFICING INFORMATION LITERACY FOR FINAL PRODUCT: FINDINGS FROM THE LILAC PROJECT

The LILAC Project is a multi-institutional study of students' information-seeking behaviors. Undergraduate and graduate student participants complete a two-part research session, responding to survey questions regarding their information-seeking training and behaviors and completing a 15-minute research aloud protocol (RAP) session that records screen capture and voice narration. The 2012 pilot study included eight first-year students whose results demonstrate a need for more focused preliminary research instruction in core classes where major research projects comprise a significant final grade percentage.

First-year participants' responses to the questionnaires show that these students perceive their IL skills as above average or exceptional; indeed, 50% rated their ability to locate information online an 8 on a 1–10 Likert scale. The remaining first-year participants rated themselves even higher with one participant ranking herself at 9 and the remaining three ranking themselves at 10. They were all also confident about their ability to evaluate online information, though they did not give themselves such high marks. Only one participant assessed himself at a 10, two participants ranked themselves at a 9, and the remaining six participants divided evenly between 7 and 8 on a 1–10 scale.

Understanding student perceptions of their own abilities is pivotal to furthering IL skills in higher education. Students who perceive their abilities to be above average may also perceive library workshops as rudimentary instruction and opt to either not attend or attend but not pay attention. Hence, it is essential to understand the differences in IL skills students *perceive* they possess and the IL skills they *demonstrate* when conducting academic research if we are to develop instruction to meet student IL needs. The second part of the LILAC Project study, the Research Aloud Protocol (RAP) begins to examine this gap.

The LILAC Project's RAP component asks students to conduct a 15-minute research session using their own research methods. Instructions offer students the chance to work with a topic for their class or use one of the six suggested topics. In sessions where students use their own topic, they identify the course and their topic; in sessions where students select from the suggested topics, we asked that students identify a class for which they might research the topic. Four first-year participants selected topics to research from the LILAC prompts: Maria[2] elected to research diversity issues; Frank, Paul, and Robert selected historical events; and Jennifer chose healthcare and health issues. The remaining three first-year participants opted to work with topics for their core courses: Robert chose his First-Year Experience class paper, a cultural analysis of Ethiopia; Laura and Heather both selected their composition class research paper topics, obesity and global warming, respectively. The RAP sessions show that students focus on the final product requirements and that this may hinder their ability to develop crucial IL skills, specifically the ability to define and articulate needed information and the ability to locate the needed information efficiently.

Focus on the final product occurs throughout LILAC's first-year participants' RAP sessions and offers candid insight into the role an assignment plays in students' research. Frank summarizes his research session in terms of writing a paper on John Marshall, not in terms of information learned or additional research questions; he evaluates his 15-minutes session as complete, stating "depending on how long the paper was, I'd probably get it done based off the patchwork from these websites." Robert avoids visiting *Wikipedia* because he was "dinged in the past" for citing this source. Laura selects specific information during her search to "use as a quote" in her obesity paper. Melinda concludes her RAP session by turning to Google Books and then to the university library databases, articulating her reason for this shift as a quest for the types of sources "teachers want." Focus on the final product in RAP sessions suggests students do not engage with early research, and this lack of engagement may continue throughout the research process if the Citation Project's (2011) initial results and McClure and Clink's (2009) findings are any indication. This focus may also determine students' search terms, leaving them to locate quick information rather than creating effective searches for credible, relevant information.

Focus on the final product removes a critical focus on early research as a narrowing technique. Participants' research does not include reading and engaging with sources; instead, they skim bullets or bolded headings to determine a source's usefulness, copy information from websites based on assignment needs, discard lengthy sources, and avoid visiting websites forbidden in the final product. Laura copies and pastes statistics about an increase in obesity among southern states into a Word document, but she does not read this information and misses an opportunity to consider more focused research. Robert avoids *Wikipedia*, preventing him from gaining a background understanding of Ethiopia, a background essential to writing a cultural analysis. Maria discards a book source simply because it is a book, since books represent more time investment because of length, especially when the book is not a familiar textbook where students can quickly locate information from previous readings. Melinda narrows her topic to global warming and rivers, but she turns to Google Books and the library databases as a rote shift, not an articulated need. Assessing sources in terms of the final product does not further students' understanding of *why* specific sources are appropriate for academic assignments, nor does this focus help students recognize the types of research needed and best methods for accessing the needed information.

Focus on the final product by LILAC first-year participants also leads to rote, superficial searches for information rather than narrowed and advanced searches to work toward a more narrowed research focus. Google searches for information begin with participants searching for their topic at large and using whatever words may appear in that topic. Laura's search for "obesity" returns 345 million results, and Michael's search for "World War 2" returns 136 million. Participants who begin with more words in their initial searches fare no better; Frank's search for "the importance of John Marshall's Supreme Court appointment" yields 3 million, and Robert's search for "cultural analysis of Ethiopia" yields 1 million. These first-year participants do not acknowledge the numbers as they begin working with the results and continue with similar search terms throughout their RAP sessions. Search terms change slightly with new searches, but not in a way that assists in topic narrowing. For example, Frank's search terms change to "the effect of John Marshall's Supreme Court" when his first search does not provide needed information. Robert's search terms change to "Geert Hoftstede analysis of Ethiopia" for the same reason. Laura shifts her focus to "obesity statistics" after determining these are necessary for the final paper. Similar search term changes occur with all first-year participants, and each time searches return millions of results and the students view only those on the first pages of Google—a clear indication these students do not even understand, let alone perceive the need for, more sophisticated search methods.

STARTING ON THE RIGHT PATH: PRELIMINARY RESEARCH ASSIGNMENTS

Students do not enter college with the scholar's curiosity nor with the scholar's sophisticated research skills; thus, determining the amount of information needed may very logically seem to require no more than checking the assignment handout. Head and Eisenberg (2010) find students define a situational context directly from the research assignment. This situational context includes how much time to devote to research, how to meet assignment expectations, how to get a good grade, and how to submit the final paper (p. 5). Immediately, the differences in how students and scholars determine the extent of information needed for a research project creates a significant gap between student products and educator expectations. Such distinct differences need addressing. Scholars do not begin research projects with a formal, final paper in mind, but with a topic or question and an expectation of devoting copious amount of time to researching. Student research needs a similar focus. Educators need to separate the preliminary research and topic narrowing from the final assignment, encouraging a research process that narrows an interesting topic, determines the information needed, and effectively locates needed information. Sandra Jamieson's chapter in this collection emphasizes the lack of student engagement with sources, and this lack of engagement is one area the preliminary research sequence presented in this chapter seeks to address. Beginning instruction with a focus on research, rather than emphasizing the final research project, provides better opportunities to talk about the process of research, foster better IL skills, and encourage better engagement with and comprehension of sources.

Students need opportunities to internalize preliminary research strategies, dialogue with other students, and distinguish differences in preliminary research and research to locate more specific support for an established claim. Separating the preliminary research from the formal research assignment and introducing low-risk, *graded* preliminary research assignments aids students' IL skills while also opening classroom discussions about the research process—laden with struggles, hurdles, complications, intrigues, and successes.

The preliminary research assignment I incorporate involves three short, graded assignments: preliminary research, focusing research, and source browsing. Together, these assignments comprise 10% of the students' final grades in research-focused composition courses. Through this recursive sequence, students locate preliminary sources, reflect on research, and develop new search strategies. The stepping stones taught in these assignments are common expectations in composition classes, but students traditionally do not demonstrate proficiency until they submit their research proposals and/or annotated bibliographies. In contrast, the preliminary research assignment sequence improves IL skills by removing the focus of research from the formal assignment and placing this focus on the research. I theme my course around the broad topic of surveillance and mass media because theming the course creates more cohesive class discussions and collaboration. Prior to the assignment introduction, we read and discuss Gary T. Marx's (2002) "What's New about the 'New Surveillance'?," Anders Albrechtslund's (2008) "Online Social Networking as Participatory Surveillance," and excerpts from Michel Foucault's (1975) *Discipline and Punish*; these works form the foundation for the preliminary research sequence and the beginning of class discussions, emphasizing ways to read complex sources, determine a variety of source types, and articulate relevance to the conversation. From the syllabus and class discussions, students know that their preliminary research begins something larger, yet the absence of final project requirements maintains a focus on the current assignment and the needed research skills rather than the specific requirements of a formal product.

RESEARCH ASSIGNMENT 1: PRELIMINARY RESEARCH

Students begin their research project with the Preliminary Research assignment (see Appendix A) designed to get students reading basic information on a broad topic and thinking about this information. There are no limitations beyond conducting research on surveillance; the research emphasizes reading and thinking, not locating certain types of sources. Students create a map of their search process, keep a list of the search terms and websites, and make research notes. Through note taking, they begin to internalize active research: moving from the passive skimming of webpage headlines to reading the webpage, following links relevant to their research topic, and collecting notes from relevant sources. Active research skills are then reinforced when they turn their notes into an informal two-page analysis. The analysis paper creates an entry point for discussing new knowledge about surveillance, problems they encountered, and questions they have about the topic. At the end of class, I reassign students the same work for researching mass media. In the next class period, students discuss the information learned and intersections between surveillance and mass media students find interesting. The focus on surveillance and mass media leads students to an array of topics, and they declare they want more research on "Twitter surveillance" or "reality television." These broad topics open discussions about what happens when these topics enter Google. As a transition to the next assignment, I google several student suggested topics and ask how they plan to read all the results before the next class. Discussion turns to what students read—Google's first page—and we problematize this approach. Students agree the approach is not the best and admit they know no other way. This dialogue begins the introduction to the next assignment as students express their need for better search methods.

RESEARCH ASSIGNMENT 2: FOCUSING RESEARCH

The second component of the preliminary research sequence, Focusing Research (see Appendix B), introduces students to more sophisticated search methods with Google—skills that create more efficient searches. This assignment structure follows the pattern set in the Preliminary Research assignment; students receive no parameters on what they can view or the number and types of sources. Again, students construct search maps, record their keywords, jot down questions, and write another two-page analysis of their work for subsequent class discussions. Students become members of topic-related small groups where they discuss their interests in the topic and begin to form a more narrowed focus that combines course theme and student interest. "Reality television" narrows to a focus on children on reality shows; "Google surveillance" narrows to a focus on the newest Google gadget. Students leave class to complete the Focusing Research assignment a second time, using their new topic focus.

Submitting their second advanced search map and analysis leads students to a new class discussion focused on developing a single, focused research question. I show Paul's LILAC session video, selected because Paul asks several closed questions of Google. From this video, we begin a dialogue about good research questions, and we workshop students' developing research questions. The workshop begins with students discussing the merits of their own questions, eliminating closed-ended questions and gathering proposal question feedback from their small groups. In many instances, students select their research question from peer group discussion. The weeks we spend on these first two assignments encourage peer collaboration; students begin their research in the same areas and recognize the benefits of class discussion to their current and future research. Less viable research questions receive less discussion, fewer ideas, and do not engage peer discussion. Students take the weekend and consider the class discussion and their research questions, returning to class with their tentative research question.

When students return with their tentative research question, they vocalize hesitations about *how* they answer this question. Several students confess to typing the question into Google and getting nothing helpful, while others express doubts that anything on the Internet can aid in answering their question. These confessions and doubts lead to discussion about the academic nature of the questions and the need for sources that provide insight into the question rather than an answer. This discussion becomes the introduction to the final component of their preliminary research sequence.

ASSIGNMENT 3: SOURCE TRAILS

The Source Trails assignment (see Appendix C) comes at a research stage where students need the bridge from Google to more sophisticated academic research. Lee (2008) discusses ways research participants use the concept of shelf browsing in the physical library to locate additional research materials. Participants in his research study knew "books on similar topics were shelved nearby and browsing after retrieving one book on a specific topic gave them the opportunity to discover other books on the same or closely related topics" (p. 214). The concept of shelf-browsing adapts for online research in a similar way, and the Source Trails assignment uses a series of workshops to teach techniques for reference browsing. The first workshop for this assignment teaches students to use the bibliographies of relevant sources to create a list of other relevant materials. Students generate a list of pseudo-citations that provide abbreviated, necessary information (title, author, year, journal) and include the author of the originating source so students can return to the original reference page when more information is needed. Students download or print sources to read and annotate, and noting the location in the pseudo-citation helps them to organize their research. During the second workshop, students learn the use of the databases' "related articles" feature, add relevant titles to their bibliography, and locate available sources. In the third workshop, I introduce Google Scholar, and students search for sources unavailable through the library using Google's "related" and "cited by" features. The previous process repeats, and only a few listed sources remain. For these sources, students learn to use the interlibrary loan feature and make requests for the remaining sources. Students turn in an in-progress list of their source trails; I do not give a specified number, though most students submit, on average, 15 sources for this work.

NEXT STEPS

After submitting their source trails, students take part in a class workshop for library database immersion. Students use the class period to research their topic while familiarizing themselves with the library databases. The goal is not to locate further information, though students perceive this as the task; rather, the goal is for students to discover what they know about the college's library databases and what they need assistance learning about the college's library databases. I prepare students for the upcoming library workshop by bringing them to the understanding that vast differences exist between Google searches and library database searches. Students show an improvement in IL skills by beginning this work using more advanced search terms than just the one or two words connected to their topic; they employ strategies learned in the Source Trails workshops. Students also begin to generate questions for the upcoming library workshop. These questions better engage students in the upcoming library workshop and help librarians shape the workshop. At the end of this class period, students submit the questions they have regarding library research skills, and I pass these along to the librarian leading the workshop. In turn, this leads to a library workshop that better develops the students' IL skills.

The library workshop takes place during the next class period. This workshop requires a huge commitment from the librarians leading the session; the workshop is not a traditional one-shot session, but rather a session focused on just-in-time instruction, answering student questions and building from knowledge and obstacles that arose during the class workshop. This does, however, provide the librarian more insight into where students are struggling with IL skills. Students attend this workshop humbled by the experience from the previous days, and some even admit the college's library database is much more complex than their high school's database. The workshop is guided by the students' questions from the previous class period but includes additional information the librarians know will further expand students' IL skills. For example, one student question regarded generating better keywords, which led to the librarian teaching the class how to read the Library of Congress Subject Headings (LCSH) listed within an individual result and how to combine and narrow multiple LCSHs to locate new material. Such a specific area of instruction does not come up in one-shot library workshops, but proved timely and useful to the students while also expanding their IL skills and abilities within the databases.

After the library workshop, I reassign the second and third research assignments, Focusing Research and Source Trails, with a restriction on students only using the library databases. This not only furthers students' familiarity with the library databases, but also reiterates the role these two assignments play in recursive research. At the conclusion of these next steps, students have approximately 25 sources beneficial for their research.

The next steps resemble more traditional composition courses. I present students with a hybrid research proposal and annotated bibliography that draws from materials previously submitted rather than beginning from scratch. They repurpose and revise in-class short writings for the formal product and present a bibliography and rhetorical summaries for Internet and library sources. The bibliography also includes current Source Trails sources, a book reference, and interlibrary loan requests for unavailable sources. The bibliography and proposal are the capstone project for the course.

PRELIMINARY IMPROVEMENTS TO INFORMATION LITERACY

The Preliminary Research sequence succeeds in improving students' IL skills because it shifts the research focus away from a formal research paper and allows students to focus on the research as a separate assignment. The sequence reinforces steps common to research projects: narrow the topic, create a focused research question, and use a variety of sources. Taken all at once, this information overwhelms students, especially when presented with the assignment that comprises a significant percentage of the course grade. However, working through early stages of research as separate assignments improves students' IL abilities while also helping students learn ways they can conduct more efficient research for all academic papers.

The first assignment, Preliminary Research, introduces students to three of the *Framework for IL* threshold concepts—Information Creation as a Process, Information Has Value, and Authority Is Constructed and Contextual; simultaneously, this assignment builds the classroom scholar community and helps students begin to think through semester research topics. Class discussions allow students to take risks and learn that these risks have no grade-related repercussions.

For example, one student discusses information learned through *Wikipedia*, though he must admit he did not include any of the information in the assignment. Other students admit to the same omission or admit including *Wikipedia* but fearing a reduced grade. Class discussions about the role *Wikipedia* can have at different stages of academic research encourage students to take the site into consideration as a resource while understanding why educators frown on its inclusion in academic papers. The conversations further students' understanding of authority as contextual and information as having value by acknowledging that *Wikipedia* does contain helpful knowledge for topic narrowing while also illustrating the differences in constructing authority in academic writing as significantly different than *Wikipedia's* constructed authority. These discussions build confidence in risk taking and discussing stumbles as well as successes, a necessary discussion for building IL skills through the subsequent assignments.

Through the assignment and corresponding class discussions, students begin to test their own authority, offering suggestions to peers when they have information related to a peer's early topic. At the early stage of the Preliminary Research assignment, such information is offered up with the qualifier "I read somewhere," before peers encourage the student to locate the specific source and share the information to the collaborative online space students use to share their research. Such actions are peer-motivated and peer-supported, encouraging students to show *how* they develop authority on even a single piece of information, encouraging peer support through the creation of information and individual authority, and emphasizing the value of information from specific sources. This assignment allows for early emphasis on the *Framework for IL* in ways that help students to better internalize IL skills without the daunting fear of a final grade for a lengthy research paper.

Through the Narrowed Focus and the Source Trails assignments, students begin to shape their broad topics into focused research questions that guide their semester research and writing; simultaneously, they work toward internalizing another American Library Association (ALA) concept—searching is strategic. Students begin to shape their broad topics into questions that will shape their semester research. For instance, the topic "medical surveillance" becomes the question "how does medical surveillance protect us?" Not long into frustrating Google searches for their questions, students begin to reconsider what, more specifically, they need to ask Google. Medical surveillance becomes a single search with over 13 million results; medical surveillance protection becomes a separate search with over 6.5 million results. These activities take place through Google because students already use the site for everyday and academic research and are more receptive to learning how to use Google more efficiently and are more receptive to advanced strategies on a familiar site.

Effective Internet search techniques, such as including phrases in quotation marks and incorporating Boolean Operators to further narrow or broaden results, parallel those students will learn for library databases, thus the library databases become less intimidating for students and more risks are taken with library database searches when assignments make this turn. These strategies teach students how to narrow their topic while also teaching them how to think more critically and strategically about the questions they need answered and the search terms that will help them answer these questions, encouraging both brainstorming for research terms and refining existing search strategies. "Medical surveillance," now enclosed in quotation marks to indicate a phrase to Google now returns under 400,000 results before strategic thinking about the topic narrows the search terms to "medical surveillance" AND "United States." Though Google automatically combines search terms, I prefer to encourage students to use this Boolean Operator with Google to better prepare them for the library databases, thus helping students understand the benefit of search strategies before applying them to the unfamiliar and less forgiving library databases.

Teaching students to use the bibliographies of relevant sources and the related research aspects of Google Scholar and the library databases adds another layer that emphasize additional methods for developing effective search strategies and also introduce students to the *Framework for IL*'s threshold concept that scholarship is a conversation. Students relate to this activity often through their covert use of *Wikipedia* as a starting point for academic research; knowing they cannot use *Wikipedia*, students learn from a peer or are self-taught in the skill of locating academically acceptable sources through references on a *Wikipedia* page. Miriam Laskin and Cynthia R. Haller's chapter in this collection further emphasizes the need to teach source trails, as junior-level students in their study still do not engage in this type of research. Thus, students know how the process works, but the Source Trails assignment makes this process a more sophisticated research activity that illustrates how and why specific sources are cited. Students are familiar with the sources they use for the Source Trails assignment through their readings in the previous assignments; therefore, they have a basic knowledge of how the sources are used in the article's content. When considering sources for the Source Trail assignment, students give consideration to how the source relates to their own research as they begin to frame their research in the scholarly conversation. Understanding the relationship between a source and their own research leads to interrogating their sources' sources and considering how their own research enters this larger conversation.

A student researching police surveillance with an emphasis on the African American community, is an excellent example of Source Trails at work. A source she described in her final project as "influential to her project" mentioned a source that argued the Rodney King case was instrumental to the rise of hip-hop. With no knowledge of Rodney King, the student identified the source as potentially useful to her research and, through this additional source and further research about Rodney King, revised her research question to the role of the Rodney King video in implementing police car surveillance cameras. The Source Trails assignment illustrates how scholarship builds a conversation between scholars and how students can strategically locate relevant sources through the references contained, which teaches students to search more effectively and efficiently, thus furthering their ability to meet the *Framework for IL*. Further, students are not looking quickly for the specific number of sources required for a course paper since the paper remains unassigned, but continue looking for more information on their focused research questions. Students learning to locate information more efficiently also begin to expand their ability to meet each IL threshold concept outlined in the *Framework for IL*, while engaging with more complex, interest-driven research rather than seeking sources that assist in meeting assignment guidelines. Students focusing on research itself, not a specific number of sources for a final paper, spend more time reading sources relevant to their specific research interest. Students recognize the Source Trails assignment as work that will help them answer their question, and they recognize the strategy of following the conversation through cited sources as a strategy they can implement for other academic research.

Acknowledging that a single source will not answer their question leads students to think more critically about the breadth and complexity of information. They create new searches, repurpose old searches, and discard located and read sources based on their current research needs. They begin to articulate an understanding of research as a process of inquiry—a process motivated by curiosity when the subject engages them. Sources providing no information relevant to the research question do not enter the annotated bibliography and are not quote mined for the final paper. My students are not at a point where they necessarily articulate a need for theory in their research; however, using Foucault's theory in class readings and discussions provides an understanding of how theory can apply to the work. Two students in the pilot implementation of this sequence located and incorporated the work of Deleuze and Barthes in their research, works they located through their source trails and recognized, after reading, as pertinent to their own research.

PRELIMINARY SUCCESS

The preliminary research sequence precedes an annotated bibliography and a proposal for a more formal research project the students might undertake; these documents form the capstone project for the semester, thus further emphasizing the *Framework for IL*'s threshold concepts of Research as Inquiry and Scholarship Is a Conversation while simultaneously enhancing the students' critical thinking skills. The annotated bibliography includes rhetorical summaries for 10 academic sources and 10 Internet sources; also included are the students' 10 most current Source Trails and at least one book reference and one interlibrary loan request. The proposal includes a brief statement of the students' narrowed research topics, an analysis of the primary materials for the research topic, and an explanation of why their research is important to an academic audience. The proposal does not include requirements for any source use, thus leaving students to decide which sources need inclusion based on their research topic, their understanding of IL skills, and their comprehension of class discussions about research. The goal for the capstone is to keep the students' focus on research related to their topic. In the pilot semester (n = 25), 23 students submitted a proposal that met the assignment guidelines, and an analysis of the sources used in the proposals illustrates the ways students incorporate research into a formal assignment following the Preliminary Research sequence.

Two students (8%) included *Wikipedia* citations in their paper. The first included the *Wikipedia* page for "Syndromic Surveillance," presenting the definition for her research topic in language more accessible to a broader audience than the reference on the Center for Disease Control (CDC) webpage. The definition preceding the *Wikipedia* citation is the student's own work, but clearly draws more from the Wikipedia language than the more complex language on the CDC page, and the student acknowledges this use, risking the reduced grade for using *Wikipedia* instead of deceptively citing the CDC page and not acknowledging knowledge gained from *Wikipedia*. The second student included a link to the *Wikipedia* page for "Computer Surveillance," not as a component of his analysis, but rather as part of a brief narrative describing how he used the *Wikipedia* page to focus this broad topic to his narrowed topic of Twitter's privacy policy. In each proposal, the selected *Wikipedia* pages reflect the discussion during the Preliminary Research sequence about the appropriate use of *Wikipedia* and its place in academic work. The use of *Wikipedia* in both proposals also illustrates the students' acknowledgement of the *Framework for IL* threshold concepts of information as having value and scholarship as a conversation. Though the students elect to use *Wikipedia* for their proposals, their strategic use and honest citation of the *Wikipedia* pages illustrates partial success for teaching IL strategies and the *Framework for IL* through the Preliminary Research sequence.

Four of the students (16%) included at least one source from a scholarly journal article available through the library databases, and though this number is significantly smaller than anticipated, these students chose scholarly sources because of relevance to their paper, not because of assignment requirements. Two other students (8%), as mentioned earlier, made attempts to apply Deleuze and Barthes to their primary material analyses. These sources served as theoretical frameworks in other scholarly articles they used, and the students, recognizing the potential role the theory might play in their own research, sought out these works and took the risk of incorporating them into their own research. These academic and theoretical sources again emphasize the students' increased understanding of scholarship as a conversation and information as having value. In each case, the students present information relevant to their research because of the informational value and the connection to their own research, not because of the need to meet specific source requirements.

A final success of the Preliminary Research Sequence is demonstrated through the way students used common Internet sources in their work. With no source requirements for the proposal, students' inclusion of sources demonstrated their critical thinking and their progress with the *Framework for IL*'s threshold concepts. The semester theme of surveillance and mass media purposely led to research topics that both engaged students in their research and required more skillful IL skills since, in the words of one frustrated student, "everybody's analyzing Beyonce's music, not her Twitter feed!" Thus, class discussions about the relevance of the sources selected, contrasted with the *publisher* of the sources selected, anticipated and acknowledged the use of common Internet sources. In their proposals, five of the students (21%) made use only of Internet sources that comprised their primary materials—Twitter feeds, YouTube videos, news stories, and images. In four of these proposals, students also relied heavily on the class readings and discussions but did not include secondary sources to expand their argument; only one student used only the primary materials and did not incorporate any form of secondary materials. Six of the students (24%) incorporated common Internet sources that supported their argument, but did so with targeted source selection. For instance, two students writing on search engines and surveillance both located and used policies from the search engines discussed in their proposal. In one instance, this included analysis of the differences in Google, Yahoo, and Bing's privacy policies and results to a common search across all three search engines. Another student, writing on government surveillance of Internet searches, located and incorporated Google's transparency report to use as evidence in his argument. Two students (8%) relied on reliable Internet sources viable to their topic, such as the FDIC information on phishing scams in a proposal about advance-fee email fraud scams and an online English translation of a 1936 internal Soviet memo about the task of the Glavit. In both cases, the students were able to locate, read, and comprehend the importance and relevance of these sources to their research; however, neither student was able to incorporate the source itself beyond a mention and discussion of the importance of the source.

Overall, the Preliminary Research sequence did not perfect students' IL skills and their use of sources in the capstone project; however, the ways students handled source inclusion without any requirements to guide their decisions demonstrates a keener understanding of source use in academic scholarship. Early conversations about *Wikipedia*, for example, made students more aware of why the source is less acceptable in their capstone project and students were able to use more sophisticated sources, whether academic or targeted and specific Internet sources. The number of students using academic sources in their capstone projects was smaller than anticipated; however, the greater take-away from those who did use academic sources is that with better instruction, guided by the *Framework for ILs*, these students begin to recognize the role of scholarly research in academic projects independent of project requirements. In a similar way, this instruction improves the Internet sources selected for academic projects as students come to understand the role of sources in their research and learn to look more critically at the sources they read for preliminary research and the sources they use for academic writing.

KEYS TO SUCCESS

The assignment sequence presented above is not the only option for incorporating successful preliminary research into a course. Patrick Corbett's (2010) "What about the 'Google Effect'?" presents a similar approach to focusing students on the research task separate from a formal writing task. Corbett incorporates more formal writing assignments throughout the semester, but focuses these on the work completed with the narrowed research. The build up to more formal research, Corbett reports, allows students "to take chances with their ideas that they otherwise would not have taken for fear of a harsh evaluation" (p. 273). The chances Corbett's students willingly take reflect the chances my own students take during their preliminary research when the current research assignment, not the final, formal paper is at stake. Other sequences can aid the teaching of IL and helping students internalize a more robust process that moves from initial curiosity to narrowed research questions. Rachel Rains Winslow, Sarah Skripsky and Savannah Kelly's chapter on Zotero in this collection offers other ways of thinking about source use and offers another layer for teaching source browsing, specifically. These varied research assignments can each assist students in taking risks with early research—research that greatly benefits students when the final product becomes the later course focus.

The Preliminary Research Sequence engages student in research separate from the formal assignment, which furthers students' IL skills by building on their everyday research skills. Library databases do not need to be the starting point for academic research; such a new method of research at the beginning of an academic project can intimidate students, especially those in core classes conducting academic research for the first time. Preliminary research that begins with the students' existing IL skills boosts confidence by reassuring them that they do know how to begin research. Confidence in the research starting point encourages students to try new things. Similarly, scaffolding the assignments so that students learn more efficient methods for searching Google well before beginning any required library research further boosts their confidence, while also teaching students how to locate information more effectively. Starting with Google also builds confidence in reading comprehension as students begin with more general sources and the knowledge they must discuss their findings in class. The more students internalize information from sources, rather than just annotating or copying it for later use, the more confident they become in their research and defining their own next steps.

The Preliminary Research Sequence also teaches students the recursive nature of research and strategies for later research. I encourage students who find themselves stalled by a portion of their final research assignment to return to the Narrowed

Focus and Source Trails looking specifically for information related to this stall. Taking this smaller question through the research helps students locate more specific information for the paper and further emphasizes their ability to recognize the need for new information as appropriate in the midst of writing the paper.

CONCLUSION

The academic research paper remains the most common assignment in higher education and access to more information quickly does not make locating research easier for students. If anything, the abundance of readily available information makes the research process more difficult, adding additional pressure to the task of writing the 8–10 page assignment with the appropriate number and type of sources. Delaying the formal assignment and incorporating a series of preliminary research assignments furthers students IL skills by emphasizing research as a way to find a narrowed topic and sources from which students select the most appropriate to their work, not the first few they locate. Alone, delaying the formal paper does not help students understand the importance of early research; students also need the work put into this early research to reflect in their semester grade a percentage that emphasizes the importance educators place on conducting in-depth research to find the paper topic. As long as educators emphasize only the final product, both in the classroom and the grading scheme, students will continue research with that emphasis in mind. Showing students the importance of preliminary research will not instill in them the scholar's passion for research, but may, for the duration of the semester, engage them with a topic narrow and interesting enough to instill in them IL skills beneficial to their academic, professional, and everyday life.

NOTES

1. This research was supported in part by a Conference on College Composition and Communication Research Initiative Grant.
2. All names are pseudonyms.

REFERENCES

American Library Association (2015) *Framework for information literacy for higher education*. Retrieved from http://acrl.ala.org/ilstandards/wp-content/uploads/2014/02/Framework-for-IL-for-HE-Draft-2.pdf.

Biddix, J. P., Chung, J. C. & Park, H. W. (2011). Convenience or credibility? A study of college student online research behaviors. *Internet and Higher Education, 14*, 175–182.

Corbett, P. (2010). What about the "Google Effect"? Improving the library research habits of first-year composition students. *Teaching English in Two-Year Colleges, 37*(3), 265–277.

Head, A. J. & Eisenberg, M. B. (2009, December 1). *How college students seek information in the digital age.* Retrieved from http://projectinfolit.org/publications.

Head, A. J. & Eisenberg, M. B. (2010, July 12). *How handouts for research assignments guide today's college students.* Retrieved from http://projectinfolit.org/publications.

Laskin, M. & Haller, C. (2016). Up the mountain without a trail. In B. J. D'Angelo, S. Jamieson, B. Maid & J. R. Walker (Eds.), *Information literacy: Research and collaboration across disciplines.* Fort Collins, CO: WAC Clearinghouse and University Press of Colorado.

Li, Huri-Lee. (2008). Information structures and undergraduate students. *The Journal of Academic Librarianship, 34*(3), 211–219.

Jamieson, S. (2016). What the Citation Project tells us about information literacy in college composition. In B. J. D'Angelo, S. Jamieson, B. Maid & J. R. Walker (Eds.), *Information literacy: Research and collaboration across disciplines.* Fort Collins, CO: WAC Clearinghouse and University Press of Colorado.

Jamieson, S. & Howard, R. M. (2011). *Initial data from the Citation Project study of student use of sources in researched papers from sixteen US colleges and universities.* Retrieved from http://citationproject.net/CitationProject-Sixteen_School_Study-Sources_Selected.pdf.

McClure, R. & Clink, K. (2009). How do you know that? An investigation of student research practices in the digital age. *portal, 9*(1), 115–132.

Winslow, R.R, Skripsky, S. & Kelly, S. L. (2016). Not just for citations: Assessing Zotero while reassessing research. In B. J. D'Angelo, S. Jamieson, B. Maid & J. R. Walker (Eds.), *Information literacy: Research and collaboration across disciplines.* Fort Collins, CO: WAC Clearinghouse and University Press of Colorado.

APPENDIX A: PRELIMINARY RESEARCH ASSIGNMENT

Goal: Locate research on surveillance and write an informal analysis of your findings.

Task: Search for sources you would use to discuss the topic of surveillance. As you search, create a map of your search that includes specific information on search engines you use, keywords, usefulness of the search, websites visited, key information learned, questions raised, problems encountered, and any other information relevant to the search. [You should be able to hand your map to a peer who can completely retrace your steps and learn the same things you learned.]

Time frame: Long enough to be able to discuss the topic knowledgeably in class.

Task Part 2: Using your search map, write an informal analysis of the information search. Your analysis should discuss what you learned, where you learned the information, effectiveness of keywords, problems encountered, questions raised, relevance and credibility of sources, and anything else you found relevant to your search. This should be approximately 2 pages of text.

Formatting: Double-spaced, 12 point font. Include a paper heading that includes your name, my name, the course number and section, date. Use the assignment number and title for the title of your paper.

Turn in:
- A hard copy of your search map
- A printed copy of your information analysis
- Final Reminders and Assessment
- This is your homework and attendance verification for class.
- To receive an "adequate" rating, your information search must demonstrate you completed the search *and* familiarized yourself with the websites in order to write the analysis, but the familiarization and analysis are relatively superficial.
- To receive an "above average" rating, your information search must demonstrate that you delved further into the search (e.g., visited links beyond the first page of Google) and further explored the links to write the analysis.
- To receive an "outstanding" rating, your information search demonstrates a broader search for understanding of surveillance (relying on more than just Google for your search) and further research when needed (knowing who compiled the page, potential bias of the page, etc.) to write your analysis.

APPENDIX B: NARROWED RESEARCH ASSIGNMENT

Goal: Locate research on a course-related topic of interest and write an informal analysis.

Task: Select a topic of interest related to our course theme and use Google's advanced search options to locate relevant research to your topic. As you search, create a map of your search that includes specific information on your advanced searches (e.g. tell me what exact phrases you searched and/or what words you omitted), usefulness of the search, websites visited, key information learned, questions raised, problems encountered, and any other information relevant to the search. [You should be able to hand your map to a peer who can completely retrace your steps and learn the same things you learned.]

Time frame: Long enough to be able to discuss your topic knowledgeably in class.

Task Part 2: Using your search map, write an informal analysis of the information search. Your analysis should discuss what you learned, where you learned the information, effectiveness and/or ineffectiveness of advanced searches, problems encountered, questions raised, relevance and credibility of sources, and anything else you found relevant to your topic research. This should be approximately 2 pages of text.

Formatting: Double-spaced, 12 point font. Include a paper heading that includes your name, my name, the course number and section, date. Use the assignment number and title for the title of your paper.

Turn in:
- A hard copy of your search map
- A printed copy of your information analysis
- Final Reminders and Assessment
- This is your homework and attendance verification for class.
- To receive an "adequate" rating, your information search must demonstrate you used advanced search features and familiarized yourself with the websites in order to write the analysis, but the familiarization and analysis are relatively superficial.
- To receive an "above average" rating, your information search must demonstrate that you delved further into the search (e.g., visited links beyond the first page of Google) and further explored the links to write the analysis.
- To receive an "outstanding" rating, your information search demonstrates a broader search for understanding of your topic (relying on more than just Google for your search) and further research when needed (knowing who compiled the page, potential bias of the page, etc.) to write your analysis.

APPENDIX C: SOURCE TRAILS ASSIGNMENT

Goal: Learn to read a bibliographic entry, use the library's Interlibrary loan system, and expand your research on your specific surveillance and mass media topic.

Task: You will search for additional scholarly sources related to your research using four methods: reference pages from current research, the library's book and journal databases, Google Scholar's "cited by," and Google Scholar's "related articles." You will locate at least ten new sources, create progressive citations (author, title, year, search location) from these sources, and request unavailable articles through Interlibrary Loan.

Time frame: This week's lab will be a hands on workshop on using the features and the Interlibrary loan request page. You will submit your progress on this assignment at the beginning of class Wednesday and Friday.

Research Components (Complete in the order provided)

Bibliography Trails: Begin your source trails with the bibliographies for the research you collected during the library database workshop. You want to use the sources you've read and rated as helpful to your research. Look through the bibliographies and/or notes where the author(s) provide bibliographic information for their references. Mark all sources that have titles that indicate they may be helpful to your research, and indicate with your markings whether these sources are books, scholarly journal articles, or websites. Your focus for this assignment is on the books and scholarly articles.

Once you have marked these sources, create a progressive citations bibliography, listing the source in which you found the new sources as the location. Include at least the author's name for the location, but if you have more than one source from the same article, list the first few words of the title as well.

Library Searching: Use your progressive citations to locate the sources you have access through via the university databases. Some of these may be readily available through the databases, but others will require you to use the library's search option. When you search, you will sometimes receive a list of scholarly articles related to your search. If you receive such a list, add relevant articles to your progressive citations and include related by with the location (article author and title you were searching).

Locate everything you can through the library databases. Download the scholarly articles you can access and add the database name *at the end* of your progressive citation. (Do not replace the original location, but add the database after this location.) Add call numbers for the books you found available through the university library.

Google Scholar: [Read the information below on "cited by" and "related articles" again before beginning this portion of the research. You want to complete all three of these processes for each article. Working through all three for one article before moving on to another article will save you significant time.]

Continue looking for materials from your progressive citation bibliography on Google Scholar (scholar.google.com). Continue looking for the articles you have not found. Placing the title in quotation marks should help Google Scholar locate the article easily. To the right of the entry will be a listing of where the article is located if you have access. Pay careful attention to whether the article is available to you, and whether it is available in an HTML or a PDF format. If the article is available via PDF, download this, and add Google Scholar to the end of your location. If available in HTML, add Google Scholar, and then the web address of the actual source.

Google Scholar Cited by: Beneath the listing for your source, you will have a "cited by" link. This link will provide you a list of scholarly articles that include the article you searched in their bibliography. Follow this link and read through the titles and blurbs provided for the results. Add relevant articles to your progressive citations using the location format above using the article title/author you searched and Google Scholar as your location. Be sure to add "Cited by" at the end of this location and, if you have access to this article, additional information listed above.

Google Scholar Related Articles: Google Scholar listings will include a "related articles" link beside the "cited by" link. This link will show you other articles Google determines are related to your source. Read through these results for your articles and, again, add relevant articles to your progressive citation bibliography using the format above and including "related articles" in the location.

Interlibrary Loan (ILL) Requests: You should request any remaining scholarly articles from your bibliography through Interlibrary Loan. Before you make a request, make certain the article is not available through any means listed above. The best way to do this (and the most efficient for requesting materials via ILL) is to search the library databases for the article again. If the database has the information, it will auto-fill your request. Once you have completed requesting your remaining articles, log in to ILL system via the Interlibrary loan link on the library homepage or directly through your web browser. Print a copy of the "Outstanding Requests" page and submit this with your bibliography. This is the page that automatically loads when you login to ILL. You may also navigate to this page by selecting the link under the "View" menu on the left-hand side menu.

Formatting: Double-spaced, 12 point font. Include a paper heading that includes your name, my name, the course number and section, date. Use the assignment number and title for the title of your paper.

Turn in:
- A hard copy of your progressive citations bibliography progress (Wednesday and Friday)
- A printed list of your outstanding ILL requests (either with your progressive citation bibliography on Friday or with your research proposal on 15 March).
- Final Reminders and Assessment
- This is your homework and attendance verification for class both Wednesday and Friday.
- To receive an "adequate" rating, your information search must demonstrate you are actively working toward your Source Trails by submitting your Bibliography Trails list Wednesday and your library research by Friday.
- To receive an "above average" rating, your information search must demonstrate you are actively working toward your source trails by sub-

mitting your Bibliography Trails and library research by Wednesday and your Google Scholar research by Friday.
- To receive an "outstanding" rating, your Source Trails assignment is complete and submitted Friday with your "Outstanding Requests" printout.

CHAPTER 8
APPROXIMATING THE UNIVERSITY: THE INFORMATION LITERACY PRACTICES OF NOVICE RESEARCHERS

Karen Gocsik
University of California-San Diego

Laura R. Braunstein and Cynthia E. Tobery
Dartmouth College

In a seminal essay, David Bartholomae (1985) asserts that novice writers need to "invent the university by assembling and mimicking its language" (p. 135), noting that they do so by various "successive approximations" of academic conventions and practices:

> What our beginning students need to learn is to extend themselves, by successive approximations, into the commonplaces, set phrases, rituals and gestures, habits of mind, tricks of persuasion, obligatory conclusions and necessary connections that . . . constitute knowledge within the various branches of our academic community. (p. 146)

Instructors and librarians who work with beginning academic writers confirm Bartholomae's assertion. Michelle Simmons (2005) has described how beginning researchers are outsiders to disciplinary discourse, arguing that traditional approaches to information literacy (IL), such as the "one-shot" library instruction session, may put these students at a disadvantage. In Simmons's view, novice writers need to see research "not as a task of collecting information but instead as a task of constructing meaning" (p. 299). Simmons argues for *critical* IL, which is not merely a matter of acquiring context-independent research skills, but of "learning . . . discursive practices within the context of an academic discipline" (p. 299). Our research asks how, precisely, novice writer-researchers go about inventing the university *before* they have an understanding of the disciplines in which they are asked to work. In other words, through which particular "successive approximations" do students transform information into meaningful disciplinary knowledge? Our careful coding of a collaborative wiki project across several years suggests that novice writers in the first steps of knowledge construction tend to mimic the *structures* of knowledge, rather than to create coherent *narratives* of understanding. This finding has implications not only for how we understand student learning, but also for how we teach students to find, make sense of, and compose knowledge.

CONTEXT AND AIMS

This particular project situates itself within Rolf Norgaard's call to "write information literacy"—a call for Writing Studies and IL professionals to co-envision and co-shape the instructional practices of composition and research (2003). While presenting his call, Norgaard identifies two key misconceptions about both writing and IL—first, that IL, like writing, is often viewed as a technical skill that is merely functional or performative; and second, that IL skills, like writing skills, are perceived to be lacking among our incoming students when in fact these students bring rich and complicated practices with them to the university (Norgaard, 2003). As instructors and researchers, we found ourselves preoccupied by these problems. Like other scholars (Fister, 2013; Melzer & Zemliansky, 2003; Fister, 1995) we had long recognized the first-year research paper as a problematic "performance"—not of knowledge but, as Bartholomae suggests, of the *approximation of knowledge*. We also realized that students were drawing from an established variety of research practices by which they were (productively or not) inventing their university (see Biddix et al. 2011; Corbett 2010; Head & Eisenberg, 2009; McClure & Clink, 2009). Informed also by the "think aloud" protocols that had been employed most notably by Linda Flower and John Hayes (1981), we aimed to develop a project that would help us make visible the research and compositional decisions of our novice writers, teasing out their various threads, uncovering what patterns of practice these novices were employing, and then exploring with them how these practices were facilitating or obstructing their learning. Bolstered further by the work that the Council of Writing Program Administrators (WPA) had done in defining its outcomes for first-year composition in 2000 and 2008, and also by the work that the Association of College and Research Libraries (ACRL) had done to develop its IL competency standards (2000), we sought a project that would help us map how our students work to construct knowledge from information—a project that might then assist us in reforming our research and writing instruction from the more traditional product-oriented model to a process model that situated research as both a generative and rhetorical endeavor.

Our aspirations were supported and informed by the particular structures of our institutional environment. While the tensions between the fields of Writing Studies and IL have been well documented (see Ivey, 2103; Meulemans & Carr, 2013; Kotter, 1999; among others), our work benefitted from an institutional "Kairos" (Baker & Gladis; Chapter 16, this collection; Norgaard, 2004) afforded by the fact that our library, our writing program, and our far-reaching teaching and learning center were aligned in their commitment to developing pedagogies that positioned writing as inquiry and research as rhetorical. We had in place the various criteria that Ruth Ivey (2013) acknowledges as central to a working collaboration: shared, commonly defined goals; trust and respect; competent partners; and ongoing, institutionally sustained conversation. Though many classes at our institution still embrace the sort of methods that Norgaard (2003) describes—where research papers are assigned and assessed as products rather than by the processes that informed them, and literacy is measured (at least in part) by how correctly one's sources are cited—we were able to develop our teaching and research in a climate where Writing Studies and IL colleagues met regularly, both informally and in regular professional development workshops, to discuss how our methods and pedagogies might inform each other. This wiki project—undertaken by a writing instructor, a librarian, and an educational developer from the teaching and learning center—was an outgrowth of these conversations about writing, research, and learning.

THE ASSIGNMENT

The aim of the assignment, given to international students in a first-year developmental writing class, was to chart the successive approximations of disciplinary discourse that novices make as they find, assess, and use information to construct knowledge (see Appendix A). In particular, we were attempting to discern to what degree students search strategically, practice research as inquiry, and appropriately contextualize and construct knowledge—three of the six "threshold concepts" articulated in the *Framework for Information Literacy for Higher Education* (ACRL, 2015). To assess these student practices, we asked the students over the course of a weekend to collaborate on a *Wikipedia*-style article on a subject that they knew little about—in this case, the history of Christianity in Early America. We gave them a reading to get them started, and then instructed them to use any credible source that would help them to build an article (which we refer to, in the assignment, as a "narrative"). We required only that they compose collaboratively, using the wiki tool embedded in the course's learning management system, and that they list the sources they used in a separate "sources" file.

In line with evolving IL practices (see Artman et al. 2010; Jacobs & Jacobs, 2009; Curzon, 2004), ours was not a "one-shot" assignment; rather, it constituted the inaugural step in the course's ongoing, sequenced instruction in research and writing. As the first, foundational step in that process, the assignment was also intended as a way that the students, the librarian, and the instructor might be challenged to re-envision and re-articulate the entire research process. Pedagogically, the assignment was challenging, deliberately designed to ask more of students than they would be able to manage. These first-year students, while intelligent, were at the very start of their academic careers and had little awareness of the academic practices through which knowledge is constructed. Moreover, as international students, they were only beginning to familiarize themselves with American history and culture. In this light, the assignment was designed to be an exercise in structured failure—an exercise by which students would confront and then assess the efficacy of the strategies that they use, or don't use, to construct knowledge. In completing the assignment and undergoing the subsequent debriefing discussion with both the instructor and the course's embedded librarian, students would begin to develop an understanding of research and writing as recursive processes that mirror and inform each other.

Over the six years that we ran this assignment (2006–2012), we engaged in ongoing, informal assessments of the assignment's success. As we did, we noted intriguing patterns in the ways that students were constructing knowledge. We ascertained that students were approximating knowledge more than they were constructing it—that is, while students organized information by creating headings and sub-headings so that their discussion *seemed* to cohere (thereby approximating what one might find in an encyclopedia entry), they were unable to construct a coherent, knowledgeable summary of the material at hand. We suspected that the assignment, though too small to enable us to draw definitive conclusions, could offer us a rich source of data that might illuminate how novice writers and researchers shape their understanding of an unfamiliar topic. As we considered the assignments' results collectively, we found ourselves returning to two important questions:

- What research and composing practices do student writers draw upon when they are engaged in the *very first steps* of knowledge construction?
- How do novices mask inadequacies in their knowledge as they attempt to approximate academic conversations?

To answer these questions, we decided to investigate further the three capabilities that the assignment was designed to assess: selecting and using sources;

assembling knowledge via basic compositional moves; and applying organizational strategies.

METHODS

In order to quantify the patterns and trends we were seeing in these three areas, we developed four distinct systems for coding: we coded for selection of sources, for use of sources, for compositional "moves," and for organizational strategies. When coding the selection of sources in the sources file, for example, we counted print sources (albeit few) and enumerated the different types of web sources that students chose: namely, *Wikipedia*, online library resources, and commercial, organizational, and personal websites. When coding students' use of sources in the collaboratively written wiki article, we were inspired by the Citation Project, a multi-year, multi-institution research study that is examining sources and citations in first-year writing (see *What is the Citation Project?* [n.d.]; Howard et al., 2010); by Randall McClure and Kellian Clink's study of student research practices (2008); and by the work of Barbara Fister (1992) and Cynthia Haller (2010), who employed interviews and speak-aloud protocol in order to conceptualize students' research processes. Our coding determined whether students were copying material directly from a source, with or without attribution; whether they were paraphrasing source material; or whether they were patchwriting, that is, "reproducing source language with some words deleted or added, some grammatical structures altered, or some synonyms used" (Howard et al., 2010, p. 181). Studies similar to ours—in that they employed coding or other forms of critical analysis to conceptualize novice research practices—are prevalent in this volume, including the work of Scheidt et al., who coded research interviews; Wojahn et al., who coded students' research journals and reflective essays; and Blackwell-Starnes, who used RAP (Research Aloud Protocol) to determine various elements in a students' research process, including what role the assignment plays and to what degree the research process focuses on the final product.

When coding for compositional moves, we examined the seven discrete wiki articles, along with all their iterations. The wikis were produced in consecutive fall terms by new classes of 16 first-year composition students; however, we were unable to code the wiki produced in the fall of 2007 due to a malfunction of the course management system. Each wiki went through a number of iterations or drafts, ranging from 66 to 131 in total, with the average number of drafts being 89 (each student therefore averaging 5.5 contributions). In order to code the wikis, we looked at every draft, each of which was saved by the course management system with changes highlighted by the system. As we coded, we compared each saved version of the document to the previous version and noted whether students were constructing knowledge by adding, deleting, moving, or revising materials. Added materials were then coded more specifically according to type:

- Content appearing in paragraph form
- Content appearing in bullet form
- Headings and subheadings
- Table of contents
- New entries in an existing table of contents
- Transitions
- Quotations/photos/videos

The coding categories were chosen after sections were analyzed by different researchers on the team; notes were then compared to normalize the coding process. The original coding scheme included subcategories for deletions as well, but deletions were so uncommon that all types of deletions were combined into one category during the analysis. All the versions for a given year were coded by the same person.

Finally, when coding students' overall organizational strategies, we noted where students were organizing material via chronology (arranging material roughly by date but without working to create a coherent narrative), classification (arranging material into categories and subcategories), narrative (arranging material into a coherent story), or analysis (arranging material around a claim, supported by evidence).

To better understand the students' attitudes toward their completed work, we developed for our final group of students an anonymous survey which asked them to assess the quality of their work according to the standards that *Wikipedia* uses for feature articles, including whether the article is well-written; focused and relevant; useful; comprehensive; well-researched; of an appropriate length; neutral; and appropriately structured (*Featured Article Criteria*, 2013). We used the students' assessment of their work as a starting point for the debriefing discussion that we held in class.

RESULTS AND INTERPRETATION

FINDING AND USING INFORMATION

The original goal of the wiki assignment was to diagnose students' baseline research skills in order to design library instruction more effectively (see Braunstein, 2009). From 2006, when the project was first assigned, the instructor and the librarian envisioned library research instruction as a collaborative, course-integrated process, anticipating recommendations in the literature of both IL

Table 8.1. Type and frequency of sources cited

Source Type	Number Cited in Sources File, all years combined
Wikipedia	108
Academic (free) website	43
Religious website	41
Government or Nonprofit website	29
Academic resource (paid library subscription)	20
Commercial or business website	14
Print book or ebook	12
Personal website	10

and Writing Studies (see Artman et al., 2010; Barratt et al., 2008; McClure & Clink, 2008, among others). Given that we deliberately did not schedule a library instruction session until after the assignment was completed, we were not surprised to find that students relied on the search tools they knew: Google and Wikipedia. Of more interest to us were the sites the students found and selected to use as sources, as shown in Table 8.1, and their expressed rationale for doing so in our post-assignment discussion. (See Appendix B for examples of the source types. Note that not all material in the document was cited in the source file.)

What concerned us about these sources was not that students overwhelmingly used websites rather than library resources (an outcome we expected), but that they so rarely analyzed the material they found. As McClure and Clink (2008) also found in their study, our students were adept at finding information, but struggled to determine its credibility in terms of authority, bias, and relevance. To address this challenge, students used their own criteria for evaluating a source's credibility. Two examples demonstrate the mixed success of this approach.

First, students from several different classes cited a page from Stanford University's archive of the papers of Martin Luther King, Jr. (Figure 8.1). The item turns out to be a class paper on the Great Awakening that King wrote as a seminarian. When questioned regarding this choice during our debriefing discussion, students replied that they thought any ".edu" website was authoritative, since, to them, it appeared to have been written by a professor. They were unfamiliar with the concept of digital archives and other materials being hosted by an academic institution—or that ".edu" sites could just as likely be authored by students like themselves. This site seemed authoritative to them for another reason: these international students came from countries in which Christianity was by no

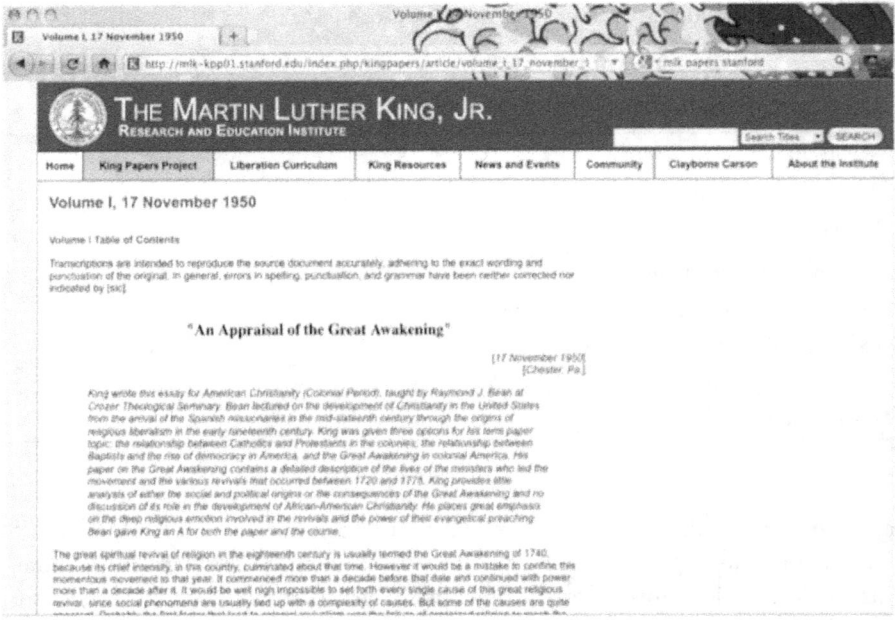

Figure 8.1. Martin Luther King, Jr.'s seminary paper. King, Martin Luther, Jr. (1950). An Appraisal of the Great Awakening. King Papers Project. The Martin Luther King, Jr. Research and Education Institute, Stanford University.

means a common religious culture. Most had never heard of figures such as Jonathan Edwards, nor were they familiar with Protestant sectarianism in colonial America. But they had heard of Martin Luther King, Jr.

A second example of students using their own criteria to evaluate sources involved the persistent (yearly) appearance of a page from *Theopedia*, on Calvinism (currently the second result in a Google search on "Calvinism") (Figure 8.2). In the years that we were employing this assignment, a striking visual similarity existed between *Theopedia* and *Wikipedia*—a similarity that springs from the practice of Wikimedia Foundation, creator of *Wikipedia*, freely distributing its engine, MediaWiki, to other groups to create collaborative encyclopedias. But clicking on "About *Theopedia*" reveals that the site is an "evangelical encyclopedia of Biblical Christianity," and that "Editors/Users are required to personally affirm the entirety of the primary statement of faith," which includes a commitment to Calvinism ("About *Theopedia*," n.d.). Students had not investigated this information. In fact, they declared in the debriefing discussion that they were unaware that an "About" link exists on many websites. Accordingly, they were unable to

Approximating the University

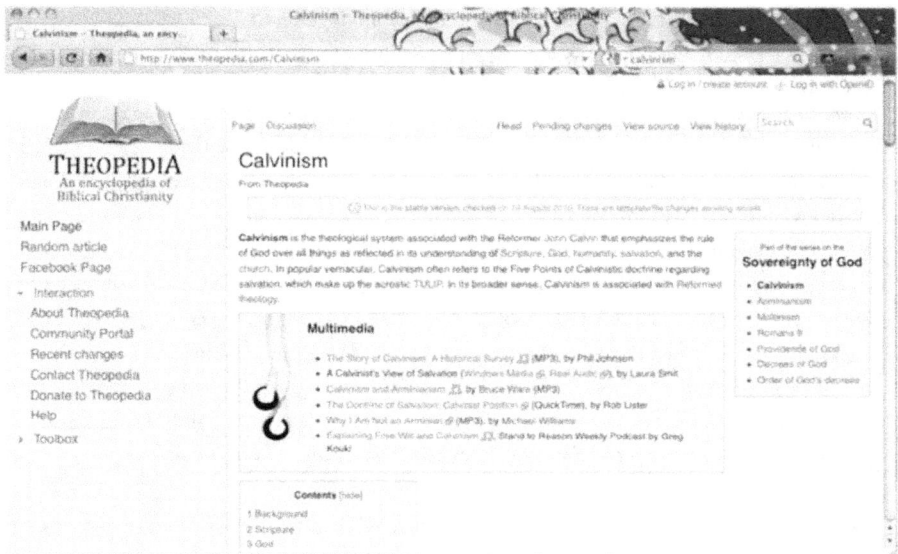

Figure 8.2. Screenshot of "Calvinism" entry from Theopedia. Calvinisim. (n.d.). Retrieved from http://www.theopedia.com/Calvinism.

place this information in its proper context—to understand how it was produced, by whom, and for what purpose. Together, the frequent appearance of the King paper and the *Theopedia* article moved us to consider how a limited understanding of contexts for writing might affect students' basic IL competencies.

Preliminary results from the Citation Project confirm our finding that first-year students struggle with context in researched writing, noting that they tend to copy, paraphrase, and patchwrite, with little or no summary of the sources they use. In terms of their interaction with sources, the Citation Project found that students are "*not writing from sources; they are writing from sentences selected from sources*" (Howard et al., 2010, p. 187, emphasis in original). Put another way, students are selecting pieces of information to use as they compose, but they are not considering that information in terms of the larger argument being made. The results—at least, in our students' work—included not only a demonstrated failure to assess a source's credibility and to represent that source fairly, but also an inability to integrate information gathered from sources into a coherent argument of their own. An analysis of the 2010 assignment (an example representative of all years) showed that the students' text was almost entirely copied or patchwritten from the websites cited in their sources file (see Table 8.2).

From one perspective, the student writing may appear to be simple plagiarism. Yet as Rebecca Moore Howard et al. (2010) suggest in their study of a set

Table 8.2. Patchwritten passage from 2010 assignment

Encyclopedia of World Biography	Student Text
Thomas Jefferson was born in Shadwell, Virginia, on April 13, 1743. . . . *At the age of seventeen* <u>he entered the</u> College of William and Mary. . . . He <u>read widely in the law</u>, in the sciences, and in both ancient and modern history, philosophy, and literature. Jefferson was admitted to the bar, or an association for lawyers, in 1767 and <u>established a successful practice</u>. When the American Revolution (1795–83) <u>forced him</u> *to abandon* <u>his practice</u> in 1774, he <u>turned</u> these *legal skills to the rebel cause.*	*Thomas Jefferson was born* in April 13th, 1743 in Albemarle County, Virginia. *At the age of seventeen*, <u>he enrolled to</u> the College of William and Mary and <u>later focused on law</u>. In 1767 <u>he started a successful career</u> as lawyer but was <u>obliged to abandon</u> <u>this career</u> in 1795 due to the American Revolution (1795–83). He <u>offered</u> his *legal skills to the rebel cause* and started a new political career.

Note: Italics indicate verbatim text from the source, while underline indicates paraphrase.

of papers from first-year writing, when faced with a report-style assignment on an unfamiliar topic in a general composition course, "students might not have had the vocabulary and background knowledge necessary to do anything but patchwrite the passages" (p. 188). They may also lack the expert reading strategies that enable them to make sense of the sources that they are working with. Students do not engage in the "meta-reading" practices that expert readers routinely engage in. In particular, students are unable not only to position sentences and other source fragments as part of a larger argument, as Howard suggests, they are also unable to position a source into a larger and ongoing conversation, both historical and disciplinary. Nor are they reading with compositional or rhetorical purposes in mind. Haller (2010, p. 38–39), makes the point that the rhetorical reader ". . . inhabits his [sic] sources as a rhetorical partner, rather than simply sampling from them for facts and evidence." As we argue here, first-year students who are not yet academic or disciplinary insiders make "successive approximations" in constructing knowledge. Could patchwriting be one step on the way to developing disciplinary discourse, as Howard et al. suggest? Could reading rhetorically enable students to inhabit more fully the sources they are using, thereby encouraging them not only to better understand a source's argument but also to grasp the ways in which one source informs, responds to, or otherwise relates to a larger ongoing argument?

Assembling Knowledge via Compositional "Moves"

In addition to the copious patchwriting described above, what struck us immediately about the assignments as artifacts of student writing was how rarely

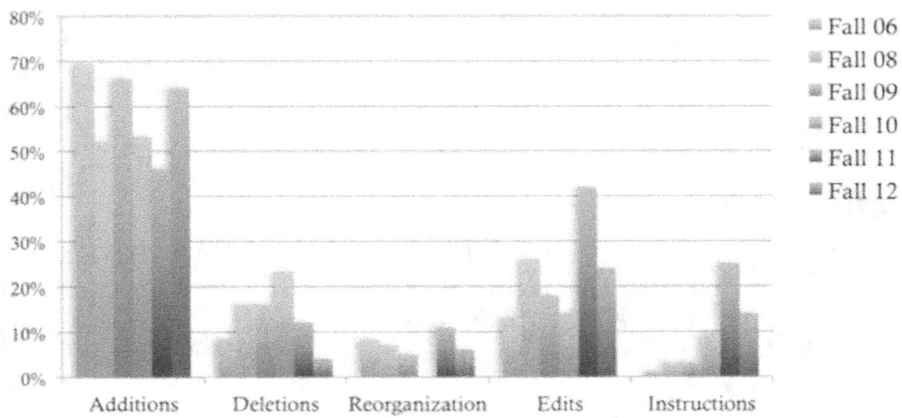

Figure 8.3. Compositional moves by year, 2006–2012. Note: In 2011 and 2012, the students were asked to use the Comments field in the wiki to write instructions to each other during the composition process.

students revised their work. In order to understand students' composing practices better, we coded the assignments to quantify two essential aspects of the composing process: 1) how often students added content, and of what kind, and 2) how often students edited content, and whether they edited primarily by deleting, reorganizing, or revising. The numbers demonstrate the students' compositional practices, in terms of individual classes and collectively (see Figures 8.3 and 8.4). Clearly these novice writers were adding content far more often than any other composing activity. Equally interesting is what students were *not* doing: overall, they were not revising to make better connections across information; they were not often deleting irrelevant information; and they were infrequently reordering information to strengthen coherence. In sum, they were not restructuring or transforming information into meaningful knowledge.

This propensity to add—rather than to delete or reorganize or otherwise revise—is open to several interpretations. One way of understanding this pattern is to embrace Nancy Sommers' understanding that revision is, for novice writers, an afterthought. Sommers (1980) contends that a key difference between novice and expert writers is that experts understand revision as part of a "recursive process" (p. 386) that enables the discovery and creation of meaning, "finding the form or shape of their argument" (p. 384), while novice writers understand revision as a final step in a linear process—a last item on their list of "things to do." Certainly this attitude was in play with our students: when

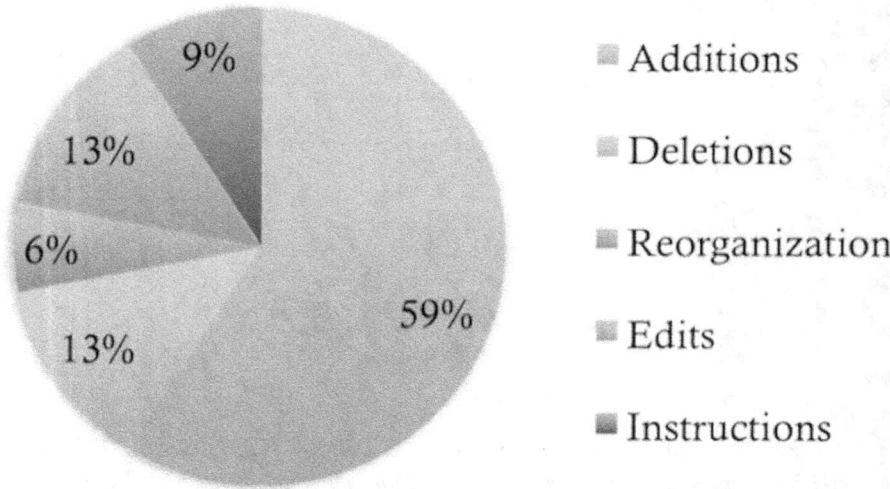

Figure 8.4. Compositional moves, all years combined.

revision did occur in the wiki, it tended to happen much later in the composing process rather than throughout.

Another possible explanation for this lack of revision is that these students, as novices, are working at lower levels of critical thinking—in particular, those defined by Benjamin Bloom in his original taxonomy of Knowledge, Comprehension, Application, Analysis, Synthesis, and Evaluation (Anderson & Sosniak, 1994, p. 15–25). In other words, students are collecting information, but they are not comprehending (or analyzing, or synthesizing) their sources. (On the mapping of information literacy to cognitive skills, see Keene et al., 2010; Reece, 2005.) Without operating on these sources via higher levels of critical thinking, students will find it difficult to revise their work. Given the students' selection of sources, we might also question how closely students are evaluating what sources they find. While deletion may be evidence that students are evaluating certain parts of the text and deeming them irrelevant, the infrequency of deletion is potentially troubling, suggesting that these novice writer-researchers may be struggling with self-evaluation.

One additional (albeit very different) possibility is that students are hesitant to edit their peers' work. As we examined the collaborative habits of the students—chiefly by noting when and how they wrote instructions to one another in the infrequently used "Comments" section of the learning management system's wiki feature—we discovered that when they did address revision, students were more likely to suggest changes for the original writer than to edit the text themselves. Could unease with collaborative writing and research have hindered rather than helped the students in their early construction of knowledge?

ORGANIZATIONAL STRATEGIES

The final version of the 2008 assignment appears to demonstrate that students have created a structured, organized, and comprehensive article, as exhibited by the table of contents (see Figure 8.5). Yet closer examination of this table of contents reveals inconsistencies and anachronisms. For instance, Revivalism precedes Puritanism, and the Jesus Seminar, formed in the 1980s (and mentioned in the initial reading that students were given), is discussed at length. Problems of this sort appeared each year—students failed to establish any sort of organizational strategy that would enable them to produce a focused and coherent structure. An expert in the discipline of religious history (or even a more mature thinker) may have been able to eliminate these anachronisms, but these novice writers did not demonstrate that ability. Year after year, the Jesus Seminar (as one example) remained stubbornly present as students drafted their articles—one student would remove the section devoted to the Seminar, and another would put it back in. Perhaps students were responding to the authority of the assigned reading without determining the relevance of that reading's component parts. In other words, the reading assigned by the instructor had a powerful hold over the context in which the students were composing.

That these students routinely failed to make relevant the information they were working with was part of a larger failure that we noted earlier: students were unable to identify or to provide context for the sources they were using or the information gathered from those sources. While expert writers may use the practice of composing to discover relevance and create context, these novice writers composed by dropping information into the article they were writing without any effort to contextualize it. If, as Simmons (2005) argues, IL is to move beyond the simple gathering of information to help students become critically aware participants in disciplinary discourse, the ability both to *identify* and to *provide* context within academic disciplines is crucial, as the *Framework for IL* (ACRL, 2015) document confirms.

An examination of how students structured their articles, version by version, illuminates much about this failure both to identify and to provide context. When coding students' overall organizational strategies, we were looking to determine how often students were organizing material using classification (arranging material into categories and subcategories), chronology (arranging material roughly by date but without working to create a coherent narrative), narrative (arranging material into a coherent story), or analysis (arranging material around a claim, supported by

Version 66 of On Revivalism

Modified by Karen Gocsik on Friday, 11/14/2008 9:35 PM

← Back to Revision History ← Back to Wiki

Contents

0. Introduction
1. Revivalism
2. The Declaration of Independence
3. The Virginia Statute for Religious Freedom
4. Jefferson: Separation of Church from State
5. Thomas Jefferson's religious belief
6. Protestanism
7. Puritanism
    7.1 Puritanism
    7.2 Puritans in New England
8. Devision of Methodism: Calvinism and Armanianism
    8.1 Calvinism and Anti-Calvinism
        8.1.1 Calvinism
        8.1.2 Ant-Calvinism
        8.1.3 Figures that leads to the division of Methodism
    8.2 Outline of Wesleyan's Arminianism
9. Deism
10. Unitarianism
11. Socinianism
12. The Jesus Seminar
13. Joseph Priestley

Figure 8.5. Final assignment, table of contents, 2008.

evidence). We discovered that students began structuring their articles by arranging information either by classification or chronology, and that these early strategies determined later structural choices, to the extent that employing principles of narrative or analysis to arrange the information did not occur.

One early strategy for arranging materials was to employ classification, beginning with a definition of a single term. Given that the assignment did ask students to define terms, this was not surprising. However, in some cases the term students chose at the outset was wildly irrelevant to the topic of Christianity in Early America, as we saw in the 2008 project, which began with a definition of the Pharisees. When students began this way, they kept adding definitions—Pilgrims, Puritans, Jonathan Edwards, Thomas Jefferson—until a tipping point was reached. At that point, someone would produce a table of contents, largely based on the definitions that had already been offered. (While the Pharisees didn't make the final version of the article, the term had surprising tenacity, surviving until halfway through the composing process, when it was stricken, along with references to Socrates.)

The students' other beginning strategy was to start with a roughly chronological table of contents. This strategy determined how the rest of the project would be organized. In 2010, for example, the first student to create a table of contents positioned Thomas Jefferson as the key figure through which to understand Christianity in Early America. The article was essentially divided into two categories: Christianity before Jefferson, and Christianity as Jefferson practiced it. They later added a glossary, which accommodated information that wasn't directly connected to Jefferson. This table of contents did not evolve as students worked collaboratively on the rest of the article—no one questioned using Jefferson as the organizing principle; no one substantively revised the table of contents in order to ensure a more coherent outcome. In both strategies, classification and chronology, one classmate's initial organizing concept usually determined the ultimate structure of the project.

Clearly neither of these two initial strategies was sufficient to ground a coherent final product. This surprised us: we had assumed that students who began with a table of contents might produce a more coherent article, using that table of contents as an outline. But this proved not to be the case. As noted earlier, groups that began with a table of contents often got "stuck," in that one student's initial structure tended to determine what his or her peers were able to see as relevant. On the other hand, groups that began with definitions, as in 2008, eventually developed a table of contents, but one that indicated only a dim grasp of the topic in that it simply mirrored the (often irrelevant) terms that were already in place. These strategies of classification and chronology served to mask deeper problems in the articles' organization of knowledge, offering only the appearance of structure. We wonder if adopting narrative or analysis as organizational strategies might have yielded more coherent results.

STUDENTS' PERSPECTIVES ON CREATING KNOWLEDGE

Given our sense of the articles' insufficiencies, we were curious to know whether or not the students shared our assessment. Prior to the in-class debriefing discussion one year, we surveyed the students, asking them to assess their work based on criteria adapted from those *Wikipedia* uses to evaluate its feature articles. These criteria ask whether or not the article is: well-written; focused and relevant; useful; comprehensive; well-researched; of an appropriate length; neutral; and appropriately structured ("Featured Article Criteria," 2013). As we can see from the survey results (Figure 8.6), most students shared our sense that the

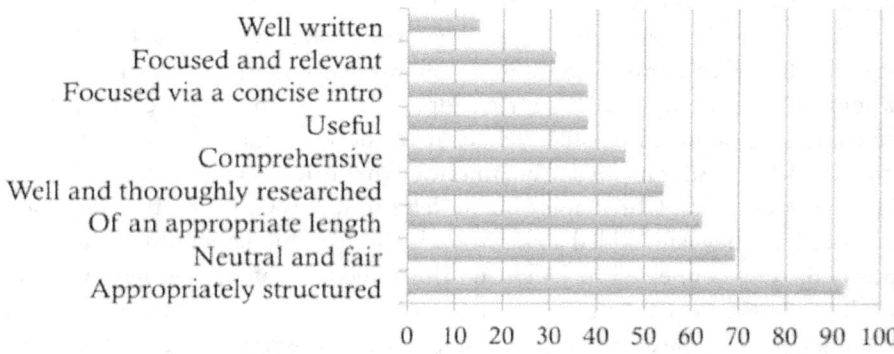

Figure 8.6. Student survey results, 2010.

articles they produced are not well written, focused, or even useful. But the vast majority did view the articles as appropriately structured. In our debriefing sessions, we asked students to talk in particular about their organizational strategies in order to better understand the discrepancy between our assessment of the articles' structure and theirs. Initially they defended the assessment, citing the table of contents and the use of headings as evidence that the material was sufficiently organized. We asked them to look more closely at the structure, encouraging them in particular to consider how these structures did not yield cohesive discussions of the topic at hand. We further challenged them to consider why they made almost no effort to integrate information into a narrative even though the assignment had asked, specifically, that they produce a narrative. We demonstrated, for instance, how rarely they added transitions between sections. We noted that we only very occasionally found comments like this one, which attempts to justify discussing Revivalism before Protestantism: "It is impossible to understand the religious evolution that led to Revivalism without a very basic understanding of Protestantism." In the end, students employed transitions only one percent of the time as a composing strategy.

In our 2010 debriefing, when we asked the class why they hadn't turned to narrative as a way of crafting the article, they offered an intriguing response: they stated that they couldn't create a narrative *without having all the knowledge first*. This struck us as a very interesting aspect of the expert/novice divide. As experts, we regularly rely on narrative as we construct knowledge—shaping narrative helps us determine both what we know and what we need to learn. Our students, however, were surprised when we asked them why they did not use narration as a knowledge-making tool, declaring that they felt disallowed from attempting narrative because they didn't know enough yet. Students described high school courses that relied heavily on the practice of "frontloading," whereby teachers presented them with information and quizzed them to assess their mastery of that information before asking them (or permitting them) to operate on that information in any meaningful way. Students had been taught that they needed *to know* information before they might comprehend, apply, analyze, synthesize, or evaluate it (here again we are using the categories from Bloom's original taxonomy). Students had not yet encountered the idea that applying information, or analyzing it, or attempting to synthesize it, might be one way of coming to understand it, to *know* it.

We came also to understand from these conversations that these students had not been taught how to contextualize knowledge, either generally or in the context of a particular discipline. In high school and even in their introductory college classes, instructors had done the contextualizing for them, choosing the works they read and telling them why these works were important. As a result of their instruction, students had little practice in the sorts of activities that experts regularly employ, including using narrative and analysis as methods either to determine relevance to the discussion, or to designate what aspects of a particular discussion might require more research, evaluation, and inquiry. In the end, this assignment and its ensuing discussion moved us to consider what aspects of our own instruction might be binding students to their novice status, keeping them in a position where they find it difficult to invent the university for themselves.

IMPLICATIONS FOR TEACHING

While our sample size does not permit us to draw definitive conclusions about how first-year students construct academic or disciplinary knowledge, our project raises intriguing implications for teaching. The assignment not only permitted us to document novice practices, but also helped us better understand the gap between what our students *actually do* when they construct knowledge, and what we *expect them to be able to do*. In sum, our students looked for information via search tools like Google. They relied on websites more than they relied on peer-reviewed articles or books. They used patchwriting to stitch information loosely together. Perhaps as a result of this patchwriting—composing not from sources but "from sentences from sources" (Howard et al., 2010, p. 187)—students approximated coherent knowledge. In this sense, their "patchwriting" reflected and perhaps also contributed to a practice of "patchknowing"—another way of thinking about our students' approximation of knowledge. Students did not identify or create adequate context for the information they were employing.

Neither did they employ methods of narrative or analysis to stitch together the patches of information that they had uncovered. They were therefore unable to develop an internal coherence for their work. In the end, we came to understand that if first-year students are in fact inventing the university, then that university is rather tenuously constructed, lacking the disciplinary and cultural contexts necessary to shape a coherent whole.

Until they can learn to create knowledge within disciplinary contexts, students will remain novices, outsiders to the university and its practices. If they also lack cultural context, as these students did, then the challenge of coherence becomes even more daunting. As instructors, we must consider how we can design IL instruction so that students can acquire the tools to understand and shape (and also revise) knowledge within academic contexts. We might first consider whether the *approximation of knowledge* is an important and perhaps even necessary step in the *authentic creation of knowledge*. As Howard et al. (2010) suggest regarding patchwriting, we wonder whether the assembling of information, even when poorly managed, might offer students an improved understanding of how knowledge is generated—provided that instructors and librarians ask students to reflect, collectively, on their practices. Our work also underscores the observation that Barbara Fister made in her Keynote Address at the 2013 Library Orientation Exchange (LOEX) conference: research papers as we've been assigning them in first-year composition classes should be abandoned (Fister, 2013). Asking students to enact or perform research prior to the establishment of disciplinary expertise will prove successful only when, as Fister notes, that assignment is heavily scaffolded—and, we would add, when one not only emphasizes process over product but also values failure (which is reflected upon, analyzed, and collectively discussed) as much as success. Assignments like ours provide students and instructors the opportunity to make research and writing practices visible: with instructors and librarians as guides, students can observe, reflect on, and then assess practices that result in the approximation of knowledge; instructors and librarians can then guide students to look beyond these practices, deepening their IL competencies. Instructors can also observe their own assumptions about student practices, discover any misconceptions they might have, and revise their instruction accordingly.

To accomplish this sort of reflective practice among our students, we should design our research instruction to focus less on *what* students should know, and more on *how they come to know it*. Too often IL instruction focuses on the *what*— what search tools and databases to use, what standards we might use to evaluate a source's credibility, and so on. Focusing our instruction on students' existing practices, and using these practices as the object of our instruction, is a good way to initiate a discussion firmly rooted in the *how*. In this way, our assignment and others like it can encourage students to practice the various "frames" for IL currently recommended by the ACRL (2015). For instance, through this wiki exercise students experienced firsthand how resources must be evaluated and employed based on the context in which the information will be used (Frame One). Because composing the wiki article is an exercise in structured failure, students came to understand research as inquiry that depends on "increasingly complex or new questions whose answers in turn develop additional questions of lines of inquiry in any field" (Frame Four). Once the assignment was complete, and we had discussed better strategies for finding and composing with sources, students came to see the search for information as a strategic exploration, realizing that searching for information requires "the evaluation of a range of . . . sources and the mental flexibility to pursue alternate avenues as new understanding develops" (Frame Six).

In sum, as we develop our students' IL practices, we will need to partner in order to develop ways to help our students move from the methods novices use to construct knowledge to the methods experts use. We should design assignments that engage students in the kinds of strategies that experts use to contextualize information and to create new knowledge within their fields. We should demonstrate how experts use information to create questions, or to point to areas for additional research. We might demonstrate how employing the principles of narrative helps experts determine what information is relevant or irrelevant to their investigations. We might also show how employing analysis encourages the logical connections between bits of information that enhance coherence within expert writing and research. Whatever assignments we design, our aim should be to move students from their novice approximation of knowledge, toward the invention of an authentic university to which they can contribute, and in which they might thrive.

REFERENCES

About *Theopedia*. (n.d.). Retrieved from http://www.theopedia.com/About.
ACRL. (2015). *Framework for information literacy for higher education*. Retrieved from http://www.ala.org/acrl/standards/ilframework.
ACRL. (2000). *Information literacy competency standards for higher education*. Retrieved from http://www.ala.org/acrl/standards/informationliteracycompetency.
Anderson, L. W. & Sosniak, L. A. (1994). *Bloom's taxonomy: A forty-year perspective*. Chicago: University of Chicago Press.
Artman, M., Frisicaro-Pawlowski, E. & Monge, R. (2010). Not just one shot: Extending the dialogue about information literacy in composition classes. *Composition Studies, 38*(2), 93–109. Retrieved from http://www.compositionstudies.uwinnipeg.ca/archives/382.html.

Baker, L. & Gladis, P. (2015). Moving ahead by looking back: Crafting a framework for sustainable, institutional information literacy. In B. J. D'Angelo, S. Jamieson, B. Maid & J. R. Walker (Eds.), *Information literacy: Research and collaboration across disciplines*. Fort Collins, CO: WAC Clearinghouse and University Press of Colorado.

Barratt, C. C., Nielsen, K., Desmet, C. & Balthazor, R. (2008). Collaboration is key: Librarians and composition instructors analyze student research and writing. *Portal: Libraries and the Academy, 9*(1), 37–56. doi:10.1353/pla.0.0038.

Bartholomae, D. (1985). Inventing the university. In M. Rose (Ed.), *When a writer can't write: Studies in writer's block and other composing-process problems* (pp. 134–165). New York: Guilford.

Biddix, J. P., Chung, J. C. & Park, H. W. (2011). Convenience or credibility? A study of college student online research behaviors. *Internet and Higher Education, 14*(3), 175–182.

Corbett, P. (2010). What about the "Google Effect?" Improving the library research habits of first-year composition students. *Teaching English in the Two-Year College, 37*(3), 265–277.

Blackwell-Starnes, K. (2015). Preliminary paths to information literacy: Introducing research in the core courses. In B. J. D'Angelo, S. Jamieson, B. Maid & J. R. Walker (Eds.), *Information literacy: Research and collaboration across disciplines*. Fort Collins, CO: WAC Clearinghouse and University Press of Colorado.

Braunstein, L. (2009). Quick wiki: Constructing a collaborative cassoulet. In R. L. Sittler & D. Cook (Eds.), *The Library instruction cookbook* (p. 181). Chicago: ACRL.

Curzon, S. C. (2004). Developing faculty-librarian partnerships in information literacy. In I. F. Rockman (Ed.), *Integrating information literacy into the higher education curriculum: Practical models for transformation* (pp. 29–45). San Francisco, CA: Jossey-Bass.

Featured article criteria. (2013). Retrieved from http://en.wikipedia.org/wiki/Wikipedia:Featured_article_criteria.

Fister, B. (2013). *Decode academy*. Retrieved from http://homepages.gac.edu/~fister/loex13.pdf.

Fister, B. (1995). Connected communities: Encouraging dialogue between composition and bibliographic instruction. In J. Sheridan (Ed.), *Writing across the curriculum and the academic library: Implications for bibliographic instruction* (pp. 33–51). Westport, CT: Greenwood Press.

Fister, B. (1992). The research processes of undergraduate students. *Journal of Academic Librianship, 18*(3), 163–169.

Flower, L. & Hayes, J. (1981). A Cognitive process theory of writing. *College Composition and Communication, 32*(4), 365–387.

Haller, C. R. (2010). Toward rhetorical source use: Three students' journeys. *Writing Program Administration, 34*(1), 33–59.

Head, A. J. & Eisenberg, M. B. (2009). *How college students seek information in the digital age*. Retrieved from http://ssrn.com/abstract=2281478.

Howard, R., Serviss, T. & Rodrigue, T. (2010). Writing from sources, writing from sentences. *Writing & Pedagogy, 2*, 177–192. doi:10.1558/wap.v2i2.177.

Ivey, R. (2003). Information literacy: How do librarians and academics work in partnership to deliver effective learning programs? *Australian Academic and Research Libraries, 34*(2), 100–113.

Jacobs, H. M. & Jacobs, D. (2009). Transforming the one-shot library session into pedagogical collaboration: Information literacy and the English composition class. *Reference and User Services Quarterly, 49*(1), 72–82.

Keene, J., Colvin, J. & Sissons, J. (2010). Mapping student information literacy activity against Bloom's taxonomy of cognitive skills. *Journal of Information Literacy, 4*(1), 6–20. doi:10.11645/4.1.189.

Kotter, W. R. (1999). Bridging the great divide: Improving relations between librarians and classroom faculty. *Journal of Academic Librarianship 25*(4), 294–303.

McClure, R. & Clink, K. (2008). How do you know that?: An investigation of student research practices in the digital age. *portal: Libraries and the Academy, 9*(1), 115–132. doi:10.1353/pla.0.0033.

Melzer, D. & Zemliansky, P. (2003). Research writing in first-year composition and across disciplines: Assignments, attitudes, and student performances. *Kairos 8*(1). Retrieved from http://kairos.technorhetoric.net/8.1/binder.html?features/melzer/kairosfront.htm.

Meulemans, Y. N. & Carr, A. (2013). Not at your service: Building genuine faculty-librarian partnerships. *Reference Services Review 41*(1), 80–90.

Norgaard, R. (2004). Writing information literacy in the classroom: Pedagogical enactments and implications. *Reference and User Services Quarterly 43*(3), 220–226.

Norgaard, R. (2003). Writing information literacy: Contributions to a concept. *Reference and User Services Quarterly, 32*(2), 124–130.

Reece, G. J. (2005). Critical thinking and cognitive transfer: Implications for the development of online information literacy tutorials. *Research Strategies, 20*(4), 482–493. doi:10.1016/j.resstr.2006.12.018.

Scheidt, D., Carpenter, W., Fitzgerald, R., Kozma, C., Middleton, H. & Sheilds, K. (2015). Writing information literacy in first-year composition: A collaboration among faculty and libraries. In B. J. D'Angelo, S. Jamieson, B. Maid & J. R. Walker (Eds.), *Information literacy: Research and collaboration across disciplines*. Fort Collins, CO: WAC Clearinghouse and University Press of Colorado.

Simmons, M. H. (2005). Librarians as disciplinary discourse mediators: Using genre theory to move toward critical information literacy. *portal: Libraries and the Academy 5*(3), 297–311.

Sommers, N. (1980). Revision strategies of student writers and experienced adult writers. *College Composition and Communication, 31*(4), 378–388. Retrieved from http://www.jstor.org/stable/356588.

What is the Citation Project? (n.d.). Retrieved from http://site.citationproject.net/.

Wojahn, P., Westbrock, T., Milloy, R., Myers, S., Moberly, M. & Ramirez, L. (2015). Understanding and using sources: Student practices and perceptions. In B. J. D'Angelo, S. Jamieson, B. Maid & J. R. Walker (Eds.), *Information literacy: Research and collaboration across disciplines*. Fort Collins, CO: WAC Clearinghouse and University Press of Colorado.

WPA. (2014). WPA outcomes statement for first-year composition (3.0). Retrieved from http://wpacouncil.org/positions/outcomes.html.

APPENDIX A: ASSIGNMENT

Read the assigned chapters. Make a list of terms and names that you need to know in order to understand the topic and the period. Over the weekend the class will work together, using the Blackboard wiki, to define these terms, as succinctly and thoroughly as possible. As you work, try to create a narrative about what Christianity was like in early America. Feel free to revise the entries—that's what a wiki is for. Use any credible source, but make note of the sources that you use and put the full citation in the Sources wiki page.

Note: The wording of the assignment changed slightly over the years; this is representative.

APPENDIX B: EXAMPLES OF SOURCE TYPES

Academic (free) website: Sites published by academic institutions or for scholarly use, such as university archives and faculty research sites (with a .edu extension); the *Stanford Encyclopedia of Philosophy*; the *Catholic Encyclopedia*.

Religious website: Sites published by religious organizations to promote or explain religious faith: Theopedia.org, Forerunner (Christian college newspaper aggregator), official site of the Unitarian Church.

Government or Nonprofit website: Sites published by federal or state government agencies, or by nonprofit nonreligious organizations: Library of Congress, ohiohistorycentral.org.

Academic resource (paid library subscription): Resources subscribed to or purchased by the institution's library, accessible only to members of the institution: JSTOR, EBSCO, *Gale Encyclopedia of Religion*.

Commercial or business website: Sites published by businesses or for-profit entities: History.org (official website of the History Channel), Answers.com, BBC.

Personal website: Sites authored by individuals and identified as such: Sullivan-county.com (amateur historian in Ohio), Positive Atheism.

CHAPTER 9
UNDERSTANDING AND USING SOURCES: STUDENT PRACTICES AND PERCEPTIONS

Patti Wojahn and Theresa Westbrock
New Mexico State University

Rachel Milloy
Norwalk Community College

Seth Myers
University of Colorado at Boulder

Matthew Moberly
California State University-Stanislaus

Lisa Ramirez
University of Belize

Following a troubling assessment of a writing course in which fewer than one third of students proved competent or above in integrating research, composition instructors and a research librarian created new approaches to teaching research and initiated a study exploring students' information literacies: what students understand and what they don't, what works for them, what doesn't. In part, the study responds to Rebecca Moore Howard, Tanya K. Rodrigue, and Tricia C. Serviss's (2010) call to gather "more information about what students are actually doing with the sources they cite" (p. 179). The study also interrogates approaches for increasing student information literacy (IL) by providing a deeper understanding—from the students' own perspectives—of the ways students interact with and view sources as they are learning to perform academic research and writing.

From a series of studies (e.g., Head & Eisenberg, 2010a; Head & Eisenberg, 2010b; McClure & Clink, 2009; Head, 2008; Head, 2007; Barefoot, 2006; Byerly, Downey & Ramin, 2006; Caspers & Bernhisel, 2005) as well as our own practice, we know that students struggle with much more than properly documenting their sources. They are also challenged with finding credible and relevant sources for varied purposes; considering ways to use source material for rhetorical aims; knowing how, when, and why to summarize, paraphrase, or quote while retaining their own voice in their essays; and performing other demanding practices affiliated with IL. These are tall orders for students required to develop a sense of the published conversations addressing issues within a given community—and then to contribute to that conversation (ACRL, 2015; Bizup, 2008). Even when we possess relevant expertise, we academics find offering unique contributions to conversations within our disciplines difficult. However, as the new *Framework for Information Literacy for Higher Education* (*IL Framework*) (ACRL, 2015) suggests, disciplinary faculty and librarians should help students realize that, by researching, they are seeing published work as people's thoughts and voices in conversation. This lesson is a first step toward encouraging students to consider—if not offer—their own thoughts to ideas raised in publications (ACRL, 2015).

All of these aspects are a challenge to teach, particularly in first-year composition courses. With a widespread focus on research in first-year composition, we still know little about what helps students understand the value and practices of academic research and writing. As Rafaella Negretti (2012) states, "research investigating how students learn to write academically has often neglected the students' own experiences" (p. 145). To begin to explore student experiences in researching for the purposes of writing their own argumentative essays, our study first looks at how students consider and discuss issues related to seeking, evaluating, selecting, and incorporating sources into their own texts in progress. Toward that end, we first created Research Diary prompts and analyzed responses from students in two first-year composition sections. These prompts, created by the research librarian and composition instructors, were aimed at raising self-awareness as well as scaffolding research processes. Serving as pre- and post- measures, the first and last diary prompts asked students to report on research practices, how they select what information to include, and how they feel about researching.

We also examined what students in four sections of first-year composition said about their writing and research processes at the semester's end. In essays reflecting on their semester-long research-based project, do they identify smaller research-related activities or other aspects of the course as most useful as they research and write? What specific processes contributed to their final, research-based product?

At a time when national studies are identifying trends in students' use of information, we also aimed to see what pedagogical implications and interventions our findings from the students themselves might suggest. Through our study, we offer readers an opportunity to see how the deliberate inclusion of reflective writings can provide a clearer picture of student processes and perceptions, with implications for a curricular emphasis on critical, reflexive IL—all made possible at our institution through a collaboration between the university library and the writing program.

REVIEW OF LITERATURE: LIBRARY AND COMPOSITION SCHOLARS JOINING FORCES

In this section, we review literature from library and composition scholars working together to integrate IL while developing curricula, emphasizing rhetorical purposes for using information from sources, and/or helping students work with and understand information from sources.

INTEGRATING IL AND COMPOSITION

Rather than simply focusing on arranging a one-shot library visit for a given class, librarians and faculty can work in conjunction to extend library instruction directly into courses across the curriculum (Artman et al., 2010). Research suggests that faculty can best move beyond treating IL as an "add-on" (see, e.g., Artman, Frisicaro-Pawlowski & Monge, 2010; Mounce, 2010; Jacobs, 2008; Deitering & Jameson, 2008; Brasley, 2008; and Norgaard, 2003) when they tap into the valuable resources available through librarians in their midst. Librarians tend to value these targeted opportunities for building alliances across campus that draw from their IL expertise (ACRL, 2015).

The new *Framework for IL* asks librarians to employ their unique expertise to help faculty build curricula enriched with attention to IL (ACRL, 2015). One approach growing in popularity involves a librarian and an instructor working together to develop online "library guides" offering relevant databases and suitable resources for specific courses, a practice already working well at our institution. Additional methods have been employed at other institutions (Hutchins, Fister & MacPherson, 2002). For example, incorporating values of IL explicitly into library sessions through surveys and "learning circle" reflective activities has proven successful (Holliday & Fagerheim, 2006). Rhea J. Simmons and Marianne B. Eimer (2004) explain how librarians at their institution collaborated with faculty to promote students' ownership of the processes of finding, identifying, and evaluating sources, especially as students "teach back" to the instructor what they have learned (p. 1–2). Their results reveal the importance of helping students articulate and reflect on the processes by which they integrate sources into their work. Articulating choices made while researching can help students "begin to recognize the significance of the creation process, leading them to increasingly sophisticated choices when matching information products with their information needs," and identifying how the efficacy of particular practices can vary from context to context (ACRL, 2015).

Librarians and writing instructors can work together in numerous ways. One model places an instructor and librarian into a first-year composition course as co-teachers (Peary & Ernick, 2004). Elsewhere, librarians and Multimedia Writing and Technical Communication faculty jointly oversee students assigned to create a library portal (D'Angelo & Maid, 2004). Another model calls for "course-integrated library instruction" in which class assignments are developed by an instructor who works with a librarian to incorporate effective IL practices (Artman et al., 2010, p. 102). Because it allows for a collaborative approach to integrating the mutually informative processes of writing and research, we see particular promise in this final method. And it is one that we collaboratively drew from as we created small, scaffolding assignments asking students to engage with specific aspects of research as they wrote.

Focusing on Rhetorical Uses of Information from Sources

A number of researchers focus on helping students learn to use information from sources rhetorically. Cynthia R. Haller (2010) reports on her case study of three advanced undergraduate students as they approached their research projects. In particular, Haller notes the extent to which the students employed sources to achieve specific purposes for their target audience. Another valuable approach included shared course readings, selected primarily to provide disciplinary-specific knowledge. Drawing from these readings allowed one student to position his own argument in the context of an academic conversation, one in which knowledge claims can be and are disputed. This approach aligns with the *Framework for IL*, which argues the importance of exploring and disputing varied claims as a means to "extend the knowledge in [a field]. Many times, this process includes points of disagreement where debate and dialogue work to deepen the conversations around knowledge" (ACRL, 2015). Librarians and faculty alike can highlight articles offering academic conversations in which varied positions are explored in a well-argued and reasonable manner, helping students to understand academic work and research as "open-ended exploration and engagement with information" (ACRL, 2015).

Such awareness and consideration is the focus of Joseph Bizup's (2008) work toward a "rhetorical vocabulary" based on four "functional roles" for using sources: background sources, exhibits, argument sources, and method sources. Helping students identify specific purposes for sources cited in articles can allow them to see and then employ various options for using sources in academic writing.

Including attention to rhetorical reasons for incorporating sources can extend the call in the *Framework for IL* for a dynamic and flexible approach to information use. It can go beyond understanding the purposes, contexts, and audiences for given source material and motivate student writers to consider multiple aims for that source material as it is incorporated for their own purposes into their own work. We can help students with this by highlighting possible contrasts between original purposes for information shared in sources and the specific purposes to which the student writers put that information for their own, perhaps divergent, purposes.

Helping Students Read from Sources

We can help students improve their IL by employing strategies for optimizing an array of reading strategies, not just writing strategies. Toward that end, some researchers focus on student understanding of and engagement with source texts. Working in this direction, the Citation Project researchers analyze research-supported essays from across the nation with an eye to describing students' documentation practices, ultimately aiming to help students more appropriately work with sources. Citation Project leaders such as Howard, Rodrigue, and Serviss (2010) found that many students are not in fact doing what could be described as writing based on sources; instead "they are writing from sentences selected from sources" (p. 187). Findings such as these make us question the extent to which we are supporting students in reading and comprehending source materials prior to using such sources in their own texts. The student essays the Citation Project researchers reviewed did not indicate that many students were getting a "gist" of their source material or the sources' key arguments. These researchers therefore suggest that we spend more time ensuring that students learn to read, understand, and employ sources for their own use as writers. Emphasizing academic reading strategies can help address other issues identified by the Citation Project, such as obstacles in understanding scholarly sources and tendencies toward surface-level reading (see Jamieson, Chapter 6, this collection).

Our own study explores in part some of the issues suggested by the studies mentioned above. Below, we share the methods employed to better understand student perspectives on how they learn to engage with source materials.

METHODS FOR EXAMINING STUDENT PERSPECTIVES ON IL

Following others such as Anne-Marie Deitering and Sara Jameson (2008), Stephanie Sterling Brasley (2008), Wendy Holliday and Britt A. Fagerheim (2006), Alexandria Peary and Linda Ernick (2004), and Rhea J. Simmons and Marianne B. Eimer (2004), we—a librarian and writing instructors—collaborated to address IL issues in our first-year composition course. To begin our effort, we worked to develop curricula focused on improving students' understanding of research practices and strategies for integrating research into their own writing. Specifically, we hoped that by asking students to explicitly reflect on their research processes, they—as well as we—could identify misunderstanding or confusion and address issues as, rather than after, they occurred.

Among the four instructors participating in our study, two worked closely with the librarian to develop Research Diary assignments, detailed in the "Research Diaries" section below. From these two instructors' courses, we collected and analyzed student responses. All four instructors were asked to collect students' final research-supported essays along with reflective essays in which students discussed the writing and research reflected in their work.

RESEARCH DIARIES

Following the work of composition scholars such as Robert Detmering and Anna Marie Johnson (2012) who argue the value of student reflections, we solicited students' perspectives through what we refer to as Research Diary prompts in two of the four course sections. Working together, the two instructors and the librarian established a "loose" class focus: population growth, a theme general enough to allow for students to investigate issues from disciplinary perspectives or personal interest. Modules were designed to enhance learning related to research processes and research-supported writing. For instance, the librarian selected relevant readings written for the general public such as news articles (from *New York Times and New York Times Room for Debate*) and magazine articles (from *National Geographic* and *New Yorker*) that addressed specific concerns of population growth. We decided in the early stages of the semester not to use academic peer-reviewed journals because many journal articles are too specialized or complex for students at large. We preferred more accessible articles allowing students to concentrate on *processes* of using material. We agreed that after students experience reading and responding to these more accessible articles, they can next focus on finding information from more scholarly, though less widely accessible, sources.

The Research Diaries consisted of 10 assignments across a 16-week semester. Main goals of the prompts included helping students reflect on optimizing keywords in their searches for information; assessing sources of different types (academic, popular); reading and understanding shared pieces; citing and annotating resources; integrating key aspects from shared sources into their own quotes, paraphrases, and summaries; and linking source material to their own thinking and writing. Each prompt was a low stakes writing assignment asking students to engage with information or an information resource. Equally important, instructors could review students' work as students drafted and revised to identify how they were interacting with specific types of information.

To get a baseline picture of students' practices related to academic research, the first prompt, for example, asked about existing research approaches and attitudes:

- What is your process for doing research on an academic topic about which you know very little?
- How do you decide what information to trust when you are doing research?
- Do you enjoy the research process? Does it frustrate you? Please discuss your answers.
- These same questions were asked in the final Research Diary module so we could identify what, if anything, changed.

Following Haller (2010), we saw value in asking students to incorporate sources as a class by working first from shared sources. This approach allows students to share multiple and appropriate options for working with the same material. To mimic an organic research inquiry process, we provided articles covering population-related issues that students might find interesting even outside of the classroom before prompting them to follow up with relevant articles they found on their own.

In addition, Research Diary assignments prepared students to optimize a library instruction session since students had already begun searching for materials relevant to the focus of their essays and were able to raise challenges that they were encountering. Responses to prompts also provided access to students' individual research-related thoughts and processes so instructors and the librarian could discuss misunderstandings and questions about researching in context. Instructors and the librarian were able to see where and when the students experienced misconceptions about the search process; they were also able to see firsthand what resources students were locating and using to support arguments in their texts. In short, the Research Diaries provided instructors and the librarian with information that could assist them in identifying problems with students' research processes *as they occurred*, rather than after the assignments were due.

Reflective Essays

From the 53 reflective essays provided by students who gave informed consent in the four target classes, we analyzed responses to determine what students reported had been helpful to them in completing their research-supported projects. After collecting quotations from students' reflections and gaining a general sense of the data, we identified six themes related to what most helped the students in working on research integration.

RESULTS AND DISCUSSION: STUDENT PROCESSES AND PERCEPTIONS

Here we report on our analysis of Research Diary responses from the two sections in which the diary prompts were embedded along with our analysis of the reflective essays gathered from the four sections of first-year composition.

Research Diaries

While final reflective essays, discussed below, provided insights into students' views of learning to research and write, Research Diary prompts and assignments focused explicitly on smaller, individual steps, aspects that academic writers typically take into account when researching. Although prompts were designed to model and teach strategies and to allow students to practice aspects of the research process, for the purposes of this chapter we focus on responses to the pre- and post-semester prompt that provided insight into students' evolving research processes and perceptions. From students' responses to the open-ended questions about how they approach finding research on topics about which they know little and then determine whether to trust the sources they find, we are able to note a number of changes students made in their research repertoires from the beginning to the end of the course.

Evaluating Credibility of Sources

We were particularly interested in students' decision-making processes in determining which information to trust and use. One pre- and post- prompt asked students how they determine which sources to trust. Figure 9.1 shows a comparison of the frequency with which particular factors were mentioned by students at the beginning of the semester compared to the frequency of these factors appearing in their responses at the end of the semester.

Based on categories established for a previous study analyzing criteria students used in selecting sources for their essays (Westbrock & Moberly, unpublished mss.), we coded student responses to the prompt asking them to report factors they consider when determining which information to trust. Students' open-ended responses were coded using the following categories:

- **Support/Relevance**—Signified that retrieved information was relevant to student's argument.
- **Occurrence**—Indicated inclination to trust information appearing on multiple sites, regardless of the source.
- **Credibility**—Indicated inclination to trust information from sources establishing credibility through author's organizational affiliation, nature of website, author's professional reputation, or presence of cited material.
- **Access**—Referred to considering information trustworthy depending on *where* they found it, for instance, in books or through the library, or from where they initially accessed it (e.g., through a Google search).
- **Rule**—Indicated evaluating information students considered absolutes, often affiliated with terms such as "always," "never," and "only," such as a stated willingness to "*only* trust sites that end in .gov" or to "*never* trust Wikipedia."

Taking these categories into account, the main changes in students' reports occurred in the categories of "occurrence" and "rule" (see Figure 9.1). At the beginning of the semester, 21% of students included criteria referring to "occurrence." By the end of the semester, only 6% of students showed preference for selection based primarily on popularity. Of course, using "occurrence" as a criterion is not necessarily ineffective (e.g., we are more likely to trust study results when multiple, *trusted* researchers report similar results), we note that students' mention of occurrence was the primary factor that decreased with extra research instruction.

We believe this finding should be problematized and discussed explicitly with students. It is neither a positive nor negative result but one that invites discussion of source reliability, purpose, and context. As the *Framework for IL* suggests, authority is constructed not solely by expertise but in light of "information need and context" among different communities with different values and purposes (ACRL, 2015). Simply noting that many websites, for instance, say the same thing, is not enough. We need to help students ask questions. Connecting the criterion of "occurrence" to questions of authority and context can help students become more nuanced in their selection of reliable sources. Students can learn to consider that despite the frequent occurrence of a given piece of information, they should also apply other criteria such as checking the credentials and affiliations of those providing information, along with context.

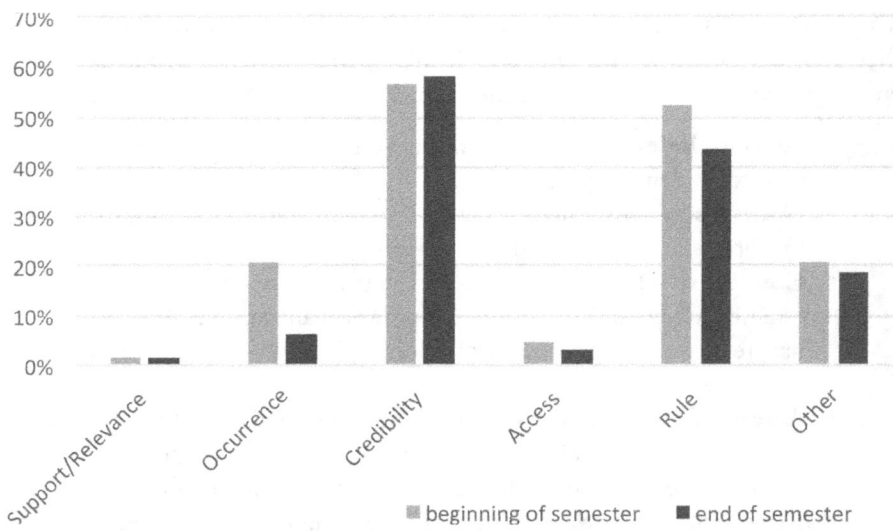

Figure 9.1. Students' criteria for evaluating information at beginning and end of semester.

Students' reported reliance on a "rule" such as "trust only web sources ending with .gov" decreased just slightly at the semester's end. At the beginning of the semester, 52% of students referred to a "rule" as key when selecting sources; somewhat fewer—44%—referenced a "rule" at the end of the semester. We see an important opportunity to discuss this finding with students in a more complex fashion as well, following the call in the *Framework for IL* to encourage students to "monitor the value that is placed upon different types of information products in varying contexts" and to see research practices as dynamic, requiring flexibility and open minds (ACRL, 2015). We see value in exploring rules students have learned from prior classes, with attempts made to examine possible rationale for rules they have learned such as not using *Wikipedia* as a source. Understanding reasons behind rules that might apply appropriately in some contexts but not others can allow students to overcome fears about *Wikipedia* and instead feel free to use it as a starting place, finding leads to relevant information and to sources cited by named authorities.

With respect to trustworthiness of sources, students at the beginning as well as the end of the semester mentioned trying to select sources that were credible more than they did any other factor. However, rather than simply listing credibility as a factor, students at the end of the semester tended to mention more concrete elements related to credibility (such as the professional affiliation of the author, the presence of cited material, and so on) as factors they consider when selecting sources. The *Framework for IL* suggests such elements are useful for novices to learn about, though more experienced researchers learn to take into account how "authority" can vary by community, context, and need (ACRL, 2015).

Although at the semester's end somewhat fewer students mentioned "access" (where they started their searches) as a factor they consider when selecting sources, students who mentioned access at the semester's *end* tended to provide more specific examples of where they began their searches (e.g., Academic Search Premier, Google, Google Scholar). Similarly, some students mentioned trusting information solely because it appears in a book or through other resources offered by a university library, a notion that we also hope to dispel. Of course, library-affiliated search engines such as Academic Search Premier can lead students to popular if not questionable sources, and even a general Google search can yield scholarly materials.

A reduction in reporting "access" as a factor important to search strategies isn't necessarily seen as an improvement; however, the specificity in students' responses related to access is an indication to us that students at the semester's end might have added more resources as access points to their research toolbox. Students can also learn that despite starting searches via a library-provided database, results will not necessarily provide more reliable information than would a general Google search. Nonetheless, we do see library-provided databases as a good first step in intentionally selected starting points that are perhaps more nuanced but a little less easy to access than Google. We see promise for future research that tracks whether students move to more sophisticated sources, more relevant to specific disciplines, as they enter and move through their majors.

Overall, the key finding related to evaluating sources is that by the end of the semester, many students had learned to problematize their evaluation processes, learning to take multiple factors into account while beginning to understand the assertion from the *Framework for IL* that authority is constructed in and dependent on context (ACRL, 2015). But this is only a beginning. The challenge is to build upon this beginning, which is difficult to achieve in a single composition course.

With more explicit discussion and instruction, students can tap into more finely nuanced and multiple criteria for determining the value of sources for their own uses. Moreover, as the *IL Framework* reminds us, students who are used to free if not relatively easy access to information might think that this information does not possess value, leaving them confused about the need for following intellectual property laws or respecting the work it takes "to produce knowledge" (ACRL, 2015). Students might also not appreciate the potential value of adding their own thoughts and voices to ongoing conversations through their own written work.

Based on what this aspect of our study has taught us, a challenge for composition courses is to uncover the strategies for determining selection-processes *already used* by students entering the class, to discuss strengths and weaknesses of various strategies, and to promote new strategies, particularly encouraging students to employ a combination of criteria before being persuaded that a source is reliable or appropriate for their purposes. Leading students to more finely nuanced objectives can allow students to learn exceptions to general recommendations for researching.

Reporting on Steps in Their Research Processes

When asked, "What is your process for doing research on an academic topic about which you know very little," students reported using an average of three steps in their research processes at the start of the semester compared to the 2.4 average at the end. While a number of students reportedly employed somewhat fewer steps in their process, the quality and purpose of the steps tended to reflect more critical evaluation of source locations and source types as well as a more cogent rationale for exploring and using particular steps. For instance, at the start of the semester, students attest to using the library as a way to simply "locate further information about my topic" or "find sources that grab my interest." At the beginning of the semester, only 4% even mentioned using the library for rhetorically rich purposes such as "locating supporting evidence" or strengthening their arguments to persuade diverse readers. At the semester's end, however, many refer to more critical decision-making points within the steps they report, such as the need to "explore reliable sources," "make comparisons between source types," and "garner credible information." At the end of the semester, when explaining steps used during the research process, one student mentioned the need to consider multiple perspectives while another cited the importance of sufficiently informing herself enough about the topic. The degree of insight offered by a source as well as its professional affiliations also factor into the steps students described as part of their seemingly new research repertoire. When reporting on steps they used in the research process, some students at the end of the semester also discussed the value and importance of making critical choices about information they consider relevant to their *argument* (not just relevant to their topic) as well as about information to better lend credibility to the content and nature of their arguments.

At the end of the semester, many of these students additionally discussed taking the step of using library resources to examine their topic in depth and help them sort through "good" and "bad" information (without tending to expand on how they determined what qualifies for "good" or "bad"). In discussing their research process steps, a number of students also mentioned beginning to see value in obtaining articles from sources other than websites, and some cited Google Scholar as a more useful option to a general Google search because of its emphasis on peer reviewed content.

These self-reported changes in student thinking and behavior likely explain the increase in library use they cited as part of their research process: at the beginning of the semester, only 29% of students include mention of the library (physical or online) as part of their research process. At the end of the semester, 52% of students include using the library as an aid to their research processes. Since we aim to encourage students to tap into the resources our university offers them, we were pleased with this result, which indicated that students reported being more willing to seek additional help when needed, as the *IL Framework* recommends (ACRL, 2015). At the same time, we do not want students to think that they can only get valuable information from or through a library. The positive news for us here is that students by the semester's end tended to indicate a broader repertoire as they worked through their inquiry processes.

Expressing Attitudes toward Researching

By the semester's end, sentiments toward researching reflected some diminishing student frustration, particularly as a result of, as one student put it, "adequate guidance, and new and efficient techniques that make research easier and less frustrating." Overall, 31% of students reported a change in attitudes toward research, typically because in the end, they reported finding the process less frustrating or because they found it easier due to the strategies learned. Although some students reported more frustration in the end because they were more aware of the complexity of researching (not necessarily a negative finding), more students mentioned feeling better equipped to navigate through the research process and attested to enjoying it more because of the potential to discover new or even "exciting" information. While quite a few students reported positive changes in their attitude toward research, 22% revealed that in the end they found the process both enjoyable and frustrating depending on the nature of the topic and the time it took to locate relevant and credible information.

Moreover, students at the semester's end reported more willingness to locate information. Some also mentioned being intrigued by the prospect of learning about a new topic. Still, students stated that they found it daunting to sift through information to locate optimal material for advancing their arguments. Many students mentioned that their interest in the topic, not surprisingly, can impact their feelings toward research. Twenty-eight percent of students at the end of the semester mentioned "interest in the topic" as a primary motivator in their quest for information. Educators have long discussed the value of finding topics that could interest and engage students (Schraw & Lehman, 2001; Wade,

1992; Dewey, 1913); student responses to the motivation question support its importance. We hope that learning to appreciate their increasing abilities to find information they are curious about will motivate students toward what the *IL Framework* advocates: "asking increasingly complex or new questions whose answers in turn develop additional questions or lines of inquiry" (ACRL, 2015).

STUDENTS' REFLECTIVE ESSAYS

One important goal of this study was to better understand students' perceptions of their own writing and research processes, particularly what they reported as most helpful to their learning and to their completion of the final research-supported essay. The reflective essays allowed students—in their own words—to contribute to our research and our understanding of their IL practices.

From our analysis of reflections, following Creswell (2007), who advocates for allowing themes to emerge (based more on perspectives of participants as opposed to researchers), we identified six key categories that students described as helping them develop as researchers: specifically, learning to

- Interact with source material.
- Improve general writing processes.
- Use library resources.
- Scaffold the research process.
- Enhance audience and rhetorical awareness.
- Develop more sound research processes.

In the following, we describe each theme, report how many final reflective essays out of 53 mentioned the given theme as helpful to them as developing researchers, and highlight students' voices through quotations.

Interacting with Source Material

In final reflective essays submitted along with their final research-supported projects, many students reported valuing instruction in learning to evaluate, integrate, and cite sources for their academic writing. This theme emerged as the most often mentioned, noted in 44 of the 53 reflective essays. Students described as most helpful activities such as learning to identify trustworthy sources, selecting relevant information, and integrating quotations and summaries into their writing. As one student explained, "[Research-related assignments] have made me read more into the articles/sources so I can understand my topic more and really pick out what I want to use in my essay. Research, for me, has been a big improvement and the audiences can trust my work." (In sharing quotes from students, we present them precisely as they were offered in students' documents.) This quote highlights student awareness of valuing outside sources: to help a writer learn more about his or her topic, to provide a writer with key information to strengthen an essay, and to build credibility. The quote also resonates with the *IL Framework* statement that "Information possesses several dimensions of value, including as a commodity, as a means of education, as a means to influence, and as a means of negotiating and understanding the world" (ACRL, 2015).

Another student wrote, "I do pay a lot more attention to how credible my source is. I used to just worry about the information that I was being given, but now I look at if they cite their sources and if they have education in the specific area or if it is biased or not." We see this student as recognizing that information is not useful merely for being related to one's topic; according to the *IL Framework*, information should also come from a reliable source suitable for a given purpose (ACRL, 2015). Still another student wrote, "I have gone from just throwing out random facts I have heard to actually researching and writing down multiple sources then choosing from the most relevant ones." We see this remark as providing evidence of a student's increased awareness of the importance of care required in selecting from a range of sources, each with potential strengths and weaknesses. This student's comments suggest other practices advocated by the *IL Framework*, including "monitor[ing] gathered information and assess[ing] for gaps or weaknesses; organiz[ing] information in meaningful ways," and "synthesiz[ing] ideas gathered from multiple sources" (ACRL, 2015).

Other students mentioned learning to integrate and cite sources as helpful for displaying multiple perspectives in the midst of their own informed views. One student explained, "Since I got into [the composition course] I was able to figure out how to [incorporate an opposing viewpoint into the essay] and still be able to get my point across and have the readers on my side and not the opposing side like I feared." Other students also mentioned valuing their new abilities in presenting an opposing or counterargument without losing an audience's support. We are encouraged by the learning such comments represent, comments that connect to themes shared in the *IL Framework*, which encourages researchers to "maintain an open mind and critical stance" as well as "seek[ing] multiple perspectives during information gathering and assessment" (ACRL, 2015).

Though not all students commented on this aspect of integrating research, most students mentioned learning to cite sources as helpful, with some students able to make connections between learning to cite material and a writer's credibility. As one student stated, "In high school we were never taught to do in text citations . . . and I never knew how easy it was. With these citations my paper makes me sound like a more reliable source than just some random person that thinks they know what they're talking about." This quotation suggests that extra practice and conversations about citation help to do more than demystify citation rules; they lead to increased confidence in writing and new awareness of how to enhance a writer's ethos. Moreover, as the *IL Framework* suggests, the citations play a role in academic conversations: "Providing attribution to relevant previous research is also an obligation of participation in the conversation. It enables the conversation to move forward and strengthens one's voice in the conversation" (ACRL, 2015). We appreciate seeing evidence that students can learn to recognize real purposes for citing, such as nodding to others involved in discussing an issue.

Improving Writing Processes

As the second most common topic to come up in students' responses related to what helped them develop as researchers, 32 of 53 students discussed benefits of their writing processes changing during the course. As one student wrote, "I used to just type it out and do all of the processes within a week and hope that it was what the teacher wanted, but now I know that it takes much more time." Our hope is that students making this type of comment will keep this in mind as they approach academic writing in the future. Another response showed that, as one student put it, "I learned that [I] have to [do] constant research and do revisions in order to make my paper better." This student's comment also reflects growing expertise in researching. As the *IL Framework* states, "Experts are . . . inclined to seek out many perspectives, not just the ones with which they are familiar" (ACRL 2015). The student's response also demonstrates something we noticed in other reflective essays: discussions of research as it relates to the writing process and written products, with research prompting more writing and more writing prompting further research.

Using Library Resources

As the third most popular theme to emerge as an aid to completing the course's final essay, using library resources encompasses activities such as learning about new databases for finding sources, gaining practice in using databases, and discussing purposes of databases and various search engines. Thirty-one of 53 students explained that learning about and using databases, search engines, or the library website aided in their completion of the research-supported, argumentative essay.

A number of students spoke of their transformation as researchers during the course of the semester due to increased awareness of resources available to them. For example, one student wrote, "Before this year, to do my research,

I would just type in the topic to Google and then just look and look until I found what I needed, but what I learned is that there is specific sources (ex. the . . . library website) that will help you narrow down your search." Another student explained, "I used to get on Google type what I was looking for then hit on the first link, but now instead of doing that I go to academic search premier or CQ researcher those two websites are my favorites to gather information." Some students noted that particular databases were useful for specific reasons, such as finding relevant peer-reviewed articles and providing information about an author's credibility. By the end of the course, some reported a new awareness of the care required to sift through information whether using academic databases or Google. Many students mentioned appreciating being explicitly taught how to use academic resources and when and why to use them as well as knowing that Google was not the only option for finding information. Other students mentioned the value of noting where a source is published and with which type of domain (i.e., .com, .edu, .gov, and .org) as a means to comprehend the context for information presented. At the same time, some students did not show much awareness of the role or value of databases, with one such student stating that "information [from databases] is correct and it will look better on a paper to a teacher verses a Google website." At the least, students showed that they were beginning to think of research as inquiry and that seeking information from multiple sources was a useful, if not desirable, option.

Learning through Scaffolding the Research Process

Twenty-eight of 53 students addressed the value of a sequence of assignments leading up to the final essay, with one student stating, "Every assignment we did in class or online was like taking little steps closer to where we needed to be in writing our final draft." Not only did students regularly mention specific helpful assignments (such as the annotated bibliography, topic proposal, audience analysis, and extended outline), but some students mentioned how helpful it was to have most of the semester to work on a final essay because they didn't "have to rush last minute to finish a paper." One student responded that "the way the instructor laid out the assignment and gave us small work to do throughout the process it made it much easier to write." Not only did students find that the sequencing and scaffolding of the entire process was beneficial, but by bringing up assignment sequencing in their responses, these students seemed to follow the *IL Framework's* assertion that each small supporting piece of the assignment informed the essay and allowed them to approach "complex research by breaking complex questions into simple ones, limiting the scope of investigations" (ACRL, 2015).

Enhancing Audience and Rhetorical Awareness

More than 40% of students (23 of 53) mentioned audience or rhetorical awareness as something that helped them during both writing and research processes. Many students talked about audiences and rhetorical considerations as new developments in their writing. One student writes, "The most important thing that I've learned this semester is how to write as a reader; to maintain a constant consideration of the reader. This has improved my writing process and the writing itself." As seen above, this increased awareness of audience also impacted students' research decisions and practices. We believe, as a number of students reported, that the deliberate inclusion of Research Diary questions about audience and argumentation within various supporting assignments throughout the research and writing processes helped students to reach this conclusion.

Developing Sound Research Processes

Overall, many students reflected on changes they had made in their research and writing processes by the end of the course; many of these students included statements such as, "Before English 111, I used to . . . but now I . . . " Fifteen students discussed how learning more academic strategies aided them as researchers. Commenting on the usefulness of initially identifying a research question, one student wrote, "I think having a specific question to be answer while looking for a source was very helpful. I don't think I ever had a specific question while looking for a source . . . this was a new method that will improve my writing if I continued to do it." Although we often assume students know, as the *IL Framework* puts it, that "the act of searching often begins with a question that directs the act of finding needed information" (ACRL, 2015), the reflections from students indicate that some have not previously been strategic in locating information but instead have simply collected information that might have some—any—connection to their topics, and not necessarily searching information for their purposes for writing, such as persuading readers.

Learning to make distinctions among source information and types is not an easy process. One student commented on this in the reflective essay, stating, "I liked how the [final essay] challenged my research skills to look for more information than I had to in the past." The *IL Framework* emphasizes the benefits of learning that "first attempts at searching do not always produce adequate results" along with benefits of observing the "value of browsing" as well as "persist[ing] in the face of search challenges," knowing when the search task for one's purpose is complete (ACRL, 2015). Also, mentioning learning, a student writes, "The research that I did helped me so much in not only to make my paper more appealing but I learned so much about this topics that I've been trying to learn about for many years." It seems, then, that slowing down the assignment pacing and dedicating time to explicit instruction on research (through Research Diaries, class discussions, library instruction, and supporting assignments) helped students understand research as an opportunity to learn much more about a topic of interest to them and then to use that information for a purpose. When we look at students' responses in the writing process and research process categories, we see students beginning to understand research as a strategic exploration, with purpose in each iterative step as indicated by the *IL Framework* (ACRL, 2015). Many students said they found learning to research just as important or helpful as learning to write as well as a process to invoke throughout writing projects, not just as something to take part in during the invention or concluding stages of writing.

Finally, one of the most surprising results from our analysis of students' reflective essays is how often students talked about research as a rhetorical act. Students explained that they now have explicit *purposes* for selecting sources, such as becoming knowledgeable about a topic, displaying ethos and appearing credible to their readers, and better understanding others' perspectives and opposing arguments. In fact, several students mentioned appreciating new abilities to incorporate an opposing or counterargument, rather than ignoring it as they had in the past. Additionally, students talked about research as a way to learn about a topic and carefully present a sound argument, rather than simply a method for "proving a point." In fact, students' reflective essays suggest many students began to understand research as a complex, iterative process integrated with writing itself. Since the course was designed with this intent, it was encouraging to see students viewing these as joint, recursive processes, equally integral to the creation of knowledge, a tenet of the *IL Framework* (ACRL, 2015).

IMPLICATIONS AND CONCLUSION

One of the most striking aspects of our exploration of students' perspectives on research-supported writing is that there is so much more to learn about what is happening "behind the scenes" and that what we stand to learn is worth the additional effort of tracking students' research processes, beliefs, and attitudes. All too often, we learn about students' IL exclusively from a final research-supported essay. As instructors have long known, however, what students do in their final products is not necessarily an indication of what they *can* do. Final products tell us little of the struggle or the logic behind any problems we might identify in the research-supported work itself. Yet tracking students' practices through interim, reflective products, as we did, allowed us to identify patterns, allowing instructors to know where students experience the most difficulty and how they gain the most. We suggest this is necessary but not sufficient.

Research Diary responses indicated great value in providing 1) space for students to reflect and report on their research practices and 2) interventions to allow a behind-the-scenes look at students' thinking about research as it is happening (Ritchhart, Church & Morrison, 2011; Wallace, Flower & Norris, 1994). Participating instructors mentioned throughout the semester how student responses helped them gauge where students were succeeding or facing challenges in researching. And a primary purpose of the Research Diary assignments—supporting students' learning *as* they researched—was also achieved. Students reported their perceptions as well as behaviors had changed, largely toward positive ends, by the semester's end.

Students' reflective essays also have important pedagogical implications concerning the ways in which we approach IL. First, with respect to assigning large research-supported essays, we saw reflective evidence for the value of breaking into steps and scaffolding research processes and assignments. Doing so, our students indicated, aids them in understanding research and writing as involved processes, and research and writing as intertwined, recursive processes in keeping with the *IL Framework* (ACRL, 2015). Second, students' reflective essays indicate student interest in learning to use library resources such as databases to locate credible information and to develop their own ethos as they work toward knowledge-making (for more on supporting such work, see Yancey, Chapter 4, this collection). When offered explanations for finding scholarly sources, students indicate they will choose to use these resources rather than using Google alone. And some mentioned that when they do use Google, they will do so more strategically.

Breaking the research process into intelligible steps also proved useful. Students indicated that including smaller assignments, such as those allowed for in Research Diary or journal entries, proved beneficial. Such assignments can prompt students to engage with sources, for instance, by reflecting on how they might use specific source material within their own texts through questioning: Can the overall argument of the article be used to support or counter a main claim in the student's own text? Can source material be used to provide background on the topic? Katt Blackwell-Starnes (Chapter 7, this collection) offers additional strategies for assignment-sequencing for supporting the research process throughout a project.

Overall, we see much evidence that students are making attempts at integrating sources into their essays but that they struggle to do so, particularly in recognizing when to cite—and how. Fortunately, the Research Diaries and reflective essays provide insights into these struggles. Students reported appreciating using a shared text for rehearsing strategies for drawing information out through summary, paraphrase, and quotes, and for practicing weaving material from that source into their own writing.

The shared text approach points to yet another implication: the need to provide more time in class for students to engage with the sources they are locating before and as they are writing their research-supported work. There are multiple ways to do so in addition to those already mentioned (Milloy, 2013). When students have engaged deeply and rhetorically with source materials, they will have a greater sense of the conversations concerning their given topics, an aspect emphasized in the *IL Framework* (ACRL, 2015). Students can then approach taking their own stance on a given issue with an informed opinion and with greater confidence.

Based on our library and writing program collaboration, we additionally argue that the importance of library and cross-curricular partnerships cannot be overemphasized. Considering the theme of this collection—*Information Literacy: Research and Collaboration across Disciplines*—we would add that IL is not just for Writing Studies faculty. As Miriam J. Metzger, Andrew J. Flanagin, and Lara Zwarun (2003) report, students across the curriculum find most of their research from online sources. We therefore encourage instructors across the curriculum to work with librarians on finding ways to optimize that practice (for more on strategies for encouraging all disciplines to improve informational literacy, see Rolf Norgaard and Caroline Sinkinson, Chapter 1), this collection.

As mentioned earlier, when we maintain boundaries between the research that students do to write and the writing that students do based on research, we are emphasizing them as distinct practices rather than showing how they can work together in an integrated process. Librarians working with writing faculty can strengthen what we can offer students with respect to writing and researching (and researching and writing) and how we offer students access to IL.

In our case, learning occurred not just among the students but also among the librarian and instructors. As one instructor put it, "I realized from the results how much we are asking of students" when we ask them to integrate material from sources into their texts. This instructor is committed to breaking down assignments as the participating librarian modeled in the Research Diaries so that students are able to practice various moves related to research and writing from sources. The writing program, also, is sharing key results so that first-year composition instructors know what types of research practices students might be employing (such as including information because it is simply "on topic" as opposed to, for instance, being able to support key arguments or provide necessary background information for target readers). The writing program is also highlighting other aspects that our study suggests students might find challenging (such as summarizing), the importance of slowing the writing/research process down by taking students through specific steps, the advantage of having students work from common sources, along with emphasizing the value of helping students initially focus on specific databases rather than sending them out to the online library "cold." Additional benefits of librarians and instructors in composition and beyond are addressed in this volume (see, for example, Scheidt, Carpenter, Fitzgerald, Kozma, Middleton & Shields, Chapter 10, this collection; Winslow, Rains, Skripsky & Kelly, Chapter 14, this collection; and Bensen, Wu, Woetzel & Hashmi, Chapter 19, this collection).

Moreover, at our institution, more librarians are now taking our results into account as they revise library session visits and targeted online guides. They are also more attuned to the rhetorical purposes to which the information students seek can be applied and to working more closely with students in considering how to determine the potential value of sources once found.

Like James Elmborg (2006), we strongly recommend the practice of reflection, in this case, reflection occurring as students are conducting research and writing based on sources. We learned much from student writing prompted in Research Diaries; we also learned much from reflective essays that were written after the final research-supported essays were completed. We encourage instructors to create these types of opportunities to learn more from the students themselves the challenges and points of confusion with integrating research into texts. Doing so can help instructors assist students at the point of need and change the ways instructors subsequently work with students learning to understand and use sources.

Our collaboration demonstrates the mutual benefit of addressing IL as integral to academic writing generally, and it puts the emphasis on student learning (Hutchins, Fister & MacPherson, 2002). The mutually informative position that information literacies and academic literacies are fundamentally intertwined leads us to conclude that a reflective posture on the parts of students, the instructors, and the librarian worked together to garner the insights we have gathered from our results, insights that allow us to see hard work, confusion, and confidence as students gain expertise in academic research and writing.

REFERENCES

Artman, M., Frisicaro-Pawlowski, E. & Monge, R. (2010). Not just one shot: Extending the dialogue about information literacy in composition classes. *Composition Studies, 38*(2), 93–109.

Association of College and Research Libraries (ACRL). (2015). *Framework for information literacy for higher education.* Retrieved from http://www.ala.org/acrl/standards/il framework.

Barefoot, B. (2006). Bridging the chasm: First-year students and the library. *Chronicle of Higher Education, 52*(20), p. B16.

Bensen, B., Wu, H., Woetzel, D. & Hashmi, G. (2016). Impacting information literacy through alignment, resources, and assessment. In B. J. D'Angelo, S. Jamieson, B. Maid & J. R. Walker (Eds.), *Information literacy: Research and collaboration across disciplines*. Fort Collins, CO: WAC Clearinghouse and University Press of Colorado.

Bizup, J. (2008). BEAM: A rhetorical vocabulary for teaching research-based writing. *Rhetoric Review, 27*(1), 72–86.

Blackwell-Starnes, Katt (2016). Beyond the internet brainstorm: Using Google to further information literacy with preliminary research. In B. J. D'Angelo, S. Jamieson, B. Maid & J. R. Walker (Eds.), *Information literacy: Research and collaboration across disciplines*. Fort Collins, CO: WAC Clearinghouse and University Press of Colorado.

Brasley, S. S. (2008). Effective librarian and discipline faculty collaboration models for integrating information literacy into the fabric of an academic institution. *New Directions for Teaching and Learning, 114*, 71–88.

Byerly, G., Downey, A. & Ramin, L. (2006) Footholds and foundations: Setting freshmen on the path to lifelong learning. *Reference Services Review, 34*(4), 589–598.

Caspers, J. & Bernhisel, S. M. (2005). What do freshmen really know about research? Assess before you teach. *Research Strategies, 20*(4), 458–468.

Creswell, J. (2007). *Qualitative inquiry and research design: Choosing among five approaches* (2nd ed.). Thousand Oaks, CA: Sage.

D'Angelo, B. J. & Maid, B. M. (2004). Moving beyond definitions: Implementing information literacy across the curriculum. *The Journal of Academic Librarianship, 30*, 212–217.

Deitering, A. M. & Jameson, S. (2008). Step by step through the scholarly conversation: A collaborative library/writing faculty project to embed information literacy and promote critical thinking in first year composition at Oregon State University. *College & Undergraduate Libraries, 15*(1–2), 57–79.

Detmering, R. & Johnson, A. M. (2012). "Research papers have always seemed very daunting": Information literacy narratives and the student research experience. *Libraries and the Academy, 12*(1), 5–22.

Duke, L. M. & Asher, A. D. (Eds). (2011). *College libraries and student culture: What we now know*. Chicago: American Library Association.

Elmborg, J. (2006). Critical information literacy: Implications for instructional practice. *Journal of Academic Librarianship, 32*(2), 192–199.

Gillaspy-Steinhilper, A. (2012). I don't have time to teach that: The benefits of faculty-librarian collaborations, *Faculty Focus: Higher Ed Teaching Strategies*. Madison, WI: Magnum Publications. July 16. Retrieved from http://www.facultyfocus.com/articles/instructional-design/i-dont-have-time-to-teach-that-the-benefits-of-faculty-librarian-collaborations/.

Haller, C.R. (2010). Toward rhetorical source use: Three students' journeys. *Writing Program Administration, 34*(1), 33–59.

Haviland, C. P. & Mullin, J. (Eds.). (2008). *Who owns this text? Plagiarism, authorship, and disciplinary cultures*. Logan, UT: Utah State University Press.

Head, A. J. (2007). Beyond Google: How do students conduct academic research? *First Monday, 12*(8). Retrieved from http://firstmonday.org/issues/issue12_8/head/index.html.

Head, A. J. (2008). IL from the trenches: How do humanities and social science majors conduct academic research?" *College and Research Libraries, 69*(4), 427–445.

Head, A. J. & Eisenberg, M. B. (2010a). How today's college students use Wikipedia for course-related research. *First Monday, 15*(3). doi: http://dx.doi.org/10.5210%2Ffm.v15i3.2830.

Head, A. J. & Eisenberg, M. B. (2010b). Truth be told: How college students evaluate and use information in the digital age. *Social Science Research Network*. http://dx.doi.org/10.2139/ssrn.2281485.

Holliday, W. & Fagerheim, B. A. (2006). Integrating information literacy with a sequenced English composition curriculum. *Libraries and the Academy, 6*(2), 169–184.

Howard, R. M., Rodrigue, T. K. & Serviss, T. C. (2010) Writing from sources, writing from sentences. *Writing and Pedagogy, 2*(2), 177–192.

Jacobs, H. L. (2008). Information literacy and reflective pedagogical praxis. *Journal of Academic Librarianship, 34*(3), 256–262.

Jamieson, S. (2016). What the Citation Project tells us about information literacy in college composition. In B. J. D'Angelo, S. Jamieson, B. Maid & J. R. Walker (Eds.), *Information literacy: Research and collaboration across disciplines.* Fort Collins, CO: WAC Clearinghouse and University Press of Colorado.

Hutchins, E. O., Fister, B. & MacPherson, K. H. (2002). Changing landscapes, enduring values: Making the transition from bibliographic instruction to information literacy. *Journal of Library Administration, 36*(1–2), 3–19.

Kellogg, R. T. (2008). Training writing skills: A cognitive developmental perspective. *Journal of Writing Research, 1*(1), 1–26.

McClure, R. & Clink, K. (2009). How do you know that? An investigation of student research practices in the digital age. *Libraries and the Academy, 9*(1), 115–132.

Metzger, M. J., Flanagin, A. J. & Zwarun, L. (2003). College student web use, perceptions of information credibility, and verification behavior. *Computers & Education, 41*(3), 271–290.

Milloy, R. (2013). Re-envisioning research: Alternative approaches to engaging NextGen students. In R. McClure & J. P. Purdy (Eds.), *The New Digital Scholar: Exploring and Enriching the Research and Writing Practices of NextGen Students* (pp. 233–253). Medford, NJ: Information Today, Inc.

Mounce, M. (2010). Working together: Academic librarians and faculty collaborating to improve students' information literacy skills: A literature review 2000–2009. *The Reference Librarian, 51*(4), 300–320.

Negretti, R. (2012). Metacognition in student academic writing: A longitudinal study of metacognitive awareness and its relation to task perception, self-regulation, and evaluation of performance. *Written Communication, 29*(2), 142–179.

Norgaard, R. (2003). Writing information literacy: Contributions to a concept. *Reference & User Services Quarterly, 43*(2), 124–130.

Norgaard, R. & Sinkinson, C. (2016) Writing information literacy: A retrospective and a look ahead. In B. J. D'Angelo, S. Jamieson, B. Maid & J. R. Walker (Eds.), *Information literacy: Research and collaboration across disciplines.* Fort Collins, CO: WAC Clearinghouse and University Press of Colorado.

Peary, A. & Ernick, L. (2004). Reading, writing, research: Incorporating strategies from composition and rhetoric into library instruction. *College & Undergraduate Libraries, 11*, 33–44.

Ritchhart, R., Church, M. & Morrison, K. (2011). Making thinking visible: How to promote engagement, understanding, and independence for all learners. San Francisco, CA: Jossey-Bass.

Scheidt, D. L., Carpenter, W., Fitzgerald, R., Kozma, C., Middleton, H. & Shields, K. (2016). Writing information literacy in first fear composition: A collaboration among faculty and librarians. In B. J. D'Angelo, S. Jamieson, B. Maid & J. R. Walker (Eds.), *Information literacy: Research and collaboration across disciplines.* Fort Collins, CO: WAC Clearinghouse and University Press of Colorado.

Schraw, G. & Lehman, S. (2001). Situational interest: A review of the literature and directions for future research. *Educational Psychology Review, 1,* 23–52.

Simmons, R. J. & Eimer, M. B. (2004). A model for promoting active learning and information literacy skills in large and small classes. *Journal of College Teaching & Learning (TLC), 1*(6), 1–8.

Wade, S. E. (1992). How interest affects learning from text. In A. Renninger, S. Hidi & A. Krapp (Eds.), *The Role of Interest in Learning and Development* (pp. 281–296). Hillsdale, NJ: Lawrence Erlbaum.

Wallace, D., Flower, L. & Norris, L. (1994). *Making thinking visible: Writing, collaborative planning, and classroom inquiry.* Urbana, IL: National Council of Teachers of English.

Westbrock, T. & Moberly, M. National problem, local solution: How libraries, writing programs, and writing centers can collaborate to help students engage with information. Unpublished ms.

Winslow, R. R., Skripsky, S. & Kelly, S. (2016) Not just for citations: Using Zotero as a portal into students' research processes. In B. J. D'Angelo, S. Jamieson, B. Maid & J. R. Walker (Eds.), *Information literacy: Research and collaboration across disciplines.* Fort Collins, CO: WAC Clearinghouse and University Press of Colorado.

Yancey, Kathleen Blake (2016). Creating and exploring new worlds: Web 2.0, information literacy, and the ways we know. In B. J. D'Angelo, S. Jamieson, B. Maid & J. R. Walker (Eds.), *Information literacy: Research and collaboration across disciplines.* Fort Collins, CO: WAC Clearinghouse and University Press of Colorado.

CHAPTER 10
WRITING INFORMATION LITERACY IN FIRST-YEAR COMPOSITION: A COLLABORATION AMONG FACULTY AND LIBRARIANS

Donna Scheidt, William Carpenter, Robert Fitzgerald, Cara Kozma, Holly Middleton, and Kathy Shields
High Point University

As other authors in this collection observe, when librarians and writing faculty teach students how to plan, conduct, and incorporate research as they write, they often do so with different working definitions of research and information literacy (IL) (e.g., Kissel et al., Chapter 20, this collection, and Norgaard & Sinkinson, Chapter 1, this collection). When Rolf Norgaard (2003) coined "writing information literacy," he argued for how our fields might contribute to one another intellectually and conceptually. Norgaard encourages Writing Studies faculty and librarians to reconsider certain conceptions of students' research, specifically as it interfaces with students' writing practices. We call this interface between writing and research "writing-research," to distinguish students' everyday practices as writing-researchers from the theoretical ideal of writing information literacy (WIL) that Norgaard articulates.[1]

All too often, whether in their own instruction or in their assignment of instruction to others, writing faculty and librarians understand writing-research as a set of skills or a product, a "generic window" on IL (Lupton & Bruce, 2010). Instead, according to Norgaard, they should consider the "intellectual and composition processes that precede and underlie that [final written] product" (p. 127) as well as appreciate students' "fairly complex (if not always effective, appropriate or productive)" practices (pp. 126–127). Our conceptions of research—and those of our students—would benefit, Norgaard insists, from the ways we understand writing—"as a recursive, goal-oriented, and problem-solving activity that involves a complex repertoire of strategies" (p. 127). The recently adopted *Framework for Information Literacy for Higher Education* (ACRL,

2015) (*Framework for IL*) reflects this concept of research. By focusing on core concepts, rather than a set of skills or standards, the *Framework for IL* represents IL as having to do with more complex intellectual practices. In light of these perspectives, it would enhance our collaborations as writing faculty and librarians instructing students on research practice to conceptualize research as we do writing, as a process that itself can be integrated with writing as a writing-research process.

Conceiving of and studying research as process is hardly a new idea to Library and Information Science, though researchers have not consistently attended to the roles of writing in research processes. Since the 1980s, Carol Kuhlthau (1988) has investigated the research processes of researchers of various ages in diverse settings, including college undergraduates. Her Information Search Process, developed out of her empirical work, has had significant influence, sensitive as it is to patterns among writer-researchers' cognitive activities and affective orientations. Yet Kuhlthau's process model privileges information seeking over meaning construction (Lupton, 2004, p. 24), and writing is largely absent as a concern. More recent studies conducted abroad, adopting a process framework (Hongisto & Sormunen, 2010) (Finland) or discovering among students a process orientation to research (Diehm & Lupton, 2012) (Australia), only tangentially address the role of writing, as an "end product" (Hongisto & Sormunen, 2010, p. 107), or as one of the "[p]rocesses for using information" (Diehm & Lupton, 2012, p. 8).

In a small-scale follow-up to Kuhlthau's work, Barbara Fister (1992) used a think-aloud protocol to interview 14 undergraduates, from freshman to seniors, who had successfully completed academic research projects, inquiring about their research and writing processes. Among her findings, she discovered, consistent with Kuhlthau, that students spent a good deal of time and energy in developing a focus for their projects. She also discovered, however, that students readily integrated research and writing, not reserving it for the final stage (as in Kuhlthau's model): "Few of the students saw any clear distinction between research and writing; they saw them as aspects of a single activity, concurrent and integrated" (p. 167). In addition to considering the implications of her findings for research and writing instruction, Fister called for additional research on research processes, especially those employed by average college students.

Recent, broad-scale U.S.-based empirical studies by Project Information Literacy (PIL) researchers suggest the importance of helping undergraduates, including freshmen, develop research strategies and processes as well as the challenges of doing so, particularly as integrated with their writing. In a survey of over 8,000 undergraduates at 25 U.S. campuses, they discovered that about half these students self-reported using processes (what researchers called "routines") for students' writing-research (Head & Eisenberg, 2010). Of those students employing processes, it was found that "[s]tudents had fewer techniques for conducting research and finding information than for writing papers" (p. 19). Also, students' processes were often more oriented to efficiency than inquiry and learning, or WIL. In a study based on interviews with nearly 2,000 college freshmen about experiences with research in their first semester, Alison Head (2013) reports that some students found themselves taking their "high school research kit"—their set of competencies and strategies—and "retooling it" to deal with the demands of college research (p.14), though not without difficulties. All too often, students' research strategies and processes are formulaic rather than responsive to situational specifics, generative of thinking and learning, and adaptable across assignments. These findings are consistent with Norgaard's call for greater collaboration in conceptualizing (and ultimately teaching) research better informed by our conceptualizations of writing, including complex and elaborated approaches to process. While acknowledging the contributions that have been made, Norgaard notes in a conversation with Catherine Sinkinson included in this volume that "we have a ways to go to foster the disciplinary dialogue and disciplinary cross-fertilization" anticipated by his earlier work (Chapter 1, this collection).

Norgaard's (2003) contribution is significant and still timely, yet its promise for actual collaborations depends on better understanding students' writing-research processes—what they are and in what respects they are most productive (most reflective, that is, of WIL) and most problematic. At this point, however, little is known empirically, especially about the processes of writer-researchers in first-year composition (FYC). Mark Emmons and Wanda Martin (2002) assessed outcomes in a FYC program employing process-oriented, inquiry-based research instruction, yet their assessment did not specifically examine students' writing-research processes. Other studies of undergraduate writing-research have examined students' activities and processes but have not focused on first-year students or students enrolled in a composition course (see, e.g., Beyer, Gillmore & Fisher, 2007; Nelson, 1993; Burton & Chadwick, 2000). Recent empirical work highlighting connections between undergraduates' research and writing has focused not on processes but on "categories" of students' orientation to research and writing (Lupton, 2004) and the extent and nature of students' reading as an attribute of their written texts (Jamieson & Howard, 2013). The need thus persists to better understand the processes of students as writer-researchers in FYC.

This chapter, itself the enactment of a research and pedagogical collaboration among faculty and librarians involved with FYC, considers how FYC students at a private comprehensive university perceive their writing-research as well as to what extent and how those perceptions change over a one-semester composition course. Specifically, we examine the "activities" that students articulate as making up their writing-research processes—what those activities are for students as a whole; what activities students discuss most and least frequently; and how students' emphases on those activities change over a semester. We also investigate what writing faculty and librarians value as WIL within those activities. The results of this study indicate that students arrive at the university with a sense of writing-research as a process. Yet generally students do not initially articulate activities critical to college-level work: working with sources in ways that might conceptually enhance their development of focus and perspective in response to an assignment. After a semester of FYC, the same students demonstrate significant gains in *how often* they discuss reading and otherwise engaging sources. They also show progress as far as *how* they discuss this and certain other activities associated with purposeful writing-research. Despite these gains, the findings demonstrate little improvement in the spectrum of other writing-research activities or WIL more generally.

In sharing our methodology and results, we hope to better understand students' writing-research processes and to operationalize what WIL means for students, writing faculty, and librarians, thereby enhancing the conceptual grounds for our own and others' pedagogical collaborations.

METHOD

This chapter reports on a one-semester mixed-methods inquiry into how FYC students at a private comprehensive university perceive research, specifically as it interfaces with their writing practices, and whether and how those perceptions change over a one-semester composition course. The study posed three initial questions:

1. What writing-research activities do students articulate in response to a research essay prompt?
2. To what extent and how do students' articulated writing-research activities reflect what Norgaard (2003) terms "writing information literacy"?
3. To what extent and how do students' articulated writing-research activities change over the course of a semester?

The study received approval from the university's Institutional Review Board (IRB) and was begun in August of 2012.

RESEARCH DESIGN

Participants

The study was conducted at a private comprehensive university located in central North Carolina. The university offers a broad range of undergraduate degrees, including those in the traditional liberal arts, business, furniture and interior design, exercise science, and education. For the academic year 2012–2013, the university enrolled 3,926 undergraduate students, 1,257 of whom were first-year students.[2]

At the beginning of the fall 2012 semester, 562 students were enrolled across 25 sections of FYC,[3] and 408 of these students consented to participate in the study. Per university IRB policies, students who were not 18 years of age at the beginning of the semester were unable to participate. Informed written consent was obtained by individual instructors during the first class session. Students who elected to participate were asked how they wanted their work cited in the study: anonymously, with pseudonyms, or with their real names. A program administrative assistant not involved with the research project created a "master spreadsheet" and assigned every consenting participant a random five-digit numerical code so that none of the participants' identities would be known to the researchers.

Online IL Modules

Before the beginning of the fall 2012 semester, the librarians created a series of five online modules in Blackboard, which were piloted in 13 of the fall composition courses. The modules addressed many of the IL concepts prioritized in FYC, such as database searches using selective keywords, identifying popular versus scholarly sources, citation, etc., and enabled the librarians to cover more content than is possible in one-shot sessions.[4]

Writing Prompt

All students enrolled in the course responded to the following process narrative prompt during the first and last weeks of the semester:

> Imagine that you have been assigned a 1500-word essay for
> this course. The essay must develop an argument about a
> current social issue and must use at least three outside sources.
> Explain how you would go about completing this assignment.
> Be as specific and detailed as possible.

Students were given 20 minutes of in-class time to respond to the prompt on a computer. They were made aware that the process narratives would not be assigned a grade. Identical prompts were used at the beginning and end of the semester.

Sampling Procedures

The process narrative prompts were administered by course instructors and collected into assignment folders in Blackboard. Instructors then sent these files to the administrative assistant responsible for the master sheet of students' identifying codes. A computer program was used to generate a simple random sample of 60 participants: 30 from the experimental sections (those who used the online modules) and 30 from control sections. All identifying information from the process narratives was removed, and they were labeled only with the students' numbers. The master spreadsheet also indicated which students were enrolled in the experimental sections. The list of 60 participants yielded 50 pre-tests and 51 post-tests (not matched in all cases), which were made available to researchers using Dropbox file-sharing software. Researchers did not know which students comprised the experimental or control groups until all coding was finished.

Coding Method

The random sample of process narratives was coded collaboratively by the six researchers: four tenure-track Writing Studies faculty and two librarians. To generate initial codes, the researchers first divided into two groups of three—one group focused on the pre-tests and the other on the post-tests. Each team included two Writing Studies faculty members and one librarian. Each team member was assigned 17 pre-test or post-test samples to ensure that all narratives were evaluated in this initial process.

After reading through the data individually doing what Johnny Saldaña (2009) describes as "initial coding" (p. 81)—making notes about patterns and themes that might offer "analytic leads for further exploration" (p. 81)—each research team met independently to discuss their results. Based on the initial coding of the samples, they collaboratively generated a list of potential codes to be presented to the larger group. All six researchers then met to develop a common list of codes (see Appendix for Code Log). Using Christopher Hahn's (2008) suggestions for organizing qualitative coding, the group identified these codes as "level 1" activities. These activity-oriented codes—a kind of coding Saldaña terms "process coding" (p. 77)—describe research-related actions that students articulate in their process narratives. Research-related actions were defined as any step in the research process, from brainstorming to citing. Writing process activities were not coded unless the activity indicated an act of writing-research. Following Saldaña's model, activities were double-coded as different level 1 codes where appropriate.

Recognizing that the level 1 codes would not alone elucidate evidence of students' WIL, and that there needed to be some way of conceptualizing the intellectual work within the students' narratives, the researchers adapted Hahn's (2008) notion of "level 2" coding (p. 6). In our study, level 2 codes relate to what Saldaña (2009) calls "elaborative coding"—"the process of analyzing textual data in order to develop theory further" (p. 168). Researchers elaborated Norgaard's (2003) notion of WIL by teasing out two concepts central to his theory: invention and inquiry. Norgaard presents these concepts as sites where Writing Studies and IL can productively overlap (p. 128–9), and researchers created level 2 codes for these terms (see Appendix). Researchers therefore agreed to double-code any level 1 activity read as "invent" or "inquire" as a level 2 code. Level 2 codes were applied where students elaborated writing-research processes meant to discover and create new ideas (invent) or to investigate and mediate ideas (inquire). For researchers, these sites demonstrated a more conceptual understanding of the activities associated with WIL; students coded for level 2 had moments when their articulated processes demonstrated an overlap between Writing Studies and IL.

After the final code log was complete, the researchers divided into three pairs, pairing faculty with librarians to the extent possible. Each pair coded pre- and post-tests for 17 students. Coding involved assigning a level 1 code, capturing all raw text data indicating the code onto the spreadsheet, and double-coding for level 2 "invent" or "inquiry" where appropriate. The paired coding process was designed to ensure that the entire data set was coded by at least two readers. When a pair of readers could not reach agreement on a code, they presented the texts in question to the entire group and a consensus was reached.[5]

RESULTS

STUDENTS' WRITING-RESEARCH ACTIVITIES AND WIL

In their narratives, students discussed 15 distinct writing-research activities, as summarized in Table 10.1. Individual students typically articulated a number of writing-research activities in their narratives, averaging 5.19 level one codes on their pre-tests. Pre-test results indicated that students frequently discussed the following activities, typically associated with the beginning of the research process: *brainstorming* prior knowledge and beliefs and finding a *topic*. With respect to finding and preliminarily working with sources, students frequently discussed determining what sources were *available*, *gathering* sources, and designating source *quality* (e.g., by naming resources considered "safe," such as databases). Frequent later-stage activities included *organizing* sources (e.g., as part of an outline) and *integrating* sources textually (e.g., introducing, quoting/paraphrasing/summarizing, or citing). As indicated in Table 10.1, each of these activities accounted for 8–10% of all codes on the pre-tests.

Table 10.1. Counts of coded activities (and as percentage of all codes)

Code	N Pre	% Pre	N Post	% Post	% Change
assignment	6	2.33%	3	1.02%	-1.31%
topic	26	10.08%	31	10.51%	0.43%
brainstorm	22	8.53%	22	7.46%	-1.07%
gather	22	8.53%	20	6.78%	-1.75%
engage	13	5.04%	37	12.54%	7.50%
learn	17	6.59%	15	5.08%	-1.51%
available	23	8.91%	21	7.12%	-1.79%
position	7	2.71%	10	3.39%	0.68%
support	14	5.43%	16	5.42%	-0.01%
different	17	6.59%	17	5.76%	-0.83%
quality	22	8.53%	22	7.46%	-1.07%
relevance	6	2.33%	10	3.39%	1.06%
organize	21	8.14%	16	5.42%	-2.72%
use	18	6.98%	22	7.46%	0.48%
integrate	24	9.30%	33	11.19%	1.89%
TOTALS	258		295		

Writing-research activities associated with working with sources in concert with students' own developing views were discussed less frequently in pre-tests. These less-discussed activities included *learning* more about a chosen topic, *engaging* sources (e.g., reading, notetaking, analyzing), locating *support* for claims, acknowledging *different* views or opinions, and *using* sources (e.g., as "facts," "information," or for other more rhetorical purposes). Discussed even less were the following: understanding the *assignment* and its tasks, determining the *relevance* of sources (e.g., to their topic or other purposes), and taking a *position*. Taken together, these activities form a snapshot of what our students emphasize in the research process as they begin their first semester in college.

Students' writing-research activities at the beginning of the term reflected WIL to different extents, as reflected in Tables 10.2 and 10.3.[6] By far, the activity most commonly identified in pre-tests with WIL was *brainstorming*, because of its association with discovery and problem-formulation—i.e., *invention*. Three other activities were often associated with WIL in pre-tests—not just with *invention* but with *inquiry* (i.e., making and mediating meaning): determining what sources were *available*, *learning* more about a chosen topic, and acknowledging *different* views.

Table 10.2. Counts of activities coded WIL (and as percentage of all codes)

Code	N Pre	% Pre	N Post	% Post	% Change
assignment	1	2.04%	0	0.00%	-2.04%
topic	3	6.12%	7	10.77%	4.65%
brainstorm	13	26.53%	15	23.08%	-3.45%
gather	1	2.04%	1	1.54%	-0.50%
engage	2	4.08%	12	18.46%	14.38%
learn	7	14.29%	4	6.15%	-8.13%
available	7	14.29%	2	3.08%	-11.21%
position	1	2.04%	2	3.08%	1.04%
support	1	2.04%	0	0.00%	-2.04%
different	5	10.20%	6	9.23%	-0.97%
quality	2	4.08%	2	3.08%	-1.00%
relevance	1	2.04%	5	7.69%	5.65%
organize	1	2.04%	0	0.00%	-2.04%
use	2	4.08%	7	10.77%	6.69%
integrate	2	4.08%	2	3.08%	-1.00%
TOTALS	49		65		

Table 10.3. Percentage of each activity coded WIL

Code	% (Pre)	% (Post)	% Change
assignment	16.67%	0.00%	-16.67%
topic	11.54%	22.58%	11.04%
brainstorm	59.09%	68.18%	9.09%
gather	4.55%	5.00%	0.45%
engage	15.38%	32.43%	17.05%
learn	41.18%	26.67%	-14.51%
available	30.43%	9.52%	-20.91%
position	14.29%	20.00%	5.71%
support	7.14%	0.00%	-7.14%
different	29.41%	35.29%	5.88%
quality	9.09%	9.09%	0.00%
relevance	16.67%	50.00%	33.33%
organize	4.76%	0.00%	-4.76%
use	11.11%	31.82%	20.71%
integrate	8.33%	6.06%	-2.27%

Students rarely articulated certain other activities in a way that suggested to researchers that they were discovering ideas, problem-solving, or making meaning in their writing-research. These low writing-information-literate activities included *gathering* sources, locating *support* for claims, and *organizing* sources.

HOW STUDENTS DESCRIBE FINDING A TOPIC AND DETERMINING THE RELEVANCE OF SOURCES

We now consider *how* students' articulated writing-research activities reflect WIL, through in-depth qualitative analysis of two writing-research activities: finding a *topic* and determining the *relevance* of sources. We chose to focus on finding a *topic* because, as indicated in Table 10.1, it was the activity that students mentioned most often in their narratives, persisting in rates of frequency from pre- to post-tests. While the activity *integrate* was coded an equal number of times overall, *topic* was double-coded for WIL at a much higher rate than *integrate* (see Tables 10.2 and 10.3). *Topic* was neither especially high nor low overall with respect to WIL, giving researchers the opportunity to richly compare instances of topic selection judged writing information literate with those that were not. Also evident in Table 10.1, *relevance* was a writing-research activity rarely coded in pre- or post-tests. (That students consider relevance all too infrequently is a finding similar to results in other studies in this collection [e.g., Goscik et al., Chapter 8, this collection; Wojahn et al., Chapter 9, this collection]). Yet as indicated in Tables 10.2 and 10.3, by the end of the semester *topic* and *relevance* would make notable gains in their association with WIL, being highly valued by researchers. This made us want to look at what students who discussed these activities were doing.

FINDING A TOPIC

Students considered to be writing information literate in finding a topic discussed their *multiple steps*: investigating, narrowing, and/or choosing. The student below first investigates a topic—thinks about or (in this case) researches possible options—and then narrows the topic, recognizing multiple possible topics and considering how to select:

> First off, I would spend a decent amount of time researching a variety of social issues that have affected not only the United States, but the world as well. I would strongly lean toward choosing an issue that can be relatable to almost everyone, or target a specific group. (A. Jones, pre-test)

Similarly, another student first investigates and then chooses a topic:

> After having the essay assigned, I would immediately start searching through news articles for a social issue that interest [sic] me. Once I come across the story that has two sides, and could be debated, I know my topic. (S. King, post-test)

These students' descriptions are not elaborate. Yet they differ from those of many students who, while noting the need to select a topic, did not explain how they would go about it.

Students also were judged writing information literate based on the *criteria* they articulated for their topic selection, especially when they articulated diverse or unusual criteria. In general, students turned most often to whether a topic was interesting, current, or controversial. Additional criteria, mentioned less frequently, included how much research was available on a topic, the quality of research on a topic, whether a topic was familiar or specific, whether a topic related to the assignment, whether a student felt a topic could be developed adequately for the essay, and whom a topic considered or addressed. These less common criteria were valued as WIL, particularly in combination with other criteria:

> After that I would then go to the library and find a current social issue that I found interesting. After coming up with some different social issues that I found most interesting I would do a little research on all three to see which one had the most information on it. (Anonymous, post-test)

This student uses a common criterion—interest in a topic—and an unusual criterion—amount of research available on the topic (i.e., "the most information"). (Other students addressing the amount of research on a topic discussed easily researched topics, or topics with enough research.)

Finally, some students identified as being writing information literate in their topic selection articulated *multiple kinds of sources*. Many students discussed using sources in their topic selection, with the resource most frequently mentioned being the Internet. Several students clarified what they were seeking online (e.g., news articles, social media, etc.), or combined online resources with other kinds of research resources, such as magazines, t.v., or even family members.[7]

One student text in particular illustrates all three aspects of WIL for topic selection—multiples steps, diverse criteria, and multiple kinds of sources:

> I would first come up with a relevant topic that would be considered a current social issue. To gather possible topics, I would first watch the world news and look for anything of interest. I

> would take note of any possible issues for later evaluation. My second source would be the local newspaper. This would give me a more local perspective on how people in my area may be reacting to national events. For the last source I would turn to the internet to find issues and conflicts that may have not been picked up by the mainstream media. This may include browsing a few independent news sites, reading through a related blog, or viewing specific eyewitness accounts on youtube. After compiling a list of possible topics, I would go through and narrow down the choices and find the most interesting, relevant, and controversal [sic] topic. (S. King, pre-test)

Investigating topics, the student turns to different kinds of sources: "the world news," "a local newspaper," and "the internet." (The student even identifies the purposes behind these differing sources—global, local, and non-mainstream coverage.) Narrowing and choosing among topics, the student employs multiple criteria, considering which topic is "the most interesting, relevant, and controversal [sic]."

DETERMINING RELEVANCE

Researchers regularly identified students' discussions of *relevance* as writing information literate, and as highly associated with "persistence." In total, only 16 text segments were coded for *relevance* codes, making it the second least applied code behind *assignment*. Yet six of these were double-coded level 2 code *inquire*, prompting a closer look at the relationship between *relevance* and WIL. In the examples where level 1 *relevance* codes were double coded with level 2 *inquire* codes, students articulated a need to be persistent in their research in order to evaluate the appropriateness of their sources in terms of their argument. Several of the students explain that this later-stage evaluation process often happens during the writing process. Some examples:

> Then once I have decided what point of view I intend to write from I will decide which of the sources would be most helpful for me to prove my point in my essay. That way I can keep the stronger sources and remove the weak sources. (A. Fortin, post-test)

> I tend to add at least two more when I'm revising my essay, or I replace sources with ones that are more relevant to my paper. (M. Maire, post-test)

These students show a willingness to give up sources already obtained in order to search for information more appropriate for their purposes. Researchers see these students as demonstrating both persistence in the writing-research process and the ability to evaluate sources in light of the rhetorical situation. In this way, students coded for *relevance* and *inquire* seem to be working squarely within Norgaard's (2003) conception of WIL.

CHANGES IN WRITING-RESEARCH ACTIVITIES AND WIL

Students averaged 5.88 codes on the post-test, a statistically significant difference from the beginning of the semester,[8] suggesting that students' end-of-semester writing-research processes were more elaborated as far as number of activities reported. However, this quantification of codes is less telling than the distribution of codes, which can be seen in Table 10.1. In particular, post-test results indicate that *engaging* with sources is where the fall 2012 FYC made the biggest difference in how students experience and understand the writing-research process.[9]

There was some difference (though not statistically significant) in how often students' activities were coded for WIL by the end of the semester.[10] Even so, results indicated notable changes from the beginning to the end of the term in the distribution of certain activities highly associated with WIL. Gains were seen in level 2 coding (*inquire*, in particular) with respect to four activities—finding a topic, engaging sources, determining the relevance of sources, and using sources, indicating changes possibly associated with FYC (see Tables 10.2 and 10.3). Other activities remained frequently coded by researchers at level 2: learning more about a chosen topic, acknowledging different points of view, and brainstorming prior knowledge or beliefs.[11] That these activities persisted as highly writing information literate is no surprise, given their ready association with inquiry and invention. Conversely, determining what is available was no longer highly associated with WIL by the end of the term, possibly suggesting an opportunity for more emphasis on research planning.

Activities infrequently associated with WIL at the beginning of the term remained so by the end of the term, including gathering sources, locating support for claims, and organizing sources (see Tables 10.2 and 10.3). These results are consistent with the ways these activities tended to contribute to student research processes that were routine and inflexible—e.g., finding a certain number of sources in order to populate an outline devised to bolster pre-formulated claims about an issue. An additional activity, however, became unexpectedly associated with low WIL by the end of the semester: understanding the *assignment*. In other words, by the end of the term, students were less frequently articulating their efforts to understand their writing-research as rhetorically and purposefully located in relationship to an assignment.

Engaging Sources

Given the gains made over the term by *engage*—both in the frequency and quality of students' articulations—researchers turned their attention to understanding how students conceived of this activity. The code log defines engage in the following way: "reading, making sense of sources, analyzing, notetaking, annotating; specific to source." However, while any of these activities could be coded engage, researchers found these activities were differentially valued as level 2 codes, with notetaking and annotating remaining a level 1 code if not accompanied by reading or making sense of sources (understanding). Upon reviewing how students who only received level 1 codes conceived activities coded engage, researchers found these students tended to emphasize annotating and note-taking:

> I would find about 5 sources about my current issues and actively take notes about each article. (Snake, pre-test)

> After finding the sources I would go through and highlight any good information or find any specific quotes I want to use. (C. Smith, post-test)

Working with texts in these ways—highlighting and taking notes—is a practice associated with active reading. But it is notable that these students highlight specific information or quotes and take notes without explicitly stating that they would take the time to first read or understand their sources. This step of articulating reading or understanding tended to differentiate the *engage* codes double-coded for *inquiry*. Here are some examples of these *engage* codes coded level 2:

> I would make sure that I spend a lot of time researching, and reading the articles carefully and thoroughly and making sure they would fit in well with my essay. (A. Jones, post-test)

> After concluding my research, I would then take the time to sit down and fully read and comprehend the articles. I personally like to have a paper copy of the sources so that I can highlight important information, take notes in the margins, and mark the text, this way I know where to look when I begin the writing process. (A. Nilan, post-test)

These students present making meaning of their sources—reading and comprehending them—as an explicit step in their research processes. The first excerpt from student A. Jones was also double-coded for *relevance*, giving an example of our interpretation of particularly complex activities. The student will "spend a lot of time researching," indicating persistence, then turn to "reading the articles carefully and thoroughly and making sure they would fit in well with my essay," articulating the step of reading, understanding, and determining relevance. Reading and understanding also tended to convert a level 1 *engage* code into a level 2 code: 10 of the 15 level 2 *engage* codes addressed reading or understanding sources, although these codes were concentrated among only seven students.

Among students only assigned level 1 codes, *engage* also tended to be perceived as "grabbing" information:

> The next step I would take is actually finding those three outside sources and grab all of the details and information I can from them. (Anonymous, pre-test)

While the above example was coded *engage*, it is typical of many activities coded *gather*, which offers a counterpoint to engage-as-inquiry. In these activities, students often referred to grabbing information and details to use in their essay

DISCUSSION

CONTRIBUTIONS AND FUTURE RESEARCH

This study makes several contributions to what we know about undergraduates' writing-research activities and processes as well as suggesting areas for further research. We turned to students' own articulations of their writing-research, which helped us to better understand writing-research from their perspective, and we did so on a much larger scale than is typical for such studies (see, e.g., Fister, 1992; Kuhlthau, 1988; Lupton, 2004; Nelson, 1993). Continued research is needed employing methods centered on students' perceptions and activities, ideally with larger sample sizes. The challenge of such research is also grounding it in students' actual writing-research contexts (one limitation of this study, given its hypothetical prompt). Wojahn et al.'s (Chapter 9, this collection) analysis of students' reflective essays and research diaries provides an innovative model of IL research grounded in students' discussions of their research processes related to specific course assignments.

The students in the sample reflected our campus's first-year population as a whole, responding to Fister's (1992) call for study of average undergraduates as well as exceptional ones. The writing-research activities students articulated were similar to those described by others. For example, our students frequently discussed finding a topic, consistent with Kuhlthau's (1988) "selection" stage and part of what Fister (1992) describes as "formulating a focus for research"— one of the most time- and energy-intensive activities of the research process (p. 164). Our close analysis of this activity contributes to what we know about students' various approaches to topic selection and what it might mean to be writing information literate in this respect. Determining the relevance of sources is also an activity consistent with earlier findings. First-year students consider relevance to be one of the most challenging aspects of research (Head, 2013). Kuhlthau (1988) describes it as part of "exploration," which she considers to be the most difficult stage of research, one during which students often give up (p. 262, 299–300). Interestingly, and responsive to Kuhlthau's observation, we judged students as writing information literate when they articulated persistence in determining relevance.

Unlike earlier studies, ours highlights the importance of students' engagement of sources, thereby contributing to a conversation on how the material practices of students' reading, notetaking, etc., implicate students' meaning making (see also Jamieson & Howard, 2013). It comes as no surprise that first-year students are challenged by reading sources, particularly scholarly sources (Head, 2013). Our findings on *engage* are consistent with the Citation Project, where through content analysis of student writing, researchers are finding that students focus on sentence-level quotations they can use rather than understanding what they read (Howard, et al., 2010; see also Goscik et al., Chapter 8, this collection). The study also traces several activities often deemphasized or found to be problematic by librarians as writing-research, perhaps because of their strong association with writing: organize, use (see, e.g., Hongisto & Sormunen, 2010), and integrate (see, e.g., Head, 2013). Further research might examine more closely how students articulated these and other activities, including what counted as WIL.[12] (One model of such research is provided by Karen Goscik and her colleagues in this collection, in their careful analysis of what it means for first-year international students in a developmental writing class to organize their writing.) This study—focused primarily on students' activities—also leaves open questions about how students group such activities, or order them in their individual writing-research processes. As librarian Catherine Sinkinson (Norgaard and Sinkinson, Chapter 1, this collection) notes the writing-research process is ideally "one in which information seeking, reading, and writing are recursive and intertwined," even though we too often "present a fragmented process to students in which writing and information may appear vastly disconnected."

The study's assumption that writing and research should be thought of and studied as blended activities in processes of writing-research is not shared by some (e.g., Kuhlthau, 1998; Stotksy, 1991). It also was a limitation in speaking to students' use of writing and research techniques, respectively (e.g., Head & Eisenberg, 2010), and to the extent of students' integration or separation of writing and research (see Fister, 1992). Nevertheless, similar to Head and Michael Eisenberg (2010), we generally observed that students' writing-research activities were more efficient than inquiring, far less articulate and elaborate than we had hoped. No doubt our generic prompt is partly to blame. And more research remains to be done analyzing multiple coded text segments for possibly rich instances of WIL, as well as the activities and processes of students who were not coded at all for IL as compared with those who were.

TEACHING AND FACULTY/LIBRARIAN PARTNERSHIPS

The study suggests areas of programmatic strength as well as opportunities for more direct and effective teaching. The pre-tests provide a useful overview of what activities students are focused on when they enter our classrooms, as well as their strengths and challenges in regards to WIL. Students initially appear to be aware of activities related to discovering a topic, finding and considering the quality of sources, and organizing and integrating those sources in their writing. They seem less focused on activities associated with making sense of sources and navigating them conceptually, given the context of an assignment and their own purposes and views. In light of this overview, faculty can create a balance between practices that lets students play to their strengths outside of class (brainstorming, finding sources) and that uses class time to help them build strategies for reading, analyzing, and otherwise engaging sources.

Additionally, the study makes clear what was valued by researchers in regards to students' WIL, suggesting what we might build on as well as change with respect to our teaching. Adopting Norgaard's (2003) WIL as a framework for the study, we were disappointed with the lack of change in students' WIL, results which suggest that the writing program in some ways maintains a view of IL as the "neutral, technological skill" that Norgaard describes (p. 125)—a "look-up skill" (p. 126). Many writing-research activities are "outsourced": left to librarians in their 50–75 minute, one-shot sessions. (The online modules were an attempt to enhance this particular instruction.) While librarians try to deliver a consistent message to all students in FYC, faculty inevitably take a variety of approaches to course assignments, and the sessions often reflect the faculty members' priorities for their assignments. Unfortunately, this is the kind of "'inoculation' approach to IL" Norgaard speaks of earlier in this collection, an approach that "tends to obscure how IL ought to be seen as a rich, multifaceted literacy that is responsive to changing contexts and opportunities" (Chapter 1, this collection). There may be a mismatch, in other words, between what is valued as WIL and what is taught and how (see Limberg & Sundin, 2006). Such a divide might be addressed programmatically by moving to a more contextual ("situated" (Lupton & Bruce, 2010)) view of writing-research that locates it among wider literacies and learning processes (Limberg & Sundin, 2006; Limberg, Alexandersson & Lantz-Andersson, 2008; Talja & Lloyd, 2010).

It is also likely that faculty and librarians have differing understandings of research and its role within a given student's writing. As just one example, relevance in terms of information might not equate to relevance in terms of rhetorical strategy and vice versa. A more situated approach to IL education and relevance in particular (e.g., Limberg & Sundin, 2006) might better align these two perspectives. The study's code log, created through intense discussion among the faculty and librarians, is an immediately beneficial product of the study that may help bridge terminological divisions between librarians and faculty noted so often in this collection. As a framework for recognizing and understanding the diverse activities within students' writing-research processes, the log provides faculty and librarians with a common language.

The *Framework for IL* provides additional opportunities for future collaborative research. The language of frames and threshold concepts used in the *Framework for IL* has the potential to promote further dialogue between faculty and librarians regarding the practices and "habits of mind" (p. 1) that both groups value in FYC. Several of the frames and their supporting documentation directly address the research and writing skills explored in our study and even use some of the same language. For example, Research as Inquiry (p. 9) mirrors our level two code "inquire." The *Framework for IL*'s emphasis on learning processes, rather than a prescribed set of skills, also allows for more flexibility in developing learning outcomes for FYC. This may enable faculty and librarians to address the disconnect between what is valued and what is taught.

Despite the practical and conceptual challenges, our research can help us and others facilitate students' WIL, by drawing on what students already know and tell us. We know, for example, that topic choice (and, surely, its teaching) involves more complexity than students often recognize—multiple steps, criteria, and kinds of sources. We have learned that relevance is about students' persistence in considering the fit of sources as their projects evolve, supporting their patience as much as their perspicuity. We are now aware that students' engaging of sources is a programmatic strength, one to build on by continuing to move students from information grabbing to purposeful reading and sense making.

Our most important work on behalf of improving students' WIL may be the strengthened collaboration between writing faculty and librarians, facilitated conceptually and pedagogically by the conversations we share—the "institutional 'sweet spot'" (Norgaard & Sinkinson, Chapter 1, this collection) we have created for ourselves. If learning is itself a dialogic act, then it can be strengthened by research activities that prioritize collaboration and promote reflective dialogue.

NOTES

1. This study is the result of a collaboration among librarians and Writing Studies faculty at High Point University. When the learning outcome "integrating sources" received new emphasis in the first-year writing program, the authors wanted to learn more about how student writers perceive research when arriving at college and how that perception might change after taking the required one-semester composition course. Professor Middleton and Professor Scheidt wish to thank the organizers of the Dartmouth Summer Seminar for Composition Research (Summer 2013) as well as High Point University for its support of this research through a course reduction, University Research Advancement Grant, and Summer Scholar Award.
2. The mean combined SAT score for these first-year students was just over 1100. 79% of them came from states other than North Carolina, and 1.3% were international students. 37% graduated from private high schools. 83.1% of students identified as white; 5.1% as African-American or black; and 2.4% as Latin American, South American, or Hispanic. The students were predominantly between the ages of 17 and 19.
3. The writing program also offered a "stretch sequence" of freshman composition offered across two semesters. Students in the stretch courses did not participate in the study.
4. The group had hoped to learn what, if any, effect the modules had on students' processes or information literacy, but the study did not provide a way of identifying or measuring any such effects. From the completion data extracted from Blackboard, researchers found that the modules were not incorporated consistently in all 13 courses. Professors did not always use them in the order suggested or assign them a grade. In addition, many of the concepts addressed in the modules were also covered in one-shot instruction sessions taught by librarians for 21 of the 25 total sections of ENG 1103, including both control and experiment sections. Although there is anecdotal evidence from faculty that they felt the modules were beneficial, the study does not provide enough evidence to claim that the modules did or did not have a significant impact on students' research processes or perceptions of research.
5. That is, "intercoder agreement" (or "interpretive convergence") depended on intensive discussion and, ultimately, consensus as suggested by Saldaña (2008, pp. 27–28) and Smagorinsky (2008, p. 401).

6. We analyzed students' WIL in two respects, both at the beginning and end of the semester: First, we considered the instances of an activity coded for WIL as a percentage of all instances coded for WIL (see Table 10.2). Second, we considered the instances of an activity coded for WIL as a percentage of all instances coded for that activity (see Table 10.3).
7. Students mentioned other research resources far less frequently, including the library, librarians, books, academic databases, and an annotated bibliography provided by an instructor. And many students did not specify what kind of research they conducted in the process of coming up with a topic.
8. The data (x) were transformed as follows: sqrt(x + 0.5). Results of a paired t-test in R on transformed data demonstrate a statistically significant difference (at alpha = .05) in the number of times activities were coded in post-tests (t(47) = 2.02, p = .04896).
9. Results of a McNemar test in R demonstrate a statistically significant difference in activities coded engage in post-tests ($\chi2(1)$ = 11.25, p = .0007962). In order to conduct the analysis, five students' pre- or post-tests were excluded, for lack of a matched post- or pre-test, so that n = 48.
10. The data (y) were transformed as follows: sqrt(y + 0.5). Results of a paired t-test in R on transformed data demonstrate a trending but not statistically significant difference (at alpha = .05) in the number of times activities were coded for WIL in post-tests (t(47) = 1.75, p = .08752).
11. While brainstorm is the activity most frequently coded for level 2, it was almost always coded for invent.
12. Such research could have significant implications for existing phenomenographic research on students' frames for understanding (or ways of experiencing) the use of sources (e.g., Bruce et al., 2006; Maybee et al., 2013). Two additional codes of particular interest are acknowledging different view or opinions and understanding the assignment and its tasks. Kuhlthau (1988) found navigating contrasting perspectives to be a significant challenge, yet Fister's (1992) exceptional students welcomed such contradictions. Nelson's (1993) case studies point to the provocative hypothesis that students' understanding of their assignments and tasks explain the difference between "valuable opportunities to extend their knowledge through critical inquiry or unchallenging exercises in gathering and reproducing information" (p.116).

REFERENCES

Association of College and Research Libraries. (2015). *Framework for information literacy for higher education*. Retrieved from http://www.ala.org/acrl/standards/ilframework.

Beyer, C. H., Gillmore, G. M. & Fisher, A. T. (2007). *Inside the undergraduate experience: The University of Washington's study of undergraduate learning*. Bolton, MA: Anker Publishing Co., Inc.

Bruce, C., Edwards, S. & Lupton, M. (2006). Six frames for information literacy education: A conceptual framework for interpreting the relationships between theory and practice. *Innovations in Teaching and Learning Computer Science, 5*(1), 1–19.

Burton, V. T. & Chadwick, S. A. (2000). Investigating the practices of student researchers: Patterns of use and criteria for use of internet and library sources. *Computers and Composition, 17*(3), 309–328.

Diehm, R. A. & Lupton, M. (2012). Approaches to learning information literacy: A phenomenographic study. *Journal of Academic Librarianship, 38*(4), 217–225.

Emmons, M. & Martin, W. (2002). Engaging conversation: Evaluating the contribution of library instruction to the quality of student research. *College & Research Libraries, 63*(6), 545–60.

Fister, B. (1992). The research process of undergraduate students. *Journal of Academic Librarianship, 18*(3), 163–169.

Gocsik, K., Braunstein, L. R. & Tobery, C. E. (2016). Approximating the university: The information literacy practices of novice researchers. In B. J. D'Angelo, S. Jamieson, B. Maid & J. R. Walker (Eds.), *Information literacy: Research and collaboration across disciplines*. Fort Collins, CO: WAC Clearinghouse and University Press of Colorado.

Hahn, C. (2008). *Doing qualitative research using your computer: A practical guide*. Los Angeles, CA: Sage.

Head, A.J. (2013). *Learning the ropes: How freshmen conduct course research once they enter college*. Retrieved from Project Information Literacy website: http://projectinfolit.org/images/pdfs/pil_2013_freshmenstudy_fullreport.pdf.

Head, A. J. & Eisenberg, M. B. (2010). *Truth be told: How college students evaluate and use information in the digital age*. Retrieved from Project Information Literacy website: http://projectinfolit.org/pdfs/PIL_Fall2010_Survey_FullReport1.pdf.

Hongisto, H. & Sormunen, E. (2010). The challenges of the first research paper: Observing students and the teacher in the secondary school classroom. In A. Lloyd & S. Talja (Eds.), *Practising information literacy: Bringing theories of learning, practice and information literacy together* (pp. 95–120). Wagga Wagga, Australia: Centre for Information Studies.

Howard, R. M., Serviss, T. & Rodrigue, T. (2010). Writing from sources, writing from sentences. *Writing & Pedagogy, 2*(2), 177–92.

Jamieson, S. & Howard, R. M. (2013). Sentence-mining: Uncovering the amount of reading and reading comprehension in college writers' researched writing. In R. McClure & J. P. Purdy (Eds.), *The new digital scholar: Exploring and enriching the research and writing practices of nextgen students* (pp. 109–131). Medford, NJ: Information Today, Inc.

Kissel, F., Wininger, M. R., Weeden, S. R., Wittberg, P. A., Halverson, R. S., Lacy, M. & Huisman, R. (2016). Information literacy community of practice. In B. J. D'Angelo, S. Jamieson, B. Maid & J. R. Walker (Eds.), *Information literacy: Research and collaboration across disciplines*. Fort Collins, CO: WAC Clearinghouse and University Press of Colorado.

Kuhlthau, C. (1988). Longitudinal case studies of the information search process of users in libraries. *Library & Information Science Research, 10*(3), 257–304.

Limberg, L., Alexandersson, M. & Lantz-Andersson, A. (2008). What matters? Shaping meaningful learning through teaching information literacy. *Libri, 58*(2), 82–91.

Limberg, L. & Sundin, O. (2006). Teaching information seeking: Relating information literacy education to theories of information behaviour. *Information Research: An International Electronic Journal, 12*(1). Retrieved from http://www.informationr.net/ir/.

Lupton, M. (2004). *The learning connection: Information literacy and the student experience*. Adelaide, AU: Auslib Press.

Lupton, M. & Bruce, C. (2010). Windows on information literacy worlds: Generic, situated and transformative perspectives. In A. Lloyd & S. Talja (Eds.), *Practising information literacy: Bringing theories of learning, practice and information literacy together* (pp. 3–27). Wagga Wagga, Australia: Centre for Information Studies.

Maybee, C., Bruce, C. S., Lupton, M. & Rebmann, K. (2013). Learning to use information: Informed learning in the undergraduate classroom. *Libraries Faculty and Staff Scholarship and Research,* Paper 41.

Nelson, J. (1993). The library revisited: Exploring students' research processes. In A.M. Penrose & B. M. Sitko (Eds.), *Hearing ourselves think: Cognitive research in the college writing classroom* (pp. 102–122). New York, NY: Oxford University Press.

Norgaard, R. (2003). Writing information literacy: Contributions to a concept. *Reference & User Services Quarterly, 43*(2), 124–29.

Norgaard, R. & Sinkinson, C. (2016). Writing information literacy: A retrospective and a look ahead. In B. J. D'Angelo, S. Jamieson, B. Maid & J. R. Walker (Eds.), *Information literacy: Research and collaboration across disciplines*. Fort Collins, CO: WAC Clearinghouse and University Press of Colorado.

Saldaña, J. (2009). *The coding manual for qualitative researchers*. London, UK: Sage.

Smagorinsky, P. (2008). The method section as conceptual epicenter in constructing social science research reports. *Written Communication, 25*(3), 389–411.

Stotsky, S. (1991). On developing independent critical thinking: What we can learn from studies of the research process. *Written Communication, 8*(2), 193–212.

Talja, S. & Lloyd, A. (2010). Integrating theories of learning, literacies and information practices. In A. Lloyd & S. Talja (Eds.), *Practising information literacy: Bringing theories of learning, practice and information literacy together* (pp. ix–xx). Wagga Wagga, Australia: Centre for Information Studies.

Wojahn, P., Westbrock, T., Milloy, R., Moberly, M., Myers, S. & Ramirez, L. (2016). Understanding and using sources: Student products, practices, and perceptions. In B. J. D'Angelo, S. Jamieson, B. Maid & J. R. Walker (Eds.), *Information literacy: Research and collaboration across disciplines*. Fort Collins, CO: WAC Clearinghouse and University Press of Colorado.

APPENDIX

Code Log
Level 1 Codes

understand *assignment* and its tasks
find *topic* of interest
brainstorm prior knowledge or beliefs
gather sources
process/*engage* sources
learn more about chosen topic
determine what is *available*
take a *position*
locate *support* for claims
acknowledge *different* views or opinions
evaluate source *quality*
determine *relevance* of sources to topic or purpose
organize/arrange/outline
use sources
integrate sources textually

Level 2 Codes

invent
inquire

PART III.
INCORPORATING AND EVALUATING INFORMATION LITERACY IN SPECIFIC COURSES

CHAPTER 11
UP THE MOUNTAIN WITHOUT A TRAIL: HELPING STUDENTS USE SOURCE NETWORKS TO FIND THEIR WAY

Miriam Laskin
Hostos Community College, City University of New York

Cynthia R. Haller
York College, City University of New York

The Association of College and Research Libraries (ACRL) has recently replaced their *Information Literacy Competency Standards for Higher Education* (*IL Standards*) (ACRL, 2000) with the *Framework for Information Literacy for Higher Education* (*Framework for IL*) (ACRL, 2015). The *Framework for IL* shifts the focus from information literacy (IL) competency standards as delineated in the *IL Standards* to a series of six threshold concepts (frames), "each consisting of a concept central to information literacy" (*Framework for IL*, p. 2). As noted in its introduction, "Threshold concepts are those ideas in any discipline that are passageways or portals to enlarged understanding or ways of thinking and practicing within that discipline" (p. 2). One of the IL threshold concepts, or frames, is Scholarship as Conversation. Our analysis of Cynthia Haller's students' research papers points to the necessity of helping students recognize that if they can identify a source network and the significant authorities in a discipline or field, they can take advantage of the "scholarly conversation" by using citation trails (i.e., source, or knowledge, networks). Three other threshold concepts relevant to our analysis are Authority Is Constructed and Contextual, Research as Inquiry, and Searching as Strategic Exploration and we will bring these concepts into our discussion as appropriate.

For this chapter, we have examined research papers written by students in Haller's Fall 2012 and Spring 2013 junior-level course, "Research and Writing for the Professions," and will describe these more fully in a later section. We find that students especially have difficulty identifying what we call a "source network"—also known as a citation trail. We define a source network as a web of interconnected texts within which a particular text occupies a single node. The source networks most important to academic research, on which we are focusing in this chapter, are the "scholarly conversations" described in the new IL frame, Scholarship as Conversation. However, we envision source networks as potentially expanding beyond the "scholarly conversations" central to disciplinary knowledge. For instance, a full source network on the neuroscience topic of memory could potentially include news and magazine articles, fiction and poetry, Internet blogs, etc. related to memory. We believe it important for students, when doing scholarly research, not only to identify the "scholarly conversation" subset of the broader source networks relevant to their chosen research topics, but also to understand how disciplinary knowledge branches out to connect to other genres and modes of text. The problems students have hooking into source networks have not been examined as fully as some of the other major difficulties they encounter in college-level research/writing, nor have source networks' connection to finding an appropriate focus and evaluating sources been fully explored.

To learn more about students' use of source networks, we analyzed nine students' three scaffolded-research writing assignments: a research proposal, an annotated bibliography, and a final, formal research paper of 10–12 pages (see Appendix A). We obtained written permission from these students to use their texts for research under the condition that they be assigned pseudonyms as authors. We discovered that none of the students used source networks, as we are defining them, even those who received the highest grades. While this was a disappointment, it has given us a chance to reflect on the need for disciplinary and library faculty to better understand how students actually search for—and choose—information sources as they do research. We realized, too, that even though it *seems* to be much easier to do research in this age of digital collections (web and databases) because of easy access to a wealth of texts, students are now floundering in an avalanche of sources that potentially obscure rather than reveal knowledge networks that might assist them in their research. Thus, the student research process—always difficult, confusing, even daunting—is complicated by the staggering number of potential sources available at the click of a mouse. Those of us who did research before there were databases and the Internet had a different, time-consuming task: we had to use print sources, and we used indexes, abstracts, and bibliographies at the end of books and journal articles to complete our research. We followed the hallowed "citation trails"—the source networks laid out in our print-based tools.

To enable our students to identify the scholarly conversations in which we expect them to participate, we must introduce them to the value of source networks, but do so in the context of the Internet and electronic research databases. It is worth noting here that students today may never have held a print journal in their hands. Somehow, we need to enable them to find the scholarly conversations, or "tacit knowledge" (Fister, 2013) that faculty possess but which their students born in 1980 or after may have no clue about because of the sea changes in how we collect, store, and retrieve information in this online, digital world. Fortunately, the tools for identifying such networks are present within electronic tools and venues; however, they must be explicitly brought to students' attention as they engage in research. Here, we suggest several ways teachers in any discipline who include formal research papers in their course curricula can better assist students in identifying and capitalizing on source networks. Students are in need of a digital age strategy for following the citation trail up that mountain of information sources.

As we noted, our study indicates that students can best be served through collaboration between academic librarians and writing faculty. Academic librarians and writing faculty, particularly those involved in writing-across-the-curriculum initiatives and writing centers, describe the problems for students and teachers alike when teaching writing is relegated to first-year writing courses and research is left to academic librarians to deal with as a focus of IL. In fact, though, research and writing should be thought of as part of the same process and not separated. James Elmborg and Sheril Hook (2005) repeatedly emphasize this point in their volume of essays on collaborations between libraries and writing centers. Elmborg correctly describes the research/writing process as recursive and notes that it is related in part to the recurring interplay between writing and information. By segregating the research process from the writing process, we obscure this fact and thereby impoverish both the writing process and the research process (Elmborg & Hook, p. 11). By working together, however, librarians and writing center professionals can enact a "shared practice where research and writing can be treated as a single holistic process" (p. 1).

Several Library and Information Science (LIS) scholars have studied and written about the difficulties undergraduate students face in identifying good sources for their research (Bodi, 2002; Leckie, 1996; Fister, 1992; among others). They make the case for disciplinary faculty becoming more aware of the gulf between being expert researchers and novices, and what those differences are. It is worth quoting Gloria Leckie (1996) from her widely read article "Desperately Seeking Citations . . . " in which she describes faculty who embody the "expert researcher model" (p. 202); they have integrated the research process and know their own fields well. To academic experts, the scholarly conversations supporting "threshold concepts" in their disciplines have become tacit knowledge; they can be so familiar that experts lose consciousness of the explicit learning by which they were originally acquired. On the other hand, their students exemplify the "novice researcher model." They

> . . . have no sense of who might be important in a particular field, and find it difficult to build and follow a citation trail. They do not have the benefit of knowing anyone who actually does research in the discipline (except for their professor) and so do not have a notion of something as intangible as the informal scholarly network. They have never attended a scholarly conference. Because of their level of cognitive development, ambiguity and non-linearity may be quite threatening. They do not think in terms of an information-seeking strategy, but rather in terms of a coping strategy. Research is conceptualized as a fuzzy library-based activity which is required of them to complete their coursework. In other words, the novice is very far from the expert model. (p. 202)

Clearly, students lack what experts have: a sound information-seeking strategy. Without an understanding of the scholarly networks that underlie writing within disciplines, they have difficulty identifying appropriate sources. They are unaware of how sources are interconnected with one another and do not understand how to discover and/or mark appropriate citation trails (our "source networks"). This problem is even more challenging for students today because they do not get the same clues, or cues, about sources when they find them online as their faculty were able to get in the print-only world of research. Unfortunately, disciplinary faculty are not themselves always prepared to help their students with these difficulties. They may have been schooled prior to the digital age and be unfamiliar with the extended tools available in electronic library resources. Their knowledge of source networks relevant to their fields may largely be tacit and thus difficult to explain unless "props" are used (for example, an actual copy of a print journal). Some simply may not have reflected upon the challenges their students encounter and/or have not been prepared to help students with the research/writing process. In her illuminating article, "Information Literacy from the Trenches: How Do Humanities and Social Science Majors Conduct Academic Research," Alison J. Head (2008) describes the results of a Project Information Literacy [PIL] study that included examining teachers' research assignment handouts. The study found

> a lack of detail and guidance in many research assignment handouts. As a whole, the handouts offered little direction about: (1) plotting the course for research, (2) crafting a quality paper, and (3) preparing a paper that adheres to a grading rubric of some kind. *Few of the handouts analyzed mentioned where students were to look for research resources.* (p. 435, italics added)

Head's article also provides insight into many other aspects of students' research and writing processes and is worth reading to enable better faculty understanding of student researchers.

In addition to (and perhaps because of) their difficulty identifying source networks, students often have difficulty evaluating sources, or they do not evaluate them at all (McClure & Clink, 2009). Academic library faculty teach how to critically evaluate information sources, but the focus is usually on evaluating the source *per se* rather than its location within a larger knowledge network. In keeping with the IL frame "Authority Is Constructed and Contextual," they teach how to apply specific criteria to a particular source in order to ascertain whether the author or creator of the source is an authority and whether the content is trustworthy and valuable. However, evaluating sources has also become an issue that should be studied as an integral part of the search process itself. This point is emphasized by Brett Bodemer (2012) in his article, "The Importance of Search as Intertextual Practice for Undergraduate Research." He is interested in the way students search, particularly in the 21st century, when students typically find an overwhelming number of sources of information both on the web and in licensed databases. Bodemer asserts that these searches are not "lower order mental activity" (p. 336) and that "the role of search" itself is part of the teaching and learning matrix, where students should know both how to find "good" sources but also to exclude sources that are not appropriate for their research (p. 337).

Bodemer's article articulates an area of the research process that needs more exploration. As a way of helping students winnow through search results that can literally number in the millions, disciplinary and library faculty have learned to urge their students to create search strategies using keywords to find articles. However, teaching students to narrow searches by manipulating keywords may not be sufficient for helping them identify networks of sources that are truly interconnected within specific knowledge networks. After our examination of Haller's students' reference lists, it is one of our conclusions that her students seem to have relied on keyword searches in a database and then looked at the first 5, 10, or maybe even 20 of the resulting articles, choosing whatever number they felt were sufficient to meet the criteria for the project and to give them enough information to fill the required number of pages. We will discuss more fully why this is a concern and how we propose to supplement teaching search behavior based solely on keyword searches.

The problem of finding and correctly using sources is discussed from a different angle by Sandra Jamieson, Rebecca Moore Howard, and the other scholars who run The Citation Project (http://citationproject.net). They explore the question of why teachers seem more concerned with plagiarism than with other difficulties in the research process. In "Writing from Sources, Writing from Sentences," Howard, Tricia Serviss, and Tanya K. Rodrigue (2010) note, "Instead of focusing on students' citation of sources, educators should attend to the more fundamental question of how well students understand their sources and whether they are able to write about them without appropriating language from the source" (177). We agree. However, we would add and emphasize that understanding a source requires not simply intratextual cognitive work of comprehension but also intertextual cognitive work that appropriately connects individual sources with one another within knowledge networks. Students' tendency to rely on loosely connected sources on their topics—e.g., that first page of results from a database or Google keyword search—contributes to their writing problems because they lack a true context and understanding of where their source material fits within larger landscapes of knowledge.

OUR RESEARCH GOAL AND METHOD OF ANALYSIS

To explore whether and how well students are able to identify, understand, and capitalize on source networks in their research, we analyzed sources cited in the research proposals, annotated bibliographies, and final research papers of students in an upper-division research writing course taught by Professor Haller. We received permission from students in her fall 2012 and spring 2013 sections to examine and publish findings about their research projects, using pseudonyms so the students would not be identified. We sought to identify where students ran into problems with source choices and incorporation, and how disciplinary faculty and academic librarians can collaborate in order to help students be more successful. We examined nine sets of three interlocking papers that were portions of the scaffolded research assignment: three in each of three grade ranges (low, mid, and high range). We were most interested in discovering aspects of how and whether students were able to find and use a "source network" during the course of their research. Did students indeed discover and use the scholarly networks Leckie speaks of in the course of doing their research? If not, what might have gone wrong?

Haller provided detailed written instructions for each of the interlocking, scaffolded assignments (see Appendix A), which address the IL Framework's threshold concepts, Authority Is Constructed and Contextual, Research as Inquiry and Searching Is Strategic. In her instructions for the 2–3 page proposal, she explained how to start finding a topic and then work on focusing it. She commented on the cyclical (recursive) nature of this stage, where reading in sources during the research process would help to focus the topic and in choosing sub-topics—which in turn would help to organize the contents of the final paper. She also instructed her students what to include in the proposal: why the topic is of interest, who the audience will be, a description of a few of their sources so far, and what keywords they would use to continue their research. The result was that most of the students' proposals appeared to be adequate or very satisfactory as a starting point for the rest of the project. It seems particularly helpful for students to find subtopics or sub-questions to keep in mind during the research and then the organization of the final paper.

The second part of the project was to compile an annotated bibliography of about 8–10 sources and again, detailed instructions were given. (Web sources were allowed, but scholarly articles needed to be included too.) The papers we examined all had satisfactory annotated bibliographies, though not without errors or problems with the citations themselves. As we mentioned earlier, emphasizing citation formats too much can be counterproductive, leading students to focus on bibliographic formatting at the expense of source understanding. However, these errors point to a problem related to students' understanding of source networks. Students often have difficulty identifying the types of sources they are using, making it nearly impossible for them to find correct bibliographic formatting in their handbooks, which organize this information by source type. Further, students do not have a clear idea of what a journal article is, and how it is different from unsigned articles from magazines, or from articles posted on informational websites and the like. As we have noted, they may never, in fact, have ever held a copy of a journal in their hands.

We are neither pining for nor advocating a return to the old days of print culture; however, it is important to recognize certain limitations electronic formats place on students' understanding of how sources are situated within knowledge networks and to compensate for those limitations. Databases collect articles from all kinds of periodicals and reference books and list them together when a keyword search is performed. In result lists, source items are embodied in a uniform format. This doesn't help students understand how information is created, distributed, and connected; it doesn't help them understand what type of source each listing represents (e.g., scholarly journal or news article); and it doesn't help them evaluate a source that appears on a result list. Bodemer makes an important point on this issue:

> Practice in searching . . . engages students in intertextual skills in the larger framework of the undergraduate paper. It involves complicated acts of evaluation and decision making. Students who learn to read and navigate the multiple points of content representation in databases are engaged in grappling with the structure of texts and the organization of knowledge at large. (p. 340)

Over time, digital copies of articles in databases have come to include visual cues that help students contextualize and evaluate their sources—e.g., actual pictures of publications are sometimes included with the sources, and pdfs reproduce the fonts, features, and visual elements of the original. However, to access these advanced versions of database articles, students must usually move beyond the results list to discover these features. In addition, material cues in electronic texts (that is, in HTML format) are only implied, whereas the embodied character of print publications disallows overlooking such cues as publication covers, size of the overall publication, and paper quality and size. Finally, paratextual cues that might help students better apprehend the knowledge networks within which sources exist are usually entirely absent in electronic formats or require further searching for discovery: editorial boards, contributor information, tables of contents, and other texts that accompany a given source text within a publication are usually absent in the result lists or item record in licensed databases.

As we compared students' annotated bibliographies with their final papers, we discovered that of the nine students' work, only one used *all* of the sources in her annotated bibliography (but added no new sources in her final paper); one student used *none* of the nine sources from his annotated bibliography (he cited 10 new sources in his final paper); and the remaining seven students used anywhere from one-half to three-quarters of their annotated bibliography sources and added from a high of 14 new citations to a low of two new cites in their final papers. This shift in sources used for the final research paper is to be expected and actually is desirable. It indicates that students were not at all finished with the research at the time they had to complete their annotated bibliographies. It also suggests (or at least we would like to hope it suggests) that students were using new sources to construct and reconstruct their understanding of their topics over time.

We analyzed the students' final research papers by noting, first, which of the sources included in the annotated bibliographies were also used in the paper and included in the references cited. We also made it a point to notice when a source was cited in-text but was left out of the references. The reason why some students didn't include some sources used within the paper in their references is not clear, though it may be a function of not knowing how to deal with material in a source that quotes and/or cites material from a prior source. Academic experts encountering this "embedded" material would generally follow up by consulting the original source and citing the original source if the material is used in their publications. Students, however, are likely not going back to the original source. Here is another indication that we are not raising their awareness of how to use citation trails to enhance their knowledge of their topics.

Finally, we moved on to the most critical portion of the analysis, looking at what we call the "intertextual index" for each paper. Specifically, for each of the sources cited, we determined whether that source cited *any of the other sources* students used. This method makes use of the idea of degrees of separation between sources to see how closely students' sources were connected to one another within knowledge networks. We see the intertextual index as only one measure of intertextuality, but one that can help to determine whether students were tapping into source networks. As research has shown, expert researchers do not simply cite individual sources but also exploit and use entire source ecologies to build their ethos and develop their lines of argument, as research by Shirley Rose (1996, 1999) has shown.

In academics' literature reviews, it is not necessarily a single source cited that identifies the knowledge network an author seeks to enter, but rather the entire constellation of sources and how they are connected to one another within larger systems of meaning—in other words, experts understand the IL frame "Authority Is Constructed and Contextual," while novice researchers have not reached that point in their understanding of the research process. We spent time looking up each citation in the list of references for each paper and, after locating it, we checked whether that source cited other sources as references or works cited at the end of the article. For even the most successful papers, we often had to struggle to locate sources because the students were not citing sources correctly, but we did our best. As we have already noted, not a single student seemed to have found a source network. Interestingly, some of the students did cite authors whom we found through our own research to be experts in their field and much cited by other writers. This finding suggests that students' searches for sources, though less sophisticated than faculty's, can indeed lead them in the direction of key experts in a field, at least in some cases. Provided students can recognize when they have happened on such an expert, they might then be taught to focus more closely on the bibliographies of these authors to lead them deeper into source networks.

One such student was Amal, whose paper on artificial intelligence (AI) was in the high-grade range. He included 10 citations in his reference list, though only one of those was from his annotated bibliography and the rest were new. Amal's reference list included two citations to two peer-reviewed articles by the same two widely published experts on AI, Shane Legg and Marcus Hutter. Upon examining the two articles by Legg and Hutter cited by Amal, we found that they cite two other writers who were also included in Amal's reference list—Ray Kurzweil (perhaps the most widely known and respected authority on AI) and Linda Gottfredson, a sociologist who writes about intelligence but has nothing to say about AI. However, the articles by Kurzweil and Gottfredson that Legg and Hutter cited are not the same articles Amal cited in his own reference list; thus, it seems likely that the apparent intertextual connections visible in Amal's cited sources were coincidental.

Amal also used two articles from a website (http://www.lucidpages.com/) that has no identified owner or creator. It seems to be a repository created in 2008 by someone who wishes to offer a wide range of unpublished pieces by someone only identified as "Dak" whose book (no title offered), it is noted, is now out of print. Thus, though Amal's paper was well-organized, the quality, authority, and reliability of his sources was very mixed: five were written by acknowledged scholars or experts in the field of AI; one was an undated, unsigned reference article on a commercial psychology portal from India; another was from an online magazine devoted to science (*New Scientist*). In addition, most of Amal's sources were published between 1994 and 2008. The only source more recent was the third (2009) edition of a widely used textbook on AI. Because of the constant work being done in AI, we believe he should have been finding more recent materials on AI. A lack of recent source material can be an indication that a student has plagiarized from an older source rather than performed fresh searches, which would likely have turned up more recent sources. The possibility cannot be ruled out; however, we did not identify indications of plagiarism in Amal's paper.

Sources used by Lee for his paper on the software patent wars and their effect on software creation for smart phones makes a good comparison to Amal's sources. Lee's paper was also in the high range, but there were differences in the ways they approached their research and in their source choices. As with Amal, it doesn't seem that Lee tapped into a source network because we couldn't link together any citations from his list of references. However, there is a good possibility that Lee found two key sources that guided his research focus and his subtopics as he described them in his proposal, thereby contributing to the quality of his paper by connecting it to ongoing scholarly conversations. Lee's research project was about U.S. laws regarding software patents, with a focus on how they make the creation of new smart phone software difficult. Two of the sources he describes in his research proposal (and which he did use for his final paper) were by well-respected experts in patent law, business and technology. The first is a book which Lee describes as an overview of the U.S. patent system. He stresses that reading it made him want to do more research on today's problematic patent laws. The second source he names in his proposal is a *New York Times* article, "The Patent, Used as a Sword," by Charles Duhigg and Steve Lohr, both prize-winning journalists and writers. The article was part of a series on the global high tech industry and it won a 2013 Pulitzer Prize. Lee notes in his proposal that reading the article helped him refine his topic to focus on software patents. We have only Lee's proposal and the final paper to use to "prove" that these were key sources and that they helped him to find his focus and refine it, but his own testimony feels like real evidence. We believe that his paper was one of the best because he found and used two key sources to the best advantage to focus his research topic.

As we examined Lee's final list of references, for instance, we noticed that of the 10 sources in his annotated bibliography, he used only seven in his final paper and added 14 more. These new sources were almost all newspaper articles or articles and reports published online by technology, patent and other relevant organizations, associations or companies. All of these were highly relevant and timely, suggesting that the early focus he achieved from the Duhigg and Lohr article may have helped him perform more focused secondary searches later as he worked on the final report. Lee did, however, go off track and make some strange choices from the web. They didn't hurt his paper, but they make us want to know more about how he actually searched for information on his topic on the web. For example, one of his sources was a Swedish website, from which he took a definition of "software patent." Another strange choice was a personal blog entry from which he got a quote from Ben Franklin's autobiography about how people should not invent new things in order to make money, but rather to do it for the public good. The blog owner describes his underlying focus as "the ineffable nature of life!"—hardly a statement attesting to the blogger's expertise on patents, though his inclusion of Franklin's quote turned out to be fortuitous for Lee. Alternatively, perhaps Lee had heard or seen the quote elsewhere and located it online in an Internet search so he could include the source in his reference list.

WHAT WE LEARNED ABOUT HELPING STUDENTS FIND SOURCE NETWORKS

We learned from our examination of Haller's students' research papers that we—disciplinary faculty and librarians—need to focus our teaching more on the actual search process, and to move beyond simply teaching students to use keywords to find sources. Today's digital world is both a blessing and a curse for researchers, especially undergraduate novices. They think they know how to find information because the entry of a word or two in a rectangular box yields a multitude of results, whether in Google or in electronic databases. However, using keywords to generate a results list is rarely sufficient for identifying how sources are interconnected within knowledge networks. Disciplinary faculty need to collaborate with library instruction faculty to teach students how to find and exploit citation trails. Because finding information in electronic formats has changed so radically from finding information in print formats, we need to use a new, modern approach for researchers, one that concentrates on finding and hooking into digital networks of related sources. The curse of digital information storage and retrieval is, of course, that many of our students are absolutely overwhelmed by the mountain of information they find from a single keyword. This difficulty has been noted many times by educators who write about the web and the critical skills needed to find the right kind of sources and be able to evaluate them for relevance and authority (Calkins & Kelley, 2007). The same "curse" applies to searching with keywords in research databases. As we have noted, Haller's students' citations seemed only loosely related to one another. They did not find source networks, in all probability because no one has taught them how to find these networks, nor shown them how valuable such networks can be to find the kind of information they need, from acknowledged experts, on their research subjects.

As it turns out, however, there are some simple ways to find intertextual connections—source networks and citation trails—both on the web and in some of the more user-friendly databases. Once a teacher or a student has seen how to do this online or in a database, they will be able to use it and to pass the techniques along to others. There are two kinds of citation trails. One is the "backward" citation trail that is found when one reads a journal article and examines the references at the end. These are citations to the sources that the writer used and because they were written before the article that contains them, we call them "backward citation trails."

In today's digital information environment, it is quite easy to find these trails, and even to find the full-text articles, especially in databases owned by Ebsco-Host that offer links to "Cited References" and "Times Cited in this Database." Each article record in Ebscohost provides both forward and backward citation trails, many of which are live links leading to the actual articles, making it relatively easy to hook into a source network that will be useful.

The source network we call the "forward citation trail" leads from a given article the researcher likes and plans to use, to articles with more recent publication dates whose authors cited the given article. The best way to find a source network that looks forward, however, is not Ebscohost but Google Scholar. Some students know about Google Scholar, but we think they may be unfamiliar with some of its useful tools, especially those that can connect them to source networks. When Google Scholar is used with a keyword search, the articles in the result list have the following links underneath each citation and the excerpt from the abstract:

Cited by [#]   *Related articles*   *All [#] versions*   *Cite*   *More*

Clicking the "Cited by [#]" link yields a new list of results—articles or books that cited that article. In our experience, about half of the results on this list also offer a link to a PDF or HTML version of the article so that the researcher does not even have to spend more time tracking down the item. In case she does, the

"More" link offers a "Library Search." Clicking on it brings up WorldCat and one can choose a nearby library (including the college library if it owns that work) that owns the item sought. There are more "goodies" available as links below Google Scholar citations that we haven't described, but we will let our readers explore them. Katt Blackwell-Starnes (Chapter 7, this collection) also finds that teaching how to use Google Scholar leads to a better understanding of the intertext—the source network—and reveals more clearly for students who the leading experts in a particular subject are, and what the context is for their research topic:

> Teaching students to use the bibliographies of relevant sources and the related research aspects of Google Scholar and the library databases adds another layer that emphasize additional methods for developing effective search strategies and also introduce students to the *Framework for IL*'s threshold concept that scholarship is a conversation. (pp. 155–156)

The writing in Haller's students' papers also indicated other issues that appear to be connected to the students' search for and use of sources. The content and organization of final papers in the middle and low grade ranges tended to veer off from their focus and the sub-questions they named in their proposals, perhaps because they did not identify source networks of related articles that spoke to the same topics and issues. Their references often included articles only loosely (if at all) relevant to their stated central focus. Perhaps they felt they should discuss the ideas in these off-topic sources since they had taken time to read them and/or wanted to include them to achieve the required number of sources, even though the sources did not really belong in the knowledge/source networks most relevant to their chosen topic. In addition, in the same low- and middle-range papers, the students often failed to synthesize, or integrate, the actual ideas and analyses from their source articles. As studies published by the Citation Project have shown, students who have not been able to comprehend an author's work tend to rely on quoting a sentence, or paraphrasing or patchwriting, and they do not summarize—which essentially points to a lack of understanding of the ideas in the sources. Our study suggests that this lack of understanding is further exacerbated by students' inability to contextualize their sources within knowledge networks.

Even assignment instruction handouts that include much helpful advice for students on how to conduct the research and how to organize and format their papers can lack one or two key aids. Instead of instructing students merely to use keywords in their database and web searches, it would be of more use to help them understand how to find the relevant source networks—the citation trails or the intertextual connections between key sources on their topics. Access to these networks helps them understand where any particular source they use is situated within the networks of knowledge about their chosen topics.

Teaming up with a librarian to show students how to use Google Scholar or a database like EbscoHost's *Academic Search Complete* to uncover the source/knowledge networks, or to see the ongoing "conversation" between scholars and professionals about their chosen field, would be a significant step for disciplinary faculty to take. Two other ways that library faculty can collaborate with their disciplinary faculty colleagues in teaching the research process come to mind. One is to get a librarian's help in teaching students to understand the types of periodicals and the usefulness of peer-reviewed journals, since Haller's students' papers led us to the conclusion that many of them didn't understand the differences in periodical types. That lack of discernment affected, among other things, the errors they made in creating their list of citations. Finally, a joint lesson or two with the teacher and a librarian to teach students why evaluating sources is important—particularly the authority of a source, whether it is a website or a digital article, is a good idea.

Librarians can teach students where to look on websites for information on the author or site owner, as well as how to apply other evaluative criteria. The disciplinary faculty member who wants to help her students focus on authority in sources can require students to include biographical and professional descriptions of authors whose sources they're using in their proposals, annotated bibliographies, or other parts of a scaffolded research project.

REFERENCES

Association of Colleges and Research Libraries (ACRL). (2015). *Framework for information literacy for higher education.* Retrieved from http://www.ala.org/acrl/standards/ilframework.

Association of Colleges and Research Libraries (ACRL). (2000). *Information literacy competency standards for higher education.* Retrieved from http://www.ala.org/acrl/standards/informationliteracycompetency.

Blackwell-Starnes, K. (2016). Preliminary paths to information literacy: Introducing research in core courses. In B. J. D'Angelo, S. Jamieson, B. Maid & J. R. Walker (Eds.), *Information literacy: Research and collaboration across disciplines.* Fort Collins, CO: WAC Clearinghouse and University Press of Colorado.

Bodemer, B. B. (2012). The importance of search as intertextual practice for undergraduate research. *College & Research Libraries, 73*(4), 336–348.

Bodi, S. (2002). How do we bridge the gap between what we teach and what they do? Some thoughts on the place of questions in the process of research. *Journal of Academic Librarianship, 28*(3), 109–114.

Calkins, S. & Kelley, M. R. (2007). Evaluating Internet and scholarly sources across the disciplines: Two case studies. *College Teaching, 55*(4), 151–156.

Elmborg, J. K. & Hook, S. (Eds.). (2005). *Centers for learning: Writing centers and libraries in collaboration.* Publications in Librarianship 58. Chicago: Association of College and Research Libraries.

Fister, B. (1992). The research processes of undergraduate students. *Journal of Academic Librarianship, 18*(3), 163–169.

Fister, B. (2013, June 25). Tacit knowledge and the student researcher. Library Babel Fish [blog]. *Inside Higher Ed.* Retrieved from http://www.insidehighered.com/blogs/library-babel-fish/tacit-knowledge-and-student-researcher.

Haller, C. R. (2010, Fall/Winter). Toward rhetorical source use: Three student journeys. *Writing Program Administration: Journal of the Council of Writing Program Administrators 34*(1), 33–59.

Haller, C. R. (2011). Walk, talk, cook, eat: What can you do with others' work? In C. Lowe & P. Zemlinansky (Eds.), *Writing Spaces: Readings on Writing. Vol. 2.* (pp. 193–209). West Lafayette, IN: Parlor Press.

Haller, C. R. & Laskin, M. (2012, March 22). Reading for research: Inhabiting the intertext. Paper presented (by C. Haller) at the Conference on College Composition and Communication, St. Louis, MO.

Haller, C. R. (2013). Reuniting reading and writing: The role of the library. In A. Horning & B. Kraemer (Eds.), *Reconnecting Reading and Writing.* West Lafayette, IN: Parlor Press.

Head, A. J. (2008). Information literacy from the trenches: How do humanities and social science majors conduct academic research. *College & Research Libraries 69*(5), 427–445.

Head, A. J. & Eisenberg, M. B. (2010, July). *Assigning inquiry: How handouts for research assignments guide today's college students.* Project Information Literacy progress report. Retrieved from http://projectinfolit.org/pdfs/PIL_Handout_Study_final vJuly_2010.pdf.

Head, A. J. & Eisenberg, M. B. (2010, Fall). *Truth be told: How college students evaluate and use information in the digital age.* Project Information Literacy progress report. Retrieved from http://projectinfolit.org/pdfs/PIL_Fall2010_Survey_FullReport1.pdf.

Howard, R. M., Serviss, T. & Rodrigue, T. K. (2010). Writing from sources, writing from sentences. *Writing & Pedagogy, 2*(2), 177–192. Retrieved from http://writing.byu.edu/static/documents/org/1176.pdf.

Jamieson, S. & Howard, R. M. (2011, August 15). Unraveling the citation trail. *Project Information Literacy Smart Talk, no. 8.* Retrieved from http://projectinfolit.org/st/howard-jamieson.asp.

Laskin, M. (2002, Winter). Bilingual information literacy and academic readiness: Reading, writing and retention. *Academic Exchange Quarterly 6*(4), 41–46.

Laskin, M. & Diaz, J. (2009). Literary research in a bilingual environment: Information literacy as a language-learning tool. In K. Johnson & S. Harris (Eds.), *Teaching Literary Research.* Chicago: ACRL Publications in Librarianship 60.

Laskin, M. & Haller C. R. (2013, May 10). Composition and library instruction faculty collaborate: Helping students develop focused research questions. Lecture presented at *Transformations in Teaching and Learning: Research and Evidence Based Practices at CUNY, Ninth Annual CUE Conference.* New York: John Jay College of Criminal Justice.

Leckie, G. J. (1996). Desperately seeking citations: Uncovering faculty assumptions about the undergraduate research process. *Journal of Academic Librarianship 22,* 201–208.

McClure, R. & Clink, K. (2009). How do you know that? An investigation of student research practices in the digital age. *portal: Libraries and the Academy, 9*(1), 115–132.

Rose, S. (1996). What's love got to do with it? Scholarly citation practices as courtship ritual. *Language and Learning across the Disciplines, 1*(3), 34–48.

Rose, S. (1999). The role of scholarly citations in disciplinary economics. In L. Buranen & A. M. Roy (Eds.), *Perspectives on plagiarism and intellectual property in a postmodern world.* (pp. 241–249). Albany: SUNY.

APPENDIX A: HALLER'S RESEARCH ASSIGNMENT INSTRUCTIONS

A. Your Research Proposal (due 8th week of class)

1. Choose a General Research Topic and Read Background Information on the Topic

Your research project should be related to an important issue in your major or professional discipline that is also of interest to you. As you explore possible topics in a preliminary way, I suggest that you move back and forth between:

a) topics that interest you, either because you've encountered them in one of your courses in your major or because you feel a personal connection of some kind; and

b) what you are able to find by exploring library databases and other online sources using keywords derived from your major or professional discipline.

That is, use the topics that you're interested in to drive your initial search strategy, then REVISE AND REFINE that topic based on what you find during the research process. This cyclical process will help you to find a topic that is both of interest to you, relevant to your major, and researchable. It's of no use to have an interesting research question but then find that there are no materials relevant to it—maybe you are years ahead of your field! But it's ALSO pointless to choose a topic that is easily researchable—there are many sources available—but which bores you to tears. Either of these approaches is a recipe for having a frustrating experience of writing a research paper, either because you can't find sources or because you are working on a topic that does not intellectually interest you. The way to avoid these twin dangers is to keep looping back between your interests and your continuing research. Start with something that intellectually interests you and is related to your major field. . . . This preliminary research process will also help you to find out the current issues in your field, including what is pretty much accepted fact, and which questions remain open and perhaps controversial. Note: An issue for which you can identify clear controversies will work best as a research topic. Remember also that you may consider social, political, economic, philosophical aspects of a particular problem, or the ways in which research is applied in your field.

2. Develop a Research Question

Once you have a general topic, start to narrow it down. To assist you in this narrowing, read some background on your topic in a specialized encyclopedia, which will help you determine possible areas you might focus on. Also consider what materials you are able to find in the databases. Remember that your goal here is to articulate a research question: a specific question which you do not know the answer to, but which can be answered through an inspection of the scholarly literature in your field. This is different from deciding on your general research topic. [Examples given, deleted here for space]

After you've been through the cycle of brainstorming/preliminary research several times, and you're beginning to get a sense of your direction, you're ready to write your research proposal.

3. Write your Research Proposal Using the Following Format

   i. **Provide a rationale for your research.** In your first section, provide some background on the topic you are choosing: what is it and why is this an important topic to research (consider social and /or medical needs). What is generally known about this topic? Who might benefit from your work? The rationale paragraph should answer the "so what?" question. Why is your topic of intellectual or social significance, and what issues are unresolved? You've picked a topic that you care about; now make me care!

   ii. **Identify your central research question and any subquestions/ related questions you've identified to guide your research.** In this section of the proposal, indicate how you have narrowed your overall research topic and what your main research question currently is (see "From general topic to research question" above). You should also be able to list several sub-questions that will guide you in finding the answer to your central question. These sub-questions will lay the groundwork for the organization of your paper. To identify sub-questions, think about some specific things you will need to find out in order to answer your big research question. If you have a logically arranged sequence of sub-questions, you are a good distance toward organizing your research paper.

iii. **Describe your audience.** In this section, provide some information about your specific audience and how your paper will help them. Your paper should have a natural audience beyond your classmates: who will be interested in this topic and why? For instance, "My paper will be directed toward a hospital administrator recommending how we can revise our patient literature to incorporate cultural diversity." Or "My paper will make a recommendation for U.S. governmental policy on genetically engineered plants, after considering pros and cons, from ecological, ethical, and economic perspectives, of genetically engineered crops in commercial agriculture. My audience will be my Senator and/or Congressman." Or "My paper will report on psychological factors contributing to overeating and recommend to counselors at a domestic abuse center how to work with overeaters."

iv. **Report of preliminary research:** This section should summarize information from two useful sources you have located that will help you answer your research question. Be very specific: name them, provide specific details about what they say, and tell what each one has contributed to your thinking about your research question. Plan on spending around ½ page summarizing each source.

v. **Explain your search strategy and keywords.** List the specific library and internet sources [e.g., specific databases, specific scholarly and trade journals] that you plan to use to develop your research paper. List the keywords and questions you've already employed to identify potential sources, along with any new keywords you've learned and plan to use. Discuss what you have found out about the types and number of sources available for this topic. Will you be able to select from many sources, or have you found just a few valuable sources so far? What kinds of books and articles are available to you? Remember that you should be researching and reading throughout the entire research process.

B. Annotated Bibliography (3–5 pages) [Due Week 10]

An annotated bibliography is a useful way to capture the essence of the sources you've located. It helps you organize your research as well. In an annotated bibliography, you summarize each of the sources you have chosen to use, provide evaluative comments on the source, and note any ways it might be useful to you in answering your research question. The annotated bibliography thus serves as both a reference guide to the sources you have collected and a stimulus for how to use those sources in your research paper.

Prepare full APA documentation for each of the items in your annotated bibliography as you would for an APA reference list. For each item, write 3–4 lines summarizing and/or evaluating the source. A sample annotated bibliography entry can be found in Hacker, The Bedford Handbook, 8th edition, p. 479.

You will need to create multiple bibliography entries like the Hacker sample, one for each of your sources. Be sure to put the sources into alphabetical order. Your Annotated Bibliography should include 8–12 good sources.

C. Drafts and Final Research Paper

Outline and Draft Section of Research Paper #1 (2–3 pages) [Due Week 11]

For this assignment, you will submit a full working outline for your paper and the draft of one section of your research paper.

Outline and Draft Section of Research Paper #2 (2–3 pages) [Due Week 12]

For this assignment, you will submit the full working outline for your paper and the draft of a second section of your research paper. After you submit this draft, we will hold the REQUIRED peer review sessions. In these sessions, we'll talk about how to take your draft sections to the next level. How can you develop your ideas further with examples and/or ideas from your sources? Do you need to consider adding an additional section or section? Is there another subquestion you need to address to answer your research question? What information do you still need to answer your research question effectively and what new sources will you use to find that information?

FINAL Research Paper [Due Week 15]

8–10 pages; minimum of 8 sources, not including background information sources (e.g., dictionaries, encyclopedias, superficial websites); sources must include a minimum of three (3) scholarly peer-reviewed journal articles selected from the York library databases, each of which must be a minimum of six (6) pages long.

The research paper is the major course assignment. It should be 8–10 pages long, not including the APA list of references or any figures/tables. While writings in lower division courses encourage students to develop a thesis and appropriately argue its merits by drawing upon appropriate sources, your research paper in Writing 303 is driven by your research question, not by the thesis.

The paper is a written report which synthesizes research findings to answer the intellectual problem you've posed for yourself in your research question. It is not an argument which seeks to persuade readers about a predetermined thesis or viewpoint. Nor should the paper be a technical report. Rather, it should explore a question related to a problem arising from the development, social application, or practice of your major or professional discipline.

The research paper is based primarily on secondary sources (e.g. books and articles). You may and are encouraged to use primary sources (e.g., interviews, etc.), but these may not count toward the 8 required sources required for your paper. While textbooks and encyclopedias (including Wikipedia) may be used to get an overview of a particular problem and can be included in your bibliography, they also may not be counted as one of the 8 required sources for the paper. You should draw on at least 8–10 sources representing a balanced mix of books, journals, both electronic and hard copy, and appropriate, reliable web-based sources. Sources must include a minimum of three scholarly peer-reviewed journal articles selected from the York library database, each of which must be a minimum of 6 pages. The number and exact mix of sources you use will depend on your topic and question. The quality of your research paper will depend to a considerable extent on the quality of your sources. I will provide feedback to you regarding the appropriateness of your sources both informally as you search for sources and also in my comments on your annotated bibliography assignment.

Your final research paper will be 8–10 pages long, not including the title page, the abstract page, and the list of references. You are encouraged to use graphics that can help you communicate what you want to say to your audience, but the graphics also DO NOT count toward the required 8–10 pages.

Your paper should address your research question in an informed, balanced manner, with consideration given to multiple perspectives regarding your question, differences of opinion and controversies, and contradictory information that you've encountered while reading your sources in relation to your question. The best research papers effectively incorporate a broad range of quality sources to support the thesis and provide responses to counterarguments as appropriate.

CHAPTER 12
ETHICS, DISTRIBUTION, AND CREDIBILITY: USING AN EMERGING GENRE TO TEACH INFORMATION LITERACY CONCEPTS

Christopher Toth and Hazel McClure
Grand Valley State University

Currently, society is swept up in an information explosion. Individuals are subject not just to a plethora of information, but also the accompanying messiness of the landscape as information streams continually from all directions in a variety of formats, media, and genres. In addition, as information is generated and distributed, it doesn't move from point a to point b to c to d and so on (the author's desk to the editor's to the peer reviewer's, back to the editor, to the printer, to the reader); it's created and published quickly and often informally and it reaches audiences via a multitude of venues. Outside the traditional academic peer review process, publication and dissemination are relatively easy and, as a result, a myriad of information is accessible. This information can take a variety of forms including, but of course not limited to, Tweets, blogs, videos, BuzzFeed lists, infographics, and news sound bites. This information reality is filled with opportunity for discovery and burgeoning conversations that transcend geographic limitations, but it also leads to an overabundance of inaccurate, time wasting information that requires a rigorous degree of scrutiny.

This new landscape puts educators into a difficult situation because we're trying to teach students to manage all of this information, not just as students, but also as citizens. There is no overarching rule to indicate whether information is "good" or "bad." Instead, we need to equip students with the skills to make their own decisions about how, when, and why to use information. One approach to this challenge is to give students a starting point by using a genre that they are familiar with and that has emerged within this new information landscape: infographics.

As an emerging genre, infographics, or information graphics as they are more formally known, can be used as a tool to empower instructors with pedagogical opportunities to teach information literacy (IL) skills. Throughout this chapter, we'll start by defining infographics and go on to show how IL allows for emerging genres like infographics to be used in educational settings. In addition, we will describe how the consumption, production, and distribution cycle of infographics relate to IL. We conclude by offering guidance on how instructors can use this genre to teach IL skills and concepts and allow students to make better, ethically informed choices.

DEFINING INFOGRAPHICS

A genre that is becoming increasingly present in information landscapes is infographics, whose popularity has exploded with the expansion of social media. While the genre is not new—it dates back to early cave drawings and Egyptian hieroglyphics (Smiciklas, 2012; Krum, 2014)—infographics open a window for teaching IL concepts in the classroom.

Infographics, as the word itself implies, merge information with graphics. They communicate by combining words and visual elements in an engaging, static, cohesive display that attempts to inform, persuade, educate, and/or entertain an audience about a particular issue. While these displays may communicate numerical or statistical data, this is not a requirement of the genre. Infographics usually contain images, text, numbers, statistics, drawings, color, linework, or some combination thereof. They are stand-alone and offer a quick snapshot of whatever topic or theme they discuss.

One special caveat of infographics is that they are static rather than dynamic. Displays that can adjust instantaneously with user input, known as interactive data displays, are related to but distinct from infographics (Rawlins & Wilson, in press; Toth, 2013). Both display information, but infographics are not adjustable by the audience. This distinction is important because this chapter will focus on static infographics. In other words, once an infographic is published, it can no longer be changed, similar to a printed journal article or book chapter.

Within the last several years, as the genre has become even more popular, and as how-to books, compilations, and other guides surface (Smiciklas, 2012; Lankow, Ritchie & Crooks, 2012; Cook, 2013; Krum, 2014), it's becoming apparent that many people are embracing the genre to communicate about their interests, products, organizations, and causes. (For examples of infographics, check out these online repositories: Cool Infographics at http://www.coolinfographics.com, Visual.ly at http://www.visual.ly), or Daily Infographic at http://www.dailyinfographic.com).

Infographics are so ubiquitous that they exist on nearly every topic imaginable, and they can be found almost anywhere: marketing campaigns, annual reports, social media sites like Twitter, Pinterest, and Facebook, promotional fliers, etc. They offer packaging that is both fun and engaging in terms of design and are capable of conveying a relatively large amount of information in a small, discreet footprint. Because of these features, they are much more readily shareable than other genres that communicate the same amount of information via text alone.

INFORMATION IN FLUX

While there are many definitions of IL, for the purposes of this chapter, we'll be using the current Association of College and Research Libraries' (ACRL) definition: "Information literacy is a set of abilities requiring individuals to recognize when information is needed and have the ability to locate, evaluate, and use effectively the needed information" (ACRL, 2000). This definition emphasizes a set of skills that an information literate person possesses and uses. This skillset is applicable not just for students in their roles as students, but also as individuals, citizens, and professionals.

In February 2015, ACRL finalized the *Framework for Information Literacy for Higher Education*. The approach of this document encourages educators to teach IL not simply as a set of skills, but also to teach within a framework that emphasizes metaliteracy and conceptual understanding of key IL threshold concepts.

IL, viewed through either a skills-based or conceptual lens, carries with it an attention and ability to critically think about the information lifecycle and the ways in which information is created, distributed, and consumed. Much like writing and research, IL skills are organic and iterative, and they reflect the rich and complex workings of the information cycle. Information (whether in the form of a song, a journal article, a painting, a tweet, or an infographic) is created and then distributed, consumed, shared, discussed, and subsequently has the potential to give rise to "new" information. The song inspires another musician, the journal article is cited, the tweet is retweeted, or the infographic is shared. Understanding how these currents move or might move in different contexts and under varying influences leads to a critical awareness of sources of information; an information literate person engages in the rhetorical act of asking questions about who the creator of any given piece of information is, the audience for whom it was created, and the purpose, in addition to using the content of the information.

The information landscape is undergoing vast changes. The sheer volume of information available can muddy the waters for students. New discovery tools mimicking the ostensible simplicity of Google provide students with easy access to millions of documents with a few taps of the keyboard, sometimes leading students to think that resource discovery is easy. However, finding a source and finding a *relevant, accurate* source are two different things. As more sources become available, it's more important than ever that students are capable of critically examining sources. In nonacademic settings, information is constantly feeding us streams of information—from the billboards on the side of the street, to the devices in our pockets—about our social, political, and financial worlds.

Access to this information is in some ways liberating and a boon to democracy. However, there are some complications. Students may be likely to find and cite information that (rightly or wrongly) simply reaffirms their own beliefs. For instance, information students find may be influenced by the phenomenon filter bubbles, where a person's search history influences his or her new search engine results (Pariser, 2011). In other ways, the vast amount of information can be frustrating and overwhelming, especially when information found can be contradictory, obviously biased, or out of date. Also, uncritically assuming that "free" information is unbiased or uninfluenced by the platforms through which the information is made available is a mistake. Some would argue that the idea of the Internet as a public good, or information commons is an illusion. Jeff Lilburn (2012) insists that "claims that social media has become our new public space, or new commons, overlook the fact that, unlike a true public square or commons, many of the most popular social media tools are privately owned and regulated" (p. 143). Awareness of the financial interests behind creators and purveyors of information is another component of information fluency.

Because information dissemination is in flux, educators who teach IL are left with some challenging questions:

- How do we prepare our students to be information literate in an information-saturated world?
- When so much information is constantly being generated, posted, reposted, tweeted, retweeted, and regenerated, how do we encourage students to slow down and engage with the facets of IL?
- How do we teach students to contribute to the information lifecycle in meaningful, accurate, ethical, information literate ways?
- How do educators guide students to interact with their source texts, analyze them, synthesize them, and then communicate them in their own meaningful contributions to the field?

CONSUMPTION

As students consume the information contained in an infographic, ideally, multiple IL skills are being used. In theory, the students know they have an information need, they seek it out, they evaluate the source and decide whether the information is reliable, and then they use and attribute it for legal and ethical reasons. However, the linearity of the process implied by the previous sentence is rarely the reality for information searches, especially in the realm of infographics. Often people encounter infographics and other information on social networking sites, and they often don't know that they even *had* a need for that particular information. For instance, someone might see an infographic about the funding of presidential candidates pop up on Twitter—they may not have known they *needed* that information, but they may be interested nonetheless. The discovery process, because of the rapid and informal publication methods of information, is imbued with elements of serendipity and complexity.

Another skill is the ability to access information. Access is perhaps the simplest part of the consumption of infographics. Rather than seeking and finding information in response to a need, people are presented with a continual flow of information. Individuals hardly have to do anything to encounter a piece of information. Content from various media washes over consumers like waves. It's impossible to engage with all of the conversations that are available, and teaching students to pick and choose what they engage with is part of the challenge. It's also essential to teach students when they need to go further to confirm information that's presented via infographic. To do this, they may need to check the sources that are cited in the infographic or track down the information in other ways that may not be as easily accessible. For instance, an infographic may illustrate the government's expenditure on a program. Before accepting this at face value and acting on or using this information, it would be beneficial for the student to confirm this in the budget or in other documentation. This fact needs to be sought; it won't present itself in the same ways that an infographic does, and it may not be easy to find, so there's still a need for educators to address discovery and access.

Infographics also present unique challenges because they have the advantage of an immediate rhetorical punch. Using a combination of colors, images, and linework, an infographic's producer can use design techniques to shape the audience's reaction about a given topic. As a result, infographics offer audiences the "illusion of trustworthiness" because of their visual nature and statistical information (Toth, 2013). People ascribe more credibility to images than text alone (Kostelnick & Roberts, 2010; Kimball & Hawkins, 2008; Tufte, 2003; Kienzler, 1997; Schriver, 1997). Images and visuals can be seductive in that audiences may not question the authority of the data that's conveyed or question its merit in the same way they might with a book or journal article. Some have even suggested that infographic producers distort data to make a stronger point and attract attention to the display (McArdle, 2011). As such, students may be

Figure 12.1. A completely fabricated statistic demonstrating the persuasive power of a visually designed piece of information.

quick to make snap and superficial decisions about the information, without fully considering its authority.

Non-information literate audiences may also be more likely to believe information presented in infographics even though source material may be questionable and/or non-existent. According to Ellen Lupton (1989), "Statistics promote the objectivity of numbers while suppressing an interest in explanation" (p. 151). For instance, if we say in this chapter that 80% of all academic librarians are female, most information literate people would want to know the source of the data. However, if we design that 80% statistic with female and male pictograms in an infographic, some people may be less likely to question the data and focus more on how the data is visually presented. As a demonstration of this, the statistic in Figure 12.1 is completely fabricated and cites no source information whatsoever, but seems viable because of its visual presentation. This example illustrates the point that designed "statistics resist the skepticism on which empirical method is founded, and project an authoritative image of self-evident factuality" (Lupton, 1989, p. 151).

Another part of the challenge is teaching and encouraging students to evaluate the information they encounter and gather via infographics. This evaluation is always an essential skill, regardless of the genre or medium of access. However, like much of the information that students encounter, there is no formal vetting process, so it's especially important to guide students to ask the essential questions behind evaluating sources of infographics.

In some cases, the information used to create the infographic may be incorrect or flawed. In other cases, the source of information for the infographic may be outdated. And while in the minority, some infographics even go as far as blatantly misleading an audience with the type of information presented either to advance a cause or sell a product.

To avoid being misled, some of the questions all information consumers need to consider are: Who are the authors? What is the purpose? Why does this piece of information exist? How does the creator of this information support claims? What interests might the creator be representing or promoting? Whose financial interests are in play? Who funded this, and who has something to gain from the distribution of this information? It's only by engaging in this scrutiny that any consumer can really decide whether to trust a source or not, whether the source of information in question is a book, a peer-reviewed article, a tweet, or an infographic.

The ethical use of information, with attention to economic, legal, and social issues, is another competency that deserves attention. When students use information from infographics, it's essential that they cite them as sources, even though, because of the information's informality, it may feel free for the taking. Citing and documenting sources, in addition to being the legal thing to do, also reminds students that information doesn't exist independently from an individual or organization with a set of biases and a particular point of view. Being aware of this can strengthen the student's attention to evaluation.

PRODUCTION

Students are not just information consumers—they're writers and communicators, so they're information producers as well. While simply consuming infographics requires the use of many of the IL competencies, the production of infographics raises issues of equal importance. Advances in technology and the ease of software programs have also made infographic production much easier for the common user. With the click of a few buttons, even a novice can generate a simple infographic. And herein lies a problem: If virtually anyone with computer access can create an infographic, there is no way to ensure the products are reliable, accurate sources of information. What we can do, however, is educate students in higher education settings to interact with infographics as consumers and producers in information literate ways.

To create an infographic, a producer needs to conduct a research process that any information literate person should undertake. After deciding on a rhetorical strategy of audience, purpose, and topic, the producer needs to determine the extent of information needed, access source material effectively and efficiently, evaluate this source material, and appropriate newly researched material for a specific purpose and audience of the infographic.

When students shift from consumers to producers, they have to make a large transition from thinking, analyzing, and using the information as consumers. They are forced to consider more deeply the rhetorical dimensions of infographics, including the audience, contexts, and purposes of the documents they create in the genre. For instance, as a consumer, a student might use an infographic to decide for whom to vote in an upcoming mayoral election. But as a producer, the student needs to make a plethora of decisions, including who the target audience is (i.e., Democratic voters, undecided voters, or Republican voters, senior citizens, first-time voters, etc.), what information will be relevant for voters (i.e., city gun rights regulations, police and fire compensation packages, funding for a new pedestrian bridge, etc.), why someone might use this information, in what context will they use this information (i.e., in the voting booth, in informal conversations, before a debate, etc.), and then present this information in a way that will allow quick and easy access. As producers of infographics, students also need to consider how to gather accurate, relevant information to inform their audience and communicate their sources of information ethically.

In effective infographics, each design element does rhetorical work so that the infographic can communicate the desired message effectively. Even though some infographics may appear as if they are for a general audience, most of them have a specific purpose and targeted audience in mind. Students are confronted with research challenges, inherent ethical concerns such as including source material and minimizing data distortion, while simultaneously deliberating on design elements of visual persuasion.

The genre, like all forms of communication, offers the producer a lot of rhetorical power. The producer also has a responsibility in terms of their ethical use of information included on the infographic. For instance, the producer should include accurate information that is taken from credible and reliable sources. But without knowledge of IL competencies, it would be easy for the producer to skew information, omit citations and/or source material, or present material from overtly biased sources.

DISTRIBUTION/REDISTRIBUTION

Technology, particularly the Internet, document design software, and social media platforms such as Twitter, Pinterest, and Facebook, has enabled a virtual explosion in the rate and amount of distribution of information. In the past, there were more gatekeepers (editors, copyeditors, publishers, etc.) in place before the information could reach intended audiences. But now audiences can receive information without as many filters. The dissemination is much quicker and easier since individuals can share and publish anything they want simply by tapping a button on the screen.

The ease with which individuals can now disseminate information is a double-edged sword. Dissemination and communication technologies have allowed many more people to express themselves and enter various conversations, arguably democratizing conversations in the public sphere to an unprecedented degree. However, because dissemination is so manageable and attainable by such a large number of people, there's a plethora of information that may not be high quality, and as a result, it takes more effort to filter the extraneous or irrelevant information.

Looking specifically at the genre of infographics, the power and resources for almost anyone to produce an infographic presents a huge potential for problems. If people don't have the IL skills to produce accurate infographics using reliable (properly cited) sources, the result is a glut of inaccurate, poorly constructed, misleading infographics that are incredibly easy to distribute. Depending on the number of followers or friends in social media circles, the distribution of inaccurate information can be far-reaching.

But the ease of distribution also presents an even more dire compounding issue: redistribution. Once wrong information is distributed for the first time, viewers of that information can redistribute the infographic to others who in turn redistribute it to more followers. Redistribution in social media networks is unthinkably simple. People can "like" or retweet or "pin" with a single click, making the spread of information (or misinformation) potentially very speedy. Because infographics are designed to be stand-alone documents, they can be emailed, tweeted, or reposted in a variety of virtual places as well. This can be a boon to public good, because if the information could help people make good decisions or avoid bad ones individuals can simply and quickly consume that information and synthesize it with their existing knowledge base. However, if the information is biased or inaccurate, this poses a problem, especially if consumers of information aren't engaging in healthy evaluation practices. For example, even news sources can be susceptible to redistributing inaccurate information, as has been shown with celebrity deaths (Decarie, 2012). Celebrities such as Tony Danza, Justin Bieber, Gordon Lightfoot, and Morgan Freeman have all at one time been reported as dead when they were, in fact, still alive.

The other potentially troubling situation is that as a result of redistribution, information becomes separated from its original context. It can sometimes be difficult to tell from the infographic itself who the creator is or for what purpose

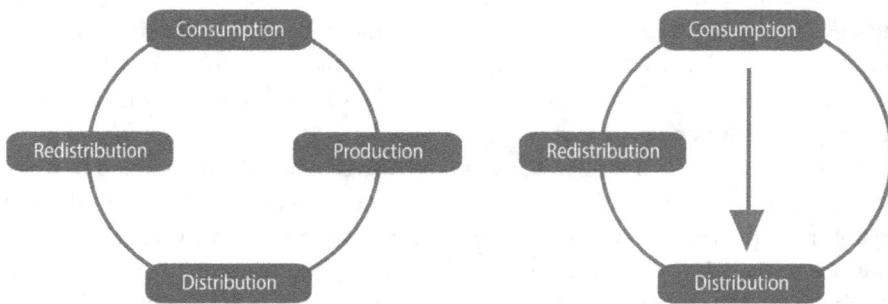

Figure 12.2. The diagram on the left shows all parts of the infographic's lifecycle, while the diagram on the right shows an unaccounted for critical step. While not all information consumers will be producers, being aware of the context of production allows for ethical use and distribution of information.

it was created. The product is alienated from its producer, relieving the producer of the responsibility (and credit) for its creation. An information literate person can do the work to track down the original source, or try to follow the trail of posting or reposting, but it sometimes isn't even possible, and many people wouldn't think to take the time to do this.

Another issue when considering redistribution is that during the act of sharing, retweeting, or reposting, an individual can easily shift from the role of the consumer of information to the distributor of information, entirely skipping the production stage or the role as producer. (See Figure 12.2.) This jump is problematic ethically because the distributor doesn't consider the rhetorical contingencies that a producer does during the creation of content. This makes distributing and redistributing incorrect or poorly constructed information easier and more prevalent.

In other words, inaccurate infographics, especially catchy ones that capitalize on emotional responses to issues, can rise to the level of pandemic. Redistribution in the worst-case scenario can be a combination of poor consumption, bad production, and quick distribution, resulting in mass communication of bad information.

AN OPPORTUNITY FOR COLLABORATIVE TEACHING OF INFOGRAPHICS

With all its difficulties and challenges, the infographic genre is incredibly exciting from an educator's standpoint for several reasons. Infographics are uniquely positioned in relation to the information cycle, involving people at multiple phases of the cycle. They also offer an engaging way to highlight the rhetorical complexities of communication and allow students to hone their visual and verbal composition skills. Moreover, infographics provide a practical solution to a challenge that educators routinely encounter by allowing for the potential distribution of students' work beyond the walls of academia. Students are thus empowered to compose for and reach real audiences if they choose.

If students are allowed to become consumers, producers, distributors (and redistributors) of information as part of an assignment to create infographics, their consumption and production of documents in this genre provides a charged moment of potential where critical awareness can blossom. The students we're teaching today will be producing information in many formats and genres in the future, and hopefully the understanding of IL they gain in relation to infographics will heighten their awareness of these issues in other genres and situations. As literate navigators of this information landscape, their future decisions and contributions to society-wide conversations will be more well-informed and of higher quality.

The genre is also exciting because it encompasses the information life cycle and allows for a moment of opportunity at which writing or document design professors and librarians can collaborate to raise student awareness and nurture skills to both consume and produce information. While a writing or document design professor's emphasis is on the rhetoric and design involved in the production of an infographic, the librarian's concern is more explicitly about the ways in which people interact with the information and the ethical implications of that interaction. We have a shared interest in educating students at this particular moment, and while our vocabularies and viewpoints may have minor differences, our ultimate goal coincides.

Recognizing this, we decided, as a writing professor and a librarian at a large, comprehensive mostly undergraduate liberal arts university, to co-teach sessions that introduce students to the genre of infographics. An ideal place to do this is in Visual Rhetoric and Document Design, a course taken by upper-level writing majors or minors. One of the major units in this course focuses entirely on infographics. Students begin as consumers and then, from the knowledge they gain, move into the role of producers and potential distributors.

Before the first day of our unit, we tell the students to begin by first viewing a sampling of infographics and selecting some that aesthetically appeal to them or interest them. After answering a series of questions to analyze the visual design components of their favorite infographics as well as to determine how they are rhetorically situated, students come to class ready to discuss particular information objects and the genre as a whole.

In class, we begin by asking students to simply look for citations on their selected infographics. After doing this, we engage them in several conversations, selecting a few of their infographics to show the rest of the class on the overhead projector. First, we discuss the facts, figures, images, and information that are not cited. Doing a quick look at many infographics that come across our radars on any given day will almost inevitably show that many infographics simply don't cite their sources.

Next, we discuss the rhetorical implications of creating a document with no cited sources. What is the effect of making a claim with no source? If any given consumer considers this issue at all, does she trust the infographic? In our experience, students notice the damage this does to the infographic's credibility. We also discuss how in some situations it wouldn't matter, depending on the rhetorical purpose of the infographic. For example, if ABC Corp. creates an infographic to promote sales of the widgets from the previous quarter, does it really make a difference that ABC has not cited themselves as the author of this information? Or, if the sole purpose of an infographic is to entertain, is it important if information is incorrect or not factual?

After discussing uncited facts, we discuss information that is cited on the infographics they're examining. We ask students to think about whether these are trusted sources, and why or why not, a similar approach we use for asking students to assess scholarly sources for a research paper. At this point, students discover that in some cases, the sources and the citations of can be problematic. For instance, there may be a citation that points to a URL for a general site that doesn't seem specific to the fact that is stated (i.e., htpp://www.nytimes.com). In other cases, there may be citations, but it is not clear to the viewer which citations are supporting which information. Some other sources are from companies with financial interests at stake, and still others are organizations with political biases.

We also ask students to pick two "facts" that are displayed on their chosen infographics and research their accuracy by checking the source materials cited and/or by doing additional research. Many students find that items presented as facts on their infographics are, in fact, not actually true or are completely misrepresented. These moments can allow students, as consumers of information, to begin to see the rhetorical motivations behind the infographic.

Beyond the information, we also ask students to find the original contexts of their favorite infographics. During this task students often find that because the infographic has been posted and reposted so many times, the origin is completely obscured. It forces them to think and move beyond the information on the infographic and act with the understanding of an information literate person, (i.e., someone who is concerned with who created the information and who is the intellectual owner). In other words, when students think explicitly about the origin of an infographic, it reinforces for them the notions of intellectual property and responsibility.

Going forward, the class is assigned to write a research proposal for creating an infographic, and then actually produce the infographic and reflect on their product. The purpose of the research proposal is for students to prove that they have a good grasp of the project by outlining the purpose of their infographic, the specific targeted audience, and the contexts in which it will function. They also have to justify their source material choices and why they deserve a place on their infographic.

Following approval of their proposals, students create an infographic about an issue of their choosing. At a minimum, their infographic must contain a strong title, a display of quantitative information, a display of qualitative information, and citations and documentation for all source material. Like any type of research, students are expected to find credible sources and cite them. The students can include any shapes, linework, color, or images to produce their final infographic, as long as all borrowed material is accurately attributed and their design choices fit within the larger rhetorical situation.

Finally, after they have constructed their infographic, students write a reflective memo where they self-assess their infographic based on the rhetorical, design, and IL issues we discussed throughout this unit. By this point, many students understand the responsibility they have as producers of information to create accurate and ethical infographics.

CONCLUSION

If educators empower students using IL principles, then they're empowered to make better political, financial, and ethical decisions, and effectively help govern our democracy as literate, critical thinking citizens. Creating assignments that engage students in thought and conversations about these challenges and working with educator partners can help prepare students to deal with the onslaught of information and hopefully help them do better work and contribute to society's conversations in meaningful ways.

Society benefits from an amazing array of information that's accessible in ways that until recently were unimaginable. There's a tremendous amount of possibility, but there are also some challenges associated with this access. As a result, educators need to instruct students to develop and use IL skills and understanding when they encounter new information as well as new forms. Infographics, and perhaps other emerging genres, allow educators a window to meet students in a realm where they're comfortable. Since students routinely encounter infographics, educators can use this genre as one of many tangible media with which to highlight IL competencies. Ideally, the lessons learned about IL from studying infographics can be applied to other forms of information.

REFERENCES

Association of College and Research Libraries. (2000). *Information literacy competency standards for higher education.* Retrieved from http://www.ala.org/acrl/standards/informationliteracycompetency.

Association of College and Research Libraries. (2015). *Framework for information literacy for higher education.* Retrieved from http://ala.org/acrl/standards/ilframework.

Cook, G. (Ed.). (2013). *The best American infographics 2013.* Boston, MA: Mariner Books.

Decarie, C. (2012). Dead or alive: Information literacy and dead(?) celebrities. *Business Communication Quarterly, 75*(2), 166–172. doi:10.1177/1080569911432737.

Kienzler, D. S. (1997). Visual ethics. *Journal of Business Communication, 34*(2), 171–187. doi: 10.1177/002194369703400204.

Kimball, M. A. & Hawkins, A. R. (2008). *Document design: A guide for technical communicators.* Boston, MA: Bedford/St. Martin's.

Kostelnick, C. & Roberts, D. (2010). *Designing visual language: Strategies for professional communicators.* (2nd ed.). Boston, MA: Allyn & Bacon.

Krum, R. (2014). *Cool infographics: Effective communication with data visualization and design.* Indianapolis, IN: Wiley.

Lankow, J. Ritchie, J. & Crooks, R. (2012). *Infographics: The power of storytelling.* Hoboken, NJ: Wiley.

Lilburn, J. (2012). Commercial social media and the erosion of the commons: Implications for academic libraries. *portal: Libraries and the Academy, 12*(2), 139–153. doi: 10.1353/pla.2012.0013.

Lupton, E. (1989). Reading isotype. In V. Margolin (Ed.), *Design discourse: History, theory, criticism* (pp. 145–156). Chicago, IL: University of Chicago Press.

McArdle, M. (2011, December 23). Ending the infographic plague. *The Atlantic.* Retrieved from http://www.theatlantic.com/business/archive/2011/12/ending-the-infographic-plague/250474/.

Pariser, E. (2011). *The filter bubble: How the new personalized web is changing what we read and how we think.* New York, NY: Penguin.

Rawlins, J. & Wilson, G. (in press). Agency and interactive data displays: Internet graphics as co-created rhetorical spaces. *Technical Communication Quarterly, 24*(2).

Schriver, K. A. (1997). *Dynamics of document design.* New York, NY: Wiley.

Smiciklas, M. (2012). *The power of infographics: Using pictures to communicate and connect with your audiences.* Indianapolis, IN: Que.

Toth, C. (2013). Revisiting a genre: Teaching infographics in business communication courses. *Business Communication Quarterly, 76*(4), 446–457. doi: 10.1177/1080569913506253.

Tufte, E. (2003). *The quantitative display of information.* (2nd ed.). Cheshire, CT: Graphics Press.

CHAPTER 13
INFORMATION LITERACY PREPARATION OF PRE-SERVICE AND GRADUATE EDUCATORS

Susan Brown
Kennesaw State University

Janice R. Walker
Georgia Southern University

With the development and adoption of the Common Core State Standards (CCSS) for K-12, there has been a shift toward challenging students to demonstrate higher-order thinking skills. This shift includes specific goals in the area of information literacy (IL). Recently, however, as one of the authors reviewed student writing in her undergraduate pre-service and graduate teacher education classes at a public suburban university, the lack of IL skills exhibited by teacher candidates at both levels was evident. This is a major concern since these are the teachers that will be expected to model and teach these skills to K-12 populations.

A large part of the problem may simply be semantic, of course, but we believe the lack of a common terminology between and among disciplines is a critical factor in what we are teaching and how we assess learning of IL skills at all levels and across disciplines. That is, while a review of standards across disciplines demonstrated some level of emphasis on IL skills, the specific terminology used to address IL varied across disciplines, and without a shared framework and terminology, the focus on IL in both K-12 and higher education is fragmented. This is evident in analysis of IL standards and review of research studies addressing interventions in pre-service and graduate educator preparation programs. Thus, the final section of this chapter includes possible solutions to begin improving IL skills in teacher preparation programs.

TEACHER PREPARATION AND IL

In pre-service undergraduate teacher education programs, the majority of students are recent high school graduates. In graduate education programs, serving both practicing teachers and career changers, there are a wide range of skills reflecting a wide range of undergraduate preparation. Both the Master of Education (M.Ed.) and the Master of Arts in Teaching (MAT) candidates come from a variety of different undergraduate K-12 teacher preparation programs, with the MAT candidates excluding undergraduate teacher preparation. The common characteristic of teacher education candidates we discuss in this chapter is a lack of IL skills acquired in previous educational settings, as also noted by Thomas Scott Duke and Jennifer Diane Ward (2009). The major focus of this chapter is to consider some of the factors impacting the IL preparation and skill level of candidates in teacher education programs and the impact (if any) of the Common Core State Standards (CCSS) on teacher education.

The National Forum on Information Literacy (NFIL) (2015) asserts that "The overarching goal of K-20 education is simple—to produce independent, self-sufficient, lifelong learners who can successfully navigate the competitive challenges of post-secondary educational and/or workplace opportunities." Marjorie M. Warmkassel and Joseph M. McCade (1997) also emphasized the importance of educator preparation in the area of IL skills to begin development of these skills before students graduate from high school.

A study by Kelly L. Heider (2009) addressed the importance of beginning instruction in IL skills as early as elementary-school years, a premise also supported by the CCSS (CCSSO, 2010), that begins with the following kindergarten-level standard: "With prompting and support, ask and answer questions about key details in a text" (ELACCKRL1 Key Ideas and Details), thereby introducing young students to the concept of providing support for their ideas, an important foundation of IL. By third grade, students are asked to build on this skill and must be able to "Use text features and search tools (e.g., key words, sidebars, hyperlinks) to locate information relevant to a given topic quickly and efficiently" (ELACC3RI5). By the time students complete high school, then, the expectation is that they can

> Gather relevant information from multiple authoritative print and digital sources, using advanced searches effectively; assess the usefulness of each source in answering the research question; integrate information into the text selectively to maintain the flow of ideas, avoiding plagiarism and following a standard format for citation. (CCSSO, 2015)

But how are teachers being prepared to teach these skills?

TEACHER PREPARATION PROGRAM STANDARDS

Warren F. Crouse and Kristine Esch Kasbohm (2004) addressed the changes in education policy that have led to the increased importance of data-driven

Information Literacy Preparation

accreditation programs. For example, the renewal of the Elementary and Secondary Education Act reauthorized in 2002, commonly referred to as No Child Left Behind, focused on accountability in K-12 public education. Schools were rated based on student performance data. As Gary Olson (2010) proposed, the focus on accountability in higher education revealed the many layers of data that could be addressed (e.g. fiscal, disciplinary). By 2013, a bill was proposed in Congress to hold institutions of higher education accountable for their four year completion rate data (see HB 1928 (https://www.congress.gov/bill/113th-congress/house-bill/1928). Although higher education and educator preparation programs had accreditation programs in place for accreditation purposes, the emphasis on completion rates and performance after graduation added another layer of accountability.

Educator preparation programs prepare for an online and onsite review every seven years to maintain Council for Accreditation of Educator Preparation (CAEP) accreditation. As part of the accreditation process, programs must meet CAEP standards, at least some of which recognize the importance of IL skills in teacher preparation, for example, "The teacher understands the demands of accessing and managing information as well as how to evaluate issues of ethics and quality related to information and its use" (CAEP, 2015). CAEP (2015) standards, however, focus on judging an institution's educator preparation program rather than setting standards of performance for individuals, as evidenced by CAEP Standard 1 which addresses expectations for the curriculum in educator preparation programs, and CAEP standards 2–5 which address the structures supporting the educator preparation programs (field experience, candidates, program impact, program capacity). CAEP Standard 1.1 includes a link to other accreditation standards: "Candidates demonstrate an understanding of the 10 Interstate Teachers Assessment and Support Consortium (InTASC) standards at the appropriate progression level(s) [i] in the following categories: the learner and learning; content; instructional practice; and professional responsibility" (CAEP, 2015). The Interstate Teachers Assessment and Support Consortium (InTASC) was formed in 1987 "to reform the licensing, preparation and professional development of teachers" (CCSO, 2011). The development of these Standards was sponsored by the Council of Chief State School Officers (CCSSO), the same organization that was involved in the development of the CCSS. The major links to IL are found in Standard 5, Application of Content, Essential Knowledge, "The teacher understands the demands of accessing and managing information as well as how to evaluate issues of ethics and quality related to information and its use," and Standard 9, Professional Learning and Ethical Practice, Performances, "The teacher advocates, models, and teaches safe, legal, and ethical use of information and technology including appropriate documentation of sources and respect for others in the use of social media." CAEP also provides a second level of accountability: "1.3 Providers ensure that completers apply content and pedagogical knowledge as reflected in outcome assessments in response to standards of Specialized Professional Associations (SPA), the National Board for Professional Teaching Standards (NBPTS), states, or other accrediting bodies (e.g., National Association of Schools of Music—NASM)" (CAEP, 2015). The relationships between accrediting organizations are represented in Figure 13.1.

The National Council of Teachers of English (NCTE) includes two relevant standards, Standards 7 and 8—"Students conduct research on issues and interests by generating ideas and questions, and by posing problems. They gather, evaluate, and synthesize data from a variety of sources (e.g., print and non-print texts, artifacts, people) to communicate their discoveries in ways that suit their purpose and audience" (std7), and "Students use a variety of technological and information resources (e.g., libraries, databases, computer networks, video) to gather and synthesize information and to create and communicate knowledge" (std8)—which refer to elements of IL as defined in the *Framework for Information Literacy for Higher Education* (*Framework for IL*) (ACRL, 2015), but do not provide a structure for how to prepare teacher candidates in IL.

InTASC Standards (CCSSO, 2011) emphasize technology merely as a tool. Amanda M. Fairbanks (2013) addressed technology as a critical element in today's schools; however, her emphasis was on the importance of digital curricula and digital tools without addressing the value of IL in selection of content and research. The International Society for Technology and Education (ISTE), the professional specialty association for technology specialists in schools, addresses the use of technology as an important component of IL, but still includes the technology-as-a-tool representation: "Model and facilitate effective use of current and emerging digital tools to locate, analyze, evaluate, and use information resources to support research and learning." As we will show in more detail later in this chapter, however, the lack of a shared vocabulary can have a constraining effect on collaboration, especially across disciplines.

INFORMATION LITERACY OF TEACHER EDUCATION MAJORS AND GRADUATES

Marcia Stockham and Heather Collins (2012), in their report on a survey of pre-service education majors (juniors and seniors) to self-evaluate their level of IL skills, note that

Information Literacy Preparation

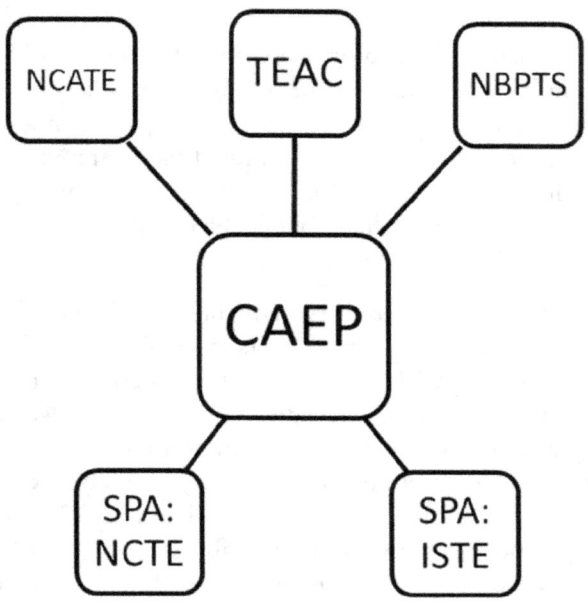

Legend:

NCATE National Council for Accreditation of Teacher Education

TEAC Teacher Education Accreditation Council

NB PTS National Board of Professional Teaching Standards

CAEP Council for the Accreditation of Educator Preparation

SPA Specialty Professional Association

NCTE National Council for Teachers of English

ISTE International Society for Technology in Education

Figure 13.1. Accreditation structure for teacher preparation programs

The fifth question [asked of pre-service teachers] was preceded by this statement: "Information Literacy Competencies for K-12 students (also called Information Power Standards,

> Handy 5, Big 6, etc.) include concepts such as: knowing how to access, evaluate and use information in order to become independent learners that allow them to become socially responsible." When asked whether the students were familiar with these concepts, only 10% indicated they were "very familiar." Fifty-one percent indicated they were "somewhat familiar" or had "heard of them," while 39% indicated this was the first they had heard of them. (p. 65)

Stockham and Collins (2012) also surveyed school media specialists to elicit their perceptions of the IL skills of new teachers in their schools. The results of the survey of school media specialists aligned with the student self-evaluations, indicating that students and new teachers did not have knowledge of IL skills. School media specialists' comments illustrate common themes in other studies as well, such as students' perception that the ability to Google demonstrates mastery of IL skills. Project Information Literacy (Head, 2013) also reported this result. Although Google represents an acceptable starting point for locating information, there was no information provided on students' ability to evaluate the sources located by a Google search.

Marlene Asselin and Elizabeth Lee (2002) discuss the common, but incorrect, assumption that preservice teachers have acquired IL skills. As they report, if this lack of IL skill development continues, teachers will not be equipped to teach their K-12 students. To address this need, they developed a teacher-librarian course for pre-service teachers that included lesson plans to develop IL skills in K-12 classrooms. Their emphasis on teacher-librarian collaboration and specific tasks (e.g., lesson plan) was recommended for future studies.

Deborah M. Floyd, Gloria Colvin, and Yasar Bodur (2008) reported on a study that began when an instructor of a field experience course "designed an assignment requiring the preservice teachers to identify real classroom problems in elementary schools and to then use professional literature to research the problems." So-called "real-world" classroom problems such as this typically include elements of effective practice by providing pre-service teachers with the opportunity to analyze student learning and research solutions to problems they will experience in their future classrooms (Coggshall, Rasmussen, Colton, Milton & Jacques, 2012). In Floyd, Colvin, and Bodur's (2008) study, the instructor provided a rubric to help students evaluate the appropriateness of sources, emphasizing recency, credibility, and relevance. Results indicated that students demonstrated mastery of addressing the real-world problems they were presented, but struggled with academic IL skills such as the use of quality professional references, especially peer-reviewed journals. This is similar to what happens in other professional fields, with students succeeding within a specific discourse community but not transferring the skills and knowledge to different communities. We expect, however, that part of what may constitute a discourse community is how it uses (and values) IL skills.

During the following semester, collaboration with library staff included an in-class IL session intended to support students in the ability to

> identify the major databases for use in education research and to be able to use them efficiently; to distinguish between peer-reviewed articles and other resources; to know how to locate articles, books, and other appropriate resources, and to be able to identify ways in which they could get assistance with their research. (Floyd, Colvin & Bodur, 2008)

Results at the end of the semester with the librarian presentation demonstrated an increase in peer-reviewed sources in projects. This is an example of the potential benefits of teacher-librarian collaboration in teacher preparation.

These studies include librarians as collaborators in development of IL skills. Librarians, as indicated in the following section, have developed structures and language to support development of IL skills. The terminology in other education fields addressed in this chapter, however, is less focused on a common definition of IL. How does this lack of a common language impact preparing K-12 teachers to prepare their students in IL skills?

SPEAKING A COMMON LANGUAGE

Although the multiple organizations impacting teacher education all include some reference to IL skills, it is interesting to note that none of them use the specific term *information literacy*. Jordan K. Smith (2013) reported on a qualitative study of secondary teachers which revealed that participants were not familiar with the term or scope of IL. Smith suggested that since the majority of IL studies were published in library and information studies publications, teachers would not have been exposed to them. The absence of shared terminology is also evident in the K-12 arena with the *Standards for the 21st-Century Learner* of the American Association of School Librarians (AASL), the professional organization for librarians serving K-12 schools, and the fragmented skills within the CCSS. If teachers are to be prepared to implement the CCSS related to IL, the adoption of a common framework or shared vocabulary across disciplines is essential for communication.

Given the growth of available information, obsolescence of information, and lack of screening of information credibility as we moved from an oral to a print and now to a digital culture, an increased emphasis on IL skills in K-12 education is essential (Warmkessel & McCade, 1997). The CCSS reflect recognition of this need to prepare K-12 students with skills for success after high school, including foundational skills (e.g., reading, and especially critical reading) essential to IL, and higher-order thinking skills required for success in higher education and careers (CCSS, 2015). The emphasis begins in kindergarten: "With prompting and support, ask and answer questions about key details in a text" (CCSS, 2015), and continues through high school content literacy standards: "Integrate and evaluate multiple sources of information presented in diverse formats and media (e.g., quantitative data, video, multimedia) in order to address a question or solve a problem" (CCSSO, 2015).

The AASL Task Force on Information Literacy Standards developed a list of competency standards to be addressed in K-12 education in 2007 that offers

> a vision for teaching and learning to both guide and beckon the school library profession as education leaders. The learning standards shape the library program and serve as a tool for school librarians to use to shape the learning of students in the school. (AASL, 2015.)

Resources, including lesson plans and an alignment, or "crosswalk," with the CCSS, are published on the AASL website. Although this crosswalk attempts to address the alignment of global AASL Literacy Standards and linked CCSS across grade levels, we believe the lack of specificity within the CCSS does not provide an adequate picture of how IL is addressed.

One problem with the attempt to connect AASL and CCSS Standards is the lack of a common terminology across disciplines. For example, as illustrated in Table 13.1, the AASL reference to an "inquiry-based process" is aligned with the CCSS standards addressing "Research to Build and Present Knowledge."

Although the two standards represent a shared vision of inquiry, the lack of shared terminology can create a barrier to collaboration between school librarians and classroom teachers. As Maggie Dugan (n.d.) notes, "Every type of science has a robust language of its own, rife with acronyms and jargon that make for efficient communication amongst peers within the field but can be confusing, misleading or off-putting to people from other disciplines."

The Association of College and Research Libraries (ACRL) also recognized the need to address IL in post-secondary education. Table 13.2 highlights similarities and differences between the elements of the definition of IL by the ACRL (2000) and the CCSS for Literacy in World History Grades 11–12.

The shared vision of IL is masked behind differences in vocabulary. Dugan (n.d.) says that "we rely on language to convey meaning, and that if we don't

Table 13.1. Comparison of AASL and CCSS standard

AASL Standard 1: Inquire, think critically and gain knowledge	CCSS English Language Arts/Literacy Standards
	Reading Informational Text Grade 6
1.1.1 Follow an inquiry-based process in seeking knowledge in curricular subjects, and make the real-world connection for using this process in own life.	CC.6.W.7 Research to Build and Present Knowledge: Conduct short research projects to answer a question, drawing on several sources and refocusing the inquiry when appropriate.

Table 13.2. Comparison of ACRL and CCSA

ACRL IL Definition Elements	CCSS.ELA-Literacy.WHST.11-12.8
• Determine the extent of information needed • Access the needed information effectively and efficiently • Evaluate information and its sources critically • Incorporate selected information into one's knowledge base • Use information effectively to accomplish a specific purpose • Understand the economic, legal, and social issues surrounding the use of information, and access and use information ethically and legally. (ACRL, 2000)	• Gather relevant information from multiple authoritative print and digital sources, using advanced searches effectively; • Assess the strengths and limitations of each source in terms of the specific task, purpose, and audience; • Integrate information into the text selectively to maintain the flow of ideas, avoiding plagiarism and overreliance on any one source and following a standard format for citation. (CCSSO, 2015)

have a shared understanding, it's harder to work together and collaborate creatively." In other words, although it appears on the surface that educators and librarians at all levels believe in the importance of a focus on IL, the lack of a shared language interferes with collaboration in providing effective IL instruction and support for students at all levels.

A key source of confusion in reviewing standards is the definition of a standard. Teacher education accrediting standards are intended to guide the self-assessment of educator preparation programs using types of results described by the Council of Writing Program Administrators (CWPA) (2014) as outcomes, but the teacher education standards do not provide the precise level of achievement described as standards by CWPA (2014). Thus aligning standards with different levels of precision requires subjective assumptions by the reader. With the recent moves by both ACRL and the CWPA to present a framework, rather than standards, for IL, we argue that teacher education programs and accrediting bodies need to review their own IL standards and consider how they may—or may not—align.

IMPROVING IL SKILLS

While it may not need saying, we nonetheless argue that in order to teach IL skills in K-20 settings, teachers must themselves first be information literate. A common characteristic of many teacher education candidates appears to be insufficient knowledge of core IL skills, according to Laura Saunders (2012) who summarized research indicating that college students did not demonstrate IL competency and university one-shot librarian presentations were not adequate to improve their skills. The lack of effectiveness of one-shot librarian presentations was also reported by Crouse and Kasbohm (2004). Duke and Ward (2009), however, report that, "many teacher educators still do not view academic librarians as collaborative partners who can help them teach information literacy skills and research strategies to pre-service and in-service teachers" (pp. 1–2). As a result, perhaps, the one-shot approach to teaching IL skills is all too often still in evidence.

As Stockham and Collins (2012) so astutely assert, "Since teachers cannot teach what they do not know, it is necessary for teacher education programs and libraries to collaborate in meeting ACRL student learning outcomes for information literacy" (p. 59). Targeted interventions have proven helpful in developing specific skills, but a more structured cross-curricular model is essential to prepare future educators so they, in turn, can better instruct information literate students. Els Kuiper, Monique Volman, and Jan Terwell (2005) suggest that

> Research on students' search skills should no longer be
> restricted to the actual search behavior of children but should
> investigate ways for students to learn search skills in an educa-
> tional situation. The research could compare the effects of var-
> ious learning environments on the acquisition of search skills.

The NFIL (2015) suggests that "Information literacy is a learner centric instructional template that, if applied strategically, can foster the development of independent, self-sufficient learners. In fact, information literacy skills instruction cuts across all disciplines." (See also Feekery, Emerson, and Gillian, Chapter 17, this collection.) To effectively ensure the development of IL skills as part of a framework, rather than as a set of fragmented skills, then, scaffolding of instruction is necessary.

Scaffolding provides support and structure for student learning at the point of need (see, for example, Douglas Fisher and Nancy Frey's (2010) extensive review and description of the instructional scaffolding approach). Smith (2013) also emphasized scaffolding of instruction as a factor for pre-service K-12 teachers and their K-12 students. A structured approach to scaffolding across the disciplines would need to engage both teachers and librarians in mapping the points of need at each level. For example, in college settings, students report their first-year composition instructors and librarians are key supporters in their development of early IL skills (Head, 2013). However, Asselin and Lee (2002) note that assumptions about student prior acquisition of IL skills can also be a barrier to effective IL instruction.

Effective collaboration between a college field experience instructor and librarian resulted in improved IL skill development of teacher education students in a job-embedded research project (Floyd, Colvin & Bodur, 2008). Similar results were reported in an early education study by Heider (2009), who found that teacher-librarian collaboration supported student IL skill development, but that a single intervention was not sufficient for continued growth. And, in a study by Angela Feekery, Lisa Emerson, and Gillian Skyrme (Chapter 17, this collection), the collaborative model was a contributing factor for student acquisition of IL skills. Asselin and Lee's (2002) research also provided a model for collaboration and relevancy in teacher education programs. Duke and Ward (2009), however, assert that

> It is not enough to simply strengthen the information literacy skills of preservice teachers; in order to prepare teachers to effectively integrate information literacy into the P-12 curriculum, teacher educators and academic librarians must model and teach information literacy pedagogy; teacher educators and academic librarians must also model and teach the collaboration necessary to support such integration. (p. 251).

Further research needs to address the impact of scaffolding IL skill instruction across the curriculum. In the NCTE *Council Chronicle*, Lorna Collier (2013) discussed the potential for the CCSS to support writing across the curriculum efforts if writing is included in content assessment. AASL Standards provide alignment with the K-12 CCSS and could serve as a first step, and collaboration between teachers and librarians is essential (Crouse & Kasbohm, 2004). Alignment of the ACRL *Framework for IL* with discipline-specific programs could also provide guidance for increased collaboration at the college level.

However, as Feekery, Emerson, and Skyrme (Chapter 17) acknowledge, there is a problem of ownership of IL skill development. This is also seen in conclusions drawn by Sharon A. Weiner (2014) after a survey of discipline faculty that addressed the importance of understanding the assumptions discipline faculty have regarding prerequisite IL skills they assume undergraduate students have already mastered. Librarians could work with faculty to develop methods to assess the level of individual IL skills that students have mastered as a pre-test to inform faculty of gaps in IL skills that would require intervention. The assessment model used by Feekery, Emerson, and Skyrme is an *example* of providing this kind of data for point of need interventions.

CONCLUSION

A common theme in research reviewed for this chapter is the lack of a common vocabulary. This interferes with communication and thus, potentially at least, with effective cross-disciplinary collaboration and continues to reinforce the development of splinter skills rather than effective IL skills. Collaboration between librarians and teachers in K-12 and higher education settings is essential. The ACRL *Framework for IL* can serve as a starting point for discussion across disciplines.

Mark Emmons et al. (2009) reported on a project that included alignment of ACRL's *IL Standards* (2000) with structured teacher/student/librarian activities and assessment across courses in an undergraduate program for dual special education/general education preparation. Although the sample size was too small to demonstrate statistical evidence, the qualitative data provide a basis for future research. An interesting outcome was the increase in rigor and expectations throughout the program. These results are in concert with Crouse and Kasbohm (2004) when they describe the natural link between library and teacher education goals, "to transfer to education department graduates the commitment to take the goals, objectives, strategies, methods, and results to their students" (p. 48).

Common vocabulary can contribute to the collaboration across disciplines that have been reported to support IL skill development. The cross-curricular model requires collaboration based on ownership of student IL skill development by all participants. The role of the teacher-librarian is essential at both the K-12 and post-secondary levels. Providing a model of collaboration for pre-service teachers is essential for their collaboration with librarians in their practice at the K-12 level. Developing a program-specific plan for scaffolding IL instruction with targeted assessment at each level could assist in providing point-of-need instruction, or what Feekery, Emerson, and Skyrme refer to as learner-centered pedagogy. Including a focus on real-world applications, as Floyd, Colvin, and Bodur have shown, can also contribute to preparation of teachers who are ready to promote higher-order thinking through problem-based learning, including IL skills as a basis for growth in their K-12 students.

Success in learner-centered and campus-specific research models can promote discussion to align with the ACRL *Framework for IL*, as described by Barbara J. D'Angelo and Barry Maid (Chapter 2, this collection), as a flexible model that can address individual program context. Future research into the separate and combined implementation of scaffolded, cross-disciplinary, teacher-librarian collaborative interventions based on shared ownership of student acquisition of IL skills within a shared framework are necessary.

REFERENCES

American Association of School Librarians (AASL). (2007). Standards for the 21st century learner. Retrieved from http://www.ala.org/aasl/standards-guidelines.

Asselin, M. M. & Lee, E. A. (2002). "I wish someone had taught me": Information literacy in a teacher education program. *Teacher Librarian, 30*, 10–17.

Association of College and Research Libraries (ACRL). (2000). *Information literacy competency standards for higher education*. Retrieved from http://www.ala.org/acrl/standards/informationliteracycompetency.

Association of College and Research Libraries (ACRL). (2015). *Framework for information literacy standards for higher education*. Retrieved from http://www.ala.org/acrl/standards/ilframework.

Coggshall, J. G., Rasmussen, C., Colton, A., Milton, J. & Jacques, C. (2012). *Generating teacher effectiveness: The role of job-embedded professional learning in teacher evaluation*. Washington, DC: National Comprehensive Center for Teacher Quality.

Collier, L. (2013). Changes in writing instruction: The challenge and the promise. *The Council Chronicle* (NCTE). Retrieved from http://www.mtsu.edu/english/forfaculty/ChangesinWritingInstructionArticle.pdf.

Council for the Accreditation of Educator Preparation (CAEP). (2015). Standard 1: Content and Pedagogical Knowledge. Retrieved from http://caepnet.org/standards/standards/standard1/.

Council of Writing Program Administrators (CWPA). (2014). WPA Outcomes statement for first-year composition (3.0). Retrieved from http://wpacouncil.org/positions/outcomes.html.

Council of Writing Program Administrators (CWPA), National Council of Teachers of English (NCTE) & National Writing Project (NWP). (2011). *Framework for success in postsecondary writing*. Retrieved from http://wpacouncil.org/framework.

Council of Chief State School Officers (CCSSO). (2015). *Common Core State Standards initiative*. http://www.corestandards.org.

Council of Chief State School Officers (CCSSO). (2011). The Interstate Teacher Assessment and Support Consortium (InTASC). Retrieved from http://www.ccsso.org/Resources/Programs/Interstate_Teacher_Assessment_Consortium_(InTASC).html#sthash.i8InXaG2.dpuf.

Crouse, W. F. & Kasbohm, K. E. (2004). Information literacy in teacher education: A collaborative model. *The Educational Forum, 39*, 44–52.

D'Angelo, B. J. & Maid, B. (2016). Threshold concepts: Integrating and applying information literacy and writing instruction. In B. J. D'Angelo, S. Jamieson, B. Maid & J. R. Walker (Eds.), *Information literacy: Research and collaboration across disciplines*. Fort Collins, CO: WAC Clearinghouse and University Press of Colorado.

Dugan, M. (n.d.). The language of creativity [blog entry]. Retrieved from http://know innovation.com/the-language-of-creativity.

Duke, T. S. & Ward, J. D. (2009). Preparing information literate teachers: A metasynthesis. *Library and Information Science Research, 31*(4), 247–256.

Emmons, M., Keefe, E. B., Moore, V. M., Sanchez, R. M., Mals, M. M. & Neely, T. Y. (2009). Teaching information literacy skills to prepare teachers who can bridge the research-to-practice gap. *Reference & User Services Quarterly, 49*(2), 140–150.

Fairbanks, A.M. (2013). Changing the role of teachers. *Education Week*. Retrieved from http://www.edweek.org/ew/articles/2013/05/22/32el-changingrole.h32.html.

Feekery, A., Emerson, L. & Skyrme, G. (2016). Supporting academics to embed information literacy to enhance students' research and writing process. In B. J. D'Angelo, S. Jamieson, B. Maid & J. R. Walker (Eds.), *Information literacy: Research and collaboration across disciplines*. Fort Collins, CO: WAC Clearinghouse and University Press of Colorado.

Fisher, D. & Frey, N. (2010) *Guided instruction: How to develop confident and successful learners*. Alexandria, VA: Association for Supervision and Curriculum Development.

Floyd, D. M., Colvin, G. & Bodur, Y. (2008). A faculty-librarian collaboration for developing information literacy skills among preservice teachers. *Teaching and Teacher Education, 24*, 368–376. doi:10.1016/j.tate.2006.11.018.

Head, A. J. (2013). *Learning the ropes: How freshman conduct course research once they enter college*. Project Information Literacy Research Report. Retrieved from http://projectinfolit.org/publications.

Heider, K. L. (2009). Information literacy: The missing link in early childhood education. *Early Childhood Education Journal, 36*(6), 513–518. doi:10.1007/s10643-009-0313-4.

International Society for Technology Education (ISTE). (2008). ISTE standards for teachers. Retrieved from http://www.iste.org/standards/iste-standards/standards-for-teachers.

The Interstate Teachers Assessment and Support Consortium (InTASC). (2011). InTASC model core teaching standards. Retrieved from http://www.ccsso.org/Re sources/Publications/InTASC_Model_Core_Teaching_Standards_2011_MS_Word_Version.html.

Kuiper, E., Volman, M. & Terwel, J. (2005). The web as an information resource in K-12 education: Strategies for supporting students in searching and processing information. *Review of Educational Research, 75*(3), 285–328.

Literate. (n.d.). In *Merriam-Webster's online dictionary*. Retrieved from http://www.merriam-webster.com/dictionary/literate.

National Forum on Information Literacy (NFIL). (2015). Information literacy skills. Retrieved from http://infolit.org/information-literacy-projects-and-programs/.

Olson, G.A. (2010). Holding ourselves accountable. *The Chronicle of Higher Education*. Washington, DC: The Chronicle of Higher Education.

Saunders, L. (2012). Faculty perspective on information literacy as a student learning outcome. *Journal of Academic Librarianship, 38*(4), 226–236.

Smith, J. K. (2013). Secondary teachers and information literacy (IL): Teacher understanding and perceptions of IL in the classroom. *Library and Information Science Research, 35,* 216–222.

Stockham, M. & Collins, H. (2012). Information literacy skills for preservice teachers: Do they transfer to K-12 classrooms? *Education Libraries, 35,* 59–72. Retrieved from http://files.eric.ed.gov/fulltext/EJ989514.pdf.

United States Department of Education (USDoE). (2015). *Elementary and Secondary Education Act.* Retrieved from http://www.ed.gov/esea.

Warmkessel, M. M. & McCade, J. M. (1997). Integrating information literacy into the curriculum. *Research Strategies, 15,* 80–88.

Weiner, S. A. (2014). Who teaches information literacy? Report of a study of faculty. *College Teaching, 62,* 5–12.

CHAPTER 14
NOT JUST FOR CITATIONS: ASSESSING ZOTERO WHILE REASSESSING RESEARCH

Rachel Rains Winslow, Sarah L. Skripsky, and Savannah L. Kelly
Westmont College

This chapter explores the benefits of Zotero for post-secondary education. Zotero is a digital research tool that assists users in collecting and formatting sources for bibliographies and notes. Existing research on Zotero reflects its influence as an efficient tool for personal research (Clark & Stierman, 2009; Croxall, 2011; Muldrow & Yoder, 2009) but has made only limited links to its use as an instructional technology for post-secondary teaching (Kim, 2011; Takats, 2009). Our study illustrates how the fruitful alliance of an instructional services librarian (Savannah), an English instructor (Sarah), and a social science instructor in sociology and history (Rachel) at Westmont College, a liberal arts college of approximately 1,200 students, has led to innovative applications of Zotero beyond its typical use as a citation aid. Our research-pedagogy partnership shows how students gain when librarians and instructors share responsibility for information literacy (IL). Rather than using IL-savvy colleagues primarily as one-shot trainers, faculty can invite them to partner in using reference managers (RMs) to reframe "research" and to interact with students' RM-accessible research choices.

Using Zotero-based research instruction in four different social science and humanities courses with 49 students total (Table 14.1), our study illustrates multiple benefits of Zotero-aided research for students' IL development. Benefits include improving students' source evaluation and annotation skills; enabling a transparent research process for peer and instructor review; offering a platform for collaboration among instructors; and creating student relationships across courses, including interdisciplinary connections that foster attention to discourse communities. Zotero's ability to showcase students' in-progress research choices allows for responses ranging from peer critique to peer emulation to instructor coaching to final evaluation. Even with such meaningful pedagogical benefits, instructors can struggle to achieve student "buy-in" if a new technique does not streamline workload. Because Zotero offers students increased citation efficiency, however, students are more willing to use it. As our study suggests, applying more of Zotero's features than just its citation aids can make a substantive difference in students' research practices. Indeed, our Zotero-aided collaboration reveals how teaching "traditional research methods" does not accurately reflect how students locate and interact with sources in the twenty-first century.

Why did we choose to implement Zotero in the classroom, as compared to other reference management systems? Though commonly used as an open-source citation tool analogous to EasyBib, Zotero is a more extensive reference manager (RM) that assists users in collecting, organizing, annotating, and sharing sources. Zotero captures in-depth bibliographic information beyond citation needs and allows users to revisit texts in their digital environments. These functions exceed those of EasyBib, which students use to cut and paste citations without capturing texts' contexts. Zotero's features mimic those of costly competitors Endnote, Papers, and RefWorks. The free RM Mendeley approximates Zotero's features, but a comparative study of four RMs (Gilmour & Cobus-Kuo, 2011) ranks Zotero higher than Mendeley in terms of fewer errors (e.g., capitalization) per citation—1.3 vs. 1.51 respectively (see Table 14.2). The same study rates these two free RMs higher in overall performance than the for-profit RefWorks (see Table 14.3). Ongoing development of Zotero and other free RMs bears watching, given their performance quality and accessibility.

George Mason University's Center for History and New Media launched Zotero in 2006 as an extension of the web browser Firefox. In 2011, Zotero developers offered a standalone version that extends its compatibility to Safari and Google Chrome. Zotero's browser-centric design allows researchers to grab source citations, full-text portable document files (PDFs), uniform resource locators (URLs), digital object identifiers (DOIs), and publisher-provided annotations while browsing (see Figure 14.1). Zotero's origin within browsers suggests assumptions about the importance of online sources in 21st-century research, and its user-friendly display mimics that of the familiar iTunes. Using rhetoric not unlike Apple's, Zotero's website stresses the connection between desired resources and everyday technology habits; its quick guide promotes Zotero as a tool that "lives right where you do your work—in the web browser itself" (Ray Rosenzweig Center, para. 1, n.d.). Once sources are gathered via browsers, Zotero gives users stable source access through a data cloud—a process that mimics not only iTunes but also Pinterest. Allowing users to tag and "relate" sources, add Notes, form groups, share research library collections, and conduct advanced internal searches, Zotero can be used as a works-in-progress portfolio for student research as well as a common platform for group projects. Zotero

Not Just for Citations

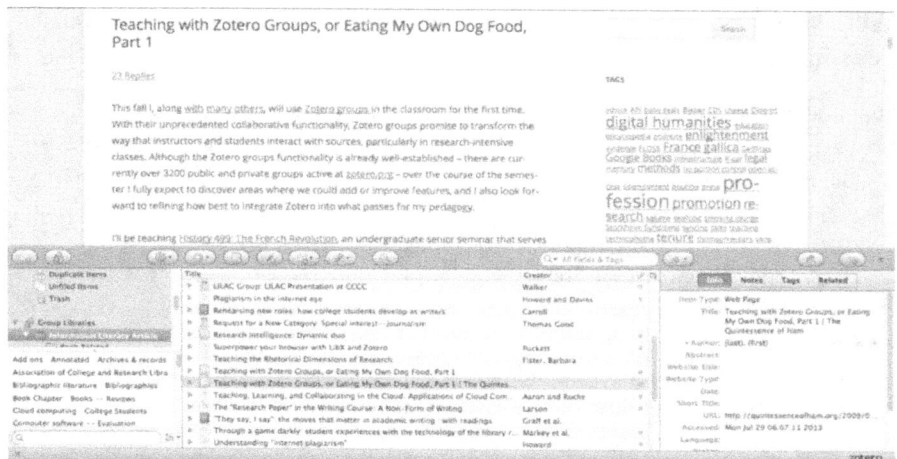

Figure 14.1. A blog entry from Zotero co-director Takats (2009), grabbed with Zotero via a browser.

serves as a potential venue for relating multiple users, course sections, or even fields of study. Indeed, Zotero's features demonstrate that the value of a citation lies not just in its format, but also as an important rhetorical device "central to the social context of persuasion" (Hyland, 1999, p. 342). As linguist Ken Hyland has found in examining citation patterns in the humanities and social sciences, scholars use citations not only to insert themselves into debates but also to construct knowledge by stressing some debates over others. Thus, citations are principally about "elaborating a context" that provides a basis for arguments situated in particular discursive frameworks.

In addition to shaping researchers' relationships to sources and peers, RMs such as Zotero are influencing academic journals and databases. For instance, the journal *PS: Political Science and Politics* started publishing abstracts in 2009 in response to RMs' emphasis on short article descriptions. Cambridge University Press has also made their journals' metadata more accessible for linking references to other articles (Muldrow & Yoder, 2009). Such developments emphasize how the research process itself is mutable; technological innovations and social context continually reshape research practices. As discussed by Katt Blackwell-Starnes in this collection, even Google searches can be applied and refined as part of a scaffolded pedagogy. Using Google to bridge students' current practices with more information-literate research attentive to source trails resembles our use and assessment of Zotero.

Table 14.1. Courses targeted in our Zotero-aided research teaching and assessment project

English 087: Introduction to Journalism	Interdisciplinary Studies 001: Research Across the Disciplines (RAD)
• 13 students completed, 2 more enrolled but failed to complete • Sarah Skripsky, Instructor • G.E. (Writing Intensive); Major elective for English and Communication Studies • Lower-division course, 4 credits • WAC/WID • Zotero-Targeted Assignment: Feature Story addressing a Social Problem	• 14 students enrolled and completed • Savannah Kelly, Instructor • Elective • Lower-division course, 2 credits • WAC/RAD • Zotero-Targeted Assignment: Annotated Bibliography
Sociology 106: Research Methods	**Sociology 110: Social Problems**
• 15 students enrolled and completed • Rachel Winslow, Instructor • Major requirement for sociology • Upper-division course, 4 credits • RID/WID • Zotero-Targeted Assignment: Original Research Project with Literature Review	• 7 students completed, 1 more enrolled but failed to complete • Rachel Winslow, Instructor • G.E. (Thinking Sociologically); Major elective for sociology • Upper-division course, 4 credits • WID • Zotero-Targeted Assignment: Policy Research Paper with Literature Review

Our assessment of Zotero extended to four classes in the fall semester of 2012 (Table 14.1), which fit into three pedagogical categories: Writing Across the Curriculum (WAC), a parallel component we term Research Across the Disciplines (RAD), and Research and Writing in the Disciplines (RID/WID). Our selection of these four courses was strategic. First, we wanted to apply Zotero in research-intensive courses with bibliography and literature review assignments engaging in scholarly conversations. Second, we wanted to test Zotero's online sharing features with peer review exercises and group projects. Third, we wanted to do a case study in interdisciplinary collaboration. Thus, we paired the English 087 and Sociology 110 courses via a key assignment in each context (Table 14.1). To assess Zotero's impact, we used a variety of methods including student surveys, quantitative annotation data, and assignment reflections. Our assessment suggests that Zotero can serve as both a general education aid for RAD/WAC and a catalyst for sustained RID/WID pedagogical progress—giving students the tools necessary to become web-savvy researchers and pursue long-term interdisciplinarity through personal citation libraries.

EVOLVING CONCEPTS OF IL IN THE CLASSROOM

Conceptions of IL have evolved over the past decade, not only at Westmont, but nationwide as academic librarians have transitioned from a library-centric to an information-centric pedagogy. For many years, Westmont librarians perceived IL as a twofold process: help students identify library resources (e.g., books, articles) and online websites for source-based assignments, and assist students with citing sources. An "information literate" student at our institution was someone who demonstrated technological competence in navigating digital content and differentiated between MLA and APA guidelines. Librarians maintained responsibility for explicating database interfaces and search engines, but spent less time, if any, introducing sources as rhetorical artifacts and exploring how such sources were used in academic argumentation.

Central to this tools-focused teaching philosophy were the 2000 *Information Literacy Competency Standards for Higher Education* (*IL Standards*) set forth by the Association of College and Research Libraries (ACRL). The *IL Standards* defined IL as an individual's capability to "recognize when information is needed and have the ability to locate, evaluate, and use effectively the needed information." The *IL Standards* sought to clarify the role of IL in higher education, but the accompanying performance indicators and outcomes were often too specific (e.g., "Constructs a search strategy using appropriate commands for the information retrieval system selected [e.g., Boolean operators, truncation, and proximity for search engines; internal organizers such as indexes for books]" 2.2.d), or broad (e.g., "Draws conclusions based upon information gathered" 3.4.c). Difficulties resulting from the *IL Standards* allowed librarians to cast IL as primarily concerned with students' searching behaviors. This well-intentioned but limited understanding of the *IL Standards* facilitated a reliance on tools-based (e.g., JSTOR, Google, EBSCO) IL instruction at our institution for over a decade.

The alliance between students' information-seeking behavior and tools-based instruction informed Westmont IL practices in the classroom as librarians used technology as the primary means to identify resources and manage citations. More complex IL processes—developing research questions and incorporating source material—were rarely discussed during IL sessions. Although we advocate using technology in this chapter, Zotero is not introduced as another technological competency for students to master, but as a portal through which students gain an understanding of IL as rhetorically oriented and reflective of genuine research practices.

Academic librarians may have placed too much emphasis on IL as tools-based instruction, but classroom faculty compound the problem when they teach dated models of the research process and source credibility: e.g., requiring students to format bibliographies manually and limiting the use of web-based sources, even if reliable. It concerns us that such teaching habits can mean devoting valuable time to teaching students the minutiae of varied citation styles, especially when few may retain or reuse that information. Such citation-based pedagogy seems equally misguided in light of our own reliance on RMs as researchers. Indeed, citation-based pedagogy (and related plagiarism panic) can send a dangerous message: *if you cite a source correctly, you are a good researcher.* This reductive definition of research resembles the current-traditional model of American education that reduced "good writing" primarily to matters of style, namely clarity and correctness (Berlin, 1987; Connors, 1997). Privileging style over substance obscures the cognitive and social aspects of research and writing, and it limits students' ability to engage in both as crafts.

Whereas good writing is not simply a composite of stylistic expertise, likewise IL is not limited to technological competencies and citation mechanics. Scholars from varying disciplines have proffered alternatives to this conventional understanding of IL. Rolf Norgaard's (2003) conception of IL as "shaped by writing" (i.e., "writing information literacy") (p. 125) served as an alternate frame of reference for faculty and librarians who struggled to identify a more compelling illustration to the *IL Standards*. As a rhetorician, Norgaard has argued for a literacy in which texts are understood in their cultural contexts, research and writing are process-oriented, and IL extends beyond source acquisition. In this volume, Norgaard, along with librarian Caroline Sinkinson (Chapter 1, this collection), extends the conversation by critically evaluating the academic reception of his previous call to redefine IL and increase collaboration between writing instructors and librarians. Although progress is noted, Norgaard and Sinkinson acknowledge the continuing challenges of achieving campus-wide IL development, and argue for broader administrative support, a redefinition of librarians' and writing teachers' roles, and an extension of IL concepts beyond the academy and into the public sphere.

In early 2012, Westmont library instruction program outcomes were revised to align with Norgaard's (2003) IL perspective—writing information literacy. The decision to embrace Norgaard in lieu of the *IL Standards* was welcomed by librarians at our institution and provided an alternative model for advancing IL on our campus. An example outcome was that "students assess the quality of each source through a rhetorical framework (audience, purpose, genre) and evaluate its relevance to their research claim" (Westmont College Voskuyl Library, 2013). This conceptual shift improved IL communication between faculty and librarians and resonated with students across disciplines.

Whether academic communities embraced the traditional *IL Standards* or alternative interpretations of IL, change was imminent: as early as June 2012, an

ACRL Task Force recommended revising the *IL Standards*. A second task force, officially charged with updating the document, followed in 2013. The resulting outcome was the *Framework for Information Literacy for Higher Education* (*Framework for IL*) (ACRL, 2015) which was presented to the ACRL community throughout 2014. After several iterations, the ACRL Board approved the *Framework for IL* early 2015. The *Framework for IL* challenges traditional notions of IL by proffering six broad frames based on "threshold concepts," which are "ideas in any discipline that are passageways or portals to enlarged understanding or ways of thinking and practicing within that discipline" (ACRL, 2015). These frames—Scholarship as Conversation; Research as Inquiry; Information Creation as a Process; Authority is Constructed and Contextual; Information Has Value; and Searching as Strategic Exploration—are highly contextualized, emphasizing students' participation in knowledge creation over knowledge consumption (ACRL, 2015).

The *Framework for IL* emphasizes the necessary collaboration between faculty and librarians in advancing IL in the classroom. Since we instructors previously aligned our conception of IL as contextual and rhetorically oriented, the shift from our 2012 Norgaard-inspired outcomes to the *Framework for IL* is welcomed and will continue to support our use of Zotero in the classroom.

When we teach Zotero, we host conversations about gauging the reliability of sources and can model those evaluative practices in real time—all while demonstrating the ease of access that students have come to crave. We encourage students to consider the rhetorical choices surrounding source citation without bogging them down in details such as whether and where to include an issue number. We emphasize source selection in relation to students' research claims and have them classify texts according to BEAM (i.e., background, evidence, argument, or method source) criteria (Bizup, 2008). Such source selection, however, is still challenging in an online environment where students must learn to sift through information and extract credible evidence, e.g., separating peer-reviewed sources on racial profiling from the unrefereed, hastily formed opinions widely available. In fact, compositionists Rebecca Moore Howard, Tricia Serviss, and Tanya K. Rodrigue (2010) highlight significant problems in undergraduate source evaluation. Their analysis suggests that students rarely summarize cited sources and that most write from *sentences within sources* rather than writing from sources more holistically read and evaluated—i.e., they often quote or paraphrase at the sentence level without assessing a source's main claims. Students' sentence-level engagement with sources suggests that ease of access to quotable text may be the key criterion in their evaluative process, if such can even be deemed evaluative. Howard et al.'s concerns were pursued on a larger scale in the cross-institutional Citation Project study of U.S. college students' source-based writing habits. Drawing on Citation Project data, Sandra Jamieson, in this collection, claims that most students engage sources shallowly even when they have selected suitable sources.

When taught in combination with suitable writing assignments such as scaffolded research projects (Bean, 2011), Zotero can nurture students' rhetorical sensitivity about the nature of sources, conversations among sources, and opportunities for source integration in writing. In a study of engineering research papers, Kobra Mansourizadeh and Ummul K. Ahmad (2011) discovered that differences in how expert and novice writers employed citations signaled a need for targeted pedagogies. Without the experts' "breadth of cumulative knowledge," novices require explicit instruction on the different purposes and "rhetorical functions of citations" (pp. 152–161). For novices to advance, they must identify a context for their "interpretive knowledge" and make the epistemological leap from writing for themselves to writing for others in a discourse community. Gerald Graff and Cathy Birkenstein's popular textbook *They Say, I Say* (2009) helps novices make this leap beyond self; yet even with effective instruction, this transition is difficult. As argued by John C. Bean (2011), both conceptual and procedural difficulties with research can lead to a vicious cycle of misperception and dread for students and instructors alike (pp. 227–229). Zotero supports novices' development both conceptually and procedurally. It gives them a central platform for building their own "cumulative knowledge." Further, in redirecting time from formatting source citations to source selection, purpose, and rhetorical integration, Zotero refocuses novices' energies from style to substance.

PERSONALIZED CITATION LIBRARIES AND INTERDISCIPLINARITY IN RESEARCH INSTRUCTION

By helping students retrieve and organize sources in individual or group libraries, Zotero sustains source accessibility and productive research habits across typical course structures. A study of undergraduates who used Zotero in a Chemical Literature course revealed that students embraced the creation of "personalized citation libraries" that strengthened their understanding of scientific literature (Kim, 2011). These libraries function as e-portfolios of research that benefit students in terms of source capture, organization, and evaluation as well as allow others to assess their choices. For example, in Savannah's RAD course (IS 001), asking first-year students to develop Zotero libraries facilitated research organization, opportunities to name and develop their academic interests, a stable record of scholarship, and pursuit of topical inquiries across courses. In terms of support, requiring first-year students to set up Zotero libraries typically means that instructors or other partners must address first-time user challenges—e.g., browser compatibility, user errors, and Zotero library syncing. Planning to support "learning curve" pitfalls increases the likelihood that first-year students will use and benefit from Zotero throughout college.

Over time, as a mechanism for personalized citation libraries with space for shared folders, Zotero orients undergraduates toward interdisciplinary innovation. Students can relate back to archived sources when starting new projects. For instance, one student in our study kept a record of books that she did not use for her sociology paper because she thought they could be useful for a religious studies project. As instructors, we emphasize the value of saving tags and notes for future projects that explore similar themes. Since Zotero's Notes are keyword searchable, we point out that students can use them to develop research across semesters. Once students chose topics such as immigration or foster care, we encouraged them to pursue those lines of inquiry not only in journalism but also in future social science courses.

For our paired ENG 087 and SOC 110 courses, Zotero file sharing enabled interdisciplinary peer review as well as students' self-reflection on projects' varied aims and need for evidence. The dual-course group library, Social Problems Research Topics, was accessed by 24 users—two course instructors (Sarah and Rachel), a supporting instructor (Savannah), 13 journalism students, and eight sociology students. As library co-administrators, we established group folders for umbrella research topics: adoption, foster care, hate movements, immigration, and incarceration. We then "salted" the folders with a few sources: first, to model Zotero file sharing for students and, second, to generate topical teaching conversations. Without a particular requirement for the number of sources to gather, the 24 users contributed a total of 112 sources to the group library, i.e., an average of 4.7 sources per user.

We also assisted students in developing subfolders with relevant subtopics for focusing their projects (Figure 14.2). After sociology students noticed that the journalism students were mainly posting popular media articles, Rachel discussed with students why a media account would not provide enough evidence for a policy paper. Though not all shared sources were suitable for all projects, Rachel told the sociology students that perusing relevant media could be useful, especially in reframing their research questions and linking policy narratives to current events. In a project on cyberbullying, a student drew on Zotero library sources related to social media to complicate her initial research questions. In turn, journalism students benefitted from reviewing academic journal articles posted by sociology students whose familiarity with social problems was grounded in months of instruction in those content areas.

Despite the benefits of such interdisciplinary collaboration, we observed several limitations. When reviewing the shared Zotero library, we noticed

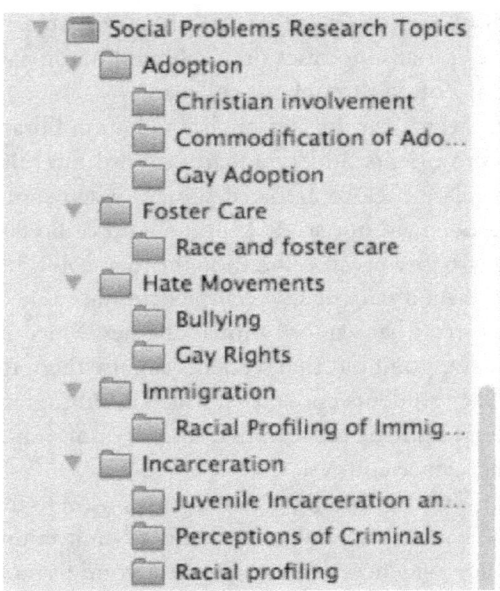

Figure 14.2. Subfolders developed in a Zotero group library for ENG 087 and SOC 110.

that fewer journalism than sociology students were participating. In part, this imbalance is consistent with the varied development of those in an introductory versus an upper-level course. In retrospect, however, the journalism assignment (writing a feature story related to social problems) was not a natural fit for Zotero use. Since one of Zotero's virtues is quick capture of secondary sources from databases, its limitations in collecting primary sources (e.g., the interviews conducted by journalism students and statistical data on government websites) likely contributed to journalism students' limited Zotero use. These source-capture constraints suggest that Zotero, especially when used in groups, is better suited for assignments such as literature reviews for which secondary sources are essential. A revised version of the ENG 087 feature story assignment asks students to prepare for interviews by creating annotated bibliographies of relevant secondary literature. Such scaffolding prompts source use more suitable for Zotero and writing of more astute interview questions. This revision promotes a dialogic model of research and enhances WID development for journalists.

Notably, students initiated interdisciplinary connections we did not require. Of the 23 students introduced to Zotero in the two sociology classes, 13 (or 56.5%) used the program in other classes that semester without any such coaching, and 20 students (or 86.9%) said they planned to use Zotero in future classes. Many students organized their personal folders by topic, rather than class, suggesting that they could envision those topics crossing disciplinary boundaries. Such activity is encouraging in a liberal arts context. A junior reported that he had created Zotero folders for anticipated projects on sexuality, family formation, and civil liberties. Equipping students for sustained topical inquiry prepares them for a range of future endeavors, including graduate school research and contributing to conversations within and beyond the academy.

WATCHING RESEARCH UNFOLD: TRANSPARENCY IN ZOTERO-AIDED PEDAGOGY

Zotero group libraries make research trails visible to faculty instructors, partner librarians, and students' peers, thus, enabling a review process in multiple moments and models of instruction. Although some process-oriented faculty may require the creation of research logs or writers' memos to accompany source-based assignments, few use RMs such as Zotero for research evaluation. In contrast to a traditional log or memo, limited to student self-report, Zotero group libraries publicize students' research choices and afford access to the sources as well. Research choices may be reviewed in an instructor's office hours when a student feels stalled; together, they can troubleshoot those choices without relying solely on the student's memory of what has already been tried. Rather, by double-clicking on sources stored in Zotero, they can retrace existing research trails and also pursue new ones (e.g., by using peer choices as samples or by modeling strategies left untried). In effect, Zotero libraries offer an archive of student research choices that, with instructor interaction, fosters IL development. Instructor-librarian teaching partners can share access to Zotero libraries as they mentor students in IL concepts and choices. Shared IL instruction can benefit teaching faculty, instructional librarians, and students alike, and Zotero helps facilitate these opportunities by offering efficient resource management and communication tools. Zotero's file sharing does not eliminate the need for capable research instruction. Rather, its ability to survey student researchers in motion (as demonstrated in Figures 14.3, 14.4, and 14.5) can redefine the IL roles of librarians and instructors, from one-shot source locators and citation doctors to research observers and coaches. This redefinition reflects our process orientation in IL instruction and supports the approach envisioned by the *Framework for IL*.

Through Zotero, students collect enough information to revisit where a source was accessed, and instructors can use this research-trail feature to introduce the idea of discourse communities. We can then reassess Zotero-gathered sources as "conversation pieces" among authors rather than static documents. We encourage this rhetorical perspective on sources by teaching Zotero's tags and "related" features, which prompt students to trace relationships among sources. For students to develop as researchers, they must tailor source selection to their rhetorical purposes. We asked students to use Zotero's Notes feature to explore these source relations and applications via annotation writing.

Annotating sources via Zotero's Notes feature may be formal and standardized (responding to instructor-provided heuristics) or more informal and organic (arising from students' inclinations). Two teaching procedures illustrate the value of instructor-guided evaluation and annotation; a later analysis of a RAD student's extra annotations (Figure 14.6, Student I) will show a more organic response with a split evaluation strategy. After explaining concepts like "peer-reviewed" and "refereed" in reference to source credibility, Rachel gave sociology students 30 minutes to collect sources in Zotero under her supervision and to begin the work of annotation. For annotation, she introduced a writing template from *They Say, I Say* (Graff & Birkenstein, 2009) in which a writer summarizes what relevant sources argue (i.e., what "they say") and then adds his or her voice to the conversation (i.e., what "I say" in response). Once students each completed a Zotero Note, they tagged it with relevant keywords linking it to related sources. Thus, Rachel introduced students to Zotero-aided annotation with a *They Say, I Say* protocol suited to literature review writing.

With a related teaching model, Savannah required that each RAD student upload ten sources to a Zotero folder for an annotated bibliography project. Students were asked to classify and annotate according to Bizup's (2008) BEAM criteria, which evaluates how a source functions in the context of an argument; i.e., a source may supply background (B) information, provide evidence (E) acceptable to a particular discipline, propose a nuanced argument (A), or advance theoretical or methodological considerations (M). BEAM-based annotations not only encouraged students to relate sources to research questions, but also allowed for comparisons across sources, but within Zotero folders. In both annotation exercises, deliberative processes stress that "research" means participating in an ongoing conversation. Via its Notes feature (shown in Figures 14.3, 14.4, and 14.5), Zotero offers a consistent platform not only for organizing sources but also for assessing them with imbedded annotation. When synced consistently with the Zotero.org website via a group folder, such Notes are accessible both to the individual researcher and to peers to use as a model.

Our content analysis of the RAD students' Zotero-based annotations reflects their varied quality; yet overall, these students demonstrate attention to source summary and rhetorical contexts. While the weakest annotations simply

Not Just for Citations

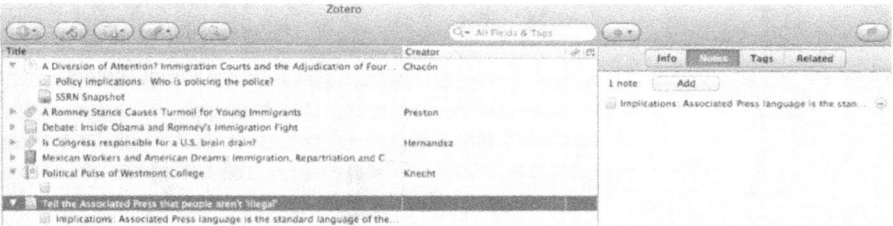

Figure 14.3. A Social Problems student's use of a source-specific Note in Zotero.

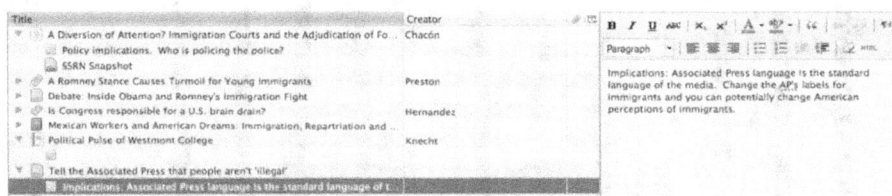

Figure 14.4. Once selected, the user can see the full-text Note appear.

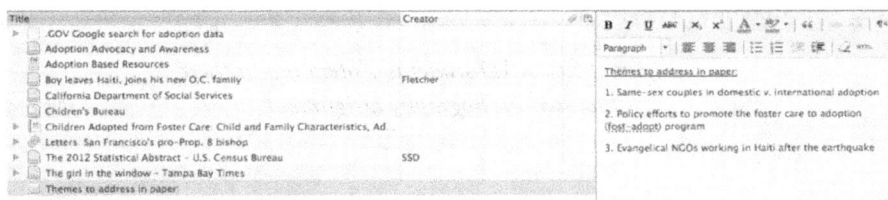

Figure 14.5. Users can also create standalone Notes related to overall research and writing plans.

reproduce source quotations (reflecting Howard et. al.'s 2010 analysis of students' habitual, sentence-level source use), satisfactory annotations include accurate summaries of sources' claims. More advanced annotations not only provide summaries but also attend to BEAM criteria or appropriateness for a student's argument. Exceptional annotations offer summaries as well as references to both the BEAM criteria and the student's argument. Such annotation writing redirects citation anxieties and helps students to resist "writing from sentences" habits. Students are then able to invest in summary writing and rhetorically sensitive evaluation related to their writing goals.

Quantitative data related to the 14 RAD students' source gathering and annotation writing (Figure 14.6) show promising effects for Zotero-aided research. Nearly 86% of RAD students used Zotero to complete their required annotations, while two students asked permission to write annotations in Microsoft

299

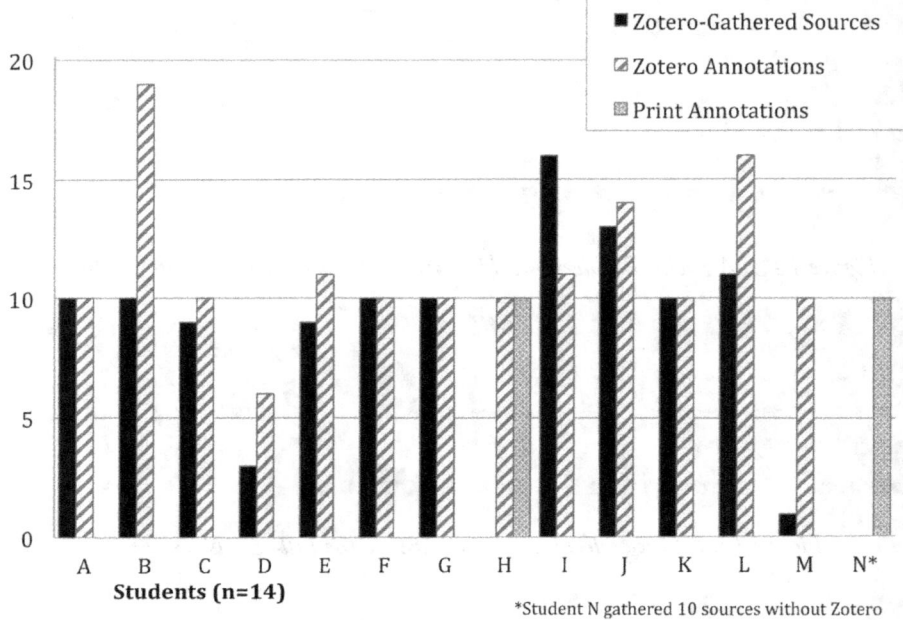

Figure 14.6. RAD students' Zotero use in their annotated bibliography assignment.

Word. (This request reflected technological literacy difficulties in adopting Zotero.) Over two-thirds of students (71.4%) met the requirement of annotating at least 10 sources. Only two students failed to annotate at least five sources. One-third of students exceeded requirements, either gathering or annotating more than ten sources.

Atypical results merit consideration. The five RAD students who exceeded requirements in source gathering, annotation writing, or both were using Zotero. This correlation suggests that Zotero's ease of source capture and note writing is related to a productive research process. In addition, Student I added a total of 17 annotations to only 11 gathered sources. In dividing Notes by type—either as "background," "evidence," and/or "argument" or, alternately, as "QUOTES" (i.e., direct quotations)—this user independently distinguishes between holistic source evaluation and source excerpts useful for quotation or paraphrase. Student I's divided Notes method could be taught to others to reinforce this useful distinction. Overall, the RAD class data links Zotero use to more sustained, holistic, and evaluative research behaviors than those typical of undergraduates, as characterized by Howard et al. (2010) and Jamieson (Chapter 6, this collection). The results summarized in Figure 14.6 suggest that Zotero facilitates students' research processes so that they gather more sources, annotate more sources, and craft higher quality annotations.

After students gather and annotate sources, how can peers review their choices profitably? In all four courses we taught for this assessment, our review activities were facilitated via Zotero group libraries' shared folders, which allow students to view the research choices, tags, and source notes of their peers. When a student performed any of these actions within a group library, that action became public to course participants. While emphasizing the need for rigorous source evaluation, we used Zotero-aided peer review to promote a culture of mutual encouragement and accountability. In Savannah's RAD course, paired students exchanged feedback on source selection and shared annotation techniques. Additionally, students described how each source would support a research argument. Although these exercises were informal, students provided suggestions and affirmations about the relationships between sources and peer-research goals—reinforcing the contexts of research choices. Sarah offered a variation on Zotero-aided peer review in an introductory composition course in spring 2013. She provided a research review handout for each student to complete first as a researcher (noting research choices and contexts), then exchange with a partner, and next complete as an evaluator of the partner's research choices (offering at least one suggestion). During this session, reviewers had access to shared Zotero folders in order to evaluate the peers' chosen sources, not just their annotations' *account* of the sources (a limitation common in annotated bibliography reviewing). Once handouts were returned, partners discussed research choices and exited class with action plans for improved research. Such Zotero-aided peer review activities prompt student researchers to identify relevant contexts, to evaluate others' choices, and even to mentor their peers.

Though we did not directly assess students' research motivations, our results suggest that motivation may increase with Zotero-aided collaboration and peer review. Students learn to identify quality sources while considering what would be accepted by peers and instructors. As Betsy Palmer and Claire Howell Major (2008) contend, peer review can increase motivation, research development, and writing quality. In Sarah's journalism class, a student who failed to complete most course assignments earned an "A" on the only assignment for which students shared sources with Zotero. This student's atypical performance implies a potential relationship between Zotero-based collaboration and student motivation. Further study of this relationship bears consideration.

IMPLICATIONS AND CONCLUSIONS

As our pilot study reflects, maximizing Zotero's use in IL instruction requires strategic assignments, interdisciplinary collaboration, rigorous peer review, and strong partnerships between instructors and librarians. In our experience, Zotero-aided instruction works best in RID/RAD contexts in which students see immediate benefits for literature review annotations and source evaluation. Course and assignment suitability enhances initial buy-in to using Zotero. While it can certainly work in WAC/WID classes, Zotero pairs best with assignments that rely on secondary sources, as Sarah's mixed experience with the ENG 087 feature assignment revealed.

Students' class standings and disciplinary identities also matter when considering placement of Zotero-aided instruction. Indeed, sophomore- or junior-level students, most of whom had declared a major, could more readily identify the program's potential for capstone projects and appreciate its usefulness. While seniors grasped Zotero's benefits more quickly, they also saw fewer opportunities to use it as undergraduates. When instructing seniors with Zotero, faculty should seek ways to help students invest, e.g., coaching them about graduate school uses for their personal citation libraries. With first-year students, such as those in Savannah's RAD class, the instructor may need to work harder to achieve buy-in: undergraduates with little disciplinary experience may lack vision for Zotero's value.

RMs such as Zotero offer faculty and librarians a platform for productive, interdisciplinary collaboration. Partnering as teachers has shaped our assignments and the types of sources we read and teach. Our study illustrates not only our fruitful alliance but also how students win when librarians and instructors share responsibility for IL. Rather than using IL-savvy colleagues primarily as one-shot trainers, faculty can invite them to partner in using RMs to reframe research and to interact with students' RM-accessible research choices. When instructors teach alongside librarians in the classroom, IL is reinforced as participatory and highly contextualized. Admittedly, our small liberal arts college (SLAC) context has been hospitable to such collaboration. As noted by Jill M. Gladstein and Dara Rossman Regaignon (2012), SLAC writing programs tend to be flexible and dynamic. Our local partnerships are indeed flexible enough for innovation; suitable for the liberal arts' interdisciplinary, writing-rich curriculum; and conducive to program development with buy-in from few stakeholders.

Still, our assessment of Zotero-assisted IL instruction indicates that such work can enrich multiple curricular contexts. Zotero can help teaching partners link course sections and even academic disciplines. We suggest that it be tested further in varied program initiatives such as first-year seminars, clustered courses, learning communities, and research-intensive capstones. Regardless of context, students benefit from our IL partnerships when we make their research processes more central to instruction and connect students with experts to coach them into scholarly conversations. Yet instructors may profit most of all. Shared IL responsibility relieves faculty from carrying the full load of research instruction and reorients such instruction significantly. As we engage students in the rigors of the new *Framework for IL*, Zotero-based collaboration offers sustained access to IL partners and refocuses instruction on substance over style and process over tools.

REFERENCES

Association of College and Research Libraries. (2000). *Information literacy competency standards for higher education*. Retrieved from http://www.ala.org/acrl/standards/informationliteracycompetency.

Association of College and Research Libraries. (2015). *Framework for information literacy for higher education*. Retrieved from http://www.ala.org/acrl/standards/ilframework.

Bean, J. C. (2011). *Engaging ideas: The professor's guide to integrating writing, critical thinking, and active learning in the classroom* (2nd ed.). San Francisco, CA: Jossey-Bass.

Berlin, J. A. (1987). *Rhetoric and reality: Writing instruction in American colleges, 1900–1985*. Studies in Writing & Rhetoric. Carbondale, IL: Southern Illinois University Press.

Bizup, J. (2008). BEAM: A rhetorical vocabulary for teaching research-based writing. *Rhetoric Review, 27*(1), 72–86.

Blackwell-Starnes, Katt (2016). Preliminary paths to information literacy: Introducing research in core courses. In B. J. D'Angelo, S. Jamieson, B. Maid & J. R. Walker (Eds.), *Information literacy: Research and collaboration across disciplines*. Fort Collins, CO: WAC Clearinghouse and University Press of Colorado.

Clark, B. & Stierman, J. (2009). Identify, organize, and retrieve items using Zotero. *Teacher Librarian, 37*(2), 54–56.

Connors, R. J. (1997). *Composition-rhetoric: Backgrounds, theory, and pedagogy*. Pittsburgh, PA: University of Pittsburgh Press.

Croxall, B. (2011, May 3). Zotero vs. EndNote. ProfHacker. *The Chronicle of Higher Education*. Retrieved from http://chronicle.com/blogs/profhacker/zotero-vs-endnote/33157.

Gilmour, R. & Cobus-Kuo, L. (2011). Reference management software: A comparative analysis of four products. *Issues in Science and Technology Librarianship, 66*(66), 63–75.

Gladstein, J. M. & Regaignon, D. (2012). *Writing program administration at small liberal arts colleges*. Anderson, SC: Parlor Press.

Graff, G. & Birkenstein, C. (2009). *They say/I say: The moves that matter in academic writing* (2nd ed.). New York: W. W. Norton & Company.

Howard, R. M., Serviss, T. & Rodrigue, T. K. (2010). Writing from sources, writing from sentences. *Writing and Pedagogy, 2*(2), 177–192.

Hyland, K. (1999). Academic attribution: citation and the construction of disciplinary knowledge. *Applied Linguistics 20*(3), 341–367.

Jamieson, S. (2016). What the Citation Project tells us about information literacy in college composition. In B. J. D'Angelo, S. Jamieson, B. Maid & J. R. Walker (Eds.), *Information literacy: Research and collaboration across disciplines.* Fort Collins, CO: WAC Clearinghouse and University Press of Colorado.

Kim, T. (2011). Building student proficiency with scientific literature using the Zotero reference manager platform. *Biochemistry and Molecular Biology Education, 39*(6), 412–415.

Mansourizadeh, K. & Ahmad, U. K. (2011). Citation practices among non-native expert and novice scientific writers. *Journal of English for Academic Purposes, 10*(3), 152–161.

Markey, K., Leeder, C. & Rieh, S. Y. (2012). Through a game darkly: Student experiences with the technology of the library research process. *Library Hi Tech, 30*(1), 12–34. doi:10.1108/07378831211213193.

Muldrow, J. & Yoder, S. (2009). Out of cite! How reference managers are taking research to the next level. *PS: Political Science and Politics, 42*(1), 167–172.

Norgaard, R. (2003). Writing information literacy: Contributions to a concept. *Reference & User Services Quarterly, 43*(2), 124–130.

Norgaard, R. & Sinkinson, C. (2016). Writing information literacy: A retrospective and a look ahead. In B. J. D'Angelo, S. Jamieson, B. Maid & J. R. Walker (Eds.), *Information literacy: Research and collaboration across disciplines.* Fort Collins, CO: WAC Clearinghouse and University Press of Colorado.

Palmer, B. & Major, C. H. (2008). Using reciprocal peer review to help graduate students develop scholarly writing skills. *Journal of Faculty Development, 22*(3), 163–169.

Ray Rosenzweig Center for History and New Media. (n.d.). *Zotero quick start guide.* Retrieved from http://www.zotero.org/support/quick_start_guide.

Takats, S. (2009, August 7). Teaching with Zotero groups, or eating my own dog food, Part 1. The quintessence of ham. [blog comment]. Retrieved from http://quintessenceofham.org/2009/08/07/teaching-with-zotero-groups-or-eating-my-own-dog-food-part-1/.

Westmont College Voskuyl Library. (2013). *Library instruction.* Retrieved from http://libguides.westmont.edu/content.php?pid=262274&sid=2165021.

CHAPTER 15
QUANTITATIVE REASONING AND INFORMATION LITERACY IN ECONOMICS

Diego Méndez-Carbajo
Illinois Wesleyan University

INTRODUCTION

The Association of College and Research Libraries' (ACRL) *Framework for Information Literacy for Higher Education* (*Framework for IL*) (2015) defines information literacy (IL) as a "spectrum of abilities, practices, and habits of mind." Articulating IL as a framework—as opposed to a set of standards or learning outcomes—ACRL articulates six different frames. Each frame identifies a threshold concept central to IL and includes learner-based recommended knowledge practices ("demonstrations of understanding") and aspirational dispositions (e.g., attitudes and values). As ACRL emphasizes "flexible options for implementation" of the *Framework for IL,* it effectively outlines an open-ended learning process while providing abundant reference checkpoints.

My 17 years of teaching undergraduate economics has led me to interpret and articulate ACRL's *Framework for IL* along pedagogical lines that closely overlap several of the literacy categories created by Jeremy J. Shapiro and Shelley K. Hughes (1996) as well as the streamlined IL process outlined by Tom W. Goad (2002). In addition, the central role that statistical data plays in the discipline of economics makes the concept of quantitative literacy, or numeracy, very relevant for our students. The National Numeracy Network (NNN) (2015) defines quantitative literacy as the "comfort, competency, and 'habit of mind' in working with numerical data," and the skill of IL is a critical means to achieve this kind of numeracy in economics.

Three frames in the *Framework for IL* are central to the education of economics majors: Searching Is Strategic emphasizes research as a process; Information Has Value underlines the social and historical context of information; and Research as Inquiry highlights the management and synthesis of information. ACRL (2009) references the work of Shapiro and Hughes (1996) in order to communicate the "substance and breadth of information literacy" to faculty and administrators, and I find it useful to borrow their language in order to relate the *Framework for IL* to the undergraduate instruction of economics. Shapiro and Hughes list a series of desirable characteristics in an IL curriculum, namely: tool literacy, resource literacy, social-structural literacy, research literacy, publishing literacy, emerging technology literacy, and critical literacy.

Given that the ACRL Instruction Section Information Literacy in the Disciplines Committee (ACRL IS) (2012) reports that it "is not aware of information literacy standards in this area," I propose adopting the dimensions of literacy put forward by Shapiro and Hughes (1996). Desirable as they all are in an "enlightened" liberal arts curriculum, three are particularly relevant in the context of the social sciences curriculum in general and of that of economics in particular. Describing resource literacy as "the ability to understand the form, format, location and access methods of information resources," these authors speak to the use of both text/qualitative information and data/quantitative information that students and researchers must employ in their work. Closely related to this dimension of literacy is that of social-structural literacy, described as "knowing that and how information is socially situated and produced." The difference between for-pay (i.e., proprietary) and public-access information, for example, becomes critical when attempting to operationalize a research project in economics. Finally, research literacy, described as "the ability to understand and use the Information Technology (IT)-based tools relevant to the work of today's researcher and scholar" specifically references "computer software for quantitative analysis." At the undergraduate educational level this quantitative analysis is frequently performed through the use of spreadsheets.

These particular dimensions of literacy underpin the "information literacy strategy" outlined by Goad (2002, p. 36) through a series of sequential tasks. These are: (i) formulating a question, (ii) pinpointing what you really want to know, (iii) organizing information, (iv) planning a search for relevant information, and (v) evaluating the appropriateness of materials. As the work of Goad (2002) fully articulates the connection between IL and workplace performance, I will argue that the multi-step information search and analysis process that he describes closely overlaps several of the desirable learning goals of the economics curriculum. Encapsulated in the phrase coined by John J. Siegfried et al. (1991) "thinking like an economist," these goals include "acquiring and using knowledge that cuts across disciplinary boundaries" and include—among others—the threshold concepts of "knowing something about the measurement of economic variables (methods of data collection, reliability, etc.)" and "being able to organize, work with, and manipulate data for purposes of comparison" (Siegfried et al., 1991, p. 216). Moreover, "the use of analytical methods to utilize information" is identified by Dale Cyphert and Stanley P. Lyle (Chapter 3, this collection) as one of the skill gaps of greatest concern to employers. For an in-depth discussion of the expected proficiencies of the economics academic major I direct the reader to the seminal work of W. Lee Hansen (1986). His influence in shaping the contemporary effort to "educate economists" is explicitly stated in the collected works edited by David Colander and KimMarie McGoldrick (2009). In sum, the instructional challenge lies in designing course assignments that help students develop the aforementioned intellectual proficiencies, relating numeracy to information literacy.

The pedagogical approach that I propose is based on the educational taxonomy originally proposed by Benjamin Bloom (1956) and it employs case method teaching in an intermediate macroeconomic theory course. The work of Lorin W. Anderson and Lauren A. Sosniak (1994) provides a helpful 40-year retrospective on the impact of Bloom's taxonomy on a wide-range of pedagogical issues and practices. Along those lines, I will posit that the use of quantitative case studies as a pedagogical resource in intermediate macroeconomics helps students analyze and evaluate theoretical constructs in economics. Specifically, the collection, manipulation and analysis of data compiled by different statistical agencies illustrate for students the connection between the theoretical and empirical dimensions of this particular social science. I believe that the process of building such a connection relies heavily on the parallel development of a basic set of IL skills.

From the course instructor's perspective, the overall goal of the proposed pedagogical strategy is to move students from Bloom's (1956) lower-order cognitive processes of knowledge, comprehension and application of intermediate macroeconomic abstract formal thinking to the higher-order cognitive processes of analysis, synthesis and evaluation of this mode of thinking. In the discipline of economics, as in almost all social sciences, the analysis and evaluation of theoretical constructs are based upon the statistical manipulation of data. In economics, these data are generally quantitative (rather than qualitative) and, depending on the topic of study, may have been generated by the researcher (e.g., surveys) or collected from public agencies such as statistical agencies. In the sub-field of macroeconomics all the data are generated and collected by public agencies.

In order to bridge the cognitive gap between the discussion of theoretical concepts and the manipulation and evaluation of these concepts I propose to borrow from the case method teaching pedagogy. As described by Melvin Copeland (1954), it was originally created in a business and management learning environment whereas, nowadays, Geoff Easton (1983) and James A. Erskin, Michiel R. Leenders, and Louise A. Mauffette-Leenders (1998) show the case method spread to many other disciplines. In essence, cases are context-rich real world stories that students, usually working in groups, analyze in order to answer a question or solve a problem. These cases provide students with quantitative information but unlike problem sets or examples they do not have a unique "correct" answer. The case method teaching pedagogy has three main components: the case itself, the students' preparation for the case, and the discussion that takes place in the classroom. It is the collaborative nature, both outside and inside of the classroom, of this evidence-based exercise that improves the grasp of theoretical concepts and their application to real-world situations. Katt Blackwell-Starnes (Chapter 7, this collection), provides a discussion of course assignment design in relation to IL. Blackwell-Starnes' study of IL skills applied to undergraduate research leads her to endorse assignment design. In the course activity that I describe in the following sections, students apply a series of economic concepts to sketch the actual macroeconomic profile of a country.

Although many teaching faculty members will argue that there is "no room in the syllabus" for the inclusion of explicit IL goals in a standard course in intermediate macroeconomic theory I envision—as discussed above—the proposed pedagogical strategy to be closely aligned with several frames in the *Framework for IL*. Later on in their academic and professional careers, when students develop independent research projects showcasing their "thinking like an economist" skills, they are likely to be savvier gatherers and users of information.

The work of Pam McKinney (2013) summarizing the lessons learned from a multi-year, multi-disciplinary curriculum development effort gives credence to the usefulness of "inquiry-based" learning to the development of IL skills. For a complete discussion of how to teach IL for inquiry-based learning I direct the reader to Mark Hepworth and Geoff Walton (2009). By presenting students with a series of questions to answer and argue, the quantitative case study method that I propose exposes students to what McKinney describes as "collaborative inquiry." The kind of longitudinal data that she analyzes offers evidence of how inquiry-based learning increases student appreciation of IL competencies. Unfortunately, I currently lack her ability to track student skills as they move through our curriculum.

In what follows, I will outline the challenge that motivates my particular pedagogical approach, assess its impact on exam performance, and relate its implementation to the development of numeracy, resource literacy, social-structural literacy, and research literacy among students of Intermediate Macroeconomics. This research was approved by the Institutional Review Board at Illinois Wesleyan University on December 3rd, 2012.

THE PROBLEM

In the course sequence for a minor or a major in economics, students at my institution start with an Introduction to Economics (ECON 100) course. Frequently, the content of this course is split into two separate courses, Introduction to Microeconomics and Introduction to Macroeconomics, which exposes students to a wide spectrum of microeconomic and macroeconomic concepts. Whether in a single course or in a two-course sequence the purpose of this introduction is widely acknowledged to be the initiation of students into what is commonly referred to as "economic thinking": an analytical comparison of costs and benefits of different choices regarding the allocation of scarce resources. This course is mostly devoid of mathematics and only makes superficial use of abstract thinking through algebra. Graphical analysis is limited to supply and demand diagrams and to the plotting of time series data in order to illustrate either trends or relative values.

After completing the introductory course, a student at my institution interested in economics as a major field of study is required to complete two courses covering intermediate-level economic theory: Intermediate Microeconomics (ECON 201) and Intermediate Macroeconomics (ECON 202). As outlined by David Colander and KimMarie McGoldrick (2009), in these units of the standard disciplinary curriculum the focus turns to the theories and identities underpinning the basic concepts discussed in the introductory course (p. 29–30). Two examples would serve to illustrate this point. The introductory discussion of economic growth is now enriched through the articulation of the Solow growth model where Robert Solow (1956) provides a theoretical model of economic growth that has become the basic framework for research since. Also, the interplay between nominal and real variables is now presented through the stylized fact of the Phillips Curve where William A. Phillips (1958) argues that there is a secular negative relationship between the inflation rate (a nominal variable) and the unemployment rate (a real variable). His work was subsequently replicated by Milton Friedman (1968) and Edmund Phelps (1970) and sparked a fierce intellectual debate in the discipline. (For a summary of both economic concepts, please see the *Palgrave Dictionary of Economics* online.) In order to develop these theoretical concepts an Intermediate Macroeconomics course makes frequent use of algebra—for purposes of manipulating concepts in symbolic form—and may even employ calculus to derive the different equations that compose the Solow growth model. Graphical analysis is also more complex, employing diagrams with multiple lines and curves intersecting at different points, as well as plotting time series data in order to illustrate cycles. For a discussion of statistical data visualization pedagogy I direct the reader to my article on data visualization and the FRED database (Méndez-Carbajo, 2015).

My experience has been that students tend to struggle when confronted with the sequential tasks of learning the economic theories and concepts, applying these theories and concepts to specific problems, and using evidence to discuss the limitations of the theories and the applicability of the concepts. The work of Ann D. Velenchik (1995) discusses these issues in detail. The aforementioned learning tasks are more demanding of our students than those they were faced with in ECON 100, not only because they employ more formal mathematical analysis but also because their application is more fluid and less clear-cut. For example, the discussion of historical shifts of the Phillips Curve requires referencing a historical context usually external to the course content and potentially controversial in and of itself. In addition, students are faced with the need to develop a new vocabulary, that of quantitative information. Continuing with the example of the Phillips Curve, students learn about how U.S. inflation increased three-fold in the 1970s and are expected to compare that figure with a doubling of the unemployment rate during the same period. In other words, students need to learn to evaluate issues of magnitude and proportion.

Finally, there is, the challenge of "thinking in macroeconomic terms"—as opposed to "thinking in microeconomic terms." In an introductory course we as instructors undertake considerable efforts to make the course material relevant and engaging through the use of examples and illustrations close to the students' "micro" reality, for example, discussing opportunity cost in terms of hours of sleep versus hours of study. Because students are familiar with these kinds of information they tend to find "thinking in microeconomic terms" rather easy and, to an extent, intuitive. At the same time, I would argue there is a large information deficit when it comes to the "macro" reality that the students live in. In my experience, beginning-of-the-semester student surveys on current inflation or GDP growth rates reveal great gaps in students' familiarity with macroeconomic information. I would argue that this degree of information ignorance makes the task of "thinking in macroeconomic terms" more difficult. In the detailed introduction to their book, Colander and McGoldrick (2009) discuss the traditional lack of "context" in the teaching of intermediate macroeconomic theory. Describing this information deficit as pervasive they argue for improved pedagogical practices that "enhance the use of context and application" (Colander & McGoldrick, 2009, p. 33)

THE ACTIVITY

The ECON 202 course where I implemented this pedagogical innovation is organized around four units of content: (1) Introduction (4 class periods), (2) Long-Run Economic Performance (6 class periods), (3) Business Cycles and

Macroeconomic Policy (8 class periods), and (4) Macroeconomic Policy (6 class periods). There are bi-weekly online quizzes and two in-class partial exams, week 6 and week 12, as well as a comprehensive final exam, week 16. As a voluntary activity for extra credit, during the last week of classes students can deliver a group presentation on the macroeconomic conditions of the country that they are assigned to at the beginning of the semester.

During the first class period of the semester the students meet the academic librarian who serves as the liaison with the Economics Department for a research instruction session at the library's computer lab. There, the students are introduced to the database that they will use to gather the data for the quantitative case studies and are assigned to one of four different work groups. The academic librarian focuses on the area of resource IL, discussing with the students the means of access, the forms, and the formats of quantitative information relevant to this course. At this point, the *Framework for IL's* "Searching Is Strategic" frame is most prominently highlighted. This research instruction session also serves to introduce the academic librarian to the students in order to encourage them to seek her/his assistance with database needs throughout the semester. See also Alison S. Gregory and Betty L. McCall's (Chapter 18, this collection) discussion of a teaching faculty/librarian collaborative approach to teaching IL skills in the context of a sociology capstone course.

The library subscribes to the International Financial Statistics (IFS) online database maintained by the International Monetary Fund (IMF), and I have found this resource very convenient for the purposes of my course. In order to keep the data analysis and the size of the work groups manageable each semester I identify four or five different countries for the students to study. I purposely select countries at varied stages of economic development in order to highlight socio-structural differences in economic performance. During the research instruction session at the library all students work on gathering data on the GDP components for the U.S., also becoming familiar with the online teaching platform Moodle, locating the discussion questions for the quantitative case studies, and importing their data into Microsoft Excel for purposes of analysis. This first quantitative case study, and all that follow, is structured around a one-page handout that I distribute in class. Table 1 in Appendix A contains a list of the topics of study, the variables that students extract from the database, the manipulations that students must perform on the series, and the discussion questions that they need to answer based on the graphical representation of their data. I will discuss these tasks in sequence.

Currently, I have incorporated a quantitative case study component for each of the following seven topics in a standard intermediate macroeconomics course: (1) GDP components, (2) Uses of Saving, (3) Productivity, (4) Growth, (5)

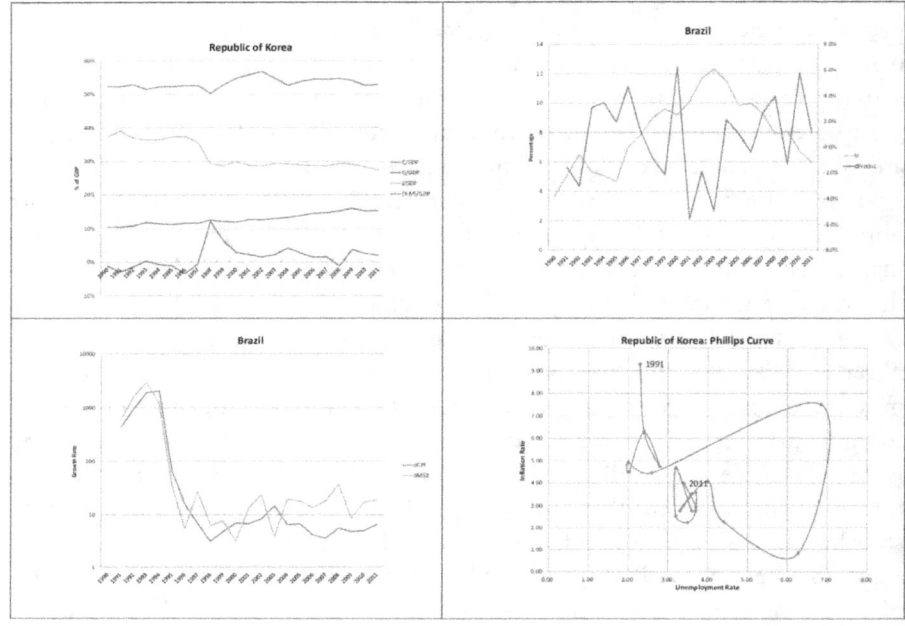

Figure 15.1. Sample data plots

Inflation, (6) Interest Rates, and (7) the Phillips Curve. Each of these concepts and topics are first presented from a conventional theoretical perspective and immediately compared against their historical record in the United States. I then direct students to compile, after class, the relevant data from the IFS database and to plot those data into Microsoft Excel spreadsheets. Figure 15.1 presents a sample of those plots.

Depending on the topic, students are asked to compute ratios between variables (topic 1), rates of growth (topics 2, 3, and 5), sums or subtractions (topics 2, 4 and 6), or to generate a scatter plot (topic 7). The use of spreadsheets for data manipulation and plotting is common practice in the discipline and this element of the activity contributes to the development of research literacy skills. At this point, the *Framework for IL's* Research as Inquiry frame is most prominently highlighted. Also, it is usually at this stage when students begin to be aware of matters germane to social-structural IL. For example, changes in the methodology of data collection, or even a change in the definition of the object of study (e.g., Germany pre-and-post 1990), result in discontinuities in the series—or even gaps. In a similar light, time periods when the variables are very large in magnitude (e.g., Brazil's hyper-inflation in the 1990s) dwarf the rest of the data, making their visual interpretation much more difficult. Although these data-related issues are sometimes frustrating to some students, they are excellent educational opportunities to develop a historical context to the study of macroeconomics.

After the data is plotted, students use the graphs they have generated to answer a series of discussion questions highlighting how quantitative evidence validates—and sometimes challenges—the theoretical relationships focus of the course. Table 2 in Appendix A contains the list of discussion questions per topic. These questions are posted on an online discussion forum hosted on the Moodle teaching platform. Only students registered in the course have access to these questions and the forum is set up in a "Q&A" format, which prevents individual students from seeing their peers' answers to the common set of questions until they have posted their own work. Students have no less than 48 hours to complete the data collection, plotting, and analysis before the submission of their answers is blocked. In other words, their work must be completed and uploaded to Moodle by the time the class convenes the following day. The discussion questions associated with each quantitative case study cover a range of issues. Some questions ask the students to describe visual aspects of the data (e.g., "which GDP component is the largest?") and aim to be prompts for discussion of economic structures when different countries' data are compared. Some questions (e.g., "Is the country a net lender or a net borrower?") require the application of theoretical concepts discussed in class to the changing reality of different economies. Finally, some other questions (e.g., "Do the growth rate of labor productivity and the unemployment rate move in the same direction? Why not?") aim to bring to the fore the theoretical relationships object of the course.

During the class period when the quantitative case studies are discussed the students' work—both their data plots and their answer to the discussion questions—are projected on video screens. Over the last three semesters I have made use of a technology-intensive classroom setup with multiple video projectors and a digital whiteboard. Those are not essential components of this activity but they facilitate the visualization of trends, cycles, and degrees of association between variables. Moreover, I believe the fact that students see their work projected for everybody else to see serves to produce a certain degree of peer pressure that marginally improves the average quality of their work. It is during the class period when the case studies are discussed that quantitative literacy, or numeracy, becomes central to the course. As the students work through their individual discussion questions they gain confidence in reading and interpreting the data associated with the assignment. Also, as the same discussion question is addressed across different countries students are able to observe different orders of magnitude, proportion, and signs of macroeconomic magnitudes under study, effectively developing a true context for their theoretical study of economics. At this point, *Framework for IL's* Information Has Value frame is most prominently highlighted.

ASSESSMENT

For the purpose of this chapter I will focus on the challenges associated with the discussion of a standard production function, the derivation of the concept of labor productivity, its connection to the demand for labor, and, finally, to the concept of the unemployment rate. This is the quantitative case study number 3 summarized in Table 1 in Appendix A.

Over the years, most of my in-class exams have included questions on these concepts. The phrasing of the questions has evolved but the focus remains on the same issue: economic theory teaches us that as productivity increases, other things being equal, the unemployment rate decreases. In my experience, students tend to struggle with the notion that as workers become more productive the demand for their labor increases. Their "micro" thinking, discussed earlier in this chapter, leads them to conclude that employers demand fewer workers once these workers become more productive.

In the fall semesters of 2008 and 2009, prior to the inclusion of quantitative case studies in the course, I asked students to identify in a diagram the impact of an increase in total factor productivity on output and on the marginal productivity of labor. Although, in general terms, the students displayed their knowledge of the concepts at stake through a proficient replication of the graphs discussed in class, they struggled when confronted with the task of evaluating a reporter's statement contradicting intermediate macroeconomic theory. In fact, as the students were asked to analyze information, rather than to replicate material covered in lectures, the average scores on these specific questions dropped from 75% to 34% and their standard deviations increased from 0.15 to 0.25 with population sizes (N) of 8 in both semesters. Due to the small size of the populations under study I will not attempt to draw conclusions about the statistical robustness of these figures. Nevertheless, one could argue that as students were pushed up the skill pyramid representing Bloom's (1956) taxonomy of learning objectives they faltered at the more demanding task.

In the fall semesters of 2011 and 2012, after the inclusion of quantitative case studies in the course, I asked students to identify in the same sets of diagrams the impact of decreases in either capital expenditure or in total factor productivity on output, the marginal productivity of labor, and the unemployment rate. The phrasing of the questions was more specific than in previous tests but it also demanded that students relate changes in production and in labor productivity to changes in the unemployment rate. The average scores on these questions were 57% in 2011 and 62% in 2012, with associated standard deviations of 0.41 and 0.29. Population sizes (N) were 14 and 17, respectively. Notice that although the standard deviations of the post-quantitative case study test scores have increased relative to the pre-quantitative case study test scores, the 2009 and 2012 values are very similar.

Student reflections on the use of quantitative case studies have been overwhelmingly positive. Quoting from the university's standard anonymous course evaluations, students state that: "I feel using real data to help support economic theories was extremely useful," "I also liked the discussion questions because they helped apply and reinforce ideas," "Learning how to analyze graphs and data and how to properly interpret that data were valuable skills to learn," and "I feel like putting the effort to read notes and work on the IMF forums [i.e., the discussion questions on the IFS-IMF data-based quantitative case studies] paid off and led me to learn/understand more about macroeconomics." In the form of suggestions, some students state their desire for "more in-class activities or assignments along the way" or notice how the course was "more lecture-oriented rather than discussion-oriented." I believe that at this point in time it would be very difficult to introduce more of these activities without substantially impacting the primary goal of the course (i.e., the mastering of intermediate macroeconomic theory). Having said that, the benefits of addressing *Framework for IL* threshold concepts through this particular pedagogical strategy are observable through the student's appreciation of the intellectual tasks of "understanding" rather than memorizing, "interpreting" rather than mimicking, and "analyzing" rather than replicating.

DISCUSSION

The goal of introducing elements of case method teaching into an intermediate macroeconomic theory course has been to make student thinking more sophisticated and context-rich. The design of activities where students collect, manipulate, and analyze data also contributes to develop critical IL skills. Replacing many of the exercises aimed at rote replication of the content of lectures, the activities organized around quantitative case studies require from students a more extended and sophisticated engagement with the material. Thus, I will argue, students more effectively apply theories and concepts to specific problems and are more capable at using quantitative evidence to discuss the limitations of the economic theories. Moreover, the nature of the case method and its use of real data allow the instructor to present students with the fact that macroeconomic concepts and theories are frequently dynamic and thus mutable. Finally, I believe that the continued exposure to macroeconomic data, their sources, and even orders of magnitude, builds a framework of reference for students that help them start to develop the desirable quality of "thinking in macroeconomic terms."

Although it is not listed as an explicit learning goal of the course I consider the described quantitative case studies a solid pedagogical strategy in the education of my students in matters of IL in the discipline: by providing instruction on the form, format, location, and access of quantitative data as a central part of the course assignments my students develop resource literacy; by discussing the process of creating and organizing statistical information and knowledge across countries and across time my students develop socio-structural literacy; and by understanding and using spreadsheets to perform quantitative analysis of the statistical information that they have collected my students develop research literacy. These literacy skills are not presented as ends by themselves, yet they become—in my opinion—critical means to develop quantitative literacy, or numeracy, among the students. Finally, as the students locate and use effectively the quantitative information that they need to evaluate intermediate macroeconomic concepts, they are in effect developing the connection between theories and empirical evidence that underpins the social science of economics.

In future iterations of the course I will consider highlighting explicit issues of social-structural literacy, creating discussion questions specific to the social situation and production of the data of each assignment. These questions may ask students to identify the agency compiling the data, the highest frequency that the data are available, and potential reasons for changes in collection methodology. By doing so I hope to draw student attention to the fact that social groups create and organize information as I continue to teach the students how to manipulate and interpret that information. Also looking forward, I hope to develop, in collaboration with the academic librarian liaison to the Department and as part of the multi-year assessment effort of our student learning goals, a rubric for IL outcomes in our program. Since we already enjoy a long history of collaboration in the delivery of instructional sessions on locating, evaluating, and using text/qualitative information as part of the capstone (i.e., senior-level) course, I believe our academic library liaison to be a key partner in this effort. As a first step I will suggest borrowing from the ACRL-guided work in other social sciences, such as political science, to develop a research competency guide for our discipline.

REFERENCES

Association of College & Research Libraries (ACRL). (2009). *Information literacy for faculty and administrators*. Retrieved from http://www.ala.org/acrl/issues/infolit/overview/faculty/faculty.

Association of College & Research Libraries Instruction Section (ACRL IS). (2012). *Information literacy in economics*. Retrieved from http://wikis.ala.org/acrl/index.php/Information_Literacy_in_Economics.

Anderson, L. W. & Sosniak L. A. (Eds.). (1994). *Bloom's taxonomy: A forty-year retrospective*. Chicago National Society for the Study of Education. Chicago, IL: University of Chicago Press.

Blackwell-Starnes, K. (2016). Preliminary paths to information literacy: Introducing research in core courses. In B. J. D'Angelo, S. Jamieson, B. Maid & J. R. Walker (Eds.), *Information literacy: Research and collaboration across disciplines*. Fort Collins, CO: WAC Clearinghouse and University Press of Colorado.

Bloom, B. (1956). *Taxonomy of educational objectives: the classification of educational goals*. United Kingdom: Longman.

Colander, D. & McGoldrick, K. M. (Eds.). (2009). *Educating economists: The Teagle discussion on re-evaluating the undergraduate economics major*. Northampton, MA: Edward Elgar.

Copeland, M. (1954). The genesis of the case method in business instruction. In M. McNair & A. Hersum (Eds.), *The case method at the Harvard Business School* (pp. 25–33). New York, NY: McGraw-Hill.

Cyphert, D. & Lyle, S. P. (2016). Employer expectations of information literacy: Identifying the skills gap. In B. J. D'Angelo, S. Jamieson, B. Maid & J. R. Walker (Eds.), *Information literacy: Research and collaboration across disciplines*. Fort Collins, CO: WAC Clearinghouse and University Press of Colorado.

Easton, G. (1983). *Learning from case studies*. London: Prentice Hall.

Erskine, J., Leenders, M. & Mauffette-Leenders, L. (1998). *Teaching with cases*. London, Ontario: Ivey Publishing.

Friedman, M. (1968). The role of monetary policy. *American Economic Review, 58*(1), 1–17.

Goad, T. (2002). *Information literacy and workplace performance*. Wesport, CT: Quorum Books.

Gregory, A. S. & McCall, B. L. (2016). Building critical researchers and writers incrementally: Vital partnerships between faculty and librarians. In B. J. D'Angelo, S. Jamieson, B. Maid & J. R. Walker (Eds.), *Information literacy: Research and collaboration across disciplines*. Fort Collins, CO: WAC Clearinghouse and University Press of Colorado.

Hansen, L. (1986). What knowledge is most worth knowing for economics majors? *American Economic Review, 76*(2), 149–152.

Hepworth, M. & Walton, G. (2009). *Teaching information literacy for inquiry-based learning*. Oxford: Chandos Publishing.

McKinney, P. (2013). Information literacy and inquiry-based learning: Evaluation of a five-year programme of curriculum development. *Journal of Librarianship and Information Science*. Retrieved from http://lis.sagepub.com/content/early/2013/05/08/0961000613477677.full.

Méndez-Carbajo, D. (2015). Data visualization and the FRED database. *Journal of Economic Education, 46*(4), 420–429.

National Numeracy Network (2015, April 22). *What is numeracy/QL/QR?* Retrieved from http://serc.carleton.edu/nnn/resources/index.html.

Phelps, E. (1970). Money wage dynamics and labor market equilibrium. In E. Phelps (Ed.), *Microeconomic foundations of employment and inflation theory* (pp. 124–166). New York, NY: W. W. Norton.

Phillips, W. A. (1958). The relation between unemployment and the rate of change of money wages in the United Kingdom, 1861–1957. *Economica, 25*(100), 283–299.

Shapiro, J. J. & Hughes, S. K. (1996). Information literacy as a liberal art: Enlightenment proposals for a new curriculum. *Educom Review, 31*(2).

Siegfried, J. J., Bartlett, R. L., Hansen, W. L., Kelley, A.C., McCloskey, D. N. & Tietenberg, T. H. (1991). The status and prospects of the economics major. *Journal of Economic Education, 22*(3), 197–224.

Solow, R. M. (1956). A contribution to the theory of economic growth. *Quarterly Journal of Economics, 70*(1), 65–94.

Velenchik, A. (1995). The case method as a strategy for teaching policy analysis to undergraduates. *Journal of Economic Education, 26*(1), 29–38.

APPENDIX A

Topics of Study, Variables, Manipulation, and Discussion Questions

Table 1. GDP components

Concept	Variable Name	Unit
C	Private Final Consumption Expend., Nominal	National Currency
G	Public Final Consumption Expend., Nominal	National Currency
I	Gross Capital Formation, Nominal	National Currency
X	Exports of Goods and Services, Nominal	National Currency
M	Imports of Goods and Services, Nominal (-)	National Currency
GDP	Gross Domestic Product (GDP)	National Currency

Computing a Ratio: (e.g. C / GDP)
New column = Column with C / Column with GDP
Number format is %

Discussion Questions:

- Which GDP component is the largest? Which is the smallest?
- Is there a trend in their evolution over time? Does this trend change direction?
- Are there any noticeable peaks or troughs that you can identify?
- Do net exports (NX=Exports-Imports) add or detract from overall GDP?
- What events could have caused specific ups and downs in the series?

Quantitative Reasoning and IL in Economics

Table 2. Uses of saving

Concept	Variable Name	Unit
CA	Current Account, Income, Credit	US Dollars
I	Corp., Househ., and NPISH, Gross Fixed Capital Formation, Nominal	National Currency
ER	National Currency per U.S. Dollar, per. aver.	National Currency per US Dollar

Computing a Sum or a Difference: (e.g. I + CA)
New column = Column with I + Column with CA

Discussion Questions:
- Is there a trend in the series? What does such a trend mean in terms of economic growth?
- Is there a noticeable cycle in the series? What could have created such a cycle?
- Do I and CA have the same sign? Do they move in the same direction?
- Do I and S have the same sign? Is one larger/smaller than the other?
- Is the country a net borrower or a net lender?

Table 3. Productivity

Concept	Variable Name	Unit
EMP	Employment	Thousands
UMP	Unemployment Rate	Percentage
GDP	Nominal Gross Domestic Product (GDP)	Billions National Currency
GDEF	Gross Domestic Product Deflator	Index Number

Transforming into Real Values

New column (rGDP) = Column with Nominal GDP / (Column with GDP deflator / 100)

Computing a Growth Rate

Growth rate (in %) = [(New value − Old value) / Old Value] * 100
New column (dProduc) = % growth rate of Column with rGDP/Emp
Number format is %

Discussion Questions:
- Which of the two series is more volatile: the growth rate of labor productivity or the unemployment rate?
- Can you identify one (or several) cycles in the series? For what dates?
- Do the growth rate of labor productivity and the unemployment rate move in the same direction? Why not?

- Do they move "at the same time"? Does one "lead" the other? Why?
- What can you infer about overall economic activity based on the evolution of the unemployment rate?

Table 4. Interest rates

Concept	Variable Name	Unit
CPI	Consumer Price Index	Index Number
DR	Bank/Discount rate (or Fed Funds rate)	Percentage
MMR	Deposit rate (passive)	Percentage
LR	Lending rate (lending)	Percentage

Computing a Growth Rate: (e.g. Rate of Inflation)

Growth rate (in %) = [(New value – Old value) / Old Value] * 100
Number format is %

Computing a Real Rate of Return: (e.g. Real Interest Rate)

Real interest rate = Nominal (reported) bank rate – Inflation rate (dCPI)

Discussion Questions:

- Is there a trend in the evolution of real interest rates over time?
- Are there cycles in the evolution of real interest rates over time?
- Which real interest rate is highest? Which is lowest? Why?
- What does it mean for a real interest rate to be negative?
- What does it mean for the financial system when the real deposit rate and the real lending rate are almost identical?

Table 5. Growth

Concept	Variable Name	Unit
GDP	Gross Domestic Product (GDP)	National Currency
GDEF	Gross Domestic Product Deflator	Index Number
EMP	Employment	Thousands
POP	Population	Millions

Computing the Real GDP per capita: (i.e., Real GDP / Population)

New column (rGDPcap) = Column with Real GDP / Column with Population

Computing the growth rate of real GDP per capita

New column (drGDPcap) = % growth rate of Column with rGDPcap
Number format is %

Discussion Questions:
- Which of the two series is more volatile: the growth rate of labor productivity or the growth rate of per capita GDP?
- Can you identify any trends or cycles in the series? For what dates?
- Do the growth rate of labor productivity and the growth rate of per capita GDP move in the same direction? Why?
- Do they move "at the same time"? Does one "lead" the other? Why?
- Consider how labor productivity is calculated (i.e., rGDP/EMP). How can you explain spikes in its value (i.e., large increases in its growth rate)?

Table 6. Inflation

Concept	Variable Name	Unit
CPI	Consumer Price Index	Index Number
MS2	Money Supply: Aggregate #2	Billions of local currency

Computing a Growth Rate: (e.g. Rate of Inflation)

Growth rate (in %) = [(New value – Old value) / Old Value] * 100

Discussion Questions:
- Is there a trend in the evolution of these variables over time?
- Are there any significant ups and downs?
- Do the rate of growth of money supplied and the rate of growth of prices move in sync?
- What policy factors affect M2 growth?
- What "real" factors affect M2 growth?

Table 7. Phillips Curve

Concept	Variable Name	Unit
CPI	Consumer Price Index	Index Number
U	Unemployment Rate	Percentage

Computing a Growth Rate: (e.g. Rate of Inflation)

Growth rate (in %) = [(New value – Old value) / Old Value] * 100

Discussion Questions:
- What is, generally speaking, the slope of the spaghetti line connecting all the data pairs?
- For which years does the concept of the short-term Phillips curve hold true?

- During which years does the short-term Phillips curve seem to "shift"?
- What could explain the fact that for some years the short-term Phillips curve slopes upward?
- Based on the visual examination of your plot, what is the natural rate of unemployment?

PART IV.
COLLABORATING TO
ADVANCE PROGRAMMATIC
INFORMATION LITERACY

CHAPTER 16

MOVING AHEAD BY LOOKING BACK: CRAFTING A FRAMEWORK FOR SUSTAINABLE, INSTITUTIONAL INFORMATION LITERACY

Lori Baker and Pam Gladis
Southwest Minnesota State University

INTRODUCTION

Infusing information literacy (IL) into the curriculum is long, hard, and often frustrating work. At our small, public liberal arts university, faculty have been crafting the pieces of an IL initiative for the past 10 years. Moving from the theoretical ideal of IL to an on-the-ground working reality takes much thought, time, and effort. Through trial and error, reflection and research, our campus is slowly moving forward toward what we would term an "institutional" model of IL appropriate for our university.

What we are finding is that this process is one of starts and stops, slowly shifting the culture to recognize the roles that all university stakeholders have in IL. Though we have not fully integrated IL, we are, we believe, building a framework that supports institutional IL, one that meshes well with the new Association of College and Research Libraries' (ACRL) *Framework for Information Literacy for Higher Education* (*Framework for IL*) (2015) and will enable our institution to adapt as the process on our campus moves forward.

We have found two key factors associated with this move to an institutional model: 1) a required shift in perspective about agency connected with IL; in other words, who is responsible for what, who does the work of IL and in what form; and 2) the importance of *kairos*, a Greek term often translated as "opportune moment," and the factors that helped lead our university to its opportune "moment" to take on institutional IL. These two reflective frames are useful even as the guidelines for IL shift, for they are not dependent on the model of IL in place but rather serve as heuristic lenses enabling us to identify any blind spots. Reflecting on these issues of agency and *kairos* has helped us to recognize the cultural factors related to IL at our institution that have influenced our work so far and how we can advance those efforts. At our university, a rural, regional school of nearly 3000 on-campus students with a strong union presence and orientation towards shared governance, that means shaping an institutional IL initiative that is driven by the faculty and integrated throughout the curriculum.

In this chapter we will describe what we mean by "institutional" IL, overview the issues of agency related to IL, and describe the exigencies leading to our institution's focus on IL. We will examine how these practical and theoretical considerations relevant to our institution's perspective ultimately led to the curriculum model our university adopted. Finally, we will describe the lessons learned and next steps in pursuing an IL initiative at our university.

RECOGNIZING AN "INSTITUTIONAL" MODEL OF IL

At many universities, currently including ours, a standard model for IL often consists of the on-demand (Curzon, 2004), one-shot "inoculation" (Jacobs & Jacobs, 2009, p. 75) approach, or what William Badke (2010) terms "short-term remedial" (p. 130). This approach, while helpful to individual faculty, students, and classes, does not lead to fully developed IL skills and understanding. As Barbara Fister (2008) asserts, the one-shot model makes it "difficult to build a systematic program for developing sophisticated information literacy skills" (p. 94). Describing findings from a case study of a Quality Enhancement Plan (QEP) project centered on IL at Trinity College, Anne E. Zald and Michelle Millett (2012) also draw this conclusion: "Ultimately, a library instruction program built entirely upon course-level partnerships is not sustainable and cannot support consistent student achievement of institutional learning outcomes" (p. 127). While we do not discount the value of individual or course-level collaborations, the goal of producing information literate students cannot be sustained by that model alone.

Recognizing the limitations of the one-shot model, Susan Carol Curzon (2004) and Stephanie Sterling Brasley (2008) describe eight additional models for delivering IL ranging from an introduction model, in which baseline IL skills are taught in perhaps several sessions, to credit-bearing courses taught by librarians. A model often illustrated in the literature involves programs working with librarians to develop program-specific IL (see examples in Brasley, 2008; D'Angelo & Maid, 2004a, 2004b; Peele, Keith & Seely, 2013; Winterman, Donovan & Slough, 2011). Exemplifying an approach that helps students to develop foundational skills within their discipline, Alison S. Gregory and Betty

L. McCall McClain's chapter in this collection (2016) describes the vertical curriculum in the Sociology-Anthropology program at their institution. Programmatic IL efforts such as this are important endeavors that contribute to the broader work of developing IL.

As Curzon (2004) notes, a comprehensive IL initiative would consist of several models of IL blended together (p. 43) in order to ensure that all students are meeting IL outcomes at all stages of their higher education experience. We call this an "institutional" model of IL. This institutional model approach would build from the four qualities necessary, according to Patricia Senn Breivik (2004), for developing a successful IL initiative:

- sharing responsibility for IL learning across faculty and beyond the library;
- close working relationships between faculty and librarians at the curriculum design and delivery levels;
- assessing IL based on "campus-determined" IL outcomes;
- and ensuring that IL is "institutionalized across the curriculum" through "departmental or college-wide planning for strategic integration of learning initiatives." (p. xiii)

Much like the matrix model described by William Miller and Steven Bell (2005), an institutional model, then, includes existing collaborations but moves beyond individual faculty or program collaboration to take a university-wide, collective approach of embedding and assessing IL throughout the curriculum. This institutional model thus aligns with the *Framework for IL*. The *Framework for IL* acknowledges the "information ecosystem" in which IL should be grounded. It advocates that IL should be contextualized to an institution and "developmentally and systematically integrated into the student's academic program at various levels" (2015, p. 10).

THE NEED FOR COLLECTIVE IL AGENCY

Moving to an institutional model of collaboration requires acknowledging and, likely, challenging existing notions of agency and ownership of IL found on a campus. Historically, librarians have been the traditional agents in the IL movement, an outgrowth from their work in bibliographic instruction that took root in the 1960s (Hardesty, 1995, p. 340). A review of the literature indicates that the majority of IL writing and research is published in the realm of library publications. As Badke (2010) notes, the limited publication of IL-related material outside of a library audience creates a "library silo" effect (p. 138), making it more difficult to raise awareness of IL and to influence other academic areas' practices.

Broader faculty culture also contributes to the traditional view of librarian ownership of IL. Larry Hardesty's (1995) study about bibliographic instruction indicated limited faculty acceptance of library instruction sessions. Curzon (2004) notes that because IL seems basic to faculty and "so much a part of the fabric of their academic life that they take it for granted" (pp. 32–33), that they often do not recognize or prioritize the need to participate in institutional IL efforts. Even within Rhetoric and Writing Studies, a discipline that has a marked interest in IL, faculty do not usually take an institutional perspective as they address IL within their programs. For example, Margaret Artman, Erica Frisicaro-Pawlowski, and Robert Monge (2010) note that within first-year writing programs, "it is still common practice to either disregard the expertise our librarian colleagues may lend to IL instruction or, conversely, to 'farm out' lessons in IL to one-shot library instruction sessions" (p. 96). These studies and comments indicate a reluctance to include librarians in a systematic way with IL skills instruction. In broad terms, faculty either teach it, don't think they need to teach it, or won't give the time (Van Cleave, 2007, p. 179).

Librarian culture certainly plays a role in limiting the expansion of IL as well, as numerous researchers have shown and as Rolf Norgaard and Caroline Sinkinson discuss in this collection (Chapter 1). Courtney Bruch and Carroll Wetzel Wilkinson (2012) explain how some librarians are caught "between the traditional librarian dharma emphasizing service preeminence, and new librarian dharma emphasizing educator responsibilities" (p. 17). Breivik (2004) and Kendra Van Cleave (2007) state that it may be difficult for librarians to share responsibility or collaborate. Nancy H. Seamans (2012), writing to librarians, notes "one of the most important components of sustaining an information literacy initiative is also one that we find most difficult, and that is the willingness to give primary responsibility to others if that's what will ensure the program's success " (p. 227). Even when librarians attempt to lead institutional IL efforts, they often have difficulty making headway due to traditional academic hierarchies and structures, such as the lack of faculty status or teaching department or program structure, which can keep librarians from having a direct impact on curriculum development (D'Angelo & Maid, 2004b).

What we have found in trying to move to an institutional model of IL is that these traditional concepts and structures related to IL agency constrict what might be possible to achieve. Van Cleave noted the same roadblock in 2007, stating that "Often the biggest stumbling blocks are a lack of an institution-wide focus on information literacy, as well as territorialism over curriculum and classroom control" (p. 179). Francia Kissel et al. (Chapter 20, this collection) further explore the issues related to faculty-librarian collaboration in their chapter in this collection. Ultimately, librarians and faculty "must have a mutual interest

... and see a mutual benefit" to IL (Curzon, 2004, p. 29). When IL is seen only as the purview of the library and librarians, or when faculty are dismissive of working with IL, it is more difficult to attain an institutional model of IL. What is needed instead is a collective IL agency, one in which both the faculty and librarians have a full understanding of IL and how it is infused in the curriculum. Faculty and librarians act in concert; they understand what IL is, where it is in the curriculum, how it can be taught, who will teach it, and how it will be assessed. This collective version of IL agency can only succeed if aided by a structural framework that supports it. This is similar to what Zald and Millett (2012) term "curricular integration" (p. 127). Such integration can only happen when IL becomes the responsibility of faculty as well as librarians, and not only within courses or programs, but across the institution. A collective sense of purpose and ownership of IL extends beyond individuals who might be in charge and resonates throughout the faculty and curriculum.

Examples of institutional IL do exist and more are emerging, with some being published beyond traditional library literature and in interdisciplinary venues (see Black, Crest & Volland, 2001; Brasley's 2008 description of Wartburg College; Lindstrom & Shonrock, 2006; Winterman, Donovan & Slough, 2011; Zald & Millett, 2012). The shifting perspective on agency can also be found in the LILAC Project's research design involving faculty, librarians, and students (Walker & Cox, 2013) as well as the revision process of the ACRL standards, which began in 2011 in an effort to update the standards first published in 2000. The organization reached beyond library professionals to include "non-librarians from university departments, higher education organizations, and an accreditor" as task force members (Bell, 2013, para. 5).

While "the autonomous culture of academia can enable resistance to collaboration," (Van Cleave, 2007, p. 179), institutions need to consider how agency and ownership of IL is structured or implicit on their campus. At our university, we are moving away from traditional, library-only ownership to a collective agency. Through a series of events, we are beginning to craft an institutional framework that infuses IL into the curriculum, regardless of who teaches it.

ACKNOWLEDGING *KAIROS* IN THE MOVE TO INSTITUTIONAL IL

Moving to an institutional IL approach, however, has not come easily or quickly, and, looking back, could not have even been put in motion without the key mix of elements and timing that occurred. Rhetoricians refer to the blend of circumstances and timing as *kairos*, "a situational kind of time" (Crowley & Hawhee, 2004, p. 37) that creates an advantageous moment in which to act.

When we consider how changes occur in academic institutions, usually they do not come unexpectedly but are in response to some kind of initial stimulus or dialogue. These might be national trends, accreditation criteria, professional organizations' push for different practices, or research studies which provide a rationale for change, which could be espoused by accreditors or new administrators or faculty; all of these factors take place in a given time and context that come together to create the opportunity for change. This unique blend of time, place, and influences produces a kairotic moment.

However, we must keep in mind that *kairos* is not the same as chronological time: "the temporal dimension of *kairos* can indicate anything from a lengthy time to a brief, fleeting moment" (Crowley & Hawhee, 2004, p. 37). On a university campus, a kairotic moment might happen when, for example, a new provost institutes an innovative program and provides a strategic and well-funded immediate plan of action. However, many university initiatives are not that neat and tidy, and the kairotic moment is not so much a single moment in chronological time as a series of moments, each contributing to the overall attainment of a larger goal.

This is particularly true of institutional IL movements, which take ongoing effort. For example, the creation of a community of practice as described in Kissel et al. (Chapter 20, this collection) in this collection started with a faculty member's concern about students' IL needs. The chapter describes how the resulting dialogue and partnerships are contributing to enhanced awareness of IL. Austin Booth and Carole Ann Fabian (2002) highlight the kairotic blend of factors and time that it takes to move an IL program forward, stating, "Initiation of campus-wide curriculum-based information literacy programs is a multi-layered, incremental, repetitive process" (p. 127). While something might occur to spark an institutional IL movement, persistence is needed to ensure that the full IL initiative comes into being. In other words, the larger kairotic event culminating in institutional IL might actually consist of a number of smaller kairotic moments spread over time.

Recognizing these moments can aid an institution in moving its efforts forward. By identifying the factors and moments that have been key in bringing IL into focus, institutions can ensure that the IL initiatives do not drop off or fade away. In other words, it is useful to look back in order to move ahead. In Eleanor Mitchell's (2007) chapter entitled "Readiness and Rhythm: Timing for Information Literacy," she reviews the kinds of external and institutional factors and "rhythms and pulses" (p. 77) that must be considered in planning a successful IL program. While Mitchell is generally focused on identifying the best time to "launch" a program, attention to timing is useful in reflecting back on the progress of IL at an institution. We see different kairotic points that have led to the place we are today; this helps us become aware of how those kairotic moments are taking shape *now*, so that we can refine the processes and framework needed to sustain institutional IL at our university.

CREATING AN INSTITUTIONAL FRAMEWORK FOR IL: LOOKING BACK TO MOVE AHEAD

A kairotic lens helps us to identify the convergences of who was involved and what circumstances or influential moments have shaped our institution's IL efforts. Our university's engagement with institutional IL began in 2004 when an external accreditation review indicated our Liberal Arts Curriculum (LAC), our general education equivalent, required an overhaul. IL itself was not directly noted in the accreditation review; however, the general education revision process provided the opening for IL to take root. In retrospect, the natural fit of IL coming into the process at this time makes sense. As noted by Ilene F. Rockman (2004), the national IL movement, having kicked off in 1989, had established itself with the 2000 release of the Association of College and Research Libraries' *Information Literacy Competency Standards for Higher Education* (*IL Standards*); this was followed in 2004 by Rockman's prominent publication titled *Integrating Information Literacy into the Higher Education Curriculum*. At the time of our accreditation review, IL was certainly on the minds of our librarians, who were by then aware of the new standards. Together with the *IL Standards* coming into being, an "instruction paradigm" shifted to a "learning paradigm" in libraries (Bruch & Wilkinson, 2012, pp. 5–6). This paradigm shift was occurring at the same time that accrediting agencies were emphasizing learning outcomes and assessment. The need to focus on learning outcomes and develop an LAC assessment plan based on those outcomes was paramount in our institution's accreditation review. Our university, though reaffirmed for 10 more years of accreditation, had to submit a progress report regarding general education to the accrediting agency.

This required our union-oriented faculty to closely examine and revamp the core of our institution's educational programming. Our institution is known for its strong faculty presence and the faculty's insistence, per the union contract, on being responsible for curriculum matters. The administration offered support but did not dictate any part of the process. As Lynn D. Lampert (2007) notes, "the curricular reform typically involved in overhauling general education programs is messy business fraught with campus politics and academic departments jockeying for position within the structure of course offerings to guarantee necessary enrollment levels" (p. 106). Our college's experience affirms that statement. The revision of the LAC was set up in stages, beginning with identification of liberal education outcomes, followed by objectives for each. A broad curriculum design was then initially established, and finally creation and approval of courses that met the outcomes took place. The initial process of developing and agreeing upon the outcomes and objectives spanned over a five-year timeframe with numerous meetings, brainstorming sessions, and discussions among faculty. It was time-consuming and at times exhausting work, but the faculty took the charge to revise the curriculum seriously.

An early step in the process was the establishment of a LAC Transformation Committee. The nine-member committee was comprised of seven faculty members, a staff member who belonged to a different union of "administrative and service faculty" representing student services, and the associate provost assigned to represent the administration and charged with writing the follow-up progress report to the accrediting agency. Of the seven faculty members, one was a faculty librarian. At our institution, a faculty librarian (4–5 full-time faculty librarians were on staff during this time out of approximately 130 full-time university faculty) has historically served on all of the major committees on campus. Having a librarian on this high-profile, high-impact committee was the first step in IL gaining a foothold in the new curriculum. As noted in Lampert's quote above, politics and departmental jockeying can greatly impact the institutional dialogue; however, the librarian on the committee held an institutional view rather than a territorial perspective on protecting credits and courses. She was able to prompt conversations about IL within the committee, as well as at departmental meetings, to ensure others were on board and the topic of IL did not remain only in the library realm; she was actively pursuing buy-in. As Curzon (2004) indicates, "Most information literacy programs fail because they are parochial and eventually come to be seen as only a library effort. To prevent this, savvy librarians will deploy a strategy that makes the information literacy program part of the educational strategy of the university, not just part of the service program of the library" (p. 35). We have little doubt that the strong and consistent library voice on the committee made an impact on the development of the revised outcomes.

That being said, the librarian on the committee was not solely responsible for the inclusion of IL concepts in the new outcomes. While the librarian was carrying forward the ACRL *IL Standards*, fortuitously, a number of departments on campus were also working with IL concepts, though they would not necessarily have called them that by name: 1) The English Department had been conceptualizing a new first-year writing program in order to align with the Council of Writing Program Administrators' *Outcomes Statement for First Year Composition*, first published in 1999 and formally adopted by Council in 2000. Several of the outcomes shared commonalities with the *IL Standards* (see Corso, Weiss & McGregor, 2010, for a description of the overlaps). 2) Faculty in the sciences had identified a lack of research and writing skills in their senior students and had revised their lower-level curriculum to address this concern. 3) During both the outcomes development phase as well as later during the curriculum design phase, the Philosophy Department engaged the faculty community in a consideration of the national dialogue on critical thinking and the best approach for representing it in the curriculum. All of these various efforts were ongoing at the same time as the general education program revision and in essence represent shared concerns about IL. This institutional conversation filtered back to the transformation committee, which was itself engaged in researching national standards, including partnering with the Center of Inquiry in the Liberal Arts at Wabash College. Together, these concurrent efforts were focused on helping our students develop IL skills, even though the different entities involved might not have labeled them as such. Looking back, we see how IL was starting to shift from the focus of the library to departments and across the institution as the transformation committee developed the first draft of what came to be called the Liberal Education Program (LEP) outcomes.

Throughout the LEP revision process, the transformation committee was vigilant in reporting to the full faculty body at union meetings. (Our union meetings replace a traditional faculty senate structure found elsewhere; our faculty union is responsible for all curriculum decisions as well as the kind of labor considerations more typically associated with union governance.) A majority of the full faculty were equally vigilant in attending open forums, drafting components of the new LEP outcomes and objectives, and commenting on proposed curriculum design.

Ten LEP outcomes were approved by faculty in 2007. Another year was spent developing the specific objectives to support each outcome. Along the way, faculty agreed that IL was an important component; they included IL-related objectives within two of the LEP outcomes, accepted an IL rubric, and listed IL as one of three core skills (along with communication and critical thinking) common to all areas of the LEP (see Table 16.1 SMSU Core Skills, LEP Outcomes, and Related IL Objectives). Because of union processes and transparency, the majority of faculty were thus involved in the inclusion of IL in the new LEP. Though the concept of IL was initially led by a librarian, by the conclusion of the revision of the LEP outcomes and objectives, all faculty had been exposed to and agreed to the importance of IL. In this manner, our faculty demonstrated their collective belief that "developing students' IL is an important aspect of their school's academic mission and programs," a factor emphasized by Arthur H. Sterngold (2008, p. 86) as vital to IL success.

Table 16.1. SMSU core skills, LEP outcomes, and related IL objectives

SMSU Core Skills

Communication, Critical Thinking, and Information Literacy are the core skills common to all areas of the liberal education program.

SMSU Liberal Education Program Outcomes§

Understand the techniques and habits of thought in a variety of liberal arts disciplines	Understand both physical and social aspects of the world and their place in it
Communicate effectively	Embrace the similarities among peoples and appreciate the diversity that enriches the human experience.
* IL-related objective: Determine the nature and extent of information needed to formulate and develop a coherent and unified thesis.	Analyze moral judgments and engage in moral discourse
Be creative thinkers able to identify, formulate, and solve problems using interdisciplinary perspectives	Practice responsible citizenship in their local and global communities
	Continue life-long learning
Be critical thinkers who evaluate information wisely and examine how assumptions and positions are shaped	Integrate mind, body, and spirit, the essential elements of a flourishing life
* IL-related objective: Demonstrate information literacy by accessing, utilizing, formatting, citing, and documenting relevant material accurately and correctly.	§In 2015, the faculty voted to revise the outcomes; 1, 9, and 10 were integrated into a values statement instead, although the curriculum did not change.

Following the passage of the outcomes and objectives, the difficult work of actually constructing a curriculum took place over the next academic year. Again, looking back, we see a number of factors that affected the eventual curricular design. While requiring credit-bearing IL courses is a model that some universities employ, this was not an option. During the curriculum design process, the state had decreed that all universities must reduce the number of credit hours to graduate from 128 to 120. This put pressure on several programs whose members lobbied that the LEP not grow much beyond 40 credits. In addition, there simply were not enough faculty librarians to handle such a load, and tensions already existed on campus regarding hires in other areas during difficult budget years. Other factors that possibly affected the curriculum design related to library personnel issues. Regrettably, shortly before the course design phase, the University Librarian unexpectedly passed away. During the design phase another instruction librarian retired and her position was not immediately filled. These factors, though not all explicitly discussed in the faculty debate about curriculum design, can in retrospect be understood as having affected the form IL took in the revised curriculum.

Over the course of the discussion about outcomes and objectives, the faculty had determined that the new LEP should guide our students over the full four years at the university, and not only for the first two years of general education. The result was the creation of interdisciplinary first and senior year LEP classes, both of which are to incorporate IL as one of the core skills. IL is also designated in the curriculum as one of the core skills to be revisited in a required sophomore-level or above writing-focused course and in a core skills course that each major program has to designate in their requirements. (See Table 16.2 SMSU LEP Curriculum Framework.) This aligns with an underpinning of the *IL Standards* (ACRL, 2000): "Achieving competency in information literacy requires an understanding that this cluster of abilities is not extraneous to the curriculum but is woven into the curriculum's content, structure, and sequence" (p. 5). The new LEP design thus provides a curricular framework upon which institutional IL can be built. Further, although unknown at the time of its initial development, the scaffolded design should align well with the newer *Framework for Information Literacy for Higher Education* (ACRL, 2015) model based on threshold concepts and moving individuals from novice to expert. The scaffolded design allows for students to develop IL skills over the whole of their time at the university, a developmental approach akin to "the way many other knowledge-based skills develop—from a combination of instruction and practice over a period of time" (Badke, 2010, p. 132).

The foundation of our redesigned framework is the first year LEP course, First Year Seminar (FYS): "The purpose of FYS is to encourage critical thinking, introduce information literacy, and involve students in the SMSU Liberal Education Program" (Southwest, 2013, p. 2). This course, then, was designed to introduce IL as one learning outcome of the class. FYS, a theme-based course, is taught by faculty from all disciplines with the understanding that they will work to meet the course objectives, including an introduction to IL. Requiring IL in FYS provides an exigency for librarians and faculty to identify together how to meet the IL learning outcome. For us, "[l]ibrarians would create the foundation that supports faculty, and enables them to integrate information literacy effectively into their own courses" (Miller & Bell, 2005, p. 3). In addition, having faculty from all areas addressing IL in FYS also makes them more conscious of integrating IL in their major courses. The FYS course requirement is a foundational element of our institutional *Framework for IL*, and the joint work of the librarians and faculty furthers the collective agency necessary for sustainable institutional IL.

Table 16.2. SMSU LEP curriculum framework

LEP Course	Primary LEP Outcome(s) and Purposes
The following two courses are to be completed by the end of the student's first year at SMSU	
LEP 100 First Year Seminar	Critical Thinking; introduction to all 10 outcomes and initial assessments
ENGL 151 Academic Writing	Communicate Effectively
The following course is to be completed by the end of the student's second year at SMSU	
COMM 110 Essentials of Speaking and Listening	Communicate Effectively
One course, with lab, chosen from approved list; three courses, chosen from approved list	Understand the techniques and habits of thought in a variety of academic disciplines
Two courses, chosen from an approved list	Embrace the similarities among peoples and appreciate the diversity that enriches the human experience
One course, chosen from an approved list	Analyze moral judgments and engage in moral discourse; Practice responsible citizenship in their local and global communities
One course, chosen from an approved list	Understand both physical and social aspects of the world and their place in it
One course chosen from an approved list in either History and the Social and Behavioral Sciences, or Humanities, Foreign Language, and Fine Arts	Develop further understanding of the liberal arts
One course, at the sophomore level or above, chosen from an approved list, focused on writing instruction that develops all the core skills	Develop the LEP core skills; provide formative assessments of the core skills
LEP 400 Contemporary Issues Seminar Chosen from an approved list (taken by students after completing at least 60 credits, including 30 credits of the MTC, and the three foundational courses)	Be creative thinkers; provide assessment of communication, critical thinking, and integration skills
Each major must include one or more upper-level courses that emphasize the Core Skills of written and oral communication, information literacy, and critical thinking	Develop the core skills

Note: Not all ten LEP outcomes were associated directly with a course. In addition, courses chosen by students must meet Minnesota transfer curriculum requirements and total 40 credits.

ADVANCING INSTITUTIONAL IL: REFINING ONGOING EFFORTS

Even though we approved a curriculum in 2008, teasing out the IL pieces has continued to be that "multi-layered, incremental, repetitive process" that Booth and Fabian described (2007, p. 127). At the time FYS was approved through our faculty assembly, the emphasis during the faculty assembly debate had centered on the critical thinking portion of the class, leaving the IL component an assumption. The other courses besides FYS that are to feature IL in the LEP (ENG 151, COMM 110, sophomore level-or-above writing course, course in the major emphasizing core skills, and LEP 400) have been created or identified; course proposals were vetted by the LEP Committee. However, the IL component in this process was included broadly, requiring only a description of what research and writing would be incorporated in the course. Different instructors and programs have approached the inclusion of IL in a variety of ways. Looking back, we can see that while the verbiage of IL had been inserted into the outcomes and core skills language for the LEP, there was not enough specificity provided for how it should be addressed or assessed.

Although IL is named as a core skill and ostensibly taught by faculty from across campus, we continue to define and identify exactly how that is or should be done. After the new LEP curriculum was in place for two years, the LEP Committee reviewed how well LEP 100 FYS was meeting its objectives. Results from a pilot critical thinking assessment and questions from the student senate about the FYS class created the impetus for the review. The committee decided that more specific training in critical thinking as well as a more standardized approach to introducing IL was needed.

The result was an opportunity to address IL in FYS as one component of a workshop held with the course instructors. Prior to the spring 2013 workshop, the three teaching librarians determined that a set of seven *IL Standards* outcomes would be most appropriate to address in the FYS course. The librarians recognized that in the previous semesters not all FYS faculty had chosen to bring their class to even one library session. However, the librarians described their desire to maintain a presence in the course in order to make contact with students early in their college experience. At the workshop, the librarian from the LEP committee led a session on IL outlining the library skills and specifically the seven IL outcomes to be introduced in FYS (see Appendix A). This introduction was meant to both introduce faculty to the described IL skills as well as foster a librarian and FYS faculty opportunity to "have a shared responsibility in injecting IL into their curriculum," but "do so meaningfully in close collaboration with the experts in the library" (D'Angelo & Maid, 2004b, p. 216).

The workshop session was a first step in continuing to systematize and scaffold how IL is being delivered. In the first year following the workshop the majority of the faculty teaching FYS preferred to have a librarian lead the IL sessions. However, that could morph as the instructors and librarians continue to develop ways to integrate those baseline IL skills into the course, and further as the institution works to adopt the new threshold concepts and *Framework for IL*.

Applying our kairotic lens, we now recognize additional avenues for continuing to emphasize and scaffold IL at the university. Assessment and accountability imperatives primarily driven by reaccreditation requirements present an exigency as well as a means for identifying and refining institutional IL efforts. The task at hand is to include IL assessment within the relevant LEP outcomes assessment, which will entail making certain that IL objectives related to critical thinking, communication, and creative thinking are clearly identified, measured, and reported. In addition, several programs have identified gaps between the introductory work done in LEP core classes and the new LEP upper-division communication requirement in their majors. A number of major programs are adding sophomore-level "introduction to the discipline" requirements, including research and writing components. These courses present another platform for scaffolding IL requirements from the LEP through the majors. Further, a faculty-wide conversation regarding academic freedom, assessment, and the contractual limits of standardized curriculum has emerged from the general education assessment team's initial undertakings; the discussion provides yet another possible kairotic moment to move the collective faculty forward in recognizing the importance and place of IL across the curriculum. We recognize that a kairotic moment is shaping right now; these assessment and curriculum initiatives, as well as integrating the new *Framework for IL*, provide key opportunities for faculty and librarians to continue their collective IL work.

Looking forward, we can see a number of steps yet to accomplish in order to fully frame out and operationalize institutional IL:

- educating the faculty about the ACRL threshold concepts
- identifying how the concepts are being addressed and developed in courses
- ascertaining which course- and program-specific learning outcomes align with the threshold concepts
- distinguishing how the assessment of those learning objectives might inform the assessment of IL, and
- ensuring that we are not only building "horizontally (across the curriculum)" but also "vertically (with the major)" (Curzon, 2004, p. 17), with the goal of helping to move students from novices to experts over their time at the university.

Having looked back at the kairotic moments that have shaped our university's efforts so far, we recognize that the embedding of IL concepts within key courses' learning objectives, scaffolded across the curriculum, creates the possibility of a much more sustainable approach to IL than the on-demand collaborations with individual faculty. We know that moving forward is only likely to happen if librarians and faculty continue to work together, through our union processes and collective recognition of the importance of the efforts.

CONCLUSION

As has become evident, our institutional approach to IL builds largely upon a blend of the introduction, general education, learning outcomes, and faculty focus models described by Curzon (2004, pp. 38–41). At other universities, an institutional approach might include the use of different models such as an entrance requirement model that Curzon describes or credit-bearing courses (see for example Eland, 2008; Mackey & Jacobson, 2007). Our move away from on-demand, one-shot IL to institutional IL is dependent on our faculty continuing to recognize and embrace their roles in sharing responsibility for IL with the library. Even though we are not approaching IL from the critical literacy standpoint described by James Elmborg (2012), we agree with his description of IL not as a "thing" but as something we "do" (p. 78); ultimately, we want IL to become a natural extension of "what we do here," a part of what faculty and librarians together expect to and do address, rather than an added-on component or dismissed altogether. As Curzon (2004) asserts, and we believe, "Regardless of the model or models that are chosen to teach information literacy, librarians and faculty must partner to teach students information literacy skills" (p. 44).

Creating an institutional approach to IL is not an activity that can take place in the vacuum of the library; it requires "a complete paradigm shift" . . . in order to "foster sustainable consistency and alignment throughout the curriculum" (Bruch & Wilkinson, 2012, pp. 13–14). It has taken our university nearly a decade to recognize, institute, and begin to refine IL. As we look back at how our university has arrived at the place where it is today, we do not see failures or missed opportunities; we see steady progress, dependent on large and small kairotic moments that kept IL in the picture and moved it forward. Perhaps a dearth of published accounts of institutionally based IL is because institutional IL tends to continually evolve and is simply not attainable quickly; it takes time, and not only chronological time, but an understanding of institutional time, the kind of time involved when we view institutional IL from a kairotic perspective. Though we know our experience at our small, public university with a strong faculty union influence will be different from other institutions' journeys, viewing IL through the lenses of agency and *kairos* is helping us to be purposeful as we move forward with our institutional approach to IL and perhaps could prove a useful approach for other institutions working to implement the ACRL *Framework for IL* and threshold concepts.

REFERENCES

Artman, M., Frisicaro-Pawlowski, E. & Monge, R. (2010). Not just one shot: Extending the dialogues about information literacy in composition classes. *Composition Studies, 38*(2), 93–110.

Association of College and Research Libraries. (2000). *Information literacy competency standards for higher education.* Chicago, IL: ACRL.

Association of College and Research Libraries. (2015, February 2). *Framework for information literacy for higher education.* Retrieved from http://www.ala.org/acrl/standards/ilframework.

Badke, W. (2010). Why information literacy is invisible. *Communications in Information Literacy, 4*(2), 129–41.

Bell, S. J. (2013, June 4). Rethinking ACRL's Information Literacy Standards: The process begins [blog entry]. Retrieved from http://www.acrl.ala.org/acrlinsider/archives/7329.

Black, C., Crest, S. & Volland, M. (2001). Building a successful information literacy infrastructure on the foundation of librarian–faculty collaboration. *Research Strategies, 18*, 215–225. doi:10.1016/S0734-3310(02)00085-X.

Booth, A. & Fabian, C. (2002). Collaborating to advance curriculum-based information literacy initiatives. *Journal of Library Administration, 36*(1/2), 123.

Brasley, S. S. (2008). Effective librarian and discipline faculty collaboration models for integrating information literacy into the fabric of an academic institution. *New Directions for Teaching & Learning, 2008*(114), 71–88. doi:10.1002/tl.318.

Breivik, P. S. (2004). Foreword. In I. F. Rockman (Ed.), *Integrating information literacy into the higher education curriculum: Practical models for transformation* (pp. xi–xiv). San Francisco, CA: Jossey-Bass.

Bruch, C. & Wilkinson, C. W. (2012). Surveying terrain, clearing pathways. In C. Bruch & C. W. Wilkinson (Eds.), *Transforming information literacy programs: Intersecting frontiers of self, library culture, and campus community* (pp. 3–44). Chicago, IL: Association of College and Research Libraries.

Corso, G. S., Weiss, S. & McGregor, T. (2010, July). *Information literacy: A story of collaboration and cooperation between the Writing Program Coordinator and colleagues 2003–2010.* Paper presented at the National Conference of the Council of Writing Program Administrators, Philadelphia, PA.

Council of Writing Program Administrators. (1999). WPA outcomes statement for first-year composition *WPA: Writing Program Administration 23*(1–2), 59–66.

Crowley, S. & Hawhee, D. (2004). *Ancient rhetorics for contemporary students* (3rd ed.). New York, NY: Pearson Longman.

Curzon, S. C. (2004). Developing faculty-librarian partnerships in information literacy. In I. F. Rockman (Ed.), *Integrating information literacy into the higher education curriculum: Practical models for transformation* (pp. 29–45). San Francisco, CA: Jossey-Bass.

D'Angelo, B. J. & Maid, B. M. (2004a). Beyond instruction: Integrating library service in support of information literacy. *Internet Reference Services Quarterly, 9*(1/2), 55–63.

D'Angelo, B. J. & Maid, B. M. (2004b). Moving beyond definitions: Implementing information literacy across the curriculum. *Journal of Academic Librarianship, 30*(3), 212–217.

Eland, T. (2008). A curricular-integrated approach to information literacy. In C. N. Cox & E. B. Lindsay (Eds.), *Information literacy instruction handbook* (pp. 103–112). Chicago, IL: Association of College and Research Libraries.

Elmborg, J. (2012). Critical information literacy: Definitions and challenges. In C. Bruch & C. W. Wilkinson (Eds.), *Transforming information literacy programs: Intersecting frontiers of self, library culture, and campus community* (pp. 75–95). Chicago, IL: Association of College and Research Libraries.

Fister, B. (2008). Course-related instruction. In C. N. Cox & E. B. Lindsay (Eds.), *Information literacy instruction handbook* (pp. 94–103). Chicago, IL: Association of College and Research Libraries.

Gregory, A. S. & McClain, B. L. M. Building critical researchers and writers incrementally: Vital partnerships between faculty and librarians. In B. J. D'Angelo, S. Jamieson, B. Maid & J. R. Walker (Eds.), *Information literacy: Research and collaboration across disciplines*. Fort Collins, CO: WAC Clearinghouse and University Press of Colorado.

Hardesty, L. (1995). Faculty culture and bibliographic instruction: An exploratory analysis. *Library Trends, 44*(2), 339–367.

Jacobs, H. M. & Jacobs, D. (2009). Transforming the one-shot library session into pedagogical collaboration: Information literacy and the English composition class. *Reference & User Services Quarterly, 49*(1), 72–82.

Kissel, F., Wininger, M. R., Weeden, S. R., Wittberg, P. A., Halverson, R. S., Lacy, M. & Huisman, R. K. (2016). Bridging the gaps: Collaboration in a faculty and librarian community of practice on information literacy. In B. J. D'Angelo, S. Jamieson, B. Maid & J. R. Walker (Eds.), *Information literacy: Research and collaboration across disciplines*. Fort Collins, CO: WAC Clearinghouse and University Press of Colorado.

Lampert, L. D. (2007). Searching for respect: Academic librarians' role in curriculum development. In S. C. Curzon & L. D. Lampert (Eds.), *Proven strategies for building an information literacy program* (pp. 95–111). New York, NY: Neal-Schuman.

Lindstrom J. & Shonrock, D. D. (2006). Faculty-librarian collaboration to achieve integration of information literacy. *Reference & User Services Quarterly, 46*(1), 18–23.

Mackey, T. P. & Jacobson, T. E. (2007). Developing an integrated strategy for information literacy assessment in general education. *JGE: The Journal of General Education, 56*(2), 93–104.

Miller, W. & Bell, S. (2005). A new strategy for enhancing library use: Faculty-led information literacy instruction. *Library Issues, 25*(5), 1–4.

Mitchell, E. (2007). Readiness and rhythm: Timing for information literacy. In S. C. Curzon & L. D. Lampert (Eds.), *Proven strategies for building an information literacy program* (pp. 77–93). New York, NY: Neal-Schuman.

Norgaard, R. & Sinkinson, C. (2016). Writing information literacy: A retrospective and a look ahead. In B. J. D'Angelo, S. Jamieson, B. Maid & J. R. Walker (Eds.), *Information literacy: Research and collaboration across disciplines.* Fort Collins, CO: WAC Clearinghouse and University Press of Colorado.

Peele, T., Keith, M. & Seely, S. (2013). Teaching and assessing research strategies in the digital age: Collaboration is the key. In R. McClure & J. Purdy (Eds.), *The new digital scholar: Exploring and enriching the research and writing practices of nextgen students* (pp. 313–327). Medford, NJ: Information Today.

Rockman, I. F. (2004). Introduction: The importance of information literacy. In I. F. Rockman (Ed.), *Integrating information literacy into the higher education curriculum: Practical models for transformation* (pp. 1–28). San Francisco, CA: Jossey-Bass.

Seamans, N. H. (2012). Information literacy reality check. In C. Bruch & C. W. Wilkinson (Eds.), *Transforming information literacy programs: Intersecting frontiers of self, library culture, and campus community* (pp. 221–244). Chicago, IL: Association of College and Research Libraries.

Southwest Minnesota State University. (2013). *Instructor's manual for LEP 100: First-Year Seminar.* Compiled by the Southwest Minnesota State University Liberal Education Committee and Instructors of First-Year Seminar. Retrieved from http://www.smsu.edu/resources/webspaces/academics/liberaleducationprogram/fys/fys%20manual%20feb%202013.pdf.

Sterngold, A. H. (2008). Rhetoric versus reality: A faculty perspective on information literacy. In J. M. Hurlbert (Ed.), *Defining relevancy: Managing the new academic library* (pp. 85–95). Westport, CT: Libraries Unlimited.

Van Cleave, K. (2007). Collaboration. In S. C. Curzon & L. D. Lampert (Eds.), *Proven strategies for building an information literacy program* (pp. 177–190). New York, NY: Neal-Schuman.

Walker, J. R. & Cox, K. (2013). Remixing instruction in information literacy. In R. McClure & J. Purdy (Eds.), *The new digital scholar: Exploring and enriching the research and writing practices of nextgen students* (pp. 349–368). Medford, NJ: Information Today.

Winterman, B., Donovan, C. & Slough, R. (2011). Information literacy for multiple disciplines: Toward a campus-wide integration model at Indiana University, Bloomington. *Communications in Information Literacy, 5*(1), 38–54.

Zald, A. E. & Millet, M. (2012). Hitching your wagon to institutional goals. In C. Bruch & C. W. Wilkinson (Eds.), *Transforming information literacy programs: Intersecting frontiers of self, library culture, and campus community* (pp. 119–130). Chicago, IL: Association of College and Research Libraries.

APPENDIX A

During the May 2013 all-day workshop for the faculty teaching the First Year Seminar (FYS) course, the instruction librarian presented the following information literacy skills as the minimum to be addressed in the course.

The instruction librarian requested that faculty focus on three primary library/information literacy areas that cover seven of the ACRL outcomes as part of the IL aspect of the course. The broad coverage areas of these three sessions include Article Databases, Online Catalog/Finding Materials, and Source Evaluation. It was explained the session goals were twofold:

1. Concrete skills
    a. Introducing seven (7) outcomes from three (3) of the Information Literacy Competency Standards for Higher Education
2. Intangibles
    a. Relationship building with librarians
    b. Comfort level using the aspects of both the online and physical library and asking for assistance

The librarian provided a demonstration of an active learning component for each session. Each instructor could decide whether to offer each session as librarian-led, instructor-led, or as a flipped classroom.

The ACRL Information Literacy Competency Standards for Higher Education introduced in FYS:

STANDARD ONE: THE INFORMATION LITERATE STUDENT DETERMINES THE NATURE AND EXTENT OF THE INFORMATION NEEDED.

Performance Indicator 1: The information literate student defines and articulates the need for information.

Outcome c. Explores general information sources to increase familiarity with the topic.

Performance Indicator 2: The information literate student identifies a variety of types and formats of potential sources for information.

Outcome c. Identifies the value and differences of potential resources in a variety of formats (e.g., multimedia, database, website, data set, audio/visual, book).

STANDARD TWO: THE INFORMATION LITERATE STUDENT ACCESSES NEEDED INFORMATION EFFECTIVELY AND EFFICIENTLY.

Performance Indicator 3: The information literate student retrieves information online or in person using a variety of methods.

Outcome a. Uses various search systems to retrieve information in a variety of formats.

Outcome b. Uses various classification schemes and other systems (e.g., call number systems or indexes) to locate information resources within the library or to identify specific sites for physical exploration.

Performance Indicator 5: The information literate student extracts, records, and manages the information and its sources.

Outcome c. Differentiates between the types of sources cited and understands the elements and correct syntax of a citation for a wide range of resources.

Outcome d. Records all pertinent citation information for future reference.

STANDARD THREE: THE INFORMATION LITERATE STUDENT EVALUATES INFORMATION AND ITS SOURCES CRITICALLY AND INCORPORATES SELECTED INFORMATION INTO HIS OR HER KNOWLEDGE BASE AND VALUE SYSTEM.

Performance Indicator 2: The information literate student articulates and applies initial criteria for evaluating both the information and its sources.

Outcome a. Examines and compares information from various sources in order to evaluate reliability, validity, accuracy, authority, timeliness, and point of view or bias.

CHAPTER 17
SUPPORTING ACADEMICS TO EMBED INFORMATION LITERACY TO ENHANCE STUDENTS' RESEARCH AND WRITING PROCESS

Angela Feekery, Lisa Emerson, and Gillian Skyrme
Massey University, Palmerston North, New Zealand

INFORMATION LITERACY IN NEW ZEALAND

Information literacy (IL) is recognized by librarians and IL advocates as a cornerstone of learning and research in higher education (Association of College and Research Libraries (ACRL), 2000; Bruce, 2008; Lupton, 2004; Secker & Coonan, 2011a, 2011b). However, the importance of explicit IL instruction is largely unacknowledged outside the library: while faculty support IL as a concept, many—if not most—teachers tend to believe responsibility for developing IL lies elsewhere. IL instruction, therefore, remains on the periphery of university curricula (Markless & Streatfield, 2007; Webber & Johnston, 2000). This chapter extends the conversation on embedding IL into the disciplines into the New Zealand (NZ) tertiary context. Prior to this research, little was known about how IL is perceived and taught by NZ faculty. Through participatory action research (PAR), our research addresses this gap by capturing unique insights into faculty's lived experiences as they adapted curricula and assessments to support students' IL development and learning in the New Zealand university context. Like much of the post-2000 literature, our research focuses on making stronger connections between IL and learning, and adopts learner-focused pedagogies that encourage reflective, experiential, and collaborative learning. We aimed to shift IL beyond the library by drawing on literature from library research, writing across the curriculum, transition to tertiary study, socio-cultural and constructivist teaching theories and pedagogy, and research connecting IL to learning. We explore IL development from a faculty perspective, and consider pedagogical and curriculum factors which both support and hinder embedding IL across an undergraduate degree.

In this chapter, then, we raise themes of concern to tertiary educators in NZ, and internationally: our study highlights the importance of IL in students' research, writing, and learning processes, examines key issues in tertiary teaching and student learning, and outlines successes and challenges in collaborating with and supporting academics to embed IL development into disciplinary courses.

PARTICIPATING PROGRAM

The participating program for this research was the Bachelor of Resource and Environmental Planning (BRP), an accredited professional degree in a NZ university. Program leaders had been challenged by an accreditation review which outlined short-comings in graduate capabilities, including IL competencies. Consequently, BRP faculty identified a need to implement change within pedagogy and curriculum design to support students' IL development.

The BRP is cohort-based and therefore presented a structure that would support scaffolded IL instruction systematically over the four-year degree. Participants in this research included five participating faculty, students, two librarians and the research team. Students were invited to be part of the conversation because, as Mills (2007) argues, "an obvious condition for doing action research and effecting educational change is that the outcome of any change effort must benefit students" (p. 158).

DEVELOPING A RESEARCH CONTEXT

The tertiary education sector in NZ (broadly defined as a single sector encompassing all post-school education) caters to over half a million (predominantly domestic) students, a third of whom are enrolled in one of eight national research universities (Goedegebuure et al., 2008; Ministry of Education, 2012a). University entrance requirements are determined by National Certificate of Educational Achievement (NCEA) credits in approved subject areas, including literacy (Ministry of Education, 2012b; NZQA, 2013), although any NZ or Australian citizen aged 20 or over can gain special admission without an entrance qualification (Healey & Gunby, 2012; Universities New Zealand, 2013). New Zealand university degrees are typically three-year programs (though vocationally focused degrees may take 4–6 years) and most have no general education component or foundation year to transition students into academic literacy (Universities New Zealand, 2013).

In recent years, NZ universities have changed in similar ways to those reported in the US (Weimer, 2003), UK (Angier & Palmer, 2006; Biggs & Tang, 2011; Secker, Price & Boden, 2007), and Australia (Brabazon, 2007; Devereux & Wilson, 2008), namely changing teaching practices, widening participation, and increasing concerns over student readiness. Successive governments over the last 30 years have taken proactive steps towards widening participation for under-represented groups, including Māori and Pasifika (Goedegebuure et al. 2008). The perceived widening gap between high school and university is also a feature of discourse around university preparedness in NZ (Ladbrook & Probert, 2011; Jansen & van der Meer, 2012), suggesting non-traditional students may struggle to transition into university successfully (Healey & Gunby, 2012; Jansen & van der Meer, 2012).

SITUATING IL IN THE RESEARCH

Recent literature on IL shows a shift to holistic views of IL and stronger connections between IL and learning (Andretta, 2005; Bruce, 2008; Martin, 2013). These views recognize a range of behavioral and cognitive competencies that characterize an information literate individual engaged in tertiary study (Secker & Coonan, 2011a; Hepworth & Walton, 2009).

Two key studies in this shift to a holistic model are the informed learning agenda (Bruce, 2008) and the "A New Curriculum for Information Literacy" (ANCIL) framework (Coonan & Secker, 2011a, 2011b, 2013). Christine Bruce's (2008) holistic concept of "informed learning" emphasizes interaction with, and use of, information in learning. Through informed learning, effective engagement with information is evolving and transferable, and information use and learning are inseparable (Bruce, 2008; Bruce, Hughes & Somerville, 2012). Bruce (2008, p. 183) describes informed learning as "both an approach to learning and the experience of learning through information use."

The ANCIL framework (Secker, 2011; Secker & Coonan, 2013) was designed as a practical IL curriculum to meet the needs of undergraduate students and reconceptualizes IL as central to academic disciplines (Secker & Coonan, 2011a, 2013). The ANCIL model (Figure 17.1) represents the importance of extending IL beyond information retrieval and towards key competencies fundamental to using information to learn. Central and unique to the model is transition, both into university and the workplace, and from dependent to independent learning (Martin, 2013; Secker & Coonan, 2011a, 2013).

Both ANCIL and Bruce's model position the learner at the center of the learning process, in alignment with the Association of College and Research Libraries' (ACRL) *Framework for Information Literacy in Higher Education* (2015).

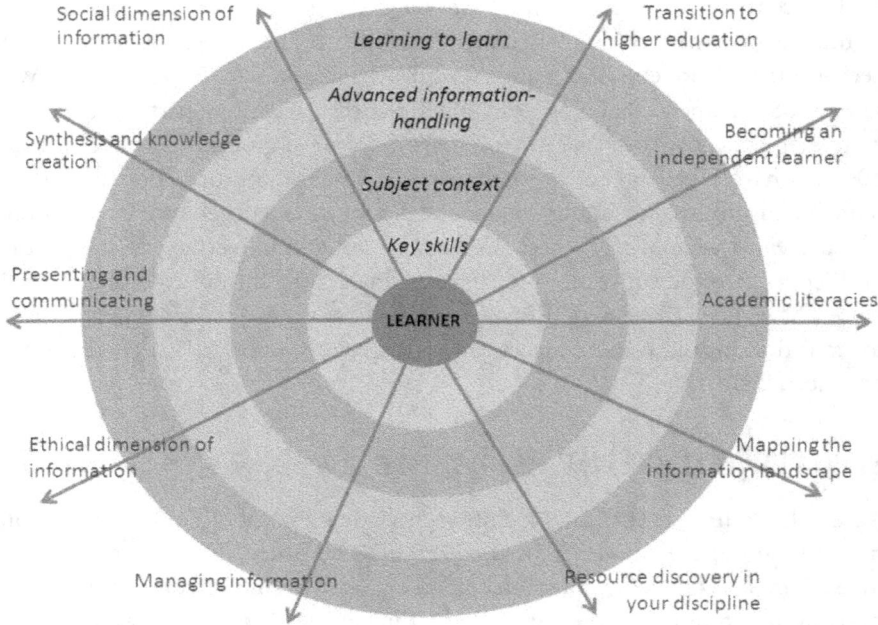

Figure 17.1. The ANCIL framework. Source: Secker & Coonan (2013).

These models take a broader holistic view of IL and recognize the joint responsibility for students, faculty, and librarians to engage in the "dynamic and often uncertain information ecosystem" (para. 1) that underpins learning in the digital age. Both ANCIL and Bruce's models informed our focus on learner-focused pedagogy as a means of embedding IL development into the BRP.

LEARNER-FOCUSED PEDAGOGY

Throughout western universities, there has been an observable movement away from traditional transmission modes of education toward a more learner-focused pedagogy (for example, in the US, Huba & Freed, 2002, and Weimer, 2003; in the UK, Biggs & Tang, 2011, and Secker et al., 2007; in Australia, Bruce, 2004, and Lupton, 2004, and in NZ, Zepke, Leach & Prebble, 2006). This same movement towards a learner-centered focus is also manifest at lower levels of NZ education. The Ministry of Education (MOE) promotes learner-focused pedagogy, recognizing the joint responsibility for learning between the instructor and the student. Learner-focused approaches are promoted at the secondary school level by the MOE's Te Kete Ipurangi[1] (TKI) guidelines:

> The success of teaching and learning is founded on the quality of the relationship built between the teacher and the student. The teacher manages the motivational climate of the classroom to foster a learning-focused relationship with students, with a shared ownership of and responsibility for learning. This provides students with the maximum opportunity to build their own motivation to learn. (Ministry of Education, (n.d.).

Learning as collaboration connects to the Māori concept of *ako*, effective and reciprocal teaching and learning:

> The concept of ako describes a teaching and learning relationship, where the educator is also learning from the student and where educators' practices are informed by the latest research and are both deliberate and reflective. Ako is grounded in the principle of reciprocity. (Kā Hikitia[2], Ministry of Education, 2009)

Despite this policy shift towards learner-focused pedagogy, in some NZ institutions including the one in which this study took place, a transmission style of lecturing prevails. Our research promoted a shift to pedagogies which adopt constructivist, experiential, reflective, and socially constructed views of learning to enhance students' IL development at university.

A key constructivist learning principle drawn on in this research sees reflection as an essential part of the learning process in higher education and professional practices (Moon, 2001; Wang, 2007). Reflection promotes higher-order thinking skills, including problem-solving, evaluation and critical analysis, synthesis of ideas, and meaning making (Burns, Dimock & Martinez, 2000), key aspects of IL within the ANCIL framework.

In adopting learner-focused pedagogy, we also needed to consider the impact of assessment on learning. Because assessment is a central focus for students (Dolan & Martorella, 2003), formative "assessment for learning" is a key to promoting learning and can be designed to help students learn by identifying errors and reinforcing correct understanding (Dolan & Martorella, 2003). Encouraging a focus on process through formative assessments can help students identify the stages in the research and writing *process*. This was a key consideration in the interventions designed for our research and runs parallel with Rolf Norgaard and Caroline Sinkinson's observation (Chapter 1, this collection), that effective IL development requires a process-oriented approach rather than focusing solely on product.

Effectively embedding and implementing IL across the curriculum requires collaboration between faculty, librarians, and wider university administrative bodies (ACRL, 2000; Secker & Coonan, 2013; Turner & Fisher, 2002). Many

IL researchers promote collaboration to ensure that IL is spread throughout the courses and consistently reinforced across the full degree (McCartin & Feid, 2001; Secker, 2011). Lori Baker and Pam Gladis (Chapter 16, this collection) refer to such collaboration as "collective agency," namely the collective understanding by faculty and librarians of what IL is within each discipline and how it can be fully integrated into curriculum design.

Participatory Action Research

PAR (McNiff & Whitehead, 2011; Seymour-Rolls & Hughes, 2000; Wadsworth, 1998) was identified as a suitable methodology for this research because a desired outcome was to collaboratively implement a necessary change within pedagogy and curriculum design. Participatory action researchers are committed to defining problems and informing, evaluating and changing both their own and others' behaviors and practices (McNiff & Whitehead, 2011), leading to lasting impact on practice (Burns, 2005). In this research, PAR enabled non-threatening, open discussion and reflection on all aspects of teaching and learning, and helped bridge the gap in librarians' and faculty understanding of and approaches to IL.

An initial review of action research definitions in various studies (Avison, Lau, Myers & Nielsen, 1999; Bunning, 1994; Creswell, 2005; Herr & Anderson, 2005; Kemmis & McTaggart, 1988; McKay & Marshall, 2001; McKernan, 1996; McNiff, 2002; McNiff & Whitehead, 2011; Oja & Smulyan, 1989; Selener, 1997; Seymour-Rolls & Hughes, 2000) led to the identification of six key characteristics (the "6 Cs") of PAR central to this research: Cyclical, Collaborative, Context-specific, Combining theory and practice, Critically reflective, and Change-focused (Feekery, 2014). The 6 Cs supported this research by recognizing the uniqueness of the context, allowing changes within the BRP to be monitored over 2 cycles, supporting collaboration and engaging in conversation that encouraged critically reflective practice, and promoting pedagogical change supported by educational theory and local data.

Data collection took place over four semesters, July 2010—June 2012. Data were collected through a range of qualitative and quantitative means drawing on techniques outlined in Mills' (2007, p. 73) taxonomy of action research qualitative data collection techniques, including:

- Experiencing: through class observations and meeting notes,
- Enquiring: the researcher asking questions via faculty interviews, reflective feedback and meeting notes, and student focus groups and surveys, and

- Examining: using and making records via instructor and student reflective journals and document analysis of course outlines, websites and handouts, and student assessments.

Data collected from participants captured attitudes, assumptions and responses to change throughout the research. Data were thematically analyzed and manually coded (Mills, 2007) for common patterns, meanings, or themes. The themes identified were guided by semi-structured interview, focus group and journal questions, and additional themes emerging through conversations. Triangulation (McNiff & Whitehead, 2011) combined the perspectives of all those involved and provided a coherent frame on which to evaluate evidence and draw conclusions.

Drawing on Judy McKay and Peter Marshall's (2001) dual-focus action research model, the complete data set was used for two purposes:

- The Action Focus: to identify the key successes and changes needed for subsequent modification of the interventions during, between, and after each cycle.
- The Research Focus: to analyze the data for a deeper sense of the research process and interventions. This included identifying shifting faculty attitudes and understandings of IL and their role in supporting students' IL development.

THE ACTION FOCUS OR "WHAT WE DID"

The process of working with BRP faculty revealed key factors impacting on the level of change they were willing and able to facilitate. Thus, a key aspect of this research was to understand participants' expectations and concerns around student performance and learning, views of teaching and learning, attitudes towards supporting IL development, and expectations of students' independence.

Participating faculty collaborated with the librarians and researchers to integrate IL development across the four-year degree. The interventions took two forms: library workshops and assessments.

Library Workshops.

Prior to our research, a review of student outcomes revealed that existing library sessions had failed to provide an in-depth introduction to effective information search strategies. Furthermore, IL competencies were not consistently extended within the four-year BRP program. We recognized that the first-year library lecture needed to be developed into interactive workshops that would allow students to attempt searches connected to assessment tasks with support from

Table 17.1. Final interventions developed for each participating course

Course	Year	Semester	Interventions
Course 1-1	1	1	Library Workshop—2 hour introduction to information searching and evaluation A: Source Justification
Course 1-2	1	2	B: Reflection on Values—draft writing submission, group discussion C: imap—research and writing process—visual model D: Worksheets for oral presentations—active listening / critical thinking
Course 2-2	2	2	E: Reading and Learning Log—critical review of information
Course 3-1	3	1	Library Workshop—Voluntary F: Reflective Logs—learning process / critical thinking / source justification
Course 4-1	4	1	G: Assessment for Group Project Report—Reflective Practitioner, Client Folder
Course 4-D	4	1/2	Library Workshop—2 hour advanced information searching and evaluation for research (modification of existing course component).

*Course coding: Course 1-1 is Year 1, Semester 1; Course 1-2 is Year 1, Semester 2 and so on. Course 4-d is Year 4, Double Semester.

librarians and faculty. Additional library workshops were added at the third and fourth years of the program (Courses 3-1 & 4-D) to ensure that IL competencies were revisited and extended as research demands on students increased.

Table 17.1 indicates the interventions developed, trialed, and modified over two semesters per course in Cycle One and Two.

The refocused library workshops offered throughout the BRP aimed to:

1. *Encourage greater student interaction and engagement in the sessions.* Common approaches to increasing interactivity include creating opportunities for learning by *doing* (conducting live searches as part of the session) and *reflecting* (Biggs & Tang, 2011, Diehm & Lupton, 2012, McCartin & Feid, 2001).
2. *Connect more closely to discipline-specific sources and immediate task requirements.* We tailored library interventions to the specific assessment tasks for each course and delivered them at point of need (Macklin, 2001).
3. *Increase input by participating faculty.* When faculty attend library sessions students value the session more (Turner & Fisher, 2002). Furthermore, faculty can offer advice to students on content-specific enquiries.

4. *Increase focus on evaluating source quality and relevance.* Students had been encouraged to identify credibility indicators and evaluate source quality using criteria commonly found in evaluation checklists. However, many checklist style evaluation tools ask questions students may lack the knowledge to answer (Meola, 2004; Metzger, 2007), and as Gocsik, Braunstein, and Tober (Chapter 8, this collection), also recognized, many students struggle to effectively evaluate sources. Therefore, we helped students conduct effective source evaluation by stressing the value of information to their discipline and connecting to the "research as conversation" metaphor (Fister, 2011; Gaipa, 2004; McMillen & Hill, 2005).

Assessments

Participating faculty brought a range of teaching approaches and experiences to the collaborative process and were willing to explore ways to adapt curriculum and assessments to support IL development within their content courses. All BRP faculty had concerns about student performance across the program but had limited understanding of how academic skills were being developed across the program. Therefore, the focus for each participant was to identify key competencies being developed and assessed within their own courses.

To consolidate skills introduced in the library workshops, a series of assessment tasks were created in each course to help students further develop IL within the research and writing process. All participating faculty changed their assessments to support the development of IL and reflective learning. The assessment interventions (Table 17.1, A-G) were designed to:

- increase awareness of IL competencies,
- focus on the research and writing process,
- provide opportunities for formative feedback,
- scaffold the development of IL competencies across the four year program,
- encourage wider and deeper reading of quality sources,
- promote the importance of clear, concise academic writing,
- encourage increased reflection on learning,
- create opportunities for collaborative learning.

It is beyond the scope of this chapter to discuss all the interventions, but three examples illustrate the innovative approaches developed to support students' academic and information literacy.

The first-year source justification task in Course 1-1 (see Appendix C) required students to select five key sources for their essay, identify key points relevant to the assignment question, and justify the selection of the source using quality indicators such as credibility, currency, and authority. The task required students to reflect on both source selection and personal learning. Students commented:

> I think that finally being assessed on your selection actually helped because it made me think that I am actually looking at the right material. (Focus Group, Course 1-1, 2011)

> No other lecturers have ever asked us to think about the sources we are using before. (Focus Group, Course 1-1, 2012)

To reinforce the importance of selecting quality information and to encourage students to make connections between sources in the first year of study, the information map (or imap—Emerson, Stevens & Muirhead, 2008; Walden & Peacock, 2006) was added into Course 1-2 (see Appendix D and Figure 17.2). The imap focused on key stages of the research process students often bypassed in last-minute assignment completion and encouraged them to reflect on their research process, thereby increasing students' awareness of IL competencies.

Students identified significant values from the imap:

> For me what [the imap] does, I can improve my timings, because if I can do that for every assignment I can see where I spend quite a lot of time. . . . [and] maybe I can improve through time. At least for me it was really really useful because at the end what I saw from that was that I should have written about this, this, and this, and I thought actually I didn't. (Focus Group, Course 1-2, 2010)

The second-year Professional Reading and Learning Log (see Appendix E) then extended the importance of critical evaluation by requiring students to find, read, and reflect on discipline-related aspects evident in their information sources to connect classroom learning with real-world situations and research. Students recognized the value of this task:

> It made me read more to do with Planning instead of just reading something and go, "Oh, that had Planning issues." [We have] to actually go, "What was the Planning issue? Tell me, explain it to me, give it to me in depth." So, I found that really helpful for understanding. (Focus Group, Course 2-2, 2011)

Faculty viewed the interventions as a valuable addition to the curriculum, and they continue to modify and create new interventions to ensure students have the opportunity to develop IL and engage with reflective learning.

Supporting Academics to Embed IL

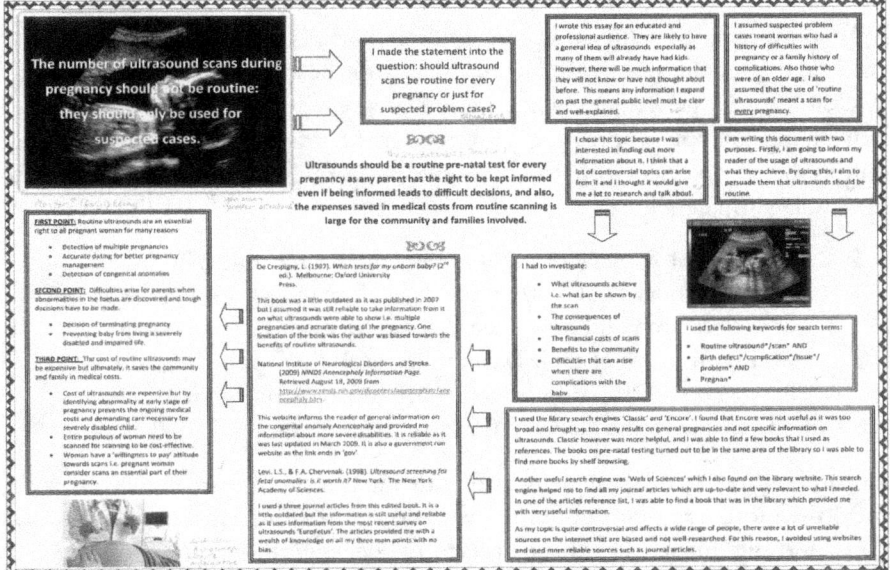

Figure 17.2. Example of an imap.

he involvement in this research has had negligible impact on my time—and in fact it has saved me time, by helping me design a smarter and more constructive lecturing programme. (Faculty Reflective Feedback, 2012)

Student responses to the formative assessments were also largely positive; they developed greater awareness of their research and writing processes and valued the scaffolded support.

> There's probably so many things you do that are just a process and you can go through the motions without really thinking about it. But this does make you go back and kind of analyse it and what you are doing, so it has been helpful. (S1, Focus Group, Course 1-1, 2012)

> I think I am open to spending more time on research. I'm viewing it as more like and experience of something to gain, rather than, you know, bamming through it to write an essay. (S2, Focus Group, Course 1-1, 2012)

The Research Focus or "What We Learned"

PAR was central to achieving change within the BRP and allowed participating faculty and the research team to learn from both successes and challenges (McNiff, 2002), particularly when ideas that seemed ideal in theory were more challenging to apply in practice. Throughout the research, we saw a significant shift in the way participating faculty viewed their roles in developing key IL and academic competencies:

> I hadn't consciously thought about [my responsibility to develop students' IL competencies] before becoming involved in the research and now I see that I have quite a clear responsibility in terms of their learning to teach them about IL, and how to be information literate, and how to actively incorporate that into the lectures. (Faculty Meeting Notes, 2010)

Although all participants engaged with the notion of learner-focused pedagogy (the ideal) as a result of our conversations, the constraints of faculty workloads, and the impact these have on faculty pedagogical development (the reality), were apparent.

> The challenge for me . . . is to manage the demands on our time from changes to our courses to allow for new IL skills development. Aside from the initial "start-up" costs of the time involved in . . . re-design of assessment packages, there is the more significant demand associated with new, more labour-intensive forms of assessment. Any instructor has a finite amount of time for professional development, for marking, for delivery of course material. If more time is needed for IL skills development, even with "economies" that come from the use of technology, then other aspects of teaching may be compromised. (Faculty Reflective Feedback, 2011)

As the research progressed, the value of conversation in facilitating change led to the emergence of a 7th C of PAR—Conversation-driven. Conversation is recognized as a valid method of data collection in PAR (Feldman, 1999; McNiff, 2002). However, in this research, it was the catalyst for initiating, promoting, and facilitating the change we achieved, and was thus elevated beyond a data collection method. If faculty had participated in solitary reflection characterized by journal writing, the depth of negotiation, debate, and understanding inherent in our conversations may not have occurred.

Conversations in this research served numerous functions. Recorded conversations during scheduled meetings about how IL instruction was perceived to be taking place were used to reflect on actions and design assessment modifications. They helped identify ways faculty could amend their pedagogy or assessment towards learner-focused pedagogies. Through conversation and observation, problems identified by faculty provided opportunities for further investigation. An example of this is the debate around the provision of course readings connected to student independence:

> I refuse to provide [readings] in paper. . . . I say explicitly say it in my reading guide that these are what I have found is useful. While you are going through trying to find these things you just might actually find something even better or even more interesting on the way. And for God's sake at this stage it's 3rd and 4th year—we should be well past the nappy changing and spoon feeding stage. (Faculty Interview, 2011)

Following this initial conversation, the participating instructor and the lead researcher regularly debated the nature of independent learning and scaffolded learning support, making reflection on effective teaching and learning a greater part of the research.

Each faculty member chose whether to adapt their teaching in response to the conversations and reflection. If they chose to trial a new teaching style for example, discussion of the outcomes helped determine if the intervention had been successful. Informal conversations were important for relationship building and further exploration of ideas around teaching and learning. Finally, conversations with students in focus groups helped determine the value of the interventions in enhancing their IL competencies.

Conversations revealed a lack of understanding of how students learn at university and mismatches between faculty assumptions and the realities of student experience. One significant mismatch concerned participating faculty's desire for students to learn academic competencies independently by using university learning support services, and students' limited use of such services.

> Instructor: I tend to think that students need to take more responsibility for using these generic services which I feel provide appropriate support for students from professionals. That leaves me free to focus on the course content. (Faculty Reflective Journal, Course 1-1, 2011)

> Student: I don't really go and get help. . . . I maybe look at [the text] a little bit and then [the online resources] but that would be it. I don't really go and ask other people. (Focus Group, Course 1-1, 2011)

IMPLICATIONS

Several implications identified in this research may contribute to the wider understanding of effective ways to enhance students' IL development and support them to become informed learners.

First, this research confirmed the notion that supporting students' IL development relies on how faculty promote and develop IL within their curriculum. Adopting learner-focused pedagogy may actively focus students on the research process. Providing embedded IL development into content courses via formative assessments may help students succeed in their transition into academic literacy and understand how disciplinary knowledge is created. As the gap between high school and university appears to be widening and more students seem unprepared for the demands of higher education (Brabazon, 2007; Secker, 2011, van der Meer, Jansen & Torenbeek, 2010), it is essential to provide explicit opportunities to support university transition into IL (Jansen & van der Meer, 2012; Weimer, 2003).

Second, this research found that faculty who are introduced to holistic views of IL can perceive a role for themselves in the development of disciplinary-focused IL development for their students. Furthermore, when explicit support in designing learning tasks and assessments that facilitate IL development is provided, student engagement in IL is improved.

Third, this research confirmed collaboration as an effective means of teaching IL. When faculty are pro-active in driving IL development, and embed IL development with the support of librarians, students developed essential academic competencies. While initial library instruction was important, further development continued under the participating faculty's guidance, with a focus on the evaluation of sources and their value to the discipline. This extended beyond first year as the curriculum became more complex and specialized. To support faculty to actively engage in designing IL initiatives, they needed to become aware of the centrality of IL in learning and then be more pro-active in initiating collaboration with librarians. They also benefitted from professional development around learner-focused pedagogy to identify how IL could be effectively embedded into existing curricula.

Finally, faculty need professional development to facilitate IL development within the curriculum and assessment. In this research, such support was provided through building trusting relationships that facilitated in-depth conversation and reflection, and through research-focused professional development. We saw a significant shift in the way faculty viewed their role in developing IL and other essential academic competencies as they created explicit, developmental, active-learning opportunities. This change in focus needs to be widely encouraged in higher education to enable students to become information literate in a world of ever expanding information. To enable such a change, participating faculty suggested more time is needed within workload allocations for professional development on teaching academic competencies alongside content.

This research resulted in IL development being integrated into each year of the BRP, but we recognize that supporting students' learning is an ongoing process and more work remains to fully embed IL development throughout the whole program. One year since the research phase ended, the interventions have been maintained and modified as faculty become more confident in supporting IL development. Our conversations are ongoing as we continue to explore effective ways to support students towards IL and informed, reflective learning.

ACKNOWLEDGEMENTS

We would like to acknowledge Ako Aotearoa for the funding for this research over a three year period, and Facet Publishing for permission to use the ANCIL diagram (Figure 17.1) as produced in Secker and Coonan, 2013.

NOTES

1. Te Kete Ipurangi–the online knowledge basket–is the NZ Ministry of Education's bilingual education portal, which provides New Zealand schools and students with a wealth of information, resources, and curriculum materials to enhance teaching and learning, raise student achievement, and advance professional development (http://www.tki.org.nz/About-this-site/About-Te-Kete-Ipurangi).
2. Kā Hikitia is the NZ Ministry of Education's Māori Education Strategy for supporting NZ's indigenous Māori towards educational success.

REFERENCES

Andretta, S. (2005). *Information literacy: A practitioner's guide*. Oxford, UK: Chandos.

Andretta, S. (2010). Learner-centred information literacy initiatives in higher education. *Journal of Information Literacy, 4*(1), 1–5.

Angier, C. & Palmer, W. (2006). Chapter 3–Writing solutions. In S. Davies, D. Swinburne & G. Williams (Eds.), *Writing matters: The Royal Literary Fund report on student writing in higher education* (pp. 15–26). London, UK: Royal Literary Fund.

Association of College and Research Libraries (2000). *Information literacy competency standards of higher education*. Chicago, IL: American Library Association.

Baker, L. & Gladis, P. (2016). Moving ahead by looking back: Crafting a framework for sustainable institutional information literacy. In B. J. D'Angelo, S. Jamieson, B. Maid & J. R. Walker (Eds.), *Information literacy: Research and collaboration across disciplines*. Fort Collins, CO: WAC Clearinghouse and University Press of Colorado.

Bean, J. C. (2011). *Engaging ideas: The professor's guide to integrating writing, critical thinking and active learning in the classroom* (2nd ed.). San Francisco, USA: Jossey-Bass.

Biggs, J. & Tang, C. (2011). *Teaching for quality learning at university* (4th ed.). Maidenhead, NY: McGraw-Hill/Society for Research into Higher Education. Open University Press.

Brabazon, T. (2007). *The University of Google: Education in the (post) information age.* Hampshire, UK: Ashgate Publishing Limited.

Bruce, C. (2004). Information literacy as a catalyst for educational change: A background paper. In P. A. Danaher (Ed.). Lifelong learning: Whose responsibility and what is your contribution? *The 3rd International Lifelong Learning Conference.* Yeppoon, Queensland.

Bruce, C. (2008). *Informed learning.* Chicago, IL: Association of College and Research Libraries.

Bruce, C., Hughes, H. & Somerville, M. M. (2012). Supporting informed learners in the twenty-first century. *Library Trends, 60*(3), 522–545.

Burns, A. (2005). Understanding action research. In A. Burns & H. de Silva Joyce (Eds.), *Teachers' voices 8: Explicitly supporting reading and writing in the classroom* (pp. 18–26). Sydney, Australia: Macquarie University.

Burns, M., Dimock, K. V. & Martinez, D. (2000). Action reflection learning. United States: Southwest Educational Development Laboratory.

Diehm, R. A. & Lupton, M. (2012). Approaches to learning information literacy: A phenomenographic study. *The Journal of Academic Librarianship, 38*(4), 217–225.

Dolan, D. V. & Martorella, G. (2003). Discipline-based information literacy and the lifelong learner. *International Journal of Lifelong Learning, 10*, 1319–1334.

Emerson, L. E., Stevens, S. M. & Muirhead, J. (2008). *Scaffolding the writing process in a large first year science class.* Presented at Symposium on Tertiary Assessment and Higher Education Student Outcomes, 17–19 November 2008, Wellington, New Zealand.

Feekery, A. J. (2014). *Conversation and change: Integrating information literacy to support learning in the New Zealand tertiary context.* (Unpublished doctoral dissertation.) Massey University, Palmerston North, New Zealand.

Feldman, A. (1999). The role of conversation in collaborative action research. *Educational action research, 7*(1), 125–147.

Fister, B. (2011a). Burke's parlour tricks: Introducing research as conversation. Inside Higher Ed. Retrieved from https://www.insidehighered.com/blogs/library-babel-fish/burkes-parlor-tricks-introducing-research-conversation.

Fry, H., Ketteridge, S. & Marshall, S. (2003). Understanding student learning. In H. Fry, S. Ketteridge & S. Marshall (Eds.), *A handbook for teaching and learning in higher education: Enhancing academic practice* (2nd ed.) (pp. 9–25). London: Kogan Page Limited.

Gaipa, M. (2004). Breaking into the conversation: How students can acquire authority for their writing. *Pedagogy Critical Approaches to Teaching Literature, Language, Culture and Composition, 4*(3), 419–437.

Goedegebuure, L., Santiago, P., Fitznor, L., Stensaker, B. & van der Steen, M. (2008). *OECD reviews of tertiary education: New Zealand*. Paris, France: OECD

Healey, N. & Gunby, P. (2012). The impact of recent government tertiary education policies on access to higher education in New Zealand. *Journal of Educational Leadership, Policy and Practice, 27*(1), 29–45.

Hedberg, P. R. (2009). Learning through reflective classroom practice applications to educate the reflective manager. *Journal of Management Education, 33*(1), 10–36.

Hepworth, M. & Walton, G. (2009). *Teaching information literacy for inquiry-based learning*. Oxford, UK: Chandos.

Huba, M. E. & Freed, J. E. (2000). *Learner-centered assessment on college campuses: Shifting the focus from teaching to learning*. Boston, MA: Allyn and Bacon.

Jansen, E. P. & van der Meer, J. (2012). Ready for university? A cross-national study of students' perceived preparedness for university. *The Australian Educational Researcher, 39*(1), 1–16.

Ladbrook, J. & Probert, E. (2011). Information skills and critical literacy: Where are our digikids at with online searching and are their teachers helping? *Australasian Journal of Educational Technology, 27*(1), 105–121.

Lupton, M. (2004). *The learning connection: Information literacy and the student experience*. Adelaide: Auslib Press.

Macklin, A. S. (2001). Integrating information literacy using problem-based learning. *Reference Services Review, 29*(4), 306–314.

McCartin, M. & Feid, P. (2001). Information literacy for undergraduates: Where have we been and where are we going? *Advances in Librarianship, 25*, 1–27.

McKay, J. & Marshall, P. (2001). The dual imperatives of action research. *Information Technology & People, 14*(1), 46–59.

McMillen, P. S. & Hill, E. (2005). Why teach "research as conversation" in freshman composition courses? A metaphor to help librarians and composition instructors develop a shared model. *Research Strategies 20*, 3–22.

McNiff, J. (2002). *Action research: Principles and practice* (2nd ed.). London: Routledge/Falmer.

McNiff, J. & Whitehead, J. (2011). *All you need to know about action research* (2nd ed.). Los Angeles: Sage.

Markless, S. & Streatfield, D. R. (2007). Three decades of information literacy: redefining the parameters. In S. Andretta (Ed.), *Change and challenge: Information literacy for the twenty-first century* (pp. 15–36). Adelaide: Auslib Press.

Martin, J. L. (2013). *Learning from recent British information literacy models: A report to ACRL's Information Literacy Competency Standards for Higher Education taskforce*. Retrieved from http://mavdisk.mnsu.edu.martij2/acrl.pdf.

Meola, M. (2004). Chucking the checklist: A contextual approach to teaching undergraduates web-site evaluation. portal: *Libraries and the Academy, 4*(3) 331–344.

Metzger, M. J. (2007). Making sense of credibility on the Web: Models for evaluating online information and recommendations for future research. *Journal of the American Society for Information Science and Technology, 58*(13), 2078–2091.

Mills, G. E. (2007). *Action research: A guide for the teacher researcher* (3rd ed.). Upper Saddle City, NJ: Pearson, Merrill Prentice Hall.

Ministry of Education. (n.d) *Te Kete Ipurangi (TKI)*. Retrieved from http://www.tki.org.nz/.

Ministry of Education. (2009). *Ka Hikitia—Managing for success: The Māori education strategy 2008–2012*. Retrieved from http://www.minedu.govt.nz/~/media/MinEdu/Files/TheMinistry/KaHikitia/English/KaHikitia2009PartOne.pdf .

Ministry of Education. (2012a). *Profile & Trends: New Zealand's tertiary education sector 2011*. Wellington, NZ: Tertiary Sector Performance Analysis. Ministry of Education.

Ministry of Education. (2012b). *The national curriculum*. Retrieved from http://www.minedu.govt.nz/Parents/AllAges/EducationInNZ/TheNationalCurriculum.aspx.

Moon, J. (2001). *PDP Working Paper 4: Reflection in higher education learning*. Higher Education Academy. Retrieved from http://www.heacademy.ac.uk/resources.asp.

Norgaard, R. & Sinkinson, C. (2016). Writing information literacy: A retrospective and a look ahead. In B. J. D'Angelo, S. Jamieson, B. Maid & J. R. Walker (Eds.), *Information literacy: Research and collaboration across disciplines*. Fort Collins, CO: WAC Clearinghouse and University Press of Colorado.

NZQA. (2013). *Secondary school and NCEA*. Retrieved from http://www.nzqa.govt.nz/studying-in-new-zealand/secondary-school-and-ncea/.

Secker, J. (2011). A new curriculum for information literacy: Expert consultation report. Retrieved from http://ccfil.pbworks.com/f/Expert_report_final.pdf.

Secker, J. & Coonan, E. (2011a). A new curriculum for information literacy: Curriculum and supporting documents. Retrieved from http://ccfil.pbworks.com/f/ANCIL_final.pdf.

Secker, J. & Coonan, E. (2011b). A new curriculum for information literacy: Executive summary. Retrieved from http://ccfil.pbworks.com/f/ Executive_summary.pdf.

Secker, J. & Coonan, E. (2013). Introduction. In J. Secker & E. Coonan (Eds.), *Rethinking information literacy: A practical framework for supporting learning* (pp. xv–xxx). London: Facet Publishing

Secker, J., Price, G. & Boden, D. (2007). *The information literacy cookbook: Ingredients, tasters and recipes for success*. Oxford, UK: Chandos.

Seymour-Rolls, K. & Hughes, I. (2000). Participatory action research: Getting the job done. *Action Research e-reports, 4*. Retrieved from http://www.fhs.usyd.edu.au/arow/arer/004.htm.

Turner, K. & Fisher, T. (2002). A collaborative quest: Building information literacy initiatives at the University of Otago. Paper prepared for the TTA Information Literacy Sub-Committee Seminar, Rotorua, New Zealand. September 26–27, 2002.

Universities New Zealand. (2013) The NZ university system. Retrieved from http://www.universitiesnz.ac.nz/nz-university-system.

van der Meer, J., Jansen, E. & Torenbeek, M. (2010). 'It's almost a mindset that teachers need to change': First-year students' need to be inducted into time management. *Studies in Higher Education, 35*(7), 777–791.

Wadsworth, Y. (1998). What is participatory action research. *Action Research International, 2*(1). Retrieved from http://www.scu.edu.au/schools/gcm/ ar/ari/p-wadsworth 98.html.

Walden, K. & Peacock, A. (2008). Economies of plagiarism: The i-map and ownership in information gathering. In C. Eisner & M. Vicinus (Eds.), *Originality, imitation and plagiarism: Teaching writing in the digital age.* Ann Arbor: The University of Michigan Press.

Wang, L. (2007). Sociocultural learning theories and information literacy teaching activities in higher education. *Reference & User Services Quarterly, 47*(2), 149–158.

Webber, S. & Johnston, B. (2000). Conceptions of information literacy: New perspectives and implications. *Journal of Information Science, 26*(6), 381–398.

Weimer, M. (2003). Focus on learning, transform teaching. Change: The Magazine of Higher Learning, 35(5), 48–54.

Zepke, N., Leach, L. & Prebble, T. (2006). Being learner centered: one way to improve student retention? Studies in Higher Education, 31(5), 587–600.

APPENDIX A: DATA COLLECTION TIMELINE

Cycle 1	
Semester 2, 2010 (July–November)	Course 1-2; Course 2-2
Semester 1, 2011 (February–June)	Course 1-1; Course 3-1; Course 4-1; Course 4-D
Cycle 2	
Semester 2, 2011 (July–November)	Course 1-2; Course 2-2; Course 4-D
Semester 1, 2012 (February–June)	Course 1-1; Course 3-1; Course 4-1; Course 4-D

APPENDIX B: SAMPLE OF THEMES / DATA CODING SPREADSHEET

Themes	Focus Groups—Course 2-2			Representative Comments
	Code	Transcript	Line	
Under-standing IL	1	1/2-2/S210	5	Not really
		2/2-2/S210	5–7	No It does ring a bell
What does IL mean?	1.1	1/2-2/S210	8–11	How to use different literature to get information. I thought, I'm still a bit confused as to what it is aiming to do, and I was trying to broaden our techniques of research and gathering information and processing it, but it's still kind of hazy.

Appendix B—*continued*

Themes	Focus Groups—Course 2-2			Representative Comments
	Code	Transcript	Line	
What does IL mean? (*continued*)	1.1	1/2-2/S210	43–46	First year I found them just like what you were talking about before, I was finding them like the first kind of 5 things that were semi-related to the topic. But then through this year I have started to use more books but I still find article searching real tricky on the Massey website.
		3/2-2/S211	20–22	Yeah, yeah, I think you've covered it pretty well there; just searching for information and finding out what's relevant and how you incorporate that into you own academic work or yeah—that's what I sort of—you had a really long definition of it last time!
		4/2-2/S211	18–27	F: I guess how we make use of information researching—yeah, research how [ ] in journals and [ ] library yes? M: How support classes work, like that report writing one? I thought that was good. F: How we gather our resources for our projects and assignments and that sort of thing. M: Yeah, I've got nothing to add to that unfortunately.
How have you learned it so far?	1.2	3/2-2/S211	31–36	Yeah, I tend to use journals like it's been accumulating a lot more that my use of journals and my really specific academic literature has increased and it was quite noticeable and I find it's because like, it's you know I feel more comfortable being able to extract the information and use it properly rather than going 'oh oh what does this actually mean?' and I'll stick to the basics. So I don't know, feeling more comfortable and stepping out and using the stuff like bigger range and everything.
		3/2-2/S211	66–69	I find that I get a bit of that in the feedback from the work we do and we're being told to evaluate sources—or that's implied—but there hasn't been any instruction really or anything to say 'heh, for example, look at these two sources—how are they different' and stuff, not really—it hasn't really been driven home.

Note: Transcript code=Focus group/course/semester, year. All transcripts included line numbers. The code number was manually written on transcripts and then data transferred into spreadsheets as shown here.

APPENDIX C: COURSE 1-1–SOURCE JUSTIFICATION TASK INSTRUCTIONS

You need to be able to justify why you chose to use or reject particular sources for your essay, and show that you are starting to make connections between the different types of sources you are using.

You will need to choose 5 of your sources to complete this assessment, but you should be considering all of your sources carefully.

Pick one of each of the following source types to review:

- Scholarly source
- Government report/paper
- News item
- Popular source
- Rejected source (of any of the source types above or other sources you may find)

Sources 1 and 2 should be ones that you have selected to definitely use in your essay. For 3 and 4, you may choose to use or reject the source, and explain why. 5 is a source that you have definitely rejected for this essay.

After you have done your search, I am also asking you to reflect on your search process, and some of the successes and challenges you faced when finding and evaluating your sources. This kind of thoughtful reflection is what helps you learn and become a more successful student at university.

REMEMBER: It is important that you always think carefully about the sources you choose to use in your assessments at university.

Reflecting on the Research Process

a. What have you learned about the information searching process?
Think about what you knew about searching before you came to university, and what you know now after having the library session and completing this assessment. You may have also had other experiences in other courses that have impacted on the way you think about information that you can mention here too.
b. Describe your information search process for this essay assignment
For example, where did you start; what different search tools did you use; how did you extend your search; where did you find your best sources? Did you go to Wikipedia to understand the topic and find some PDFs there? I want to see here how you searched and if there is a method to the madness!

> **c. What was the greatest challenge for you in finding and evaluating information sources to use in this essay?**
>
> The challenges in searching are what we have to overcome to help make the process easier. For some of these challenges you can try to find solutions for yourself, but for others, you may need to get support from the librarians. The better you get at searching in first year, the easier life will be for the rest of your degree. These are skills that develop through trial and error and support. Knowing what challenges you have is the first step to overcoming them.

APPENDIX D: COURSE 1-1—IMAP INSTRUCTIONS

In addition to the essay, you will also need to produce an imap. An imap "is a way of recording the research stages of a project, focusing on the information handling process. An imap logs such things as finding sources, reading and evaluating them, taking ownership of ideas, formulating a response or argument, evaluating sources where appropriate, and building a bibliography, in a visual account of the process" (Waldon and Peacock, 2008, p. 142, cited in Emerson, Stevens and Muirhead, 2010). Information about the imap is on the following page. Further instructions will also be given in class.

The imap—An information map (imap) is a way of visually representing the process of gathering information and developing ideas for any piece of writing. It is a work in progress and should be created as you go, not at the end of the process retrospectively.

The imap will help you develop your IL skills. Making an imap will help you:

- Distinguish between different types of sources
- Identify the quality of your sources
- Create a PROCESS for doing research (the process may not be linear—you plan and revise and this is depicted in your imap)

Your imap is your own creation. It should contain:
- An early brainstorm—before the literature search
- A description of your search process
- A detailed description of your thoughts as you analyse your sources.
- Your thesis statement (may or may not include early and revised versions)
- A plan for the structure of your essay
- A list of key sources (references).

It may also include:
- Key quotations

- Illustrations
- Timeline
- Evaluation of sources
- Other thoughts / emotions regarding the assignment writing process.

The imap must represent an accurate and detailed representation of the process you went through in gathering information, developing ideas and writing your essay. It must also have a professional, eye-catching appearance.

The imap will be marked on:

1. The quality of the process, as depicted by the imap.
2. The way in which the process is depicted, i.e., the quality of the visual presentation.

APPENDIX E: COURSE 2-2—PROFESSIONAL READING AND LEARNING LOG INSTRUCTIONS

1. ASSESSMENT OBJECTIVES

- To enhance your ability to identify and evaluate planning information.
- To increase your understanding of the relationship between information and the development of knowledge.

2. THE PROFESSIONAL READING & LEARNING LOG

The aim of the Log is to get you into the habit of reading not only the material supplied as part of the course, but the many other sources of planning information. It is vital when you become a practicing planner that you read the newspaper, either in print form or on the web, as this is an important means of staying in touch with the community you are planning for. It also helps you identify what their present concerns are. While books and articles are vital information sources, radio and websites can also provide you with material on a whole range of planning and planning-related issues. I have provided some sources to get you started, but I do expect to see clear evidence that you have located some sources yourself. Letters to the Editor and cartoons are also interesting commentaries on planning issues.

I will look at your Logs half way through the process to identify if you (as an individual or the class as a whole) are having any problems with constructing good thoughtful Logs. This should ensure that everyone 'stays on task', has the opportunity to get the best grade possible and is developing the skills and knowledge that we hope you will gain from this exercise. Half of your marks will come from the first assessment and half from the second.

3. THE TASK—A READING & WRITING LOG—PART I

You are to assess 5 pieces of writing or oral productions that address a planning issue. These five pieces will include the following:

1. An article from an academic journal which **must not** be an article which has been used on any other university paper you have completed or are presently enrolled on.
2. A newspaper article selected from the list of articles that will be posted on Stream.
3. An article from an edition of *Planning Quarterly* published between 2009 and 2011.
4. An item of your own choice provided it does not fall in the 'Sources not to use' category.
5. The interview of the Prime Minster John Key on the BBC programme Hard Talk. The You Tube link will be provided on Stream.

With each of the articles or sources you have selected you must assess as follows:

1. Full, accurate APA reference
2. A concise 5 line summary (in at least a 12 point font) highlighting the issues discussed in the text or programme.
3. An identification of the planning issues that are being discussed,
    a. how and why these are planning issues and
    b. how plans and planners might respond to these issues.
4. What you have written must be presented in well-constructed paragraphs and ***not*** in bullet points.

PART II

You are to assess 5 pieces of writing or oral productions that address a planning issue that you have not used in Part I. These five pieces will include the following:

1. Your choice from the three academic/professional articles and chapters that will be posted on Stream for your use.
2. A newspaper article selected from the list of articles that will be posted on Steam.
3. An article from an edition of *Planning Quarterly* published between 2009 and 2011.
4. An item of your own choice provided it does not fall in the 'Sources not to use' category.
5. Ten Lessons from New Zealand, Miller (2011) pp. 190–200

With each of the articles or sources you have selected you must assess as follows:

1. Full, accurate APA reference
2. A concise 5-line summary (in at least a 12-point font) highlighting the issues discussed in the text or programme.
3. An identification of the planning issues that are being discussed,
4. how and why these are planning issues and
5. how plans and planners might respond to these issues.
6. What you have written must be presented in well-constructed paragraphs and ***not*** in bullet points.

4. SOME SOURCES TO CONSIDER
Quality Planning
http://www.qualityplanning.org.nz/ Go to the QP Library

Radio New Zealand
http://www.radionz.co.nz/

There are a number of programme on the National Programme addressing environmental issues. They are all available after the programme has aired via their website and most are available to download.

The following are the programmes that are worth looking at:

- Nine to Noon http://www.radionz.co.nz/national/programmes/ninetonoon
- Sunday Morning with Chris Laidlaw http://www.radionz.co.nz/national/programmes/sunday
- Nights with Bryan Crump http://www.radionz.co.nz/national/programmes/nights
- Morning Report http://www.radionz.co.nz/national/programmes/morningreport
- Checkpoint http://www.radionz.co.nz/national/programmes/checkpoint
- Saturday Morning http://www.radionz.co.nz/national/programmes/saturday
- Newspaper sources will also be useful and Stuff is obviously the first source to go to at http://www.stuff.co.nz/

Newspapers

It is worth going to the specific websites for

- The New Zealand Herald (main paper in Auckland),
- The Press (main paper in Christchurch) and
- The Otago Daily Times (main paper in Dunedin) as they often have longer features on environmental issues often on Saturday editions.
- Don't forget the local papers—The Dominion (available free daily) and the Manawatu Evening Standard.
- You can also use Letters to the Editor and Cartoons as your examples but you can only have one example of each in your Log.

SOURCES NOT TO USE

- No tweets
- No websites that are not linked to a recognised organisation. If you are in doubt then ask me.
- No blogs

5. PRESENTATION

It is up to you how you present the material but I would stress that I do not want you to waste time and effort on 'pretty' presentations. You will gain marks for the content of your Log not the way it is presented. I am look for a clear, easy to read document.

CHAPTER 18
BUILDING CRITICAL RESEARCHERS AND WRITERS INCREMENTALLY: VITAL PARTNERSHIPS BETWEEN FACULTY AND LIBRARIANS

Alison S. Gregory and Betty L. McCall
Lycoming College

INTRODUCTION

In the spring semester of 1988, a soon-to-be college graduate stared with fright at her syllabus for the "Sociology Methods" course. It required a 25–30 page paper on a topic of her choice. Nowhere in her college career had she been prepared for such a task. Some 20 years later that same student found herself teaching a sociology methods course at Lycoming College, a small, private, liberal arts and sciences college, and looking for ways to prepare her soon-to-be college graduates for writing a similar paper, but in profoundly better ways. Thankfully, in the intervening decades, a nationwide movement toward information literacy (IL) had ensued. In 2000, the Association of College and Research Libraries (ACRL) adopted the *Information Literacy Competency Standards for Higher Education* (*IL Standards*). Through the *IL Standards*, IL is defined as the ability to recognize and satisfy information needs efficiently, effectively, and ethically; while the *IL Standards* were designed for higher education, they ultimately enabled the information literate individual to be a lifelong learner.

At Lycoming College, where the once-bewildered student became a professor, there was a distinct shift in the college's approach to IL. Instead of requiring students to master the research methods of a discipline in one course, in most disciplines, IL development began to occur progressively throughout the sequences of courses leading up to the capstone requirements. The work to meet the capstone methods requirements no longer begins in the eighth semester of college; it begins in the first semester and builds skills along the way across all courses to ensure the development of IL. As Katt Blackwell-Starnes (Chapter 7, this collection) notes, students are best served by developing IL proficiencies in the preliminary research assignments of lower level courses that will better prepare them for the formal research assignment in their capstone courses.

DEVELOPING IL PROFICIENCIES

Information literacy is best learned incrementally, moving from the relatively straightforward ability to locate the full text of an article to the increasingly subjective ability to evaluate sources for quality and relevance. The discovery of a relevant research article for a paper is often the stopping point for many students; they are satisfied with their research once they have the requisite number of sources in hand. Understanding how to critique the research, to evaluate its appropriateness and quality, to utilize it to support or warrant further research, and to include it appropriately in a paper is not learned (or taught) in one fell swoop. Both librarians and faculty need to be cognizant of the fact that information-seeking and evaluation abilities need to "be developed over time and [are] not a simple content or procedure that can be handed to students during their first year and then neglected" (Gowler, 1995, p. 392).

At the University of Guelph in Ontario, Canada, the library worked to scale IL "sessions throughout the four year degree" in hopes of helping students to utilize "their maturing education to developing more advanced IL skills over time" (Harrison & Rourke, 2006, p. 602). This model allows IL to be more easily "embedded into the curriculum" and allows the library to introduce "concepts repeatedly and at an increasingly sophisticated level" over the course of the degree (Harrison & Rourke, 2006, p. 602). At York University, also in Ontario, Canada, Robert Kenedy and Vivienne Monty (2008) noted that not only should the learning outcomes for library sessions progress incrementally with the students' experience levels, but it is also important to teach the concepts of information seeking, and not just the tools, with an emphasis on easily transferable skills.

A VERTICAL CURRICULUM—SCAFFOLDING IL

Because these abilities are best learned incrementally, including them vertically throughout the curriculum is a logical step. While a horizontal curriculum indicates the various academic subject areas a student takes during a given school year, the vertical curriculum indicates the upward climb of skills, subject comprehension, and improved application of abilities that come with each new step of the course or discipline. A vertical curriculum is deliberately designed to increase mastery through small steps, with students encountering increasing difficulty at each new level. Each step in the process, through repeated practice, allows for refinement of the learner's knowledge. As students build expertise, they broaden their aptitude for more intensive work.

Another term for educational elements that conspicuously move students from an entry level to an expert level is that of "scaffolding." Scaffolding can be thought of as a "learning sequence" that can "help the student climb to the desired educational goal or behavior," wherein the teacher "fades from the learning situation" as the student climbs to ever higher levels of mastery (Callison, 2001, p. 37). Librarians and faculty are the underlying structures working together to support the construction of adeptness at IL, moving learners toward stronger overall research skills. Well-designed scaffolding can help students to see how a previously learned skill can be applied to new situations without explicit instruction, making the student a more active participant in his or her own learning (Callison, 2001). Including research competencies "gradually and cumulatively" gives students a logical way of understanding library resources, while providing them a view of research as "relevant and potentially useful in other situations" (Gowler, 1995, p. 396). Rolf Norgaard and Caroline Sinkinson (Chapter 1, this collection) note the importance of avoiding the "skills-oriented 'inoculation' approach to IL" because it can remove or obscure the contextual basis for IL applications beyond the classroom. Norgaard and Sinkinson (Chapter 1, this collection) also emphasize the importance of imparting IL abilities broadly so that learners identify information competencies as being both transferable and relevant in contexts outside of academia.

IL CHALLENGES

The *IL Standards*, developed by the Association of College and Research Libraries (ACRL) in 2000, have been the guiding principles for IL in colleges throughout the country. Although the *IL Standards* provide a solid basis for the kinds of information-seeking skills that undergraduate students ought to master, the *IL Standards* were written by, and are almost exclusively used by, professional librarians. One risk in discussing IL is the jargon the *IL Standards* use, which can limit the appeal to educators outside of the library. Another risk is a confusion of what computer or technology literacy is and what IL is—the two are not the same and a student can be highly computer literate whilst being wholly "information illiterate" (Kenedy & Monty, 2008, p. 91). Adopted in early 2015, the ACRL *Framework for Information Literacy in Higher Education* (*Framework for IL*), seeks to address some of these challenges through threshold concepts that reflect students' roles in knowledge creation, the increasingly complex dynamics of the infosphere, and a growing emphasis on information ethics. The *Framework for*

IL allows for more individualized implementation of concepts, rather than using fixed standards or skill sets.

Concerning the first risk, that of terminology, a number of groups have addressed the breadth and jargon typically associated with IL in an attempt to make the concepts more accessible, and some accrediting bodies and state higher education associations have created their own language and plans for incorporating IL into higher education. The state of New Jersey, as an outgrowth of the Lampitt Law that regulates requirements for students transferring from county community colleges to four-year colleges and universities, created a task force of librarians to develop a plan to standardize the information-seeking abilities that would accompany the standardized transfer obligations; the resultant Information Literacy Progression Standards provide a two-tiered approach for the introductory/novice level of skills and the gateway/developing level of skills (DaCosta & Dubicki, 2012). New Jersey's Progression Standards, which align well with the new *Framework for IL* language regarding novice learners and experts, are intended to denote "an ongoing process" that are not "too context-specific" and can "be elaborated on and further customized" (DaCosta & Dubicki, 2012, p. 619). Jacqui Weetman DaCosta and Eleonora Dubicki concluded that, as a result of the collaboration between librarians, faculty, and administrators, students not only have stronger IL competencies for their academic work, but also that these "information seeking and handling skills" better prepare them for the workplace (2012, p. 628).

Addressing the second risk, that of confusing computer literacy with IL, speaks to the need to teach students to use familiar technologies to identify resources and to also apply IL proficiencies. Computer literacy commonly refers to the ability to use a computer effectively for problem solving, to distinguish between hardware and software, to use software programs, and to use the Internet for information-gathering (Kershner, 2003). Because so many research resources are available through online platforms, it is necessary to have some computer and technological savvy in order to use the systems and databases for information retrieval, and it is tempting to think that because "everything" is available online, being able to access a web-based database and to retrieve the full-text of the source is the equivalent of IL. College-level research, however, necessitates going beyond the ability to retrieve search results. Information competencies are needed to evaluate search results, to determine which resources will best satisfy the information need, and to use the sources ethically, appropriately, and intellectually.

COLLABORATING AND CUSTOMIZING IL

These risks of discussing and implementing IL become lessened to a great degree with collaboration between librarians and faculty to establish consistent and effective development of IL. Students benefit from building long-term relationships with the library's human resources (Gowler, 1995) by way of working with a librarian throughout the entire course of the major. The liberal arts college where this particular collaboration took place is committed to excellence in teaching and supports a strong collaborative library instruction program. Faculty are encouraged to work with librarians to design research and writing assignments that will foster transferable lifelong abilities such as the ability to communicate effectively and to think critically, and the ability to be research- and information-competent.

To counteract the library-centric feel to the *IL Standards*, and to customize IL as we see it in a liberal arts environment, an *ad hoc* subcommittee of the Faculty Library Advisory Committee (FLAC) at Lycoming College set forth in 2006 to rearticulate the skills and abilities of the *IL Standards* into a more faculty-friendly version. FLAC, comprised of seven faculty members, the provost, the chief information officer, and the director of library services, assists and advises in the formulation of library policies and evaluation of services. Committee members promote better understanding of library concerns and needs to other constituencies within the college. The *ad hoc* committee that created the college's information standards was comprised of faculty members, guided by documents the librarians provided, but the end result was written by and for faculty members. The resultant guiding document of Research and Information Competencies (RICs) was approved by the faculty in 2007 (see Appendix A); since that time, individual academic departments have adapted the RICs to suit their disciplinary research needs and goals.

As is the case at North Harris College, a public community college, we want students to leave library research sessions with "transferable strategies for finding information" rather than situationally specific tasks, and we want students to "think critically about the information" they discover (Dodgen et al., 2003, p. 28). In his description of the library's role in the general studies program at Berea College, a small liberal arts college, Steve Gowler (1995) noted that an approach of teaching transferable research capabilities allows librarians to be very targeted in the library sessions because there is no need to "try to tell students everything they need to know about the library in each class session" (p. 397). The Lycoming College RICs statement, as included in the college's faculty handbook and noted below, makes clear the campus expectation of incorporating these practices and behaviors throughout the curriculum, both in the general education courses and in the major-specific classes, building transferable information-seeking abilities that lead to overall mastery without specifying the tools or resources.

> The Faculty of Lycoming College endorses a research and information competency commitment across the curriculum

that will enable Lycoming students to master the following skills: formulate and refine questions; acquire basic knowledge of where to begin the discovery process; know how, when and what kind of information defines effective research; synthesize, format, cite and reconcile diverse information; evaluate the quality and sustainability of information; and differentiate between types of sources and the relevance of each. (Lycoming College, 2007)

IL WITHIN THE CURRICULUM

One academic department at Lycoming College that has worked to deliberately incorporate the research and information competencies in an incremental and progressive way into its curriculum is that of sociology-anthropology. The department has devised its own learning outcomes related to information-seeking skills and behaviors, not dissimilar from the "Information Literacy Standards for Anthropology and Sociology Students" from ALA/ACRL's Anthropology and Sociology Section (2008), but written at a micro-level specific to the curriculum and goals of the department.

The focus of IL in sociology and anthropology is similar to other disciplines. As established by the Anthropology and Sociology Section of ACRL, in collaboration with the American Sociological Association, the disciplines have four specific standards: to know what kind of information is needed; to access needed information effectively, efficiently, and ethically; to evaluate information and its sources critically and incorporate selected information into knowledge base and value system; and to use information effectively and ethically to accomplish a specific purpose (ALA/ACRL/ANSS, 2008). The ability to create a plan for collecting, synthesizing, and analyzing data is strongly tied to Lycoming College's RICs statement and utilizes critical thinking skills to connect basic research competencies to the original research students need to conduct through their course sequence, and the information literacies are best learned incrementally, using "sequential mastery of tasks from an elementary to an advanced level" (Proctor, Wartho & Anderson, 2005, p. 159). The research competencies that students need to be successful in the sociology-anthropology majors and minors are mapped to specific course levels, and then are articulated within the individual courses at each level, matching where possible to the department's learning goals.

The sociology-anthropology department at Lycoming College offers a major in sociology-anthropology, with concentrations in either anthropology or sociology, as well as a major in medical sociology; it also offers three minors: sociology, anthropology, and human services. All majors within the department must take SOC 330 "Research Methods I" and SOC 430 "Research Methods II" as their capstone experience. The end goal is for the students to conduct and write about original research. The capstone project includes conducting a review of the literature, selecting and describing at least one methodology, conducting the research, describing the findings, and documenting the sources. The department has explicit learning goals for its graduates:

- Understand how race, class, gender and its intersection influences peoples' experiences within larger social institutions and across cultures.
- Articulate empirical research questions and hypotheses and develop a logical plan of data collection and analyses to address such questions and hypotheses.
- Create and deliver a professional presentation designed for a professional audience using oral, written, and visual formats.
- Hone effective critical thinking skills. (Lycoming College, n.d.)

Based on these departmental goals, sociology professor Betty McCall created scaffolded RICs goals for her courses and worked collaboratively with librarian Alison Gregory to implement them:

- 100-level courses: Find peer-reviewed articles; Identify components of research articles; Provide appropriate citation
- 200-level courses: Evaluate appropriateness and quality of research articles; Effectively synthesize research articles to support or warrant further research
- 300-level courses: Identify within research articles the connection between questions and theory; Develop unique and measurable research questions
- 400-level courses: Synthesize a research question with appropriate methodology and theory to produce original research

APPLYING IL WITHIN COURSES

As part of the collaborative culture of the library, the faculty librarians at Lycoming College offer a series of workshops in January of each year, just prior to the beginning of the spring semester. Topics for the workshops vary, but in 2008, Alison Gregory, librarian, offered one such workshop on IL as related to the Middle States Commission on Higher Education, as the college was in the early stages of a reaccreditation process, and Betty McCall, sociology professor, attended the workshop. While the two had already been paired together in library instruction sessions, this workshop was the beginning of a stronger working relationship wherein a more deliberate approach to connecting content learning goals to research competencies goals began, an outgrowth of the discussion IL related to Middle States and assessment. The partnership played to the strengths of each—as a faculty member, McCall could be the subject expert guide who could help students become more knowledgeable and independent researchers, while as a librarian, Gregory could mentor students as they honed their research abilities.

Better integrating information-seeking competencies was one goal of the collaboration between McCall and Gregory. Another goal was to improve students' critical thinking skills. While the two—information literacy and critical thinking—have a number of things in common, they are not identical. Evaluating information and developing strong search strategies are "higher level cognitive activities" built on critical thinking, and without those abilities a student's information competencies will be limited (Albitz, 2007, p. 100). Because information is reasonably tangible, IL is often taught as skills-based, while "reason, logic, and assumptions are abstract concepts" and are categorized as the more theoretical critical thinking abilities (Albitz, 2007, p. 101). The relationship between the two is symbiotic, though; one cannot be information literate without critical thinking skills, but one does not have to employ IL to think critically. This "disconnect between the definitions . . . foreshadows the differing opinions" over whether it is the librarian or the faculty member who should be teaching these "overlapping skill sets" (Albitz, 2007, p. 101), as is addressed by Lori Baker and Pam Gladis (Chapter 16, this collection), through the term of "agency" in determining responsibility for teaching IL.

In the experiences of McCall and Gregory, both faculty and librarians are responsible for the meaningful inclusion of IL in higher education. This echoes the experiences of Meggan D. Smith and Amy B. Dailey (2013) of Gettysburg College (a small private college committed to the liberal arts), who found in their faculty-librarian collaboration that students' IL expertise was significantly improved by Smith and Dailey's careful joint planning, deliberate incorporation of specific IL objectives, and the gradual introduction of the skills throughout the semester. Joyce Lindstrom and Diana D. Shonrock (2006) also noted the importance of bringing faculty and librarians together to integrate IL into programs in ways that truly bolster student learning and the development.

McCall recognized the lack of information competencies within her students not only at the introductory level, but also at the upper level courses. The Lycoming College sociology-anthropology department has a two-course research methods series that is the capstone experience. The first of the courses (SOC 330) is utilized to teach students how to write a literature review and to understand statistical analysis while the second methods course (SOC 430) has students conducting their own original research. After several years of this approach, student papers still demonstrated a lack of skills in finding good information, and showed an inability to clearly address a research question while considering the previous work in the field. Similar to what Karen Gocsik, Laura R. Braunstein, and Cynthia E. Tobery (Chapter 8, this collection) note, though students could organize the material to make it appear they knew what they were writing about, it was clear that they were not able to create truly coherent knowledge about their topics. McCall and Gregory determined that the best way to assure that students were properly prepared for the methods course sequence was to implement a vertical curriculum focusing on research and information competencies across other courses within the major.

Scaffolding assumes that one course leads into the next with a simple review in the higher level course of the skills previously learned. The dilemma, however, is that few of the 200- and 300- level sociology and anthropology courses have prerequisites. In fact, a majority of the students in these courses have not had any other sociology or anthropology course. So, to scaffold IL learning it almost had to be done from the starting point for each course. McCall faced in her courses what Gregory faced in her library sessions, teaching the same foundation material for every class while attempting to build transferable research competencies.

The collaborative efforts began in SOC 110 "Introduction to Sociology," the gateway class into the major; enrollment is open to any student and the majority of the students are non-sociology majors. The collaboration began by working with the course assignments that McCall already had in place, but it left Gregory trying to teach too many subject-specific databases during a single hour in the library. The library workshops incorporated active learning whenever possible, but the sessions were still very tool-oriented and did little to ask students to think about source quality or how the resources they were finding fit together. McCall and Gregory began to hone the assignments to bring in one element at a time and developed an incremental project that required students to first decipher a provided article to identify the common elements of a research article in sociology. This exercise was completed, evaluated, and returned to the students prior to a library session. For the library workshop, students identified a topic of interest and were given basic instruction on how to obtain one research piece on that topic. The assignment required students to "dissect" this article that they located on their own, identifying and labeling the research article elements. On the article deciphering worksheet (see Appendix B), students also had to cite the articles using the American Sociological Association (ASA) style. There was a hands-on activity during the library session to introduce students to the ASA citation style, as none of the students had used this citation style previously.

In stages, McCall and Gregory were able to move students from understanding the basic elements of a research article, to being able to efficiently locate a peer-reviewed research piece, to noting the specifics of the research conducted in the published piece, to properly attributing the source. Students were required to identify the major components of the research article, including the author(s), title, journal name, specific cited works in the article's literature review, research question, methodology, dependent variable(s), key independent variables, statistical analysis, findings, limitations, and conclusions. The students had to be able to delineate qualitative and quantitative research. By focusing their attention (and ours) on one or two elements of IL, rather than trying to cover everything a student might need in the sociology major, we were able to make more meaningful connections for the students as they took incremental steps toward becoming information literate undergraduate students. By the end of the assignment, students were able to locate peer-reviewed articles and identify specific components of the research articles that would be the stepping stones for them to be able to include in a literature review in later coursework. While McCall and Gregory's work was in sociology classes, the practice of breaking research articles down into key elements can be applied to any discipline, and is indeed similar to the experiences of Donna Scheidt et al. (Chapter 10, this collection) who found in their collaborative work with a first-year composition study that it is important to deliberately move learners from "information grabbing to purposeful reading and sense making," which will improve the overall engagement with sources and thus one element of IL.

Building on the article deciphering assignment, McCall's 200-level courses require a short literature review. (Courses at the 200-level include "Introduction to Human Services," "Race, Class, Gender and Sexuality," "Mental Health and Illness," and "Sociology of Aging.") Students are provided with a worksheet on identifying components of research articles and are encouraged to turn in the worksheet with at least one of their selected articles for their literature review. The challenges here are three-fold: students in the 200-level courses are not required to take the 100-level introductory course, the majority of the students taking these courses are not sociology-anthropology majors, and, in order to provide the opportunity for a wider array of students, there is no prerequisite in place. As a result, many of the students taking the course have not yet mastered the IL know-how acquired by those students who took the "Introduction to Sociology" course. The research and library instruction by Gregory has some overlap, with the additional goal of assisting students in finding information that is relevant to their topic and can be synthesized well into a literature review. More often than not, in the authors' experiences, students do not write a well-synthesized literature review because they do not fully understand the research they have gathered for the review. McCall and Gregory have found that asking students to master an understanding of the components of the research piece helps them to better integrate the articles into a well-designed literature review. For the 200-level courses, the outcome of the students' work is a short 4–5 page literature review on a topic of their interest that effectively integrates their new understandings of research competencies within their writing. McCall has found that those students who have completed the worksheet perform much better on the literature review. Students in any discipline could benefit from practice in identifying elements of published research articles, as these articles can then serve as models for students' own academic writing.

This specific writing requirement is replicated in the 300-level course with an additional caveat: students must develop an original research question as part of their paper. This fits the Research as Inquiry element of the *Framework for IL*, as students begin to develop the ability to identify research gaps and develop questions of appropriate scope. In the 200-level courses, the assignment is simply to write a short literature review on a topic of their choice, so students find articles that address that topic but do not necessarily answer a question they pose about the topic. In the 300-level courses, which include "Medical Sociology" as well as "American Immigration," students work to understand how to develop research questions. The library workshop with Gregory is similar to the earlier sessions, but the endeavor becomes very specific toward helping the students focus on how researchers ask questions and how students can ask their own questions. Students first complete the article deciphering worksheet for at least one article of interest to them, then they are provided 10 articles selected by McCall and Gregory; for each of these articles they must identify the research question. These are confirmed in a classroom discussion and then the students work in groups to brainstorm to generate other ideas for research questions that could be asked given the topics of the articles. Students then create their own research questions and write a short literature review based on that specific question.

All of these individual course-specific assignments are aimed at building research and information seeking abilities in order to successfully complete the senior-level capstone course. The ultimate goal of the capstone course is for students to be able to construct a research question, decipher what other research has determined about that question, and then devise and implement a plan that allows them to conduct their own research addressing their research question. This brings students into the scholarly dialogue by asking them to contribute to the discipline through these studies, which is one of the *Framework for IL* elements—"Scholarship Is a Conversation"—wherein learners recognize the ongoing nature of scholarly research and also learn to contribute to it at an appropriate level. The work involved in this endeavor is impossible to learn in one methods course; instead, it is best to teach the steps of the process progressively throughout the earlier departmental requirements. The partnership between the faculty and the library is essential for imparting IL skills in a manageable way. The collaborative approach, between librarian and teaching faculty, works well in large part because "the faculty member defines the assignments and the librarian fits and molds the resources into the research process so that those assignments can be carried out, producing the best possible results, performance is improved" (Kenedy & Monty, 2008, p. 96). Regardless of subject matter, students can benefit from an incremental approach to building their research and information-seeking competencies.

CONCLUSION

Improvement of student learning and performance was one of the goals of creating the *IL Standards* in 2000. The *Framework for IL*, with its conceptual "interconnected core concepts, with flexible options for implementation," will likely impact how information literacies are integrated at this liberal arts college. The Lycoming College's Faculty Library Advisory Committee will be tasked with revisiting the college's Research and Information Competencies statement to see if it still aligns its goals with the broader aims of ACRL and with the core concepts of the *Framework for IL*, and making revisions to the RICs statement as appropriate. The *Framework for IL* places value on contextualization of authority, knowledge creation, and research as an iterative process; this will align well with Lycoming College's mission and philosophy of building a foundation through the liberal arts that will lead to informed lives, and with the library's mission of fostering lifelong learners. The sociology-anthropology department will also continue to look anew at how the *Framework for IL* and the RICs can be best incorporated into its departmental goals, and McCall and Gregory will continually reevaluate research-related assignments to best meet the goals of both the department and the college.

Through their collaboration, McCall and Gregory hoped to impart both the broad concepts needed for thinking about information needs as well as the more narrow skills specific to the discipline of sociology. Ever a work in progress, this collaboration and the information competencies it strives to impart through a vertical curriculum or scaffolding approach has allowed for more targeted information literacy sessions, for immediate applicability to students' work, and for stronger lifelong learning and information seeking abilities.

REFERENCES

ALA/ACRL/ANSS Instruction and Information Literacy Committee Task Force on IL Standards. (2008). Information literacy standards for anthropology and sociology students. *Association of College & Research Libraries*. Retrieved from http://www.ala.org/acrl/standards/anthro_soc_standards.

Albitz, R.S. (2007). The what and who of information literacy and critical thinking in higher education. *portal: Libraries and the Academy, 7*(1), 97–109.

Association of College & Research Libraries. (2000). *Information literacy competency standards for higher education*. Retrieved from http://www.ala.org/acrl/standards/informationliteracycompetency.

Association of College & Research Libraries. (2015). *Framework for information literacy for higher education*. Retrieved from http://www.ala.org/acrl/standards/ilframework.

Baker, L. & Gladis, P. (2016). Moving ahead by looking back: Crafting a framework for sustainable, institutional information literacy. In B. J. D'Angelo, S. Jamieson, B. Maid & J. R. Walker (Eds.), *Information literacy: Research and collaboration across disciplines*. Fort Collins, CO: WAC Clearinghouse and University Press of Colorado.

Blackwell-Starnes, K. (2016). Preliminary paths to information literacy: Introducing research in core courses. In B. J. D'Angelo, S. Jamieson, B. Maid & J. R. Walker (Eds.), *Information literacy: Research and collaboration across disciplines*. Fort Collins, CO: WAC Clearinghouse and University Press of Colroado.

Callison, D. (2001). Key words in instruction: Scaffolding. *School Library Media Activities Monthly, 17*(6), 37–39.

DaCosta, J. W. & Dubicki, E. (2012). From Lampitt to libraries: Formulating state standards to embed information literacy across colleges. *Library Trends, 60*(3), 611–636.

Dodgen, L., Naper, S., Palmer, O. & Rapp, A. (2003). Not so SILI: Sociology information literacy infusion as the focus of faculty and librarian collaboration. *Community & Junior College Libraries, 11*(4), 27–33.

Gocsik, K., Braunstein, L. R. & Tobery, C. E. (2016). Approximating the University: The information literacy practices of novice researchers. In B. J. D'Angelo, S. Jamieson, B. Maid & J. R. Walker (Eds.), *Information literacy: Research and collaboration across disciplines*. Fort Collins, CO: WAC Clearinghouse and University Press of Colorado.

Gowler, S. (1995). The habit of seeking: Liberal education and the library at Berea College. *Library Trends, 44*(2), 387–399.

Harrison, J. & Rourke, L. (2006). The benefits of buy-in: Integrating information literacy into each year of an academic program. *Reference Services Review, 34*(4), 599–606.

Kenedy, R. & Monty, V. (2008). Dynamic purposeful learning in information literacy. *New Directions for Teaching and Learning, 2008*(114), 89–99.

Kershner, H.G. (2003). Computer literacy. In *Encyclopedia of Computer Science*. Retrieved from http://search.credoreference.com/content/entry/encyccs/computer_literacy/0.

Lindstrom, J. & Shonrock, D. (2006). Faculty-librarian collaboration to achieve integration of information literacy. *Reference & User Services Quarterly, 46*(1), 18–23.

Lycoming College. (2007). Research and information competencies. *Lycoming College*. Retrieved from http://www.lycoming.edu/library/about/instruction.aspx.

Lycoming College–Department of Sociology/Anthropology. (n.d.) Learning goals. *Lycoming College*. Retrieved from http://www.lycoming.edu/sociologyAnthropology/learningGoals.aspx.

Norgaard, R. & Sinkinson, C. (2016). Writing information literacy: A retrospective and a look ahead. In B. J. D'Angelo, S. Jamieson, B. Maid & J. R. Walker (Eds.), *Information literacy: Research and collaboration across disciplines*. Fort Collins, CO: WAC Clearinghouse and University Press of Colorado.

Proctor, L., Wartho, R. & Anderson, M. (2005). Embedding information literacy in the sociology program at the University of Otago. *Australian Academic & Research Libraries, 36*(4), 153–168.

Scheidt, D., Carpenter, W., Fitzgerald, R., Kozma, C., Middleton, H. & Shields, K. (2016). Writing information literacy in first-year composition: A collaboration among faculty and librarians. In B. J. D'Angelo, S. Jamieson, B. Maid & J. R. Walker (Eds.), *Information literacy: Research and collaboration across disciplines*. Fort Collins, CO: WAC Clearinghouse and University Press of Colorado.

Smith, M. D. & Dailey, A. B. (2013). Improving and assessing information literacy skills through faculty-librarian collaboration. *College & Undergraduate Libraries, 20*(3–4), 314–326.

APPENDIX A: LYCOMING COLLEGE RESEARCH AND INFORMATION COMPETENCIES

The Faculty of Lycoming College endorses a research and information competency commitment across the curriculum that will enable Lycoming students to master the following skills:

> formulate and refine questions; acquire basic knowledge of where to begin the discovery process; know how, when and what kind of information defines effective research; synthesize, format, cite and reconcile diverse information; evaluate the quality and sustainability of information; and differentiate between types of sources and the relevance of each.

The goals of this curriculum-wide implementation of research and information competencies are to develop students who do the following:

- INQUIRE—Formulating and refining questions is a fundamental research skill. As a student's research advances, by adapting queries students can assess information more efficiently and effectively. Knowing how to frame inquiries is critical to pursuing information with the appropriate resources.
- NAVIGATE—Beyond the Internet and the World Wide Web, students should acquire some basic knowledge of where to begin the discovery process. Students should be able to employ a variety of information resources such as catalogs, indexes, and bibliographies in electronic and print formats.

- FIND—Knowing how and when to access information defines effective research. Often the inability to find data can be as frustrating as the overwhelming number of resources available.
- ORGANIZE—Appropriately synthesizing, formatting, citing and reconciling diverse information is logically an essential step in the research process. Students should be vigilant in avoiding plagiarism.
- REVIEW—Evaluating the quality and the suitability of information is what distinguishes legitimate research information competency. Students should be able to identify the place, context, and time in which the information was produced, the reliability and biases of the original source of the information, and whether the information has been reviewed by trustworthy referees.
- MAKE DISTINCTIONS—Students should be able to differentiate between primary, secondary and tertiary literature and know the relevance of each. Aware of various print and electronic formats of information, students should be able to see the difference between peer-reviewed and popular literature. Students should be able to identify trustworthy sources.

The Faculty Library Advisory Committee (FLAC) is charged with gathering information and assessing progress in implementing research and information competencies.

APPENDIX B: DECIPHERING RESEARCH WORKSHEET

Quantitative Research

Article Title
Author's Name(s)
Journal Name
Article Citation
List a citation for 1 article used in their literature review
Research question
Methodology
Study population and Sample
Dependent variable(s) and how it's defined
Key Independent variables and how they're defined
Statistical Analysis utilized
Results
Conclusions
Limitations

QUALITATIVE RESEARCH

Article Title
Author's Name (s)
Journal Name
Article Citation
List a citation for 1 article used in their literature review
Research question
Methodology
Study population and Sample
Themes discovered
Conclusions
Limitations

CHAPTER 19

IMPACTING INFORMATION LITERACY THROUGH ALIGNMENT, RESOURCES, AND ASSESSMENT

Beth Bensen, Denise Woetzel,
Hong Wu, and Ghazala Hashmi
J. Sargeant Reynolds Community College

INTRODUCTION

In the late 1990s, the Governor of Virginia charged a Blue Ribbon Commission on Higher Education to make recommendations for the future of Virginia's public four-year and two-year post-secondary institutions, with the goals of improving quality, affordability, and accountability. In its final report released in 2000, the Commission recommended that the State Council of Higher Education for Virginia (SCHEV) implement a Quality Assurance Plan that would define and assess the core competencies that "every graduate of every Virginia college or university regardless of major, can be expected to know and be able to do" and that the core competencies should include "at least written communication, mathematical analysis, scientific literacy, critical thinking, oral communication, and technology" (Governor's Blue Ribbon Commission, 2000, p. 51).

In response, the Chancellor of the Virginia Community College System (VCCS) formed the VCCS Task Force on Assessing Core Competencies in 2002. The task force decided to define technology in terms of information literacy (IL) "because of the long-standing emphasis at the colleges on assessing computer competencies" (Virginia Community College System, 2002, p. 6). The task force adopted the Association of College and Research Libraries' (ACRL) *Information Literacy Competency Standards for Higher Education* (*IL Standards*) (2000) and defined IL as "a set of abilities requiring individuals to recognize when information is needed and have the ability to locate, evaluate, and use effectively the needed information" (Association of College and Research Libraries, 2000). This chapter's primary focus is on the *IL Standards* and does not address the ACRL (2015) *Framework for Information Literacy for Higher Education* (*Framework for IL*). The *Framework for IL* was filed in its final form in

February 2015. In spring 2015 Reynolds librarians began review and discussion of developing learning outcomes tied to the six IL frames.

However, in the mid-1990s James Madison University (JMU) began development of a Web-based platform for IL instruction titled *Information-Seeking Skills Test* (*ISST*) (Cameron, Wise & Lottridge, 2007, p. 230). Also in the 1990s, JMU began development of another Web-based IL application, Go for the Gold (Cameron & Evans, n.d.). Both platforms were built on ACRL *IL Standards*. Go for the Gold is composed of eight self-instruction modules with online exercises that teach students to identify and locate library services and collection, employ efficient search techniques with a variety of information sources, evaluate and cite information sources, and apply appropriate ethical guidelines to the use of the information. *ISST* is a Web-based test that is composed of 54 questions to assess student information competencies as instructed in Go for the Gold. All first year students at JMU were required to take both Go for the Gold and *ISST* as part of the general education requirements (James Madison University Libraries, n.d., para. 1). JMU used the assessment results in the Southern Association of Colleges and Schools accreditation review and to meet system-wide goals set by SCHEV (Cameron, Wise & Lottridge, 2007, p. 231).

Because the information competencies assessed by JMU's *ISST* match that of ACRL *IL Standards*, VCCS licensed *ISST* to comply with SCHEV's mandate to assess IL competencies in 2003. VCCS established a score of 37 (out of 54) as indicating overall competency and 42 as highly competent. Each of the 23 VCCS community colleges developed their own testing plan. Nine colleges chose to test graduates, six chose students in ENG 112, and eight chose one or another of their courses that would involve students from varied programs. System wide, a total of 3,678 students completed *ISST*. Among the test takers, 53.18% of VCCS-wide students and only 26.42% Reynolds students met or exceeded the required standard (a score of 37 out of 54). Although VCCS developed a tutorial titled Connect for Success based on Go for the Gold to prepare students for the test, most of Reynolds instructors and students were not aware of the tutorial. Institutional librarians were not involved in the test planning and implementation and there was no collaboration or communication between faculty and librarians. These less-than-desirable results confirmed the fact that the statewide charge for the IL competency assessment was not balanced by a corresponding institutional mandate on how to develop, provide, and assess IL competencies within the standard general education curriculum.

Prior to 2003, only a handful of Reynolds faculty requested library instruction; these requests could not be made electronically and were limited to one 50–75 minute class period, with little room for student engagement. With no uniform instructional guidelines available to them, librarians provided instruction without guarantee of consistency among themselves. Additionally, with no assessment activities in place, the efficacy of instruction could not be appropriately evaluated. Reynolds students' low scores on the *ISST* assessment coupled with inconsistency in IL instructional methods signaled the urgent need to adopt a number of remedying measures. The measures included the following:

- Development of library instruction packages based upon ACRL's *IL Standards*.
- Dissemination of an online library instruction request form that included a list of packages and skill sets, allowing faculty to tailor instruction to their research assignments and also serving as a guideline for consistency among librarians.
- Training of librarians on the delivery of effective library instruction
- Publication of a new marketing plan pertaining to the IL program: librarians presented at campus-wide meetings, emailed information to faculty, and used social networking media such as Facebook, Twitter, and blogs.
- Implementation of assessment activities, such as multiple-choice quizzes within Blackboard and various student worksheets, enabling librarians and faculty to better evaluate student learning
- Creation of research guides tailored to specific assignments, courses and subjects first through PBwiki in 2005 and then through Springshare's LibGuides in 2009. Librarians used these guides during instruction sessions and linked them to individual Blackboard course sites.
- Development of a variety of open session workshops, enabling students to register and attend sessions on their own time.
- Creation of an online tutorial in the form of seven modules based upon ACRL's *IL Standards* and titled *Research at Reynolds Library* (2015). This tutorial guides students through a complete research process from exploring topics and finding resources to evaluating and citing resources. Faculty choose to integrate all seven modules or select specific ones for their courses. Each module is accompanied by ten self-assessment questions, with the exception of Module Five, which includes seven questions.
- Dedication of computer labs at two of the college's three libraries in which students receive hands-on experience during IL sessions.

Although these remedies continue to evolve, most of the steps listed above began to take effect in 2005 and remain in place. However, despite these many efforts, Reynolds librarians still faced the same essential concerns: the absence of a college mandate for the effective delivery of IL skills, the mapping of these skills within the general education curriculum, and the assessment of student learning. Complicating matters was the lack of coordinated collaboration between librarians and faculty to align instructional resources with essential course outcomes within specific areas of the general education curriculum.

LITERATURE REVIEW: ASSESSMENT AND COLLABORATION PRACTICES

Regional accrediting agency mandates to assess core IL skills (Saunders, 2007, pp. 317–318; Saunders, 2008, p. 305), as well as academic institutions' continuing focus on assessment, presents libraries with an opportunity to play a greater role in campus-wide assessment activities and contribute to student success (Lewis, 2010, p. 74; Saunders, 2011, p. 21). Librarians that connect their assessment plans to the mission and goals of their institution will be more effective in presenting and communicating their achievements in the area of IL (White & Blankenship, 2007, p. 108). According to Patricia Davitt Maughan (2001), several critical reasons for assessing students' IL skills include developing a core set of learning outcomes as a foundation for the IL program, assessing the effectiveness of instructional methods, measuring student success within the program, and communicating data results to faculty (p. 74).

One way to address outcomes is to focus on existing outcomes as developed by the Council of Writing Program Administrators (WPA). The WPA Outcomes Statement for First-Year Composition (WPA OS), first published in 2000 and amended in 2008, includes five sections: Rhetorical Knowledge; Critical Thinking, Reading, and Writing; Processes; Knowledge of Conventions; and Composing in Electronic Environments. The most recent version of the WPA OS was published in 2014; however, the English Department relevant to this study developed Reynolds ENG 112 learning outcomes based on the amended 2008 version. This discussion will focus on the amended 2008 version with the knowledge that a more recent version exists. For the purposes of this discussion, the two sections on which we will focus are Critical Thinking, Reading, and Writing (CTRW) and Composing in Electronic Environments (CEE). Both of these sections address IL skills, with CTRW suggesting that students may develop the following skills:

- Use writing and reading for inquiry, learning, thinking, and communicating.
- Understand a writing assignment as a series of tasks, including finding, evaluating, analyzing, and synthesizing appropriate primary and secondary sources.

- Integrate their own ideas with those of others.
- Understand the relationships among language, knowledge, and power.

CEE suggests that students will develop the following skills:

- Use electronic environments for drafting, reviewing, revising, editing, and sharing texts.
- Locate, evaluate, organize, and use research material collected from electronic sources, including scholarly library databases; other official databases (e.g., federal government databases); and informal electronic networks and internet sources.
- Understand and exploit the differences in the rhetorical strategies and in the affordances available for both print and electronic composing processes and texts. (WPA Outcomes Statement, 2008).

Of importance here are the statements that focus on IL skills such as "finding, evaluating, analyzing, and synthesizing appropriate primary and secondary sources" and "[l]ocate, evaluate, organize, and use research material collected from electronic sources, including scholarly library databases; other official databases (e.g., federal government databases); and informal electronic networks and internet sources" (WPA Outcomes Statement, 2008). As this literature review establishes, existing research supports collaboration among librarians and faculty when teaching IL skills, but a more specific approach that recognizes the value of outcomes-based assessment will also integrate the WPA OS. For example, as early as 1989 the University of Dayton revised its general education program to include IL as part of its competency program (Wilhoit, 2013, pp. 124–125). Outside of the U. S., the University of Sydney adopted the WPA OS to its writing program, including IL as one of the five clusters on which it focused to encourage growth and learning (Thomas, 2013, p. 170). The program established three graduate attributes to include "scholarship, lifelong learning, and global citizenship," breaking these down to five clusters to include "research and inquiry; communication; information literacy; ethical, social and professional understandings; and personal and intellectual autonomy" (Thomas, 2013, p. 170). Eastern Michigan University (EMU) also identified a need to connect outcomes with IL. EMU developed a plan to integrate first-year composition (FYC) outcomes with the *IL Standards* (ACRL, 2000), recognizing the need to integrate key IL concepts with the research process into their first-year writing program's research courses (Dunn, et al., 2013, pp. 218–220).

Outcomes-based assessment is an effective means for evaluating writing programs; however, when planning for IL assessment, criteria guidelines should weigh both the reliability and validity of a tool as well as the ease of administering the assessment (Walsh, 2009, p. 19). Megan Oakleaf (2008) provides a thorough overview of three popular assessment methods including fixed-choice assessments, performance assessments, and rubrics, and then charts the advantages and disadvantages of each approach (pp. 233–253). For the purposes of this discussion, we will focus on fixed-choice assessments. The benefits of fixed-choice assessments in the form of multiple-choice tests include ease of administration and scoring, the ability to compare an individual's pre- and post-test results, and the ability to evaluate results over time; however, one limitation of this method is the difficulty in measuring higher level critical thinking skills (Oakleaf, 2008, p. 236; Williams, 2000, p. 333). Another benefit is that pre- and post-test data results can identify both student mastery of material covered in an instruction session as well as areas of student weakness (Burkhardt, 2007, p. 25, 31). Additionally, pre- and post-test data can be compared over time to further refine the library and IL curriculum (Burkhardt, 2007, p. 25, 28). Although benefits to fixed-choice assessments are numerous, Kate Zoellner, Sue Samson, and Samantha Hines' (2008) claims pertaining to pre- and post-assessment projects suggest that there is little or no statistical difference or significance in assessment results, which makes evident the need for continuing this "method to strengthen its reliability as an assessment tool" (p. 371). For example, Brooklyn College Library developed and administered pre- and post-quizzes within Blackboard for students in an introductory first-year composition course. Learning management systems such as Blackboard have been adopted by most academic institutions for well over a decade and have been used by many libraries as a delivery platform for IL modules and assessments. Some of the advantages of using Blackboard for IL include faculty and student familiarity with the system, convenient 24/7 access for both on and off campus students, ease of creating and revising assessment questions, automatic grading for faculty, and immediate assessment scoring and feedback for students (DaCosta & Jones, 2007, pp. 17–18; Henrich & Atterbury, 2012, pp. 167, 173; Knecht & Reid, 2009, pp. 2–3; Smale & Regalado, 2009, p. 146, 151). All students in this course attended a library instruction session and completed a research paper assignment. Students completed the pre-quiz before attending a library instruction session and prior to completing their research paper assignment. Pre- and post-quiz results revealed that although scores ranged widely, the majority of students improved their scores on the post-quiz (Smale & Regalado, 2009, pp. 148–149).

An important aspect of IL assessment is the level of faculty support and participation in these efforts. Brooklyn College Library's positive outcomes confirm collaboration is crucial to the success of library instruction programs and can lead to a greater number of more effective programs (Buchanan, Luck & Jones, 2002, pp. 148–149; Fiegen, Cherry & Watson, 2002, pp. 308–309, 314–316;

Guillot, Stahr & Plaisance, 2005, pp. 242, 245). Over the years, academic librarians have consistently discussed the important role they can play by partnering with teaching faculty to integrate library instruction programs into the curriculum (Breivik & Gee, 1989; Mounce, 2010; Rader, 1975). However, an effective cross-departmental collaboration requires that college administrators and interdisciplinary committees communicate the importance of curricular inclusion and implementation of IL (See Norgaard and Sinkinson in this collection). ACRL also recognizes collaboration as a major component in exemplary IL programs (ACRL Best Practices, Category 6: Collaboration section, 2012). As noted by Katherine Branch and Debra Gilchrist (1996), community college libraries in particular "have a rich tradition of instructing students in library use with the goal of increasing information literacy and lifelong learning" (p. 476). Librarians at J. Sargeant Reynolds Community College (Reynolds) have long embraced this tradition, and over the years, have identified collaboration between librarians and teaching faculty as the key element of a successful IL program. Joan Lippincott (2000) notes that there are a variety of factors that encourage success in cross-sector collaborative teams, including an eagerness to work together to develop a common mission, an interest in learning more about each other's expertise, and an appreciation for each other's professional differences (p. 23). Many consider integrating IL into specific courses through faculty-librarian collaboration the most effective way of improving the IL skills of students (Arp, Woodard, Lindstrom & Shonrock, 2006, p. 20; Black, Crest & Volland, 2001, p. 216; D'Angelo & Maid, 2004, p. 214, 216). While many publications exist on collaborative IL instruction, examples of collaborative IL assessment projects are limited (Jacobson & Mackey, 2007). However, the number of collaborative assessment case studies is growing, including Carol Perruso Brown and Barbara Kingsley-Wilson (2010), Thomas P. Mackey and Trudi E. Jacobsen (2010), Megan Oakleaf, Michelle S. Millet, and Leah Kraus (2011), and Maureen J. Reed, Don Kinder, and Cecile Farnum (2007).

Developing a curricular program that integrates IL skills suggests the potential exists for students to retain these skills successfully. Evidence also exists to support the targeting of first-year composition courses as an effective means for incorporating IL into the curriculum partly because first-year composition is traditionally taken by all students (Barclay & Barclay, 1994, pp. 213–214). Michael Mounce (2010) similarly focuses on IL collaboration, arguing that in the humanities, librarians collaborate most frequently with writing instructors to integrate IL into composition courses (p. 313). Additionally, Sue Samson and Kim Granath (2004) describe a collaboration among librarians, writing instructors, and teaching assistants at the University of Montana-Missoula. This collaborative effort focused on integrating a library research component into randomly selected sections of first-year composition. Assessment results from the participating sections modeled on a "teach the teacher" plan, confirm that writing instructors and teaching assistants were effective in delivering IL instruction, with the added benefit of familiarizing graduate students with the IL resources available to them (p. 150).

Existing research on IL assessment efforts further substantiates faculty-librarian collaboration as critical to successfully integrating IL into the curriculum. The literature also reveals that although IL assessment is important for measuring students' skills, there is no consensus on the best assessment methods or instruments to implement. The academic institutions examined in the literature pertaining to IL assessment developed unique assessment plans tailored to their specific situation and student population. These examples establish the framework for this study and from which Reynolds based its IL assessment practices. The following discussion of Reynolds' IL project serves as a model for other institutions and expands the literature on IL assessment and collaboration practices by examining the impact of embedding IL modules and assessments into 22 first-year composition classes during the spring 2012 semester.

BREAKTHROUGHS IN COLLABORATION

Although instructional collaboration existed between librarians and faculty at Reynolds prior to the assessment, it took the form of an informal and individualized process. A major breakthrough in the development of a structured collaborative process occurred in 2008 when Reynolds developed and implemented a campus-wide Quality Enhancement Plan (QEP) as a part of its accreditation reaffirmation process with the Southern Association of Colleges and Schools Commission on Colleges (SACSCOC). While not directly related to the SCHEV Quality Assurance Plan mentioned in the introduction to this chapter, the QEP expanded the work the SCHEV plan began in 2000. The QEP targeted the improvement of student success in online learning as its primary focus. The QEP's concentration on faculty development and student support was designed to have a broad reach and to impact student learning outcomes throughout the college. Because the college does not have a discrete population of students and faculty involved only in online learning, the designers of the plan were confident of its expanded impact; most Reynolds students and faculty combine online learning with on-campus classes, and thus resources migrate easily between the various course delivery options. Further, the QEP Team identified IL, as well as other core student learning outcomes for assessment within its broader plan to bridge multiple disciplines, including Writing Studies, Information Technologies, and Student Development. Members of the QEP Team, including librarians, college administrators, and faculty began to discuss how to align IL instructional materials with identified course outcomes with the following courses: College Composition, Information Technology Essentials, and Student Development. With this impetus as its starting point, the college has witnessed active, interdisciplinary collaboration in the area of IL instruction and assessment; college librarians are no longer simply dependent upon individual faculty requests for instruction and one-shot sessions.

Within the Student Learning Outcomes Assessments (SLOA) subcommittee of the QEP, librarians collaborated with both Writing Studies and Computer Science faculty to incorporate the *Research at Reynolds Library* (2015) modules into high-reach, high-impact courses within these disciplines. The modules consist of the following sections: "Topics," "Types of Information," "Find Books," "Find Articles," "Use the Internet," "Evaluate Sources," and "Cite Sources." In Information Technology Essentials (ITE) 115: Introduction to Computer Applications and Concepts, faculty incorporated three of the seven modules into all class sections: "Types of Information," "Find Articles," and "Use the Internet." Librarians also began discussions with writing instructors on the inclusion of all seven modules within first-year composition courses.

DEVELOPMENT OF THE COLLABORATIVE INSTRUCTIONAL AND ASSESSMENT PROJECT

During many discussions focused upon IL assessment activities, Reynolds librarians identified key guidelines for the development and delivery of content: 1) the modules should cover core IL competency skills as identified by the ACRL and SCHEV; 2) they should be comprehensive enough to cover a complete research process and be flexible enough for instructors to disaggregate the modules and incorporate them into different stages of their courses or their curricula; 3) the research guides should be easy to evaluate by instructors and easy to revise by librarians; 4) the modules should be delivered online in order to serve both on-campus and online students; and finally, 5) the evaluation process should offer ease in the administration of assessments and in the collection of data. Reynolds librarians concurred that the seven *Research at Reynolds Library* (2015) IL modules, along with their corresponding assessments, should be delivered through Blackboard in order to meet these articulated guidelines. Blackboard provided an efficient portal for all instructors and students to reach the modules directly through their established course sites.

With these essential guidelines in place, the *Research at Reynolds Library* (2015) modules were developed using Springshare's LibGuides, a Web-based content management system dedicated to improving students' learning experiences. Skill sets covered in each of the seven modules are based on ACRL's IL *Standards*, SCHEV standards, and the VCCS core competency standards for IL.

Because of the features provided by the LibGuides technology, the new modules are much more dynamic and interactive than the ones they replaced. These modules now include embedded videos, self-assessment activities, and user feedback options. Further, Reynolds librarians have found that they can create and update the modules' content with great efficiency and that these modules receive positive and enthusiastic responses from faculty. The modules cover the entire research process and contain a number of tutorials to walk students through the IL process. The content for each module is as follows:

1. Module 1: "Topics" offers an overview of the research process and developing a concept map to narrow focus for a research topic.
2. Module 2: "Types of Information" includes videos and links that explain and describe the information cycle and types of sources and the differences between scholarly and popular periodicals. Module 2 also clarifies publication dates to ensure currency and timeliness of sources.
3. Module 3: "Find Books" offers tutorials in both video and alphabetic texts on how to find books using Reynolds' online library catalog and using electronic sources such as ebooks on EBSCOhost (formerly known as NetLibrary) and Safari. Module 3 also addresses how to request titles using WorldCat and Interlibrary Loan.
4. Module 4: "Find Articles" includes videos that provide a general overview of how to search in library databases and a more specific tutorial of how to find articles in EBSCOhost databases. Module 4 also clarifies Boolean searching and locating full-text articles when Reynolds does not subscribe to a journal or does not have the full-text of an article. Additionally, Module 4 explains how to access databases when off-campus.
5. Module 5: "Use the Internet" is a comprehensive discussion about searching via the World Wide Web and briefly addresses evaluating sources. It also makes a distinction between using subscription databases and the Internet when conducting scholarly research. Module 5 includes an effective video that further discusses using search engines.
6. Module 6: "Evaluate Sources" includes a video on evaluating sources and a helpful checklist for students to follow when evaluating sources—the checklist can easily be adapted to a handout. Module 6 also addresses *Wikipedia*, including an instructional video and a satirical view of wikis.
7. Module 7: "Cite Sources" defines and clarifies what plagiarism is and the consequences of plagiarizing. Module 7 includes an instructional video and tips for avoiding plagiarism. Module 7's "Cite Sources" page addresses how to cite in MLA and APA, with helpful links, handouts, and worksheets on documentation and citing.

As the discussion of consistent IL instruction within college composition courses progressed, the SLOA subcommittee reached critical points of consensus, agreeing that 1) the *Research at Reynolds Library* (2015) modules (rather than other modules created outside of the college) were the ideal instructional resource for Reynolds students; and 2) ENG 112 (the second semester college composition course) was the ideal site for this instruction because the course guides students through the research process and thus provides an effective corresponding context for the IL modules. The committee agreed that all seven modules would be integrated within the composition course.

Librarians developed a variety of multiple choice, true/false, and matching questions that align with each module's content and that can be graded automatically through Blackboard's testing tools. Librarians from both within and outside of Reynolds reviewed all seven modules and each module's assessment questions to provide feedback and evaluation. The modules and questions were revised based upon these initial reviews. In addition to the assessment questions, satisfaction survey questions were developed for each of the seven modules to glean information on each module's user-friendliness and to improve the modules. Delivered through Google Docs, these satisfaction surveys are embedded in each module and provide useful feedback from the perspectives of the student users. Finally, a screencast video was developed using TechSmith's Camtasia Studio software, providing students with a welcome message that outlines the scope and purpose of the *Research at Reynolds Library* (2015) modules; sharing with them how to begin, navigate, and complete the modules; and encouraging them to engage actively, rather than passively, with the various resources in order to gain essential and useful skills in IL.

METHODS: COLLABORATIVE OVERVIEW

As the previous discussion establishes, Reynolds librarians and faculty worked closely to improve the instruction of IL skills across the curriculum and within disciplines, and have made great strides in providing an online platform to deliver the *Research at Reynolds Library* (2015) modules to both on-campus and online students. IL skills have indeed improved at Reynolds, yet challenges exist, as Edward Freeman and Eileen Lynd-Balta (2010) confirm: "[p]roviding students with meaningful opportunities to develop [IL] skills is a challenge across disciplines" (p. 111). Despite this challenge, it is clear that providing sound IL instruction occurs in the first-year composition classroom because such instruction is determined to be a vital component to general education (Freeman & Lind-Balta, 2010, p.109). Collaborative efforts among Reynolds faculty and staff further confirm that achieving a common set of goals "goes beyond the roles of our librarians, English professors, and writing center staff; therefore, campus initiatives aimed at fostering information literacy collaboration are imperative" (Freeman & Lynd-Balta, 2010, p. 111). Although not specifically a campus-wide initiative, the Reynolds English Department has worked toward developing learning outcomes for ENG 112 based on the WPA OS (2008). The WPA OS suggests guidelines for implementing sound writing and composing practices in the FYC classroom. The Reynolds IL study focused on developing skills pertaining to "locat[ing], evaluat[ing], organiz[ing], and us[ing] research material collected from electronic sources, including scholarly library databases; other official databases (e.g., federal government databases); and informal electronic networks and internet sources" (WPA Outcomes Statement, 2008). These skills are essential not only to the writing classroom but also to other disciplines that expect students to arrive in their classrooms possessing skills to conduct research with little assistance.

During the fall 2011 semester, the English Department's assessment committee was charged with assessing how effectively ENG 112 aligns with the teaching of IL. The QEP subcommittee recruited faculty from the writing Assessment Committee to review the modules and offer feedback from a pedagogical perspective. The writing Assessment Committee chair mapped the seven modules into the ENG 112 curriculum to provide participating faculty with guidance. Additionally, the librarians asked a number of writing instructors to review the seven library modules and to take the assessments from the perspective of a current instructor for the purposes of preparing the modules for a pilot study conducted in spring 2012. After offering feedback to Reynolds librarians and after revising the modules, the QEP subcommittee also recruited students who had successfully completed ENG 112 to review and pilot-test the modules and provide feedback. Nine students agreed to participate, and six completed the intense reviews of all seven modules successfully. Student volunteers evaluated the modules on the information and materials in each module and then completed the self-assessments to see how well they had learned the material. They then completed the feedback/satisfaction survey embedded at the end of each module. Student feedback proved to be valuable, as they offered critical reviews of the modules and the accompanying assessments from a student's perspective.

After the initial review, receipt of feedback on the modules and consequent revision process, the project organizers recruited a sufficient number of faculty teaching ENG 112 to offer a broad spectrum of course delivery options across three campuses. The committee determined the need for a treatment group that agreed to integrate all seven modules and assessments into the course design and a control group that did not integrate the modules in any way. The composition of delivery formats for the treatment group is as follows:

- Thirteen face-to-face sections
- Two online sections
- Four dual enrollment sections (college-level courses taught to high school students in a high school setting)
- Three eight-week hybrid sections
- Nine control sections

In order to participate in the study, the treatment group faculty agreed to integrate all seven modules and have students complete the pre- and post-tests and the assessments associated with each module. In addition to a variety of course delivery formats, the study included a wide representation across Reynolds campuses to include 12 course sections on a suburban campus, four course sections on an urban campus, two course sections on a rural campus, two course sections in a virtual setting, and four course sections in a high school setting.

The break-down of delivery for the control group included sections from the urban and suburban campuses. The control group instructors agreed to administer the pre- and post-test assessments without integrating the seven modules. They taught IL skills as they normally would to their individual sections. One instructor within the control group integrated one face-to-face library instructional session for her course. The primary point to keep in mind is that the control group differed dramatically from the treatment group in that they did not take advantage of the online library research guides; this distinguishing factor becomes significant when comparing the results between the two groups.

After recruiting study participants, extensive communications occurred to introduce the project to faculty and to encourage continued participation, from initial agreement to the project's completion. The committee provided support and resources for:

- understanding the ENG 112 Learning Outcomes;
- revising course schedules to demonstrate effective integration of the modules;
- raising awareness of which chapters and sections of the two textbooks in use at the time of the study corresponded with the *Research at Reynolds Library* (2015) modules;
- understanding the technologies of how to integrate the IL Blackboard course into existing sections of ENG 112; and
- submitting pre- and post-assessment scores to the QEP coordinator.

Each participating instructor was enrolled in the Blackboard course "ENG 112 Information Literacy Project." Specific Blackboard training included:

- Integration of pre- and post-tests
- Integration of all seven modules

- Integration of all seven assessments
- Integration of results into Blackboard's grade book

Although most faculty at Reynolds have experience with Blackboard, the more advanced functions in the grade book or the completion of a course copy are often not familiar to all of them. Providing initial and ongoing technical support proved to be beneficial to the study and minimized frustration that often occurs with technology. In-depth training within Blackboard's components and specifically for the grade book was important to encourage accurate sharing of data for analysis purposes.

DATA ANALYSIS: RESULTS OF THE ASSESSMENT

The collaborative effort on the part of writing instructors and librarians in both instruction and assessment resulted in several important findings. Apart from the research results themselves, however, the collaboration emphasized efficiency and effectiveness in the broader assessment process. The development of clear and specific course learning outcomes, combined with well-developed instructional resources and a solid, guided assessment process, resulted in impact upon student learning. In significant ways, the assessment project highlighted essential outcomes for both the librarian and faculty researchers: effectively communicated strategies of assessment and a well-designed collaboration among a team of researchers were critical to the development, implementation, and assessment of teaching and learning.

On a fundamental basis, the assessment confirmed that the second semester composition course is an appropriate site for the instruction of IL skills. That is, students of the institution enter ENG 112 with enough foundational knowledge to serve as a building block upon which to develop their skills. At the same time, they are not yet proficient enough in research skills to meet the challenge of conducting and completing independent researched writing. Thus the institution's efforts in mapping its general education curricula within the areas of IL were reinforced by the assessment; the results demonstrated that ENG 112 was an appropriate location for the introduction, development, and application of research and research-supported learning activities. Within this foundational course, students gain skills upon which subsequent courses and programs of study can build and strengthen research and IL skills. Further, assessment results also indicate that ENG 112 instructors are having solid and effective impact upon student learning in the area of researched writing.

Integration of the online *Research at Reynolds Library* (2015) modules proved to be quite successful; results indicated a significant rise in scores from pre-test

Impacting Information Literacy

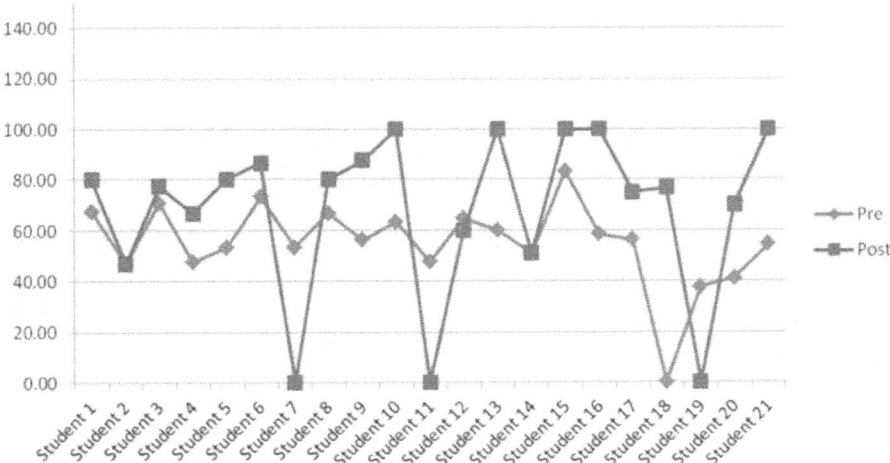

Figure 19.1. *Comparison between pre- and post-tests (face-to-face, Spring 2012).*

to post-test in both the treatment and control groups. For example, Figure 19.1 depicts the rise in scores for a face-to-face class in which fifteen of the twenty-one students enrolled in the course showed improvement between the pre- and post-tests. Only three students showed little-to-no improvement and three others did not take the post-test. Zero scores are indicative of students who either remained in the class but did not take the post-test or students who took the pre-test but withdrew from the class prior to taking the post-test.

Although not quite as dramatic, Figures 19.2 and 19.3 also depict a marked improvement from pre-test to post-test in an additional face-to-face section of ENG 112 and in a distance learning section of the same course. In Figure 19.2, nine students improved their rest results from pre-to post-test: One student achieved the same results on both assessments, and four students attained lower scores.

Figure 19.3 highlights similar improvement in learning for distance learning students. These results indicate that the IL modules impact student learning regardless of the course delivery method. Although this course section experienced a lower rate of post-test completion than the face-to face sections, the 14 students who did complete the post-test all achieved scores that were higher than their pre-test results.

Although the two summer sessions of ENG 112 that were incorporated within the study had fewer students, the post-test results indicate that the majority of students achieved higher results in the post-test, with only one scoring below his or her pre-test results and six students achieving the same results on the pre- and post-tests. Figures 19.4 and 19.5 illustrate the increase in scores between pre- and post-tests.

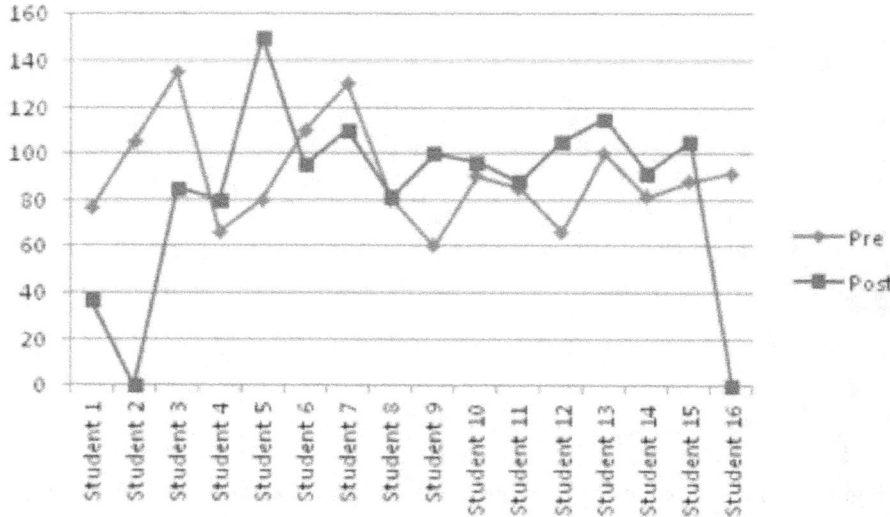

Figure 19.2. Comparison between pre- and post-tests (face-to-face, Spring 2012).

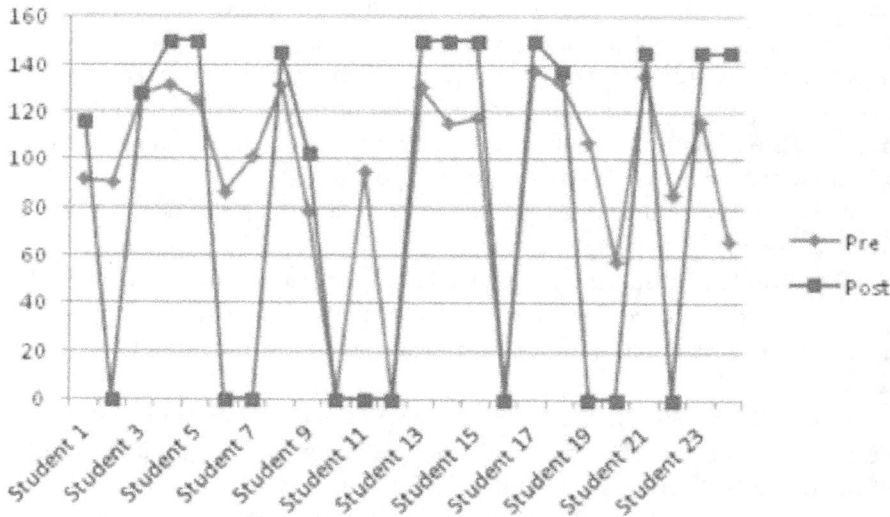

Figure 19.3. Comparison between pre- and post-tests (distance learning, Spring 2012).

Figures 19.1 through 19.5 focus upon results within individual courses that were a part of the treatment groups. Students within the control groups were also administered the pre-and post-tests, but they received in-class IL instruction only and did not have guided access to the *Research at Reynolds Library* (2015) modules. Like their counterparts within the treatment group, the majority of

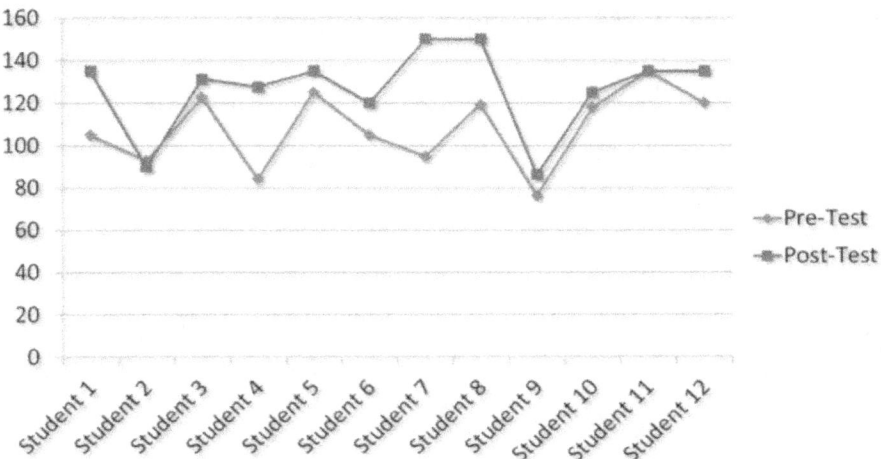

Figure 19.4. Comparison between pre- and post-tests (DL, Section A, Summer 2012).

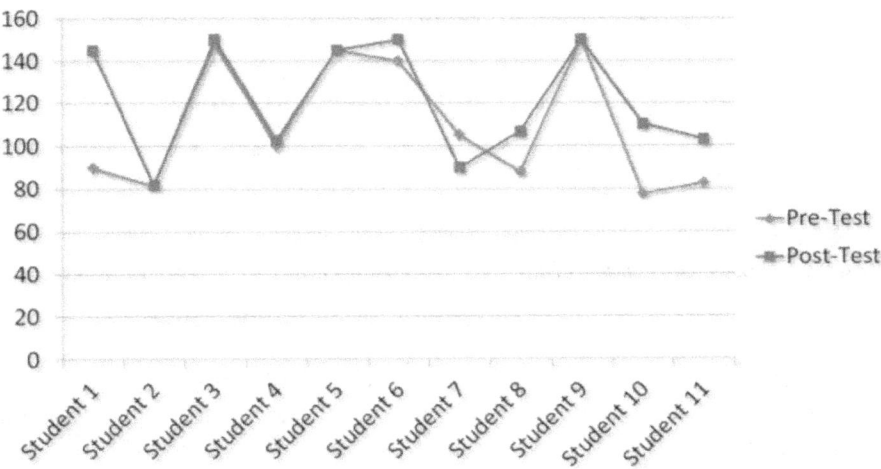

Figure 19.5. Comparison between pre- and post-tests (DL, Section B, Summer 2012).

students in the control group also demonstrated improvement between the pre- and the post-assessments. However, the students who had the added benefit of the seven online modules demonstrated a greater impact upon their learning outcomes. These students, regardless of the course delivery format of ENG 112 (online, hybrid, dual, or traditional), experienced much higher results within their post-assessment scores. Thus, while instructor-led efforts in the areas of research strategies and IL certainly impacted student learning, student

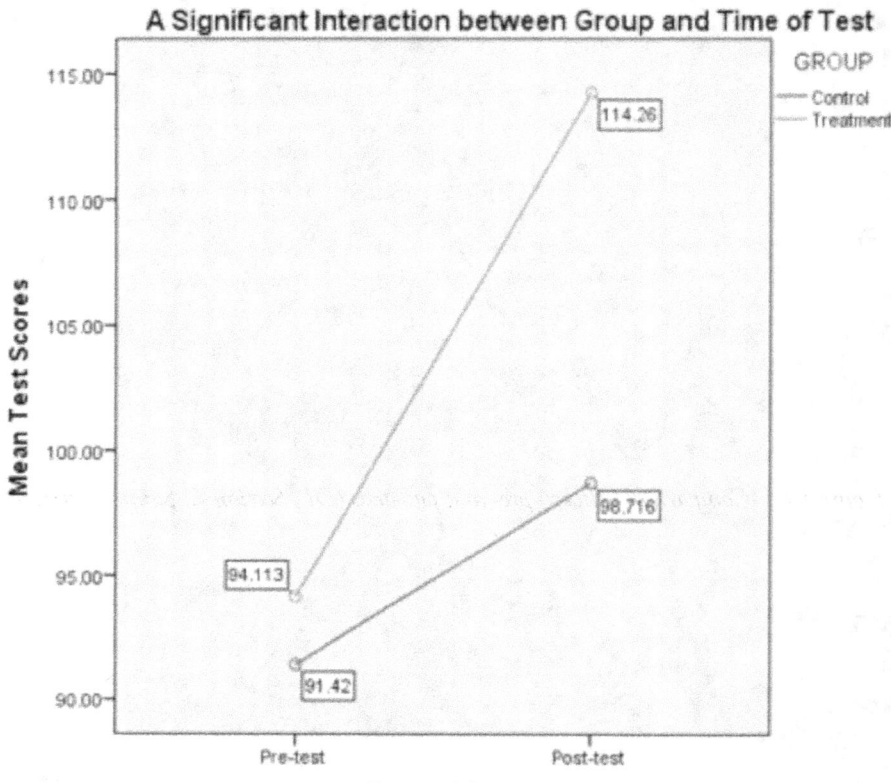

Figure 19.6. A comparison of the treatment group and the control group results.

engagement with the online, self-guided research modules yielded overall higher post-test scores. These results indicate that the students within the treatment group had developed research skills and identified effective research strategies at a rate exceeding their counterparts within the control sections. Figure 19.6 highlights this attainment of learning for both groups of students:

At pre-test time, the average scores of students in the control sections versus the treatment sections demonstrated no reliable difference between the two groups. The students in the control group began at approximately the same level as those in the treatment group. Overall, students scored an average of 93.41 points (SD=21.21 points). This score represents a typical score of about 62% correct responses on the assessment survey. By the time of the post-test assessment, both the treatment group and the control group had made significant progress:

Impacting Information Literacy

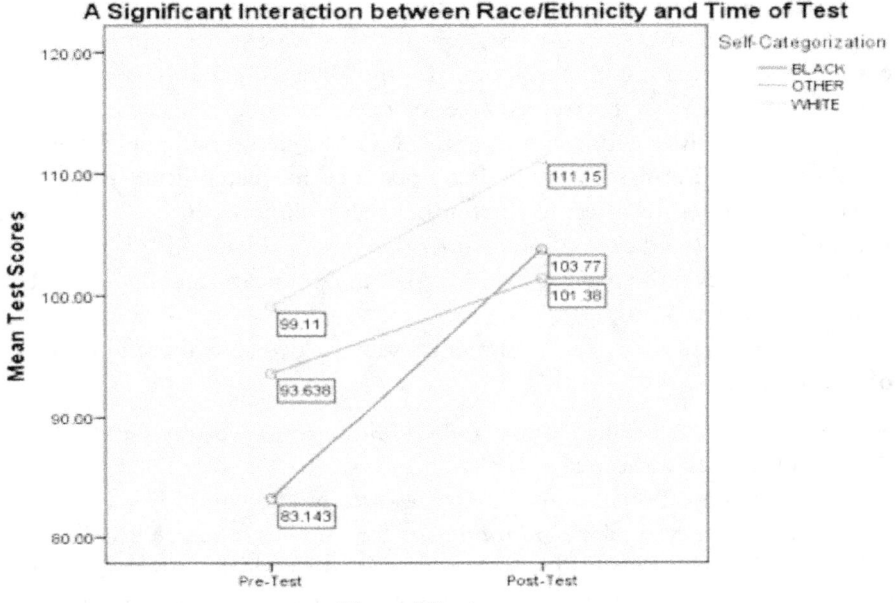

Figure 19.7. Results according to ethnicity.

- The control group improved by 7.30 points, on average.
- The treatment group improved by 20.15 points, on average.

In other words, at the time of the post-test, the treatment group achieved a solid level of competency in research skills, with an average score of 76% within the post-assessment. The control group neared "competency," averaging 66% of correct responses on the post-assessment.

An unanticipated outcome of the assessment was the significant impact that the African-American students within the assessment group. Figure 19.7 indicates that at pre-test time, African-American students scored significantly lower than White students. (The average scores of students self-classified as "Other" indicate *no reliable difference* between "Other and White," or "Other and African-American.") By post-test time, however, African-American students' scores were commensurate with the scores of "Other" students. The slope of learning representing the African-American students is steeper than the slope of the other two groups. Further, the *difference* noted in slopes representing the learning and the attainment of skills of the African-American students and the White students is statistically significant.

African-American students began the semester scoring at an average of 55% correct responses. By post-test, however, they were scoring approximately 69% correct, which is commensurate with the 74% correct average for White students and the 68% correct average for other students. By the end of the course, all ethnicities within the assessed ENG 112 classes had made progress, but African-American students had compensated for a significant initial disadvantage. The results attest to the finding that a combination of instruction within ENG 112 and the online *Research at Reynolds Library* (2015) modules are helping to level the playing field for African-American students, at least in terms of IL skills.

In its final evaluation, the assessment results yielded several useful elements of information:

- ENG112 is having a direct and significant impact on student learning outcomes in the area of IL.
- The integration of online library research guides within ENG 112 results in even *more significant gains* for students in research skills.
- African-American students begin ENG 112 with IL skills that are at a disadvantage when compared to White students and to students classified as "Other." However, African-American students make the most significant gain in learning by the end of a semester, surpass the "Other" category, and reach very close to "competency" level by time of post-test.

CONCLUDING COMMENTS

The study concluded at the end of the summer 2012 session with faculty submitting spreadsheets, indicating scores on both the pre- and post-tests from both the spring 2012 semester and the summer 2012 session. Full integration of the seven online modules along with assessment of each module reinforces twenty-first century IL skills based on the ACRL's *IL Standards* and that also conform to the VCCS core competency standards. The results of the IL assessment at Reynolds demonstrate that students who might initially be underperforming as they enter ENG 112, will perform at equivalent or higher levels than their classmates. Not only do such positive results suggest the success of the *Research at Reynolds Library* (2015) modules, but they also suggest great potential for students to be successful in upper-level courses within the community college system and in four-year college and university systems. Although the data collected for this study do not extend to students beyond a two-year college, researchers can conclude that students who successfully complete the seven online library modules are more likely to persist in college to achieve greater success in 200 level courses requiring the use of IL skills based on 21st-century literacy practices. Clearly, reinforcing IL skills is relevant to the first-year undergraduate curriculum because "[t]he ideal way to produce fully capable graduates is to embed academic skills in the first-year curriculum, then continue their application, reinforcement and further development through the degree programme" (Gunn, Hearne & Sibthorpe, 2011, p. 1). These same skills are likely to remain with them as they transfer to four-year colleges and universities. The primary goal of this study was to determine the effectiveness of the online modules, but a perhaps secondary goal to be studied further is to determine how well students retain IL skills acquired through Reynolds as they move on to 200 level courses within the community college system and beyond.

REFERENCES

ACRL Best Practices Initiative Institute for Information Literacy (2012, January). Characteristics of programs of information literacy that illustrate best practices: A guideline. Retrieved from http://www.ala.org/acrl/standards/characteristics.

Arp, L., Woodard, B. S., Lindstrom, J. & Shonrock, D. D. (2006). Faculty-librarian collaboration to achieve integration of information literacy. *Reference & User Services Quarterly, 46*(1), 18–23. Retrieved from http://lib.dr.iastate.edu/cgi/viewcontent.cgi?article=1022&context=refinst_pubs.

Association of College and Research Libraries. (2000). *Information literacy competency standards for higher education.* Retrieved from http://www.ala.org/acrl/standards/informationliteracycompetency.

Barclay, D. A. & Barclay, D. R. (1994). The role of freshman writing in academic bibliographic instruction. *Journal of Academic Librarianship, 20*(4), 213–217. doi:10.1016/0099-1333(94)90101-5.

Black, C., Crest, S. & Volland, M. (2001). Building a successful information literacy infrastructure on the foundation of librarian-faculty collaboration. *Research Strategies, 18*(3), 215–225. doi:10.1016/S0734-3310(02)00085-X.

Branch, K. & Gilchrist, D. (1996). Library instruction and information literacy in community and technical colleges. *RQ, 35*(4), 476–483

Breivik, P. S. & Gee, E. G. (1989). *Information literacy: Revolution in the library.* New York: American Council on Education and Macmillan.

Brown, C. & Kingsley-Wilson, B. (2010). Assessing organically: Turning an assignment into an assessment. *Reference Services Review, 38*(4), 536–556.

Buchanan, L. E., Luck. D. L. & Jones, T. C. (2002). Integrating information literacy into the virtual university: A course model. *Library Trends, 51*(2), 144–166. Retrieved from https://www.ideals.illinois.edu/handle/2142/8454.

Burkhardt, J. M. (2007). Assessing library skills: A first step to information literacy. *Portal: Libraries and the Academy, 7*(1), 25–49. Retrieved from http://digitalcommons.uri.edu/lib_ts_pubs/55/.

Cameron, L. & Evans, L. (n.d.). Go for the Gold: A web-based instruction program. Retrieved from http://www.ala.org/acrl/publications/whitepapers/nashville/cameronevans.

Cameron, L., Wise, S. L. & Lottridge, S. M. (2007). The development and validation of the information literacy test. *College & Research Libraries, 68*(3), 229–237. Retrieved from http://crl.acrl.org/content/68/3/229.full.pdf+html.

DaCosta, J. W. & Jones, B. (2007). Developing students' information and research skills via Blackboad. *Communications in Information Literacy, 1*(1), 16–25. Retrieved from http://www.comminfolit.org/index.php?journal=cil&page=article&op=view&path%5B%5D=Spring2007AR2.

D'Angelo, B. J. & Maid B. M. (2004). Moving beyond definitions: Implementing information literacy across the curriculum. *Journal of Academic Librarianship, 30*(3), 212–217. doi: 10.1016/j.acalib.2004.02.002.

Dunn, J. S., et al. (2013). Adoption, adaptation, revision: Waves of collaborating change at a large university writing program. In N. N. Behm, G. R. Glau, D. H. Holdstein, D. Roen & E. W. White (Eds.), *The WPA Outcomes Statement: A decade later* (pp. 209–229). Anderson, SC: Parlor Press.

Fiegen, A. M., Cherry, B. & Watson, K. (2002). Reflections on collaboration: Learning outcomes and information literacy assessment in the business curriculum. *Reference Services Review, 30*(4), 307–318. doi:10.1108/00907320210451295.

Freeman, E. & Lynd-Balta, E. (2010). Developing information literacy skills early in an undergraduate curriculum. *College Teaching, 58,* 109–115. doi: 10.1080/87567550903521272.

Governor's Blue Ribbon Commission on Higher Education (2000, February 3). *Final report of the Governor's Blue Ribbon Commission on Higher Education* (Rep.). Retrieved from State Council of Higher Education for Virginia website: http://www.schev.edu/Reportstats/final_report.pdf.

Guillot, L., Stahr, B. & Plaisance, L. (2005). Dedicated online virtual reference instruction. *Nurse Educator, 30*(6), 242–246. doi:10.1097/00006223-200511000-00007.

Gunn C., Hearne, S. & Sibthorpe, J. (2011). Right from the start: A rationale for embedding academic literacy skills in university course. *Journal of University Teaching and Learning Practice 8*(1), 1–10. Retrieved from http://ro.uow.edu.au/jutlp/vol8/iss1/6/.

Henrich, K. J. & Attebury, R. I. (2012). Using Blackboard to assess course-specific asynchronous library instruction. *Internet Reference Services Quarterly, 17*(3–4), 167–179. doi:10.1080/10875301.2013.772930.

Jacobson, T. E. & Mackey, T. P. (Eds.). (2007). *Information literacy collaborations that work.* New York, NY: Neal-Schuman.

James Madison University Libraries. (n.d.). Freshmen information literacy requirements. Retrieved from http://www.jmu.edu/gened/info_lit_fresh.shtml.

Knecht, M. & Reid, K. (2009). Modularizing information literacy training via the Blackboard eCommunity. *Journal of Library Administration, 49*(1–2), 1–9. doi:10.1080/01930820802310502.

Lewis, J. S. (2010). The academic library in institutional assessment: Seizing an opportunity. *Library Leadership & Management, 24*(2), 65–77. Retrieved from http://journals.tdl.org/llm/index.php/llm/article/view/1830/1103.

Lippincott, J. (2000). Librarians and cross-sector teamwork, *ARL bimonthly report*, (208/209). Retrieved from https://www.cni.org/wp-content/uploads/2011/07/team.pdf

Mackey, T. P. & Jacobson, T. E. (Eds.) (2010). *Collaborative information literacy assessments: Strategies for evaluating teaching and learning.* New York, NY: Neal-Schuman.

Maughan, P.D. (2001). Assessing information literacy among undergraduates: A discussion of the literature and the University of California-Berkeley assessment experience. *College & Research Libraries, 62*(1), 71–85. Retrieved from http://crl.acrl.org/content/62/1/71.full.pdf+html.

Mounce, M. (2010). Working together: Academic librarians and faculty collaborating to improve students' information literacy skills: A literature review 2000–2009. *Reference Librarian, 51*(4), 300–320. doi:10.1080/02763877.2010.501420.

Norgaard, M. & Sinkinson, C. (2016). Writing information literacy: A retrospective and a look ahead. In B. J. D'Angelo, S. Jamieson, B. Maid & J. R. Walker (Eds.), *Information literacy: Research and collaboration across disciplines.* Chapter 1. Fort Collins, CO: WAC Clearinghouse and University Press of Colorado.

Oakleaf, M. (2008). Dangers and opportunities: A conceptual map of information literacy assessment approaches. *Portal: Libraries and the Academy, 8*, 233–253. Retrieved from http://meganoakleaf.info/dangersopportunities.pdf.

Oakleaf, M., Millet, M. & Kraus, L. (2011). All together now: Getting faculty, administrators, and staff engaged in information literacy assessment. *Portal: Libraries and the Academy, 11*(3), 831–852. Retrieved from http://meganoakleaf.info/portaljuly2011.pdf.

Rader, H. (1975). Academic library instruction: Objectives, programs, and faculty involvement. In Papers of the fourth annual Conference on Library Orientation for Academic Libraries. Ann Arbor, MI: Pierian Press.

Reed, M., Kinder, D. & Farnum, C. (2007). Collaboration between librarians and teaching faculty to teach information literacy at one Ontario university: Experiences and outcomes. *Journal of Information Literacy, 1*(3), 29–46. Retrieved from http://ojs.lboro.ac.uk/ojs/index.php/JIL/article/view/RA-V1-I3-2007-3.

J. Sargeant Reynolds Community College (2010 March). The ripple effect: Transforming distance learning, one student and one instructor at a time (Quality Enhancement Plan). Retrieved from http://www.reynolds.edu/who_we_are/about/qep.aspx.

Research at Reynolds Library (2015, June 14). Retrieved from http://libguides.reynolds.edu/research.

Samson, S. & Granath, K. (2004). Reading, writing, and research: Added value to university first-year experience programs. *Reference Services Review, 32*(2), 149–156. doi: 10.1108/00907320410537667.

Saunders, L. (2007). Regional accreditation organizations' treatment of information literacy: Definitions, collaboration, and assessment. *Journal of Academic Librarianship, 33*(3), 317–318. doi: 10.1016/j.acalib.2008.05.003.

Saunders, L. (2008). Perspectives on accreditation and information literacy as reflected in the literature of library and information science. *Journal of Academic Librarianship, 34*(4), 305. doi:10.1016/j.acalib.2008.05.003.

Saunders, L. (2011). *Information literacy as a student learning outcome: The perspective of institutional accreditation.* Santa Barbara, CA: Libraries Unlimited.

Smale, M. A. & Regalado, M. (2009). Using Blackboard to deliver research skills assessment: A case study. *Communications in Information Literacy, 3*(2), 142–157. Retrieved from http://www.comminfolit.org/index.php?journal=cil&page=article&op=viewArticle&path%5B%5D=Vol3-2009AR7.

Thomas, S. (2013). The WPA Outcomes Statement: The view from Australia. In N. N. Behm, G. R. Glau, D. H. Holdstein, D. Roen & E. W. White (Eds.), *The WPA Outcomes Statement: A decade later.* (pp. 165–178). Anderson, SC: Parlor Press.

Virginia Community College System. (2002, July 18). *Report of the VCCS task force on assessing core competencies.* Retrieved from http://www.pdc.edu/wp-content/uploads/2012/02/VCCS_Task-Force-Report.pdf.

WPA Outcomes Statement for First-Year Composition. (2008, July). *WPA outcomes statement for first-year composition.* Retrieved from http://wpacouncil.org/positions/outcomes.html.

Walsh, A. (2009). Information literacy assessment: Where do we start? *Journal of Librarianship & Information Science, 41*(1), 19–28. Retrieved from http://eprints.hud.ac.uk/2882/.

White, L. & Blankenship, E. F. (2007). Aligning the assessment process in academic libraries for improved demonstration and reporting of organizational performance. *College & Undergraduate Libraries, 14*(3), 107–119. Retrieved from https://www.academia.edu/784402/Aligning_the_Assessment_Process_In_Academic_Libraries_for_Improved_Demonstration_and_Reporting_of_Organizational_Performance.

Wilhoit, S. (2013). Achieving a lasting impact on faculty teaching: Using the WPA Outcomes Statement to develop an extended WID Seminar. In N. N. Behm, G. R. Glau, D. H. Holdstein, D. Roen & E. W. White (Eds.), *The WPA Outcomes Statement: A decade later.* (pp. 124–135). Anderson, SC: Parlor Press.

Williams, J. L. (2000). Creativity in assessment of library instruction. *Reference Services Review, 28*(4), 323–334. doi:10.1108/00907320010359641.

Zoellner, K., Samson, S. & Hines, S. (2008). Continuing assessment of library instruction to undergraduates: A general education course survey research project. *College & Research Libraries, 69*(4), 370–383. Retrieved from http://crl.acrl.org/content/69/4/370.full.pdf+html.

CHAPTER 20

BRIDGING THE GAPS: COLLABORATION IN A FACULTY AND LIBRARIAN COMMUNITY OF PRACTICE ON INFORMATION LITERACY

Francia Kissel, Melvin R. Wininger, Scott R. Weeden, Patricia A. Wittberg, Randall S. Halverson, Meagan Lacy, and Rhonda K. Huisman
Indiana University-Purdue University Indianapolis

INTRODUCTION

Why do students perform poorly on research assignments? How can librarians and faculty best help their students develop confidence and competence in finding and using information? Concerns like these led a number of faculty and librarians at Indiana University Purdue University Indianapolis (IUPUI) to form a community of practice, a voluntary group which met regularly to investigate issues in effective teaching of information literacy (IL) and to propose solutions. Members began with disparate and sometimes conflicting ideas about how to accomplish this goal, including how to quantify the goal in the first place. Does student success equal accurate citation, use of scholarly sources, or expeditious searches in academic databases? Or is it something more amorphous: that through practice and recursive steps, students finally *get it* and are able to select and use disciplinary knowledge in ways that disciplinary experts recognize as valid?

The community members' struggles to understand each other and find common ground exemplify the larger problem that IL practitioners and stakeholders are facing: reconciling one view, that IL is composed of discrete skills and competencies with measurable outcomes, with an alternate view, that IL is comprised of interconnected threshold concepts, where success is more difficult to identify. To IL practitioners, these two points of view are represented by the *Information*

Literacy Competency Standards for Higher Education (*IL Standards*) (ACRL, 2000), standards which are being superseded by the *Framework for Information Literacy for Higher Education* (*Framework for IL*) (ACRL, 2015). Although the *IL Standards* and the *Framework for IL* are familiar to most academic librarians, faculty may find that defining, teaching, and assessing IL is puzzling or even futile. Even if librarians thoroughly adopt the *Framework for IL* itself, "Each library and its partners on campus will need to deploy [the] frames to best fit their own situation" (ACRL, 2015). As a result, faculty/librarian cooperation in teaching and promoting IL at the university level is crucial for student success.

Collaboration is difficult, the members of the community of practice discovered, as they worked through misunderstandings, assumptions, and territoriality described in the case study presented later in this chapter. Individual faculty and librarians, nonetheless, grew into a community by discussing their preconceived notions, clarifying shared language, and agreeing to use assessment to investigate current knowledge and to strategize future initiatives. The community of practice has forged a mutually supportive partnership promoting IL on the campus. They have worked together to initiate assessments to discover the campus climate in relation to taking responsibility for IL, and they have sponsored professional development for both faculty and librarians at their home institution and from other institutions across the state.

The work of the community of practice is not yet complete. But this work has opened a new conversation shared by librarians, faculty, and administration on the campus level, a conversation that will help lead students to become confident users of the complicated contemporary world of information. The experience of the community of practice at IUPUI demonstrates ways other institutions can form campus-wide partnerships in order to embed IL into the curriculum. Adding to previous literature about librarian and faculty collaboration, this example of a community of practice model is useful because it shows ways that faculty can partner with librarians in the teaching of IL.

LITERATURE REVIEW

How can librarian/faculty collaboration be bolstered, overcoming the barriers and providing concerted action to improve IL acquisition for all students? Although librarians may be familiar with the literature on student development in IL concepts, many college faculty are not, since much of the IL literature comes from library-related articles and presentations (Artman, Frisicaro-Pawlowski & Monge, 2010, p. 95, and as noted by Norgaard & Sinkinson in this collection). Faculty may not have heard about recent research describing students' actual research practices, librarian-led assessments based on national standards, or even debates about the place of IL in the curriculum. Faculty are also unlikely to know that librarians sometimes see them as barriers impeding students' opportunities to learn appropriate IL practices. If collaboration between faculty and librarians is crucial, significant collaboration may well mean reading each other's literature in order to unpack assumptions and see more integral relationships between disciplines and their dependence on IL.

The IUPUI community of practice began meeting with most members unaware of the concept of "community of practice" beyond its use on campus as an organizing and naming tool. They also did not share the record of two important literatures: studies of the attempts to bridge the librarian-faculty gap and studies of the gap between students' perceptions of IL and the sense shared among faculty and librarians that students don't practice IL very well. A brief review will help to set the context for how the IUPUI community of practice sought to address some of the issues that emerge in that record.

The Gap between Student Self-perception and Faculty/Librarian Views

Faculty often observe that students have less developed research skills than they need for success in college courses, and recent research investigates why. In sum, students do find and use information, but they do not engage in the ways they are using it to make meaning, with the result that they are overconfident in their work, both in the context of courses and their imagined futures.

Project Information Literacy, over a series of six national studies beginning in 2008, found that students brought high school research practices to college, and that many continued to use the same routines and the same limited resources for paper after paper (Head, 2013, p. 475). Not only do college students have difficulty finding manageable topics and locating and evaluating resources (Head, 2013, p. 474), they often don't use the resources effectively. For example, the Citation Project examined papers of first-year writing students and found that most writing from the sample failed to engage source texts in meaningful ways, with 70% of the citations derived from the first two pages of a source and most sources cited only once per paper (Jamieson & Howard, 2011). This superficial use of sources indicates the students may not understand the source ideas well enough to integrate them within their own work. Similarly, the chapters by Katt Blackwell-Starnes and by Miriam Laskin and Cynthia Haller (Chapter 11) describe how students tend to focus on the final product requirement for a minimum number of references, using Google's first page results mechanically to fulfill this requirement without knowing how to gauge the relationship between the sources they cite or knowing how to fit them into ongoing scholarly discourse. They seem to be operating under the assumption that when IL matters, it will be evaluated only for its representation of a set of discreet skills.

Adding to student confusion about finding and using sources is the increasing amount of information available to students from the Internet. Students may think they can evaluate web resources for reliability and authority, but another study reveals participants used arbitrary and "highly subjective evaluation criteria" (Wang & Arturo, 2005, as cited in Badke, 2012, p. 35). Furthermore, less proficient students have high confidence in their own research skills (Gross & Latham, 2009, p. 336, and in this collection, Blackwell-Starnes). College graduates who bring inexpert research skills to the workplace can frustrate employers (Head, 2013, p. 476). The 2013 LEAP poll of employers conducted by Hart Research Associates found that 70% of employers surveyed wanted universities to place more emphasis on IL knowledge, including "evaluation of information from multiple sources." Job skills which depend on finding and using information have changed with the proliferation of media technology, as has the very nature of information (Andretta, 2012, pp. 57–58).

The independent, sophisticated, and ethical use of information marks college students and graduates as competent and fluent, even if they are only emerging as experts in a field. The issue that remains undecided in many institutions is when, how, and from whom students are to learn the range of knowledge and practices they need. Students like those interviewed by Melissa Gross and Don Latham (2009, p. 344), who enter college with very little training, often regard themselves as self-taught. Students also learn from peers, including those with whom they have a prior relationship, and "from strangers who appear available to talk and approachable" (Gross & Latham, 2009, p. 343). Some faculty may think student self-instruction is sufficient, or that undergraduates should be able to learn research skills and habits in the process of an assignment, with advice from supervising faculty (McGuinness, 2006, p. 577). However, students who actually do learn the research skills contained within the context of one assignment may not see the transferability of those skills to another course (Saunders, 2013, p. 139).

Where do the information professionals—librarians—fit in this picture? Project Information Literacy found that students do not turn to libraries and librarians very often (Head, 2013, p. 475). These findings point to several gaps: the gap between student self-perception of their skills versus their actual abilities, the gap between faculty goals for student accomplishment in research and lack of faculty instruction to support that accomplishment, and the gap between the availability of research knowledge from librarians and students' reluctance to call upon librarians for assistance. These gaps lead to the questions of who should teach IL and how it should be taught.

The Gap between Librarians and Faculty

Examples of partnerships between librarians and discipline faculty in library journals to address those gaps are inspiring, but the successful ones are often the work of pairs or small teams. Barbara D'Angelo and Barry Maid (2004) comment that these efforts "are not sustainable" on a wider scale (p. 213). Examples of campus-wide initiatives, on the other hand, like the IL assessment at Trinity College (Oakleaf, Millet & Kraus, 2011), enjoy administrative support and wide faculty buy-in, but these examples are much more rare. William Badke (2005) summarizes: "The fact is, and the vast literature confirms it, effective [librarian-faculty] collaboration is simply not the norm" (p. 68). The conviction that librarians and faculty share the responsibility for teaching IL is wide-spread, arising from the common-sense idea that the best instruction occurs when students put new knowledge and skills into repeated practice for relevant purposes. However, real collaboration on IL instruction can be difficult to achieve because of two persistent tensions.

First, language can be an impediment to collaboration (Anthony, 2010, p. 84); even the term *information literacy* may confuse the uninitiated. Rolf Norgaard and Caroline Sinkinson, in this collection, stress that a shared definition of IL is "a prerequisite" to conversations between cross-disciplinary colleagues. Norgaard has been pointing to this fundamental barrier to collaboration since his two seminal articles in 2003 and 2004. In them, specifically referring to the fields of IL and Writing Studies, he argues that the lack of familiarity of one another's disciplines can result in misidentifying theoretical connections and lead some to settle for seeing IL the same way that students seem to, as a "neutral, discrete, context-free skill" (p. 125), where success is measured by products, such as successful information searches and correct citation. Instead, Norgaard defines IL in terms of practices that should be an integral part of the writing process, helping writers to solve problems and make meaning through their writing (p. 127). Similarly, Badke (2012) stresses the need for faculty to teach research processes, so that students understand how disciplines identify and use knowledge, learning "to *do* higher education disciplines, rather than acquiring just what constitutes a discipline's knowledge base" (p. 93). To "do" a discipline, he suggests, students must not merely parrot scholarly discourse, but learn to participate in a scholarly conversation in the discipline. Faculty-librarian collaboration can help merge content and process within instruction so that students learn how to *think* in their discipline and recognize themselves as *creators* of knowledge and not merely consumers. The shift from viewing IL as skill to viewing it as practice is unsettling for librarians and faculty, as well as for the students they share.

Second, surveys of both faculty and librarians list some common and conflicting assumptions about each other's roles that impede effective instructional partnerships. Librarians at times have perceived that faculty apathy, time constraints, or culture contribute to difficulties of collaboration. For example, librarians may see faculty as territorial about their classes, limiting librarian access to students (Julien & Given, 2003 and 2005, as cited in McGuinness, 2006, p. 574). On the other hand, faculty may view librarians themselves as territorial, wishing "to retain ownership of information literacy" (Saunders, 2012, p. 227). A related issue is status: Librarians may be suspicious of faculty who encroach or miss the target when faculty seek to "integrate *our* [librarian] standardized skills into *their* curriculum" (Gullikson, 2006, p. 584). In addition, some faculty may not want librarians to teach, thinking that librarians are not trained to instruct, while other faculty may not see themselves as having any responsibility for teaching IL (Saunders, 2013, p. 137).

A Model of Collaboration for Bridging the Gaps

Faculty and librarians alike desire to narrow the gap between their shared perception of students' IL and students' commonly held self-perception. The problem that librarians and faculty both want to solve together is, however, embedded in the problems of their relationship—partly caused by differences in language and focus and partly created by their roles in the institution.

One potential solution to overcome impediments to collaboration in an institution is the community of practice model, which can develop from the grass-roots level and can encourage wide-spread teamwork. The "Community of Practice Design Guide" defines the term: "A community of practice is a group of people who share a common concern, a set of problems, or interest in a topic and who come together to fulfill both individual and group goals" (Cambridge, Kaplan & Suter, 2005, p. 1). Communities of practice are used in businesses, government units, and other policy-driven endeavors, as well as in higher education.

A campus community of practice can cross disciplinary boundaries, expand to include several members, operate on a small budget, and result in wide-spread effects. Ongoing meetings help participants build trust as they discuss common concerns, create new knowledge about the focusing issue, and take action through projects or products (Cambridge, Kaplan & Suter, 2005, p. 3). Naturally there are negatives as well; interest in a community's work may wax and wane, depending on the energy of individual members and the quality of the volunteer leadership (Wenger, McDermott & Snyder, 2001). Communities also have life cycles; sometimes the work sputters or a community disbands. However, a vital and growing community of practice can call campus-wide attention to an issue and begin conversations to investigate causes, enlist other stakeholders, and propose solutions. Such has been the experience of the Community of Practice on Information Literacy at IUPUI.

COMMUNITY OF PRACTICE ON INFORMATION LITERACY AT IUPUI
BACKGROUND

IUPUI is a large, mostly non-residential, research university located in the heart of Indianapolis. IUPUI has a high undergraduate enrollment (21,000 students) as well as graduate and professional schools (8,000 students). The campus's commitment to IL is explicitly incorporated in its foundational Principles of Undergraduate Learning, which were adopted by faculty in 1998 and are consistently used on syllabi across campus. The Principles are similar to the more recent Essential Learning Outcomes of the Association of American Colleges and University's Liberal Education and America's Promise initiative. One outcome of the first principle, Core Communication and Quantitative Skills, is that students will be able to "make effective use of information resources and technology" (Office of Student Data, Analysis, and Evaluation, 2008). As part of the campus commitment to IL, a librarian is assigned to the instructional team of each first-year seminar, reaching 90% of incoming first-time, full-time students in recent years. However, nearly 40% of students earning bachelor degrees are transfer students (Hansen, 2014), and no campus-wide program introduces them to the library or to a librarian. Moreover, the university library does not offer a centralized IL program. Responsibility for IL instruction often falls to individual faculty and librarians, some of whom proactively work to instruct students in research skills on an as-needed basis. However, even with the success of these individual efforts, a needs assessment survey distributed in 2011 to faculty teaching Gateway courses—those courses identified as having the highest numbers of first-time, full-time students—resulted in 95% of respondents agreeing that IL and an introduction to the resources of the academic library were among the most critical needs for their students (University College, 2012).

Communities of practice have been used at IUPUI since 2000 (Chism, Lees & Evenbeck, 2002, p. 39). IUPUI's communities of practice are organizational structures used to emphasize collaborative learning and problem-solving and to capitalize on the small group's work for the sake of the university's mission. Other IUPUI communities have focused on concerns like retention of first-year students, multicultural teaching, and critical thinking. These groups have served as leaders and change agents at IUPUI, bringing attention to campus needs, providing forums for public discussion, studying aspects of an identified problem, advocating best practices for solutions, and presenting and publishing their findings.

Currently, most campus community of practice groups are supported by the Gateway to Graduation Program, which provides a small budget for materials or speaker fees. Communities which receive Gateway support are expected to hold regular discussion meetings focused on an issue pertinent to students in first-year and gateway courses and to develop scholarly projects that enlarge the body of knowledge about their central question, which then leads to development and dissemination of best practices. The three aspects of the community of practice model—discussion within the group, emphasis on scholarly inquiry, and dissemination of best practices—have been crucial to the formation and work of the IUPUI Community of Practice on Information Literacy.

DEVELOPMENT OF THE COMMUNITY OF PRACTICE ON INFORMATION LITERACY

One faculty member's search to address student needs led to the formation of the Community of Practice on Information Literacy. Realizing that some of the best seniors in her sociology capstone course lacked sufficient skills to find sources for a final paper, Professor Patricia Wittberg was searching for solutions when she attended a conference workshop called "Information Literacy: The Partnership of Sociology Faculty and Social Science Librarians" (Caravello, Kain, Macicak, Kuchi & Weiss, 2007). Wittberg then approached the campus director of writing, urging an "Information Literacy across the Curriculum" program. Prior campus successes with communities of practice led the director to suggest that Wittberg form a group focused on IL. The two solicited members, including both faculty and librarians, and began meetings.

One initiative undertaken by the community of practice in 2008 and 2009 was a pilot assessment of faculty teaching practices in courses that required research assignments. The focus of this limited study was to identify classroom strategies used to foster IL and to judge the relative success of the pedagogical efforts. To that end, teachers of 14 classes in liberal arts, science, and business disciplines who regularly included IL instruction in their classes were enlisted; those instructors administered an in-class IL pre-test to their students. The pre-test, which consisted of open-ended questions asking them to describe their prior research experience, their methods of topic selection and development, and their processes for finding and evaluating sources, was taken by 478 undergraduate students. Results of the initial in-class surveys were coded by criteria arranged in a matrix to measure levels of student success in research processes. After evaluating the pre-tests, the researchers discovered that students' skills were poorer than expected, with fewer than 25% reporting practices determined adequate on the matrix. For example, 77% reported minimal, linear steps in topic selection: "Pick topic, research, write paper." In naming the first source(s) they used in research, 58% said they went to "the internet," "Google," "magazines," or the like, with no further elaboration. When asked how they judged the credibility of online sources or of journal articles, fewer than one-fifth of the students surveyed gave answers to these questions that were evaluated on the matrix as "good." The pre-test was coded so that it could be matched with a post-test using the same questions. The hope was that by comparing each student's answers at the beginning and end of the semester, the researchers could identify promising pedagogical methods for teaching IL. However, the post-test results were as abysmal as the pre-test scores; only the students enrolled in six sections of a researched argument course showed any improvement, but their gains were not statistically significant.

Although the survey results were disappointing, these early efforts were important, both for the development of the group as a cohesive community and for campus partnerships about IL. Beginning with a community of practice model, the group developed a librarian-faculty collaboration different from those seen on campus and in the literature. One of the differences was that *faculty* initiated the outreach to librarians, and in so doing affirmed the value of IL as a central issue to academics on our campus. Another difference was the size of the group, which involved several faculty and librarians working together—small-team relationships are the norm for faculty-librarian collaboration on the IUPUI campus and in much of the IL literature. The initial foray into assessment was also critical, as it shaped the group's understanding of inquiry as a process of discovering how to ask the *right* questions. Therefore, the group committed to further study and development of more effective pedagogical strategies, which built the foundation for the next iteration of the community of practice.

COMMITMENT TO DIALOGUE, SCHOLARLY INQUIRY, AND DISSEMINATION

Because life cycles of communities of practice wax and wane, new members were solicited to the community of practice in 2012 to reinvigorate the work of the group. Those who answered the call for members included an equal number of librarians and faculty. An interest survey indicated that participants were eager to investigate a variety of issues, including their own IL pedagogy, teaching of research practices in other disciplines across the curriculum, current and planned library-sponsored initiatives, students' understanding of ethical use of intellectual property, and ways faculty were currently collaborating with librarians and using library services. Respondents also mentioned some hesitation about joining, with one librarian wondering why faculty were leading the group, and an instructor admitting to fears that faculty voices would be lost with so many librarian participants. Fifteen committed to the community of practice goals of dialogue, emphasis on scholarly inquiry, and dissemination of best practices.

Dialogue

Although members found they had much in common in their desires to help students achieve competence in IL, it is not surprising that fault lines began to show up in early meetings. In fact, participants' discussions sometimes echoed the barriers to collaboration mentioned in the library literature: who owns IL? Who is responsible for teaching it? Why won't faculty give librarians more access to their students? Why do librarians *want* to come to class? Are librarians trained to teach? What use is a one-time library session, when IL needs stretch across the semester? Facing these barriers with honest discussion was a positive development for the community, as it helped members uncover assumptions. Rhetorician Kenneth Bruffee "advises that partners undergo an examination of assumptions. . .to avoid misperceptions, misunderstandings, and the like" (Brasley, 2008, p. 73). Working through the assumptions and questions that caused barriers, participants soon agreed on a foundational principle: *all* own IL and *all* bear responsibility to teach it, with the goal of helping students to be successful information users while they are learners at IUPUI and later, in their careers.

As the group moved toward articulating common objectives and a plan of work, they found that language was also a barrier. Bruffee's work emphasizes "'shared language' as an essential part of the collaborative process in order to communicate fully and reach consensus" (Brasley, 2008, p. 73). To begin with, members needed to figure out what all meant by the term *information literacy*. To do so, they focused on the Association of College and Research Libraries (ACRL) definition of IL as "a set of abilities requiring individuals to 'recognize when information is needed and have the ability to locate, evaluate, and use effectively the needed information'" (ACRL, 2013). However, faculty from different disciplines interpreted the phrase *information literacy* differently. What some found difficult in that discussion was the meaning of *literacy* as part of the term. Is IL a set of skills or a set of practices? These were differently problematized depending upon the role each thought they played in relation to the ACRL definition—whether one asked students to do something or taught them how to do it. Inevitably, members also asked, "What is information?" How has technology changed the nature of information and transformed information users and producers? Although the group did not fully resolve the definition questions, they felt confident that a shared understanding of what was at stake could now lead them toward learning what they wanted to assess and to share with colleagues across the campus.

Self-assessment

To further solidify their shared understanding of the ACRL's conceptualization of IL, both librarians and faculty agreed to participate in a pilot assessment intended to ultimately shape questions and procedures for a campus-wide assessment. In the process, faculty grappled with the five *IL Standards*, as well as the 22 performance indicators and 87 student learning outcomes supporting the standards. This study, an environmental scan led by the university library's Instructional Services Council, asked participants to carefully examine one of their courses by looking at all 87 outcomes. Faculty were asked to determine whether they teach each outcome (i.e., in class, online, through assigned reading, or through some other approach); whether the faculty member assesses the outcome (either by direct or indirect measures); whether a librarian teaches or assesses the outcome for that specific course; whether no one addresses it; or if the outcome does not apply to the course. Since each outcome was included on the survey instrument, taking the survey was time-intensive, a barrier to faculty participation also noted by Gullikson (2008, p. 585), which ultimately led to a more streamlined faculty survey instrument.

The value of participation in the pilot study for faculty in the community of practice was that the instrument forced reflection on their teaching practices, which led to a clearer understanding of the scope of the ACRL *IL Standards* and the interconnectedness of the IL practices with their own curriculum. The actual results of the survey were controversial in group discussion. Faculty taught or assessed 59.5% of the 87 outcomes, while librarians taught 2.5%. Was this difference the result of faculty territoriality, denying librarians access to their students? Were faculty teaching effectively? Were the *IL Standards* an effective way to describe or to measure IL, or would the *Framework for IL*, then in draft mode, be more helpful in understanding IL learning for IUPUI's students? The discussion ultimately led to a greater development of trust within the community of practice, as it affirmed the importance of librarians' responsibility to teach the teachers as well as the students—preparing faculty to address IL concerns in their own courses. In fact, through dialogue, the community of practice became a support system for one another with meetings as a safe place to share ideas and goals.

Campus-level Assessment

The pilot study using the ACRL *IL Standards* was part of a much broader initiative conducted by the library's Instructional Services Council and funded by a grant from the campus Program Review and Assessment Committee. This initiative intended to gather information on faculty collaboration, student learning, and adherence to campus-wide assessment and evaluation initiatives because little historical information is available at the campus level. The purpose of the initial assessments, according to the Instructional Services Council, was to shape a more intentional IL instruction program at IUPUI and engage in deeper, meaningful conversations about student learning outcomes and goals at the class, course, and departmental levels.

As previous researchers have discovered (Latham & Gross, 2012, p. 580, and Blackwell-Starnes in this collection), students tend to rate their abilities to find and evaluate information as higher than they really are. To conduct a campus-wide assessment of student perceptions of their IL knowledge, the library's Instructional Services Council worked with IUPUI's Office of Institutional Research to add questions to a biennial cross-campus assessment called the Continuing Student Satisfaction and Priorities Survey. Previous student surveys had included minimal references to IL skills; for example, respondents were asked how effective they felt they were at reading and understanding books, articles, and instruction manuals, or how effectively they believed they could recognize which ideas or materials need to be fully acknowledged to avoid plagiarizing (Institutional Research Office, 2012).

The expanded student survey was administered in spring 2013 to a randomly selected group of IUPUI undergraduates, 22% of whom responded. Student self-satisfaction with their IL abilities was high: about 9 out of 10 rated themselves as effective or very effective at identifying sources of information most appropriate for a project and at knowing how to acknowledge sources to avoid plagiarism (Graunke, 2013, p. 2). More than 80% were confident in their ability to distinguish between popular and scholarly sources, to choose and evaluate relevant information for a specific assignment, and to use reference materials appropriate to the discipline. Interestingly, although 92% claimed to have visited the library, only 33% of respondents had attended a class taught by librarians, only 21% had attended a library workshop, and fewer than 16% had made an appointment with a librarian. Despite the lack of interaction with actual librarians, 65% thought they were effective or very effective at finding contact information for a subject librarian (Graunke, 2013, p. 3). These data, although limited because they represent student self-ratings rather than actual measurement of student knowledge, are valuable because understanding student self-perception can shape new pedagogical approaches to improving information use in papers and projects.

Another campus-wide assessment collected data about faculty efforts to teach IL by adding items to a faculty satisfaction survey. Agreeing that data collection about faculty teaching of IL concepts was important, the Institutional Research Office assisted community of practice members to select and refine questions, which were then added to the 2015 version of the survey instrument. Although the IL items on the faculty survey were companion items to those on the student survey, faculty were asked, not about student competence, but about concepts they teach in a typical class. The survey was sent to all campus faculty and had an overall response rate of 43%. Results from the 795 respondents (excluding teaching librarians from this analysis) showed that the majority do intentionally teach IL concepts. The highest ranked items in the faculty survey were selecting appropriate sources of information for a topic or question (67%) and recognizing what constitutes plagiarism and how to avoid it (63%) (S. Lowe, personal communication, April 28, 2015). These items correspond with the highest ranked items on the student self-satisfaction survey, at approximately 90% each (Graunke, 2013, p. 2). The correlation suggests that students may be learning about IL concepts from faculty efforts. On the other hand, when students reported the helpfulness of various entities in their development of IL, their most helpful means of developing IL skills was self-instruction, a finding that is widely echoed in library literature. On the campus level, this gap between what faculty think they teach and how students believe they learn might be usefully examined from an instructional design standpoint to uncover new practices.

One of the benefits of the inclusion of IL concepts in both campus-wide surveys is increased visibility of the need for IL instruction across departments and schools. The survey also indicates a receptive attitude toward IL at the institutional level; administrators are aware of the work and very interested in the outcomes. Universities are feeling pressure from multiple stakeholders, including state legislators and employers, to strengthen students' lifelong uses of information. These goals are also emphasized in the Lumina Foundation's Degree Qualifications Profile, in the Liberal Education and America's Promise campaign of the Association of American Colleges and Universities, and by accrediting associations, including the Middle States Commission on Higher Education (Mounce, 2010, p. 306). These documents are opening up new discussions about the shared work of educating citizens and about the conflicts, not dissimilar to the conflicts faced by the community of practice at the outset, that continue to call all stakeholders to negotiate the meanings of degrees and of higher education itself.

Dissemination

Discussion within the community of practice about assessment resulted in an action plan to increase student empowerment in the information world by enlisting other faculty and librarians in this important endeavor. Two campus-wide workshops have brought IL experts to IUPUI to share useful and relevant strategies. After all, any plans created collaboratively by librarians and faculty must still be operationalized in classrooms and course work, using measurable learning outcomes. Building those learning outcomes and incorporating IL pedagogy in actual classroom work became the focus of the first hands-on workshop, led by Anne Zald, Head of Educational Initiatives at the University of Las Vegas libraries. Zald led a series of exercises scaffolded to allow participants to identify IL learning outcomes in an assignment or activity, then to identify the criteria for successful student work, and then to scale the criteria for grading. This first workshop was a turning point for the community of practice, bringing increased interest and energy from the campus to the community's work. Hosting a large group of librarians and faculty in the same room, all using the same language and sharing the same concerns, was remarkable, showing the inherent value of the community of practice. The workshop was also a good recruitment tool, bringing more members, which prompted a new phase in the community life cycle to continue the collaborative work of improving IL instruction across the curriculum.

A second workshop in 2014 featuring William Badke, author of *Teaching Research Processes: The Faculty Role in the Development of Skilled Researchers* (2012), drew participants from six institutions in central and southern Indiana. Badke's presentation emphasized that threshold concepts in a particular discipline include its research processes, which should be taught as centrally as the content of the discipline. Badke helped participants to understand the literacy issue inherent in the term *information literacy*, pointing out that the term denotes more than just stand-alone skills—students must be brought into the academic culture and into the cultures of their disciplines in order to learn the habits of mind and practices that constitute information literacy. This second workshop continued the transformative work of the community of practice, bringing faculty and librarians together to investigate strategies to improve students' command of research processes.

NEXT STEPS

Both workshops, Badke's and Zald's, while seemingly focused on the two different views of IL—the *IL Standards* view and the *Framework for IL* view—shape the next steps for the Community of Practice on Information Literacy. As Megan Oakleaf (2014) affirms in "A Roadmap for Assessing Student Learning Using the New Framework for Information Literacy for Higher Education," the threshold concepts identified as critical at the local level need to be "transform[ed]" into learning outcomes so that the learning can be assessed (p. 512). Oakleaf recommends that librarians seek agreement on outcomes with all stakeholders involved in the particular learning situation (p. 512). For example, if a librarian designs an IL outcome on the program level, those who administer and instruct in the program should also agree on the outcome. IUPUI librarians and faculty in the community of practice are eager to explore the potential for the *Framework for IL* to shape new understandings of teaching and learning IL in Indianapolis.

Another next step for the community of practice is analysis and dissemination of the student and faculty survey results. For the first time, the IUPUI campus has data about student perceptions of their own skills at finding, evaluating, using, and citing sources, and corresponding data about faculty efforts to teach IL. This collected data should be shared with stakeholders and followed up with more targeted inquiry as the community of practice pursues its inquiry into best pedagogical practices. Another plan for dissemination is to add to an existing online collection of sample assignments and teaching strategies that have worked well on IUPUI's campus.

At IUPUI, the Community of Practice on Information Literacy brought librarians, faculty, and administrators together to promote IL engagement. While the work is far from finished, the community continues to evolve, adding points of focus as individual members bring their own classroom experiences and research interests into the collaboration. Perhaps the most valuable benefit of the community of practice is the transformation of the pedagogy of individual members who, with increasing confidence, can facilitate real growth in students' information-using behaviors.

CONCLUSION

Other chapters in this volume have highlighted the need for conversation between librarians and disciplinary faculty, conversations that can lead to collaboration for the benefit of students. (See Scheidt et al., Norgaard & Sinkinson, Feekery, Emerson & Skyrme, and Bensen, Woetzel, Wu & Hashmi in this collection, for examples.) The community of practice model could be valuable for other institutions, helping to open up conversations about students' needs, instructional roles, and strategies for learning. Since group members determine the work to be conducted, the community of practice model can fit varying local situations. A community of practice can jump-start ideas, turning them into action, and it can lead the way to real discovery and real professional development, in the end, closing instructional gaps and benefitting students.

REFERENCES

Andretta, S. (2012). Web 2.0: From information literacy to transliteracy. In P. Godwin & J. Parker (Eds.). *Information literacy beyond library 2.0* (pp. 73–80). London: Facet Publishing. Retrieved from http://site.ebrary.com.

Anthony, K. (2010). Reconnecting the disconnects: Library outreach to faculty as addressed in the literature. *College & Undergraduate Libraries, (17),* 79–92. doi: 10.1080/10691310903584817.

Artman, M., Frisicaro-Pawlowski, E. & Monge, R. (2010). Not just one shot: Extending the dialogue about information literacy in composition classes. *Composition Studies (38)*2, 93–109. Retrieved from http://www.uc.edu/journals/composition-studies.html.

Association of College and Research Libraries. (2013). *Information literacy competencies for higher education.* Retrieved from http://www.ala.org/acrl/standards/information literacycompetency.

Association of College and Research Libraries. (2015). *Framework for information literacy for higher education.* Retrieved from http://acrl.ala.org/ilstandardsilframework.

Badke, W. B. (2012). *Teaching research processes: The faculty role in the development of skilled student researchers.* Oxford: Chandos Publishing.

Badke, W. B. (2005). Can't get no respect: Helping faculty to understand the educational power of information literacy. *The Reference Librarian, 89–90,* 63–80. doi: 10.1300/J120v43n89_05.

Bensen, B., Woetzel, D., Wu, H. & Hashmi, G. (2016). Impacting information literacy through alignment, resources, and assessment. In B. J. D'Angelo, S. Jamieson, B. Maid & J. R. Walker (Eds.), *Information literacy: Research and collaboration across disciplines.* Chapter 19. Fort Collins, CO: WAC Clearinghouse and University Press of Colorado.

Blackwell-Starnes, K. (2016). Preliminary paths to information literacy: Introducing research in core courses. In B. J. D'Angelo, S. Jamieson, B. Maid & J. R. Walker (Eds.), *Information literacy: Research and collaboration across disciplines.* Fort Collins, CO: WAC Clearinghouse and University Press of Colorado.

Brasley, S. S. (2008). Effective librarian and discipline faculty collaboration models for integrating information literacy into the fabric of an academic institution. *New Directions for Teaching and Learning, 114,* 71–88. doi: 10.1002/tl.318.

Cambridge, D., Kaplan, S. & Suter, V. (2005). Community of practice design guide. Educause. Retrieved from http://net.educause.edu/ir/library/pdf/nli0531.pdf.

Caravello, P., Kain, E., Macicak, S., Kuchi, T. & Weiss, G. (2007, August). Information literacy: The partnership of sociology faculty and social science librarians. Workshop presented at the American Sociological Association Meetings, New York City.

Chism, N. V. N., Lees, N. D. & Evenbeck, S. (2002). Faculty development for teaching. *Liberal Education, 88*(3), 34–41. Retrieved from http://www.aacu.org/liberaleducation/.

D'Angelo, B. & Maid, B. (2004). Moving beyond definitions: Implementing information literacy across the curriculum. *The Journal of Academic Librarianship (30)*3, 212–217. Retrieved from http://www.journals.elsevier.com/the-journal-of-academic-librarianship/.

Feekery, A., Emerson, L. & Skyrme, G. (2016). Supporting academics to embed information literacy to enhance students' research and writing process. In B. J. D'Angelo, S. Jamieson, B. Maid & J. R. Walker (Eds.), *Information literacy:*

Research and collaboration across disciplines. Chapter 17. Fort Collins, CO: WAC Clearinghouse and University Press of Colorado.

Gross, M. & Latham, D. (2009). Undergraduate perceptions of IL: Defining, attaining, and self-assessing skills. *College & Research Libraries (70)*4, 336–350. Retrieved from http://www.ala.org/.

Gullikson, S. (2006). Faculty perceptions of ACRL's Information Literacy Competency Standards for Higher Education. *Journal of Academic Librarianship, 32*(6), 583–592. Retrieved from http://www.journals.elsevier.com/the-journal-of-academic-librarianship/.

Hart Research Associates. (2013). *It takes more than a major: Employer priorities for college learning and student success.* Retrieved from http://www.aacu.org/leap/documents/2013_EmployerSurvey.pdf.

Hansen, M. J. (2014, November 14). *Understanding IUPUI transfer students* [Report]. Retrieved from http://osdae.iupui.edu/Student-Success-and-Learning.

Head, A. J. (2013, April). Project Information Literacy: What can be learned about the information-seeking behavior of today's college students? Paper presented at the Association of College & Research Libraries Conference, Indianapolis, IN. Retrieved from http://www.ala.org/acrl/.

Institutional Research Office. (2012). 2011 student satisfaction and priorities survey. Indianapolis: Indiana University Purdue University Indianapolis. Retrieved from http://imir.iupui.edu/surveys/reports/default.aspx/STU/STU_CSSPS/68/3/2011.

Jamieson, S. & Howard, R. M. (2011, August 15). Sandra Jamieson and Rebecca Moore Howard: Unraveling the citation trail. (A. Head, Interviewer.) *Project Information Literacy Smart Talk (8).*

Laskin, M. & Haller, C. (2016). Up the mountain without a trail: Helping students use source networks to find their way. In B. J. D'Angelo, S. Jamieson, B. Maid & J. R. Walker (Eds.), *Information literacy: Research and collaboration across disciplines.* Chapter 11. Fort Collins, CO: WAC Clearinghouse and University Press of Colorado.

Latham, D. & Gross, M. (2012). What's skill got to do with it? Information literacy skills and self-views of ability among first-year college students. *Journal of the American Society for Information Science and Technology (63)*3, 574–583. doi: 10.1002/asi.

McGuinness, C. (2006). What faculty think—Exploring the barriers to information literacy development in undergraduate education. *Journal of Academic Librarianship (32)*6, 573–582. Retrieved from http://www.journals.elsevier.com/the-journal-of-academic-librarianship/.

Mounce, M. (2010). Working together: Academic librarians and faculty collaborating to improve students' information literacy skills: A literature review 2000–2009. *The Reference Librarian, 51*, 300–320. Retrieved from http://www.tandfonline.com/toc/wref20/current.

Norgaard, R. (2003). Writing information literacy: Contributions to a concept. *Reference & User Services Quarterly (43)*2, 124–130. Retrieved from http://www.ala.org/rusa/communications/rusqinfo.

Norgaard, R. & Sinkinson, C. (2016). Writing information literacy: A retrospective and a look ahead. In B. J. D'Angelo, S. Jamieson, B. Maid & J. R. Walker (Eds.),

Information literacy: Research and collaboration across disciplines. Chapter 1. Fort Collins, CO: WAC Clearinghouse and University Press of Colorado.

Oakleaf, M. (2013). A roadmap for assessing learning using the new Framework for Information Literacy for Higher Education. *The Journal of Academic Librarianship, 40,* 510–514. Retrieved from http://www.journals.elsevier.com/the-journal-of-academic-librarianship/.

Oakleaf, M., Millet, M. & Kraus, L. (2011). All together now: Getting faculty, administrators, and staff engaged in information literacy assessment. *portal: Libraries and the Academy, (11)*3, 831–852. Retrieved from http://www.press.jhu.edu/journals/portal_libraries_and_the_academy/.

Office of Student Data, Analysis, and Evaluation (2008). Principles of undergraduate learning. Retrieved from http://osdae.iupui.edu/resources/puls.

Saunders, L. (2012). Faculty perspectives on information literacy as a student learning outcome. *Journal of Academic Librarianship, 38*(4), 226–236. Retrieved from http://www.journals.elsevier.com/the-journal-of-academic-librarianship/.

Saunders, L. (2013, April). Culture and collaboration: Fostering integration of information literacy by speaking the language of faculty. Paper presented at the Association of College & Research Libraries Conference, Indianapolis, IN. Retrieved from http://www.ala.org/acrl/.

Scheidt, D., et al. (2016). Writing information literacy in first-year composition: A collaboration among faculty and librarians. In B. J. D'Angelo, S. Jamieson, B. Maid & J. R. Walker (Eds.), *Information literacy: Research and collaboration across disciplines.* Chapter 10. Fort Collins, CO: WAC Clearinghouse and University Press of Colorado.

University College. (January, 2012). *Survey summary report: Faculty needs assessment of undergraduate education.* Indianapolis: S. S. Baker.

Wenger, E., McDermott, R. & Snyder, W. (2002). *Cultivating communities of practice: A guide to managing knowledge.* Boston: Harvard Business School Press. Retrieved from web.b.ebscohost.com

AFTERWORD

Trudi E. Jacobson
University at Albany

I am honored to have been asked to write the afterword for this important volume. We are at a time when the world of information possibilities has exploded—not just the resources available to us, which are overwhelming and often daunting, but also the roles each one of us can play in creating, collaborating, sharing, and disseminating information. As academics, these roles tend to come naturally. Our facility in engaging with information in our own fields coincides with our abilities to create and share other forms of information, and to use less traditional modes of dissemination. We may write letters to the editors of periodicals. We may contribute reflective posts on social media, be it tweets or via professional or personal-interest blogs, or contribute reviews—product, hotel, or restaurant—to help others. We understand the need for varying formats of information creation and modes of information dissemination to suit specific purposes and to reach varying audiences.

The variety of information-related roles is outlined in the outer ring of Figure A.1.

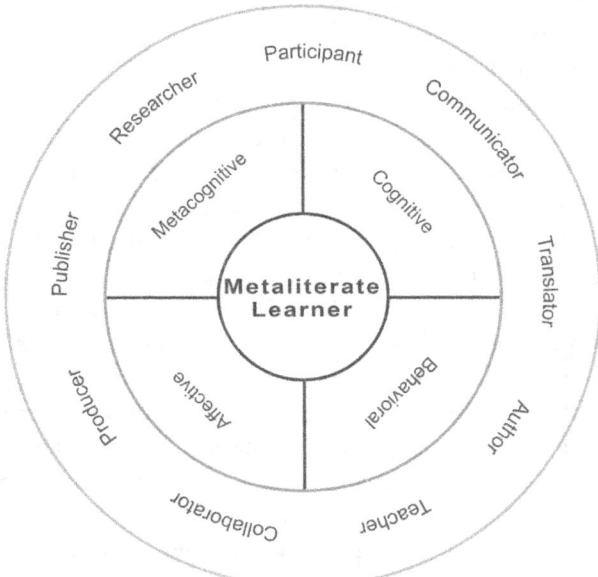

Figure A.1. The Metaliterate Learner (Mackey & Jacobson, 2014).

These roles are now open to almost everyone, but many do not see themselves as information producers and distributors nor as teachers or translators of information. Even if our students are actually engaging in these activities, they may not recognize the full potential of what they are able to do.

When students post online, for example, they don't see this as a reflection, often a lasting one, of themselves. Rather than understanding that they are shaping an online persona, they might see their utterances as disconnected and effect-neutral. And for those who do not feel comfortable participating, it leads to a loss of unique voices and perspectives in online communities. Educators have the opportunity, indeed duty, to introduce these roles to our students, and information literacy (IL) is a powerful player in these conversations.

As this collaborative collection epitomizes, IL is a shared responsibility. No longer do we consider IL to be a simple set of discrete skills connected with finding and evaluating information. Two of the themes discussed in this volume, metaliteracy and the ACRL *Framework for Information Literacy for Higher Education* (*Framework for IL*) (which was itself influenced by metaliteracy) are extending beyond and opening new vistas in the field. While the ideas encompassed by both of these constructs are not entirely new, each provides its own cohesive lens that opens up exciting opportunities for thinking about and teaching IL. The overlap between metaliteracy and the *Framework for IL* allows them to support and enhance each other.

Both metaliteracy and the *Framework for IL* address multiple domains (metacognitive, cognitive, behavioral, and affective), providing a rich scope for learning activities. As reflected in the chapters in this collection, educators are identifying potent opportunities to empower learners, and in the process, we also learn from our students. The fertile ground provided by this environment is reflected in the chapters you have just read. As you did so, you probably imagined how you might alter this piece, and tweak that, and add a dash of this, and end up with something very exciting to try out on your own campus.

As educators, we may be animated by the possibilities, but crucially, how do students respond? Section IV's chapters describe collaborative pedagogical techniques used by their author teams. The frame Scholarship as Conversation is highlighted in the first chapter in Section III, Miriam Laskin's and Cynthia Haller's "Up the Mountain without a Trail: Helping Students Use Source Networks to Find Their Way." In my own classroom I have seen that concepts critical to IL, such as this one, engage students once they understand how they relate to their academic and non-academic needs. In one of my upper-level undergraduate courses, teams of students wrestled with Scholarship as Conversation individually and through discussion, including reflecting on associated dispositions. In order to assess their grasp of the core ideas, a team-based culminating project asked them to develop a lesson plan to introduce lower-level undergraduates to this frame. The lesson plan needed to include an activity and a final project for these hypothetical students to complete. I was amazed with the teams' responses to this challenge, which included a 30-minute deadline. Their work indicated that they had grasped the core ideas contained within the frame. In addition, the students saw themselves in new roles: those of information producer and teacher. These outcomes highlight the fundamental difference between teaching students basic skills and introducing them to core concepts in the field. But teaching on this higher level requires more than just the one class period often allotted to a librarian. Collaboration in this endeavor is crucial.

The discussion about who is responsible for IL instruction is long-standing and ongoing. When the topic of the instruction was library research skills, it was clear that librarians played the key role. But IL goes far beyond library research, as is evident in the chapters in this volume. Its scope is expansive; the need permeates life, both on campus and off, as well as on and off the job. With the conceptions of IL as a metaliteracy, and the core concepts espoused by the *Framework for IL*, it becomes clear that teaching and modeling information-literate competencies is a challenge that needs to be undertaken by all educators.

I applaud the vision expressed in the Introduction: "we hoped that a collection that bridged the disciplinary divide would advance the notion of shared responsibility and accountability for IL." Conversations such as the ones that this book will initiate are vital in making IL a strong component of higher education. Give and take will be important: librarians and disciplinary faculty members will each have contributions to share, and things to learn. The terms and framing may differ, but there will be much common ground. As Caroline Sinkinson says in her chapter with Rolf Norgaard, citing Barabara Fister: we "need to trust one another and have a sense of shared ownership." Norgaard and Sinkinson are discussing collaborations between librarians and Rhetoric and Writing Instructors, but Fister's advice is pertinent for all such initiatives. The issue of language and ownership are addressed in Susan Brown and Janice R. Walker's "Information Literacy Preparation of Pre-Service and Graduate Educators" (chapter 13).

The material in this book has engaged you with the new ideas, new theories, and new terminology, introduced through metaliteracy and the *Framework for IL*, and also through the collaborations described in some of the chapters. This willingness to grapple with the new is critical in moving IL forward, and I call upon you to serve as advocates for these new theories and ideas. Your adaptation of these concepts will in turn motivate and inspire others both in your own field, as well as outside it. Please share your enthusiasms, your insights, and your experiences.

And please do so with your students as well. Provide the scaffolding they might need, but let them struggle with the nuances of the ideas and understandings that lead to the concepts and the resulting competencies.

I was struck by something that Barbara Fister said during her keynote presentation for librarians at the 2015 Librarian's Information Literacy Annual Conference (LILAC) in Newcastle, UK. She talked about the liminal space that precedes crossing the threshold for each concept in the *Framework for IL*, and the worry that librarians, in desiring to be helpful, will attempt to move learners over the threshold without their having a chance to really wrestle with the understandings they need to master. Let them flounder a bit—we all did when we first encountered these key concepts. The nature of threshold concepts is that it is hard to remember what or how we thought before we crossed the threshold. This is what I took away from one of her points during her talk. In looking for the source, to make sure my memory was accurate, I found her exact wording:

> What really caught my imagination was their focus on identifying those moments when students make a significant breakthrough in their understanding, a breakthrough that changes the relationship they have with information. If we know what those moments are, we can think about how our teaching practices can either help students work toward those moments of insight or perhaps inadvertently hinder them by describing a simple step by step process that defuses troublesomeness to make it more manageable (Fister, 2015).

Fister was referring to a 2013 Library Orientation Exchange (LOEX) presentation by Lori Townsend and Amy Hofer (see http://www.loexconference.org/2013/sessions.html#townsend). Not coincidentally, Townsend was a member of the ACRL task force that developed the new *Framework for IL*.

I highly encourage you to read the text of Fister's talk, "The Liminal Library," which she has generously provided online (Fister, 2015) She touches on many of the themes included in this collection, including students, collaboration, language, the changing nature and definition of IL including metaliteracy, the movement from the *IL Standards* to the *Framework for IL*, and more.

This is an exciting time to explore and to teach information literacy/metaliteracy. The authors whose work is collected in this volume have conveyed that energy. It is now your turn to add to the increasing dynamism in the field. And wouldn't you like to share that excitement with a partner from another discipline?

REFERENCES

Fister, B. (2015). The liminal library: Making our libraries sites of transformative learning. Retrieved September 3, 2015, from http://barbarafister.com/LiminalLibrary.pdf.

Mackey, T. P. & Jacobson, T. E. (2014). *Metaliteracy: reinventing information literacy to empower learners*. Chicago: Neal-Schuman.

CONTRIBUTORS

Lori Baker, Southwest Minnesota State University
Beth Bensen, J. Sargeant Reynolds Community College
Katt Blackwell-Starnes, Lamar University
Laura R. Braunstein, Dartmouth College
Susan Brown, Kennesaw State University
William Carpenter, High Point University
Dale Cyphert, University of Northern Iowa
Barbara J. D'Angelo, Arizona State University
Norbert Elliot, New Jersey Institute of Technology
Lisa Emerson, Massey University, Palmerston North, New Zealand
Angela Feekery, Massey University, Palmerston North, New Zealand
Robert Fitzgerald, High Point University
Pam Gladis, Southwest Minnesota State University
Karen Gocsik, University of California-San Diego
Alison S. Gregory, Lycoming College
Cynthia Haller, York College, City University of New York
Randall S. Halverson, Indiana University Purdue University Indianapolis
Ghazala Hashmi, J. Sargeant Reynolds Community College
Rhonda K. Huisman, Indiana University Purdue University Indianapolis
Trudi E. Jacobson, University at Albany
Sandra Jamieson, Drew University
Irvin R. Katz, Educational Testing Service
Savannah L. Kelly, Westmont College
Francia Kissel, Indiana University Purdue University Indianapolis
Cara Kozma, High Point University
Meagan Lacy, Indiana University Purdue University Indianapolis

Contributors

Miriam Laskin, Hostos Community College, City University of New York
Stanley P. Lyle, University of Northern Iowa
Barry Maid, Arizona State University
Betty L. McCall, Lycoming College
Hazel McClure, Grand Valley State University
Diego Méndez-Carbajo, Illinois Wesleyan University
Holly Middleton, High Point University
Rachel Milloy, Norwalk Community College
Matthew Moberly, California State University-Stanislaus
Seth Myers, University of Colorado at Boulder
Rolf Norgaard, University of Colorado at Boulder
Lisa Ramirez, University of Belize
Donna Scheidt, High Point University
Kathy Shields, High Point University
Caroline Sinkinson, University of Colorado at Boulder
Sarah L. Skripsky, Westmont College
Gillian Skyrme, Massey University, Palmerston North, New Zealand
Cynthia E. Tobery, Dartmouth College
Christopher Toth, Grand Valley State University
Janice R. Walker, Georgia Southern University
Scott R. Weeden, Indiana University Purdue University Indianapolis
Theresa Westbrock, New Mexico State University
Melvin R. Wininger, Indiana University Purdue University Indianapolis
Rachel Rains Winslow, Westmont College
Patricia A. Wittberg, Indiana University Purdue University Indianapolis
Denise Woetzel, J. Sargeant Reynolds Community College
Patti Wojahn, New Mexico State University
Hong Wu, J. Sargeant Reynolds Community College
Kathleen Blake Yancey, Florida State University

www.ingramcontent.com/pod-product-compliance
Lightning Source LLC
Chambersburg PA
CBHW070124080526
44586CB00015B/1544